Texas Wildlife Resources and Land Uses

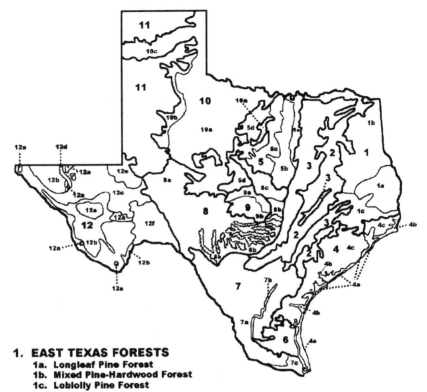

1. **EAST TEXAS FORESTS**
    1a. **Longleaf Pine Forest**
    1b. **Mixed Pine-Hardwood Forest**
    1c. **Loblolly Pine Forest**

2. **POST OAK SAVANNAH**

3. **BLACKLAND PRAIRIES**

4. **GULF COAST PRAIRIES & MARSHES**
    4a. **Dune/Barrier Islands**
    4b. **Marshes**
    4c. **Prairies**

5. **CROSS TIMBERS & PRAIRIES**
    5a. **East Cross Timbers**
    5b. **Grand Prairie**
    5c. **West Cross Timbers**
    5d. **North Central Prairie**

6. **COASTAL SAND PLAINS**

7. **SOUTH TEXAS BRUSH COUNTRY**
    7a. **Brush Country**
    7b. **Bordas Escarpment**
    7c. **Subtropical Zone**

8. **EDWARDS PLATEAU**
    8a. **Live Oak-Mesquite Savannah**
    8b. **Balcones Canyonlands**
    8c. **Lampasas Cut Plain**

9. **LLANO UPLIFT**
    9a. **Mesquite Savannah**
    9b. **Oak & Oak-Hickory Woodlands**

10. **ROLLING PLAINS**
    10a. **Mesquite Plains**
    10b. **Escarpment Breaks**
    10c. **Canadian Breaks**

11. **HIGH PLAINS**

12. **TRANS-PECOS**
    12a. **Mountain Ranges**
    12b. **Desert Grassland**
    12c. **Desert Scrub**
    12d. **Salt Basin**
    12e. **Sand Hills**
    12f. **Stockton Plateau**

Ecological Regions of Texas (modified by Ray C. Telfair II from the map of Natural Regions of Texas. Part III, p. 18 in Preserving Texas' Natural Heritage. LBJ School of Public Affairs Policy Research Project, Report 31, Part III, p. 1978).

Edited by Raymond C. Telfair II

Texas
Wildlife Resources
and Land Uses

UNIVERSITY OF TEXAS PRESS, AUSTIN

Requests for permission to reproduce material from this work
should be sent to Permissions, University of Texas Press, P.O. Box
7819, Austin, TX 78713-7819.

⊗ The paper used in this publication meets the minimum requirements of American National Standard for Information Sciences—
Permanence of Paper for Printed Library Materials, ANSI Z39.48-
1984.

**LIBRARY OF CONGRESS
CATALOGING-IN-PUBLICATION DATA**

Texas wildlife resources and land uses /
edited by Raymond C. Telfair II. — 1st ed.
    p.   cm.
  Based on revised and updated papers
from a 1982 wildlife symposium published
by the Texas Chapter of the Wildlife Society, with new topics.
  Includes bibliographical references
(p.   )
  ISBN 0-292-78159-8 (pbk. : alk. paper)
  1. Wildlife management—Texas.
2. Land use—Texas. I. Telfair, Raymond
Clark, 1941– .
SK451.T535 1999
333.95'415'09764—dc21   98-33234

Contents

Preface

The Texas Chapter of The Wildlife Society recognizes the importance of healthy environments for both human and wildlife activities. In 1982, a symposium was organized for the annual meeting of the Texas Chapter to recognize that habitat loss is the most crucial problem confronting wildlife. At that time, conservation and environmental awareness among citizens were increasing but were not as widespread and of as much concern as they are today. Wildlife habitat destruction continues to increase, even though we face the possibility that only remnants of our native landscape and associated wildlife may survive.

During the decade of the 1980's, many changes occurred in Texas that involve conservation and management philosophies, policies, and issues as well as land-use impacts on wildlife. Fifteen years after the original symposium was published by the Texas Chapter, there is an even greater demand for information, because a myriad of conservation issues affects wildlife and land resources of Texas. Therefore, the Executive Board decided that a new version—a book rather than another symposium—was needed and should be published and marketed by a well-established press. Thus, the Texas Chapter would have a splendid opportunity to provide a unique, valuable contribution to the natural resource literature of Texas.

The new wildlife management philosophy in Texas is that of providing a balance between "game" and "nongame" interest groups. The goal is landscape ecology in the broadest context, i.e., ecosystem biodiversity. The old-style management philosophy emphasized production of selected species of value to sportsmen. However, natural resources are essential to all citizens. One of the clearest lessons from history is that increasing human populations and the resulting environmental damage destroyed the resources upon which past civilizations were dependent. But, unlike earlier civilizations, we have the knowledge and educational capability to prevent a similar catastrophe if we take the initiative and make the commitment. However, there are no easy solutions, only choices based on intelligence and wisdom.

Although the new *Texas Wildlife Resources and Land Uses* advocates this ethical philosophy, it also reflects the 1982 symposium so that we can track our progress (or lack thereof) during the past and into the future. For, as Dr. John Baccus said in his preface to the proceedings, "It would be most unfortunate that our enlightenment at the symposium be forgotten and lost due to a lack of action."

All previous chapters are revised and updated. There are 7 new topics, including an entire section of 9 chapters on wildlife management on Texas public lands, which, although extremely important, comprise only about 2% of the state. New articles discuss the ecological regions of Texas, the need for a Texas land ethic, a landowner's view of wildlife and wildlife users, private lands and wildlife, nuisance wildlife and land use, and conservation organizations in Texas.

The authors present viewpoints of various governmental and private organizations that represent diverse user groups and resource areas. In some cases, they reflect differences of opinion which are important: they reveal problems that should be addressed and could result in dialogue, cooperation, coordination, and action.

I hope that *Texas Wildlife Resources and Land Uses* will be of value to all persons interested in wildlife conservation and management: landowners, government officials, agency representatives, conservationists, managers, educators, consultants, and the people of Texas. Perhaps groups of people in different disciplines will develop a new team approach to restore biodiversity to Texas ecological regions. If so, the efforts of all those involved in the production of this book will have been worthwhile.

Raymond C. Telfair II

Acknowledgments

This book is a product of cooperation and coordination of many people in diverse fields of expertise. The contributors and support staffs of many organizations provided text and illustrative materials. I deeply appreciate their interest in the project.

The book could not have been produced without the support and guidance of an excellent publisher. I am sincerely grateful to the University of Texas Press for accepting the project and working with me and the contributors during the long, arduous task of editing. I especially thank the following staff members: Shannon Davies (sponsoring editor), Leslie Tingle (manuscript editor), and Heidi Haeuser (designer).

The laborious task of reviewing the original manuscript was accomplished by the astute professional guidance and insight of Drs. Craig A. McMahan (retired, Wildlife Division, Texas Parks and Wildlife Department) and Nova J. Silvy (professor, Department of Wildlife and Fisheries Sciences, Texas A&M University).

Several colleagues graciously agreed to prepare or assist with illustrations and tables: book cover design (Carl Frentress) and artwork (Rob Fleming); frontispiece, other maps, and graphs (Cynthia Banks, Tom Boggus, Gary Burke, Greg Creacy, Jinger Knight, Duane R. Lucia, Kim Ludeke, Kathleen B. Martin, Rodney Peters, Steve Segura, and Kevin W. Storey); and tables (Jimmie R. Bybee). Information pertinent to the origin of the regional name "Cross Timbers" was provided by Charles D. Tipton of Garland, Texas. David W. Rideout checked library sources for several taxonomic references.

Appendixes of common and scientific names of plants and animals were prepared by Doris V. Harris. The appendix of threatened and endangered species was provided by Dorinda Scott, Endangered Resources Branch, Texas Parks and Wildlife Department.

Raymond C. Telfair II
Conservation Scientist, Wildlife Division
Texas Parks and Wildlife Department
Management and Research Station
11942 FM 848
Tyler, Texas 78707

Introduction: Ecological Regions of Texas: Description, Land Use, and Wildlife

Abstract: Conservation and management of Texas wildlife resources and land-use practices should be based on landscape ecology. Understanding the ecological regions of the state builds the best foundation upon which to base sound decisions. After a discussion of the biodiversity and biogeography of Texas, 12 ecological regions are described. Then, trends in land use affecting wildlife resources are discussed.

This introductory chapter is quite general in scope. The references at the end of the chapter will provide specific historical as well as biological information, some of which is extensive.

Setting

Texas is located at the crossroads of 4 major physiographic subdivisions of North America—Gulf Coastal Forests and Prairies, Great Western Lower Plains, Great Western High Plains, and the Rocky Mountain Region (Fig. 1). Topographically, with the exclusion of the Rocky Mountain Region west of the Pecos River, the state is a series of descending plains and prairies from northwest to southeast. There are 3 prominent geologic features: western mountains in the Trans-Pecos, the north-south Caprock Escarpment in the Panhandle, and the arc-shaped Balcones Escarpment in the central area of the state. The 367 miles of coastline are extensive and diverse. Prior to the 1880's, the

I

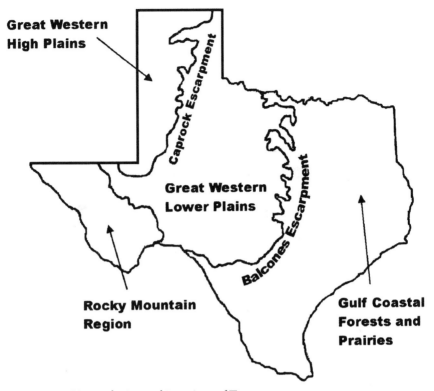

Fig. 1.1. *Major physiographic regions of Texas.*

central 80% of the state was short to tall grassland, the western 10% across the Pecos River was desert grassland, and the eastern 10% was forest land.

Contemporary landownership patterns reflect the history of the state. Because Texas retained its public lands at the time it entered the United States, the proportion of federal ownership has remained low (1.4%). Political views of Texans have traditionally stressed rights of private landownership. However, in contemporary times, individual small landowners are being joined by large corporate landowners, including foreign investors.

The Texas economy was originally agricultural, major products being cotton, corn, and cattle. Oil discovery in the early 1900's and mineral production assumed an important economic role during the next decades. Agriculture, manufacturing, and mining diversification began about 1940 and led to a high degree of steady economic stability and growth. Shifts of population from rural to urban areas provided sufficient labor markets for industrial development as well as creating area markets. Texas is cited as having the best business climate in the nation and ranks among the top 3 or 4 states in most economic activities.

Texas is the second most populated state. It also ranks as one of the fastest growing states, having an annual growth rate more than twice that of the entire nation.

About 83% of the land in Texas is devoted to agriculture, mostly grazing (61%) and crop production (21%). Although mineral extraction is a major industry, the proportion of land devoted to this use is small. Commercial forestry is located primarily in the East Texas Pine-Hardwood Forests. Texas is also a land of vast recreational opportunities because of its favorable climate and varied topography, vegetation, and wildlife, most of which is provided within the Texas State Parks System and the federal recreational lands of the National Park System, the Forest Service, National Wildlife Refuges, and reservoir lands controlled by the U.S. Army Corps of Engineers.

Texas has a greater variety of wildlife than any other state. However, public and private activities in the state have the potential to cause significant destruction of wildlife habitat, and general trends are evident. Among them are rapid population growth and continued exploitation of natural resources which include water resources development, agricultural practices, forestry practices, mineral and energy production, urban and industrial expansion, recreational or leisure developments, and transportation facilities.

Floral and Faunal Patterns

Biodiversity

The great diversity of flora and fauna in Texas (Table I.1) and their patterns of distribution within ecoregions (frontispiece) correlate with a matrix of complex environmental factors involving geology, topography, climatic zones, rainfall belts, and soil types (Tables I.2–I.4). There are 4,834 species of vascular plants, of which 425 (8.8%) are endemic. Nearly half (523) of the grass species indigenous to the United States occur in Texas. There are 247 species of freshwater fishes (14 endemic, 5.7%) and 958 species of terrestrial vertebrates (16 endemic, 1.7%).

Unfortunately, 574 species of vascular plants are introduced (11.9%), as are 42 vertebrate species (3.5%). Fortunately, few species have become extinct or extirpated since the time of Anglo-American settlement (8 fishes, 4 birds, and 9 mammals), but many species are

Table 1.1. VASCULAR PLANTS AND FRESHWATER AND

Taxa	Total species	Extinct (since Anglo-American settlement)		Extirpated (since Anglo-American settlement)	
		No.	%	No.	%
Ferns and flowering plants	4,834				
Jawless fishes	2				
Cartilagenous fishes[b]	6				
Bony fishes[b]	239	5	2.1	3	1.3
Amphibians	62				
Reptiles	148				
Birds[c]	594	2	0.3	2	0.3
Mammals[b]	154	0		9	5.8

[a] Counts from Hatch, Gandhi, and Brown 1990; Hubbs, Edwards, and Garrett 1991; Page and Burr 1991; Conant and Collins 1991; Dixon 1987; Bryan, Gallucci, Lasley, and Riskind 1991; Jones and Jones 1992; and Texas Organization for Endangered Species lists 1988, 1993.

[b] Includes 7 estuarine fishes and 1 estuarine mammal.

classified as threatened, endangered, or of special concern (Table I.1). Collectively, these include 56 vascular plants (1.2%) and 171 vertebrates (14.2%). See species lists in Appendix D.

The greatest number of species inhabit the Gulf Coast, Trans-Pecos, and eastern forest regions. The area of least diversity is the panhandle (High Plains and Rolling Plains). The largest number of endemic species (both statewide and local) occur in the Trans-Pecos, Edwards Plateau, and South Plains.

Biogeography

In general, species diversity tends to increase from areas of uniform elevation to areas of varied topography, i.e., from the relatively flat, uniform east to the relatively rugged, heterogeneous west. However, fish and amphibian species diversity increases from west to east in response to permanent water and moisture availability.

TERRESTRIAL VERTEBRATES OF TEXAS[a]

Introduced (exotic)		Endemic		Threatened[d]		Endangered[d]		Special concern[e]	
No.	%	No.	%	No.	%	No.	%	No.	%
574	11.9	425	8.8	5	0.1	23	0.5	28	0.6
				2	33.3				
18	7.5	14	5.9	19	7.9	8	3.3	15	6.3
		8	12.9	10	16.1	2	3.2	4	6.4
3	2.0	4	2.7	19	12.8	0	0	12	8.1
8	1.3	1	0.2	20	3.4	13	2.2	25	4.2
13	8.4	3	1.9	10	6.5	7	4.5	7	4.5

[c] Includes only confirmed species (excludes 6 species listed as historical and 11 species considered as hypothetical). Endemic refers to breeding only. Otherwise, there are no totally endemic bird species in Texas.

[d] Legal status (state status, Texas Parks and Wildlife Department regulations 1997).

[e] From Texas Organization for Endangered Species lists 1988, 1993.

Maximum fish species diversity corresponds with the location of river drainages (Fig. 2), which, in general, flow from northwest to southeast. Except for the longest through-flow rivers and those of North Texas and the Trans-Pecos, most river systems are east or south of the Balcones Fault zone.

Amphibians reach maximum species diversity in East-central Texas, exceeded only in parts of the extreme southeastern United States. Amphibian diversity declines rapidly to the west.

Highest reptile species diversity for Texas and the United States occurs in Central Texas in the Austin area. Then, reptile diversity declines in all directions but is most pronounced to the northwest, in the panhandle region. Most turtles are dependent upon the availability of aquatic environments, whereas snakes and especially lizards seem to be more dependent upon the structural complexity of their environment.

The number of breeding bird species is highest in the western and

Table 1.2. ECOLOGICAL REGIONS OF TEXAS—

Region	Characteristics			
	Location	Area %	Distribution (mi.) N–S	E–W
East Texas Forests	Eastern region	9.6	238–262	15–146
Post Oak Savannah	East central N–S belt	4.2	408	15–125
Blackland Prairies	East central N–S crescent	7.2	135–346	23–115
Coastal Prairies and Marshes	Coastal arc	6.0	367	3–85
Cross Timbers and Prairies	North central	9.0	208–285	62–139
Coastal Sand Plains and South Texas Brushlands	Southern region	12.6	245–269	10–225
Edwards Plateau and Llano Uplift	West central	15.0	100–200	262–323
Rolling Plains	North central & E. panhandle	14.4	223–385	25–192
High Plains	Western panhandle	11.4	292–323	77–146
Trans-Pecos	West of Pecos River	10.8	10–200	131–223

Sources: Hatch, Gandhi, and Brown 1990; Texas General Land Office &

southern regions of the state and declines eastward (matching continental trends). Mammal species diversity declines from west to east, most species being in the Trans-Pecos.

GENERAL TRENDS

Although some species are widespread, having very broad ecological tolerances, there are 3 general patterns of vertebrate distribution in Texas.

1. East vs. West

First, a major east-west discontinuity coincides with a north-south line from Fort Worth to Austin, San Antonio, and Corpus Christi. This

PHYSICAL AND CLIMATIC DESCRIPTION

Elevation (ft.)	Topography	Rainfall (in) and peak months	Frost-free days	Soil type
200–700	Level to rolling to hilly	40–56 Even	235–265	Deep acidic loams and sands
200–800	Level to gently rolling	30–45 May, Sept.	235–280	Acid loams over shallow clay pan
250–700	Nearly level to rolling	30–45 May, Sept.	230–280	Deep black, rich clay loam
0–250	Nearly level	26–56 Sept., May	245–320	Deep clays, loams, silt, and sand
500–1,500	Gently rolling	25–35 May, Sept.	230–280	Acid loams/sands basic, neutral loams
0–1,000	Nearly level to rolling	18–35 Sept., May	260–340	Many, clays to sands
1,200–3,000	Rolling, hilly, rough	12–32 May, Sept.	220–260	Basic in limestone, neutral in granites
1,000–3,000	Nearly level to rolling	18–28 May, Sept.	185–235	Soft prairie sands and clays
3,000–4,500	Nearly level high plateau	14–21 May, Sept.	180–220	Outwash sediments from Rocky Mts.
2,500–8,751	Basins, plateaus, and mountains	8–18 July, Aug. Sept., Nov.	220–245	Shallow clays to sands

Texas Nature Conservancy 1986.

faunal pattern corresponds to the abrupt elevational change along the Balcones Fault from Fort Worth to San Antonio. From there to the gulf, the line corresponds with soil (edaphic) differences. There are also climatic and floral correlations. West and south of the line the climate is xeric; to the east, mesic. Before Anglo-American settlement, the area to the east was tallgrass prairie and forest; to the west and south were plains (mixed and shortgrass prairies) and brushlands. Today, most of this area is cropland and grazingland.

2. North vs. South

The second most prominent discontinuity occurs north and south of a line from Corpus Christi to San Antonio to Del Rio. As explained

Table 1.3. ECOLOGICAL REGIONS OF TEXAS—

Region	Characteristic vegetation
East Texas Forests	Pine-oak upland, hardwood bottomlands, much variety
Post Oak Savannah	Oak-hickory belt with many small, scattered prairies
Blackland Prairies	Tallgrass prairie mostly converted to crops and pasture
Coastal Prairies and Marshes	Diverse cordgrass marshes and scattered oak mottes
Cross Timbers and Prairies	Transitional area of oak woodlands and prairies
Coastal Sand Plains and South Texas Brushlands	Thorn woodlands, shrublands, and scattered oak mottes
Edwards Plateau and Llano Uplift	Oak savannahs and woods, juniper breaks, springs, caves
Rolling Plains	Juniper breaks and midgrass prairie
High Plains	Shortgrass prairie
Trans-Pecos	Much variation related to elevation: desert scrub/grassland, pine, oak, juniper woodlands

*U/R = Unique/rare	T = Threatened	E = Endangered

Sources: *a Texas General Land Office & Texas Nature Conservancy 1986; Diamond, Riskind, and*

above, edaphic differences match the segment of the line from the gulf to west of San Antonio. From there to the Rio Grande, the boundary follows the Balcones Escarpment, which is a very rugged and abrupt topographic feature in this region.

3. Plains vs. Roughlands

The third biogeographic pattern is another north-south interface occurring farther north. From east to west, the line connects Georgetown, San Saba, Brady, Eldorado, and Odessa. This boundary is less sharp than the others. It roughly corresponds to the irregular northern edge

VEGETATIONAL PATTERN AND CONSERVATION STATUS OF FLORA AND FAUNA

Conservation status*

Plant communities^a				Species^b						
				Flora			Fauna			
Types	U/R	T	E	T	E	Ex	Ed	U/R	T	E
16	4	2		3	2		4	2	15	1
8	1			2	1		3	3	7	1
7	3	1	2				4		6	
15		1	2	3			5	2	23	9
4							2	1	7	
15		1	2	8			5	Many	28	4
13				3	1		4	Many	18	6
12		1		1			2	6	6	2
11	2	1					2	1	4	1
28	Many			5	6	1	6	Many	20	8

Ex = Extinct   Ed = Extirpated since Anglo-American settlement

Orzell 1987; ^b *Texas Parks and Wildlife Department state regulations 1997*

of the Edwards Plateau, the approximate southern limit of the Great Plains. To the south, the terrain is hilly, irregular, and more rocky. This is the region of the roughlands of the Edwards Plateau and Trans-Pecos, which are the eastern extension of the plateaus, deserts, and mountain ranges of the Southwest.

REGIONAL TRENDS

There are 4 regional trends in Texas biogeography. These occur at a lower distinction level than the 3 general trends but, nevertheless, are evident.

Table 1.4. ECOLOGICAL REGIONS OF TEXAS— LAND USES

Region	Land Use	
	Major	Minor
East Texas Forests	Pine-hardwood industry, pine plantations, cattle pastures and dairies	Farms, oil fields, lignite mines, minerals, reservoirs, recreation, poultry farms, hunting leases
Post Oak Savannah	Cattle pastures, farms	Lignite mines, minerals, deer leases
Blackland Prairies	Cattle pastures and dairies, farms	Urban and industrial centers, poultry farms, minerals
Coastal Prairies and Marshes	Farms, cattle pastures and dairies	Urban, industrial, petro-chemical centers, recreation, waterfowl leases
Cross Timbers and Prairies	Cattle pastures and dairies, farms	Sheep and goat ranches, minerals
South Texas Brushlands and Coastal Sand Plains	Cattle ranches, gardens, farms	Sheep and goat ranches, poultry farms, deer/javelina leases, minerals, recreation, winter resorts
Edwards Plateau and Llano Uplift	Cattle, sheep, and goat ranches	Deer and exotic big game leases, some farms, recreation, minerals
Rolling Plains	Cattle ranches, farms	Oil fields, upland game bird leases, minerals
High Plains	Farming, cattle ranching and feedlots	Oil fields
Trans-Pecos	Cattle, sheep, and goat ranches	Some irrigated farms, recreation, deer leases, minerals

Sources: Hatch, Gandhi, and Brown 1990; Jordan, Bean, and Holmes 1984; Texas Almanac 1996–1997; Thomas, Adams, and Thigpen 1990.

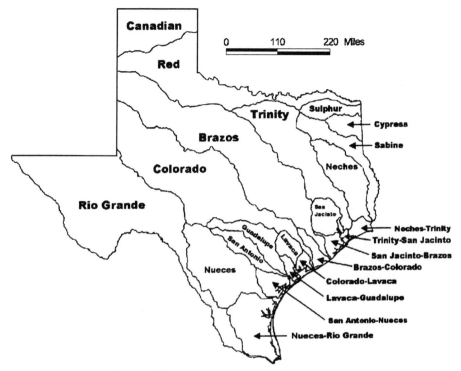

Fig 1.2. *River and coastal basins of Texas.*

1. Eastern Forest vs. Oakwoods and Prairies

This east-west segregation corresponds to a climatic gradient, primarily moisture, as well as edaphic (soil) factors that separate eastern pine-hardwood forests from western mixtures of oak woodlands and tallgrass prairies.

2. Edwards Plateau vs. Trans-Pecos

These 2 roughlands are separated by an ecotonal area, the Stockton Plateau, which divides the hilly, more mesic Edwards Plateau to the east from the more xeric deserts and mountains of the Trans-Pecos to the west. Although the shift is not abrupt, the plateau is generally lower than the lowest basin elevation in the Trans-Pecos.

3. High Plains vs. Rolling Plains

The north-south Caprock Escarpment of the panhandle forms an abrupt elevational separation of the high and low plains. The High

Plains of the west are considerably higher and relatively flat and were uniform shortgrass prairie until converted to cropland and grazing-land. The Rolling Plains to the east are more varied in topography and vegetation.

4. *Coastal Zone vs. Inland Regions*

The influence of the marine environment as it interfaces with land along the Gulf Coast creates a unique, ever-changing, dynamic coastal zone that defines a narrow region that contrasts markedly with inland regions.

Ecological Regions

Based upon physiography and vegetation, Texas can be divided into 12 ecological regions (frontispiece). This biogeographic analysis of landscape ecology is very important, because this approach could improve the probability of long-term, effective land-use decisions in the best interest of economic and ecologic considerations. Unfortunately, we are far from achieving an integrated biogeographic approach. Most people not only are unaware of the landscape ecology in the area of their residence but do not know or understand how land-use decisions in other areas also affect them as well as the state as a whole.

1. East Texas Pine and Hardwood Forests

Description. These timberlands are also known as the Pine Belt or "Piney Woods" because of the predominance of pine trees throughout much of the region. This area is part of the Southern Mixed Forest that extends westward into Texas from the Red River to within 25 miles of the Gulf Coast.

Physiognomy is medium to tall forest of broad-leaved deciduous and needle-leaved evergreen trees. Dominant vegetation is oak-hickory-pine-beech-sweetgum-magnolia. Plant community sites range from dry sandylands to permanent wetlands. There are 16 plant community types in this region, more than in any other region except the Trans-Pecos. Four community types are unique or rare (pine-oak woodlands, sphagnum shrub swamps, sandstone seeps) and 2 are threatened (American beech–southern magnolia, longleaf pine–tall grass). Three plants are endangered (white bladderpod, Texas trailing phlox, Navasota ladies'-tresses). Several factors, especially the early effects of timber industries, complicate definition and subdivision of the region. However, there are

3 definite subregions, each recognized by the dominant species of pine, all of which are fire adapted.

The northern subregion is the largest and is characterized by short-leaf pine. Islands of this subregion occur in Red River and Leon Counties in the northwest and southwest, respectively. The central, eastern subregion is dominated by longleaf pine. It includes most of the "Upper" Big Thicket, i.e., that portion in which American beech is present. The southern subregion is characterized by loblolly pine. It includes a small portion of the "Upper" Big Thicket and the "Lower" Big Thicket, i.e., that portion in which American beech is absent. Islands of "lost" loblollies also occur westward in Bastrop, Fayette, and Caldwell Counties in the southern Post Oak Savannah.

Land Use. The largest oil fields in the state are located in this region, and the value of the timber industry is second only to oil. This region also has the greatest variety of farming. Until 1945, farms were family or tenant operated and comparatively small, and livestock was commonly permitted to range freely in many localities. Since 1930, there has been a decline in the number of farms and a precipitous decrease of farms operated by tenants.

In former years, the practice of uncontrolled burning caused heavy losses of young timber and damage to wildlife habitats. Today, controlled burning is recognized as a useful tool in local rather than extensive management of both timber and wildlife.

Most timberland has been cut, and the sites are now producing the 4th generation of managed timber, primarily pines. Overcutting for saw and paper mills was once widespread in East Texas except on large private lands and on state and federal forests. Slash pine was introduced as a commercial species, and the most abundant grass, bermuda, also an introduced species, has become so thoroughly naturalized as to be popularly considered a native plant.

This region is also known as the land of "lakes," i.e., manmade reservoirs that inundate much of the original bottomland forest and associated wetlands that were large areas of fish and wildlife habitats.

Wildlife. Principal game species are eastern gray squirrel (bottomlands), eastern fox squirrel (uplands), white-tailed deer, and northern bobwhite. The eastern wild turkey was a valuable game bird during early days of settlement but was extirpated. Today, attempts are being made to reintroduce it into areas of suitable habitat. Black bears once inhabited this region but were exterminated by 1940. Important furbearers are Virginia opossum, raccoon, gray fox, and nutria (an introduced South American rodent). Minor furbearers are striped skunk and mink.

In response to the great variety of habitats within this region, there is a high diversity of nongame species. Examples of such habitat types are upland forests, forested bottomlands, pine stands, deciduous woods, mixed woods, rivers, swamps, bayous, sloughs, oxbow lakes, woodland edges, second-growth woods, open pine savannahs, sphagnum bogs, baygalls (shrub swamps), and seeps.

The only terrestrial species in Texas to become extinct since Anglo-American settlement inhabited the forests of this region (passenger pigeon, Carolina parakeet, and probably the ivory-billed woodpecker). Conservation management programs for some of the extirpated (4), unique or rare (2), threatened (15), and endangered (4) species are operational, but 1, the red-cockaded woodpecker, is very complex and controversial.

There are many complicated wildlife problems. Formerly, much of the farmland was operated by tenants who were not active participants in conservation programs. There was widespread disrespect for protective wildlife laws strengthened by the time-honored system of the open range and large blocks of "company-owned" land.

Free-ranging (feral) pigs severely damage seedlings of longleaf pine crops and compete for acorns and other important mast. If uncontrolled, these animals can greatly compete with native wildlife.

Continued conversion of poor sandy soil from cultivation to pasture would be desirable if native wildlife cover and food plants were planted and/or not removed and grazing pressure were reduced.

East Texas forests and the trend to build large reservoirs for water resource development within major watersheds make the region especially well suited for recreation and industrial expansion. This provides habitat for many aquatic and semiaquatic species but eliminates extensive habitats of many bottomland forest species. Also, reservoirs change downstream flooding patterns, which adversely impact species composition and quality of floodplain forests. Furthermore, there are local conflicts between timber, hunting, and environmental interests.

2. Post Oak Savannah

Description. This narrow oak belt is a forest, woodland, or savannah depending upon its location within the region. It is a narrow, highly irregular belt wedged between the East Texas Pine-Hardwood Forest to the east, Blackland Prairies to the west, and the Coastal Prairie and South Texas Brushlands to the south.

Physiognomy is medium to tall broad-leaved deciduous and some needle-leaved evergreen trees. The name of the region is derived from the predominant tree, the post oak. However, many other species of oak are common, as are hickories and other trees. There are 8 plant community types, of which 1 is unique (loblolly pine–post oak–blackjack oak). Two plants are endangered (large-fruited sand-verbena and Navasota ladies'-tresses). In the northern and eastern areas, timber is open and savannahlike, but in the southern and western areas, it is close and thickety. In the localities where marl (limy clay) outcrops occur, live oak is common. Farkleberry is a common understory plant in the northern area. Characteristic of the southern area is a thick understory of yaupon and eastern red cedar. Within about the last 40 years, a decided invasion of cedar has produced a noticeable scattering of this evergreen through the oaks.

Most of the plant species occur in other regions, but Post Oak Savannah soils are distinctive. The area is also known as the Clay Pan Savannah because a shallow, nearly impervious clay pan causes the soil to be unexpectedly arid. An exception is the Carrizo Sands area in Bastrop County, home of the unique "Lost Pines," a western range extension of loblolly pine. Sphagnum bogs also occur within this region.

Land Use. The Post Oak Savannah is one of the first regions that was settled by Anglo-Americans because of its transition between forest and prairie. Cultivation severely eroded its soils, and grazing caused proliferation of understory thickets of yaupon and bumelia.

From 1830 to 1888, uplands were open and parklike with waist-high grasses. Bottomlands were timbered and free of underbrush. Land not under rail fence was open range for cattle and hogs. Cultivation was primarily cotton, with smaller areas of garden crops.

By 1900, most land was fenced by barbed wire, and roads had been built. Much of the large timber had been used earlier for rail fences, fires were suppressed, and small trees and underbrush appeared.

From 1900 to 1930, undergrowth increased, and mast crops failed more regularly. From 1900 to 1944, cotton peaked and declined as the major crop, and crop diversification developed. Range was overstocked with livestock.

Since 1930, young oaks, hickories, and underbrush have dominated uplands. Loss of upland cover in cultivated areas resulted in long periods of flooding that killed large bottomland trees.

From 1950 to 1965, livestock production increased. Large tracts of hardwoods were cleared and converted to improved pastures. Since 1965, this trend has continued, and farm production has declined.

Wildlife. Prior to 1860, game in the Post Oak Savannah was apparently plentiful. Principal species were white-tailed deer, wild turkey, northern bobwhite, and eastern fox and eastern gray squirrels. At that time, as well as today, the Rio Grande wild turkey inhabited southern areas. The eastern wild turkey was originally native to northern areas, and attempts are being made to reintroduce it into suitable habitat. In winter, ducks were present, and passenger pigeons once roosted locally in large numbers.

Between 1860 and 1920, wildlife began a rapid decline with the increase of settlers. Year-round hunting with no bag limits was a common practice. Passenger pigeons were extinct by 1900, and turkeys and deer were killed in such numbers that by 1920 so few were left that hunting was unproductive. Quail and squirrels were exceptions to this trend. They were abundant and maintained their numbers during this period.

Between 1920 and 1948, quail, squirrels, and ducks were principal game. Farming practices provided optimum quail habitat, and populations thrived. Squirrels were abundant in timbered bottoms, and thousands of ducks wintered in the bottomlands.

From 1948 to the present, quail populations declined with changing land use from cropland farming to improved pastures, and this trend continues. Squirrel and waterfowl populations have maintained themselves in suitable habitat and provide abundant hunting opportunities. The deer population has continued to increase, and deer hunting provides the major recreation in this area.

Major furbearers of this region are raccoon, Virginia opossum, coyote, and striped skunk. Minor furbearers are nutria, gray fox, and American beaver. Depleted species include 1 extinct, 3 extirpated, 2 unique or rare, 7 threatened, and 3 endangered. Perhaps the best known of these is the endangered Houston toad, which is found in the Lost Pines area of Bastrop County.

Free-ranging hobs severely damage wildlife habitat and compete for food; however, "hog hunting" has recently become quite popular with many sportsmen.

Wildlife will continue to be influenced by land-use practices and can only exist as long as suitable habitat is provided. The current trend toward conversion of hardwood timber and brushland to improved pastures effectively removes this acreage from wildlife production and results in depletion of this resource. Also, as in the East Texas forest region, the trend to build large reservoirs eliminates bottomland habitats of many species.

To meet future energy demands, large areas of the Post Oak Savannah are being strip-mined for lignite. This could result in destruction or permanent alteration of productive aquatic and terrestrial habitats for wildlife unless proper protective measures are undertaken to reclaim and revegetate these areas with native plants.

3. Blackland Prairies

Description. The major Blackland Prairie extends in a southwestern direction as a broad wedge-shaped area from near the Red River in Northeast Texas to the vicinity of San Antonio (Bexar County), where it merges with the brushlands of the Rio Grande Plains. The eastern boundary is the Post Oak Savannah; the western boundary is the Edwards Plateau except in the north, where it is separated from the Grand Prairie by a narrow strip of forest—the East Cross Timbers. Minor prairies (Fayette, San Antonio, Vegua, and Washington) lie somewhat parallel and south of the major prairie.

Original physiognomy was medium-tall, rather dense grasslands with scattered open groves of deciduous trees in minor prairies. Dominant grasses were dropseeds, switchgrass, eastern gamagrass, yellow indiangrass, and big and little bluestem. There were osage orange, sugar hackberry, eastern red cedar, oaks, elms, pecan, and eastern cottonwood in scattered mottes, knolls, hills, escarps, ridges, and bottomlands. Today, in addition, honey mesquite is common throughout the prairies.

There are few unique or rare species. However, the original 7 plant community types themselves are almost gone. Only a few small, scattered parcels of a total of 5,000 acres (0.04%) of the original 12 million acres remain. The 3 basic community types are threatened with extinction (gamagrass-switchgrass, little bluestem–indiangrass, and silveanus dropseed). The rich, unique blackland soils were derived from the activities of abundant soil organisms at least as diverse as those above ground.

Land Use. The moldboard plow, perfected by Thomas Jefferson about 1800, gave settlers an implement that could turn heavy, fertile clay soils. In time, equipment improved, and heavy draft mules were brought into the region. Corn was grown to feed the mules and horses that supplied power for agriculture. The economy that motivated development of the Blacklands was "white gold"—cotton. Railroads and heavy farm equipment (steam tractors) put the area in the cotton-producing business. Peak productivity was reached in the mid-1920's but then declined due to loss of soil fertility. In the 1930's, along with general concern for soil loss, practices were developed to curb erosion and to return soil fertility.

Today, most of the Blackland Prairies are under cultivation or are being grazed. Unfortunately, much of the early soil depletion damage cannot be restored. As a result, short grasses and brush have replaced most of the originally dominant tall bunch grasses. However, a few native hay meadows have been preserved and constitute accurate representations of the composition of the original prairie vegetation. This region is the most thickly populated area in the state and contains along its western border more of the state's large and middle-sized cities than any other area.

Wildlife. Originally, the Blackland Prairies had large numbers of American bison, pronghorn, plains gray wolf, red wolf, and greater prairie-chicken. These grassland species are now gone, being incompatible with intensive agriculture. Under modern conditions, the Blackland Prairies have low game production. The wooded belts along streams once had numerous white-tailed deer and wild turkeys and still provide much of the border type of environment necessary to many species of wildlife. The mourning dove is the most important game species in this region. Northern bobwhite populations are found in "grass" years when sufficient food and cover result from plentiful rain. Eastern cottontails are a source of sport and food. Eastern fox squirrels and bullfrogs are important in areas where suitable habitat remains. Major furbearers are raccoon, Virginia opossum, and striped skunk. Minor furbearers are ringtail and eastern spotted skunk. In addition to 4 extirpated species, 6 are threatened, but none are endangered.

Floodwater-retarding structures provide satisfactory habitat for game fishes and waterfowl. With proper preproject planning and accommodations for management, excellent habitats could be provided by these water impoundments, and the impact could be significant. In recent years, the furbearer resource has been important and is an incentive for preservation of their habitats, especially bottomlands. Successful wildlife management in the Blackland Prairies depends upon intentional application of farming and grazing practices and watershed conservation to provide habitat.

4. Gulf Coast Prairies and Marshes

4a and 4b. Dune/Barrier Islands and Marshes

Description. The Dune/Barrier Islands and Marshes include a 3–20-mile-wide arc of coastal flats having smooth terrain with low relief. There are alluvial embayments, fluvial and deltaic deposits, sand beaches, barrier islands, and mud flats. Artificially created dredge spoil islands are also included in this region.

Physiognomy is open, short to medium-tall grassland with occasional shrubs and medium to very tall grassland, often very dense. There are 6 plant community types. None are classified as unique, rare, threatened, or endangered. Dominant coastal vegetation is sea-oats and seacoast bluestem. Farther inland, smooth cordgrass dominates. Other components are dwarf saltwort, sedges, crotons, coastal saltgrass, Pan American balsamscale, morningglories, rushes, wolfberries, Jamaica sawgrass, panicums, paspalums, common reed, arrowheads, bulrushes, sea purslanes, cattails, pricklyashes, and marshmillet. The floral composition is rich—about 45% of vascular species native to Texas are found within this region. The crown shape of trees, especially oaks, is greatly affected by the almost continuous salt spray and is quite noticeable around High Island and on the Aransas National Wildlife Refuge.

Although plants are abundant in this region, beneficial aquatic species and open water areas necessary for wildlife are being threatened by several introduced pest weeds, foremost of which are water hyacinth and alligator weed. Some native plants are also increasing, e.g., cattails, waterlettuce, common frogbit, American featherfoil, and waterprimroses. Habitats especially threatened are streams, canals, lakes, and ponds.

Land Use. These marshes and barrier islands contain several popular state parks and wildlife management areas and national parks and wildlife refuges. Urban, industrial, and recreational developments have increased in recent years. Most land is not well suited for cultivation because of periodic flooding and saline soils. However, much of the area is grazed, resulting in overgrazing on coastal islands.

Wildlife. Principal game species are ducks and geese. Two thirds of the waterfowl population of the Central Flyway winter in this area and the adjacent Coastal Prairie. This includes 12 species with 90% of their winter population within these regions. During the hunting season, sportsmen from many parts of the United States come to the Texas

Coast for unexcelled waterfowl shooting. Minor game birds are rails, gallinules, and coots. Important furbearers are raccoon, Virginia opossum, nutria, and muskrat.

A large number of fish and wildlife species is dependent upon this long, narrow coastal zone; some are resident, some transitory, and many aquatic species spend critical parts of their life cycles in this area. The marshes are spawning and nursery areas for fin- and shellfish. Tidal flats are important feeding grounds for many species of coastal birds. Manmade islands, created by the dumping of dredged spoil materials along the Intracoastal Waterway, are used by many species of birds for nesting. These spoil banks, when protected, are sanctuaries for a number of coastal species that have been driven from their native nesting habitats by human activities.

The West Indian manatee is extirpated from the Texas Coast. Two species are unique or rare. Twenty-three species are threatened, and 9 endangered species are dependent upon this region, the best known being green, Atlantic hawksbill, leatherback, loggerhead, and Atlantic ridley sea turtles; brown pelican; reddish egret; Arctic peregrine falcon; whooping crane; piping plover; and Eskimo curlew. Attwater's greater prairie-chicken formerly inhabited barrier islands on the upper and central coast.

The 2 most critical habitat types are wetlands and submerged grassflats. The highly productive wetlands are essential to many species, marine and terrestrial. Habitat quality has been diminished by reduced freshwater inflows due to marsh draining and filling, flood control measures, channelization, dredging, and other developments. Wildlife losses that result are often so subtle they may not be noticed until considerable change has occurred. Many species are declining in abundance, especially those dependent upon wetlands.

In 1923, only 600,000 people lived on the Texas Coast. Today, the population is about 4.5 million, or 26% of the state total. This impact has caused serious problems involving wildlife, but it has been estimated that 85% of the coast can be maintained in a healthy state by carefully planned management. Such management can provide high quality economic and aesthetic opportunities and can maintain varied vital habitat, all of benefit to mankind and wildlife.

4c. Coastal Prairie

Description. The Coastal Prairie is an almost level strip 20–80 miles inland from the zone of dunes, barrier islands, and marshes. There are

2 subregions separated near the vicinity of the San Antonio River: the wider northeastern section is nearly flat grassland prairie, and the subhumid, more narrow southern section of similar relief consists of coastal brush.

Physiognomy is medium to tall, dense to open grassland. There are 12 plant community types, of which 1 is threatened and 2 are endangered. Three plants are endangered. Dominant vegetation is seacoast bluestem and Gulf cordgrass. Other components are bluestems, three-awns, buffalograss, sedges, panicums, paspalums, indiangrasses, dropseeds, needlegrasses, and rattlebush. Within the Coastal Prairie are 575,000 acres of forests extending from Galveston County westward to the drainage of the Lavaca River in Jackson and Calhoun Counties. Principal trees are oaks, pecan, ashes, hackberries, eastern cottonwood, American sycamore, willows, and some loblolly pine. Except along the Trinity and San Jacinto Rivers, bottomland forests do not reach the coast. Deltaic deposits and banks of the lowermost stretches of other rivers are occupied by salt meadows and marshes.

Land Use. Since the early days of Anglo-American settlement, much of the southern and inland area as far north as the Brazos River has been greatly modified by agriculture. Before the period of cultivation, intensive grazing reduced the grass cover to the extent that mesquites, live oaks, pricklypears, and acacias became established and dominant. In some areas, recent brush control programs have been so effective that scarcely a trace of original prairie or secondary brushland remains. Few open prairies remain; most have been transformed into farms and ranches or absorbed into urban areas. Much of the area has been continuously grazed and invaded by exotics such as Macartney rose and Chinese tallow tree as well as native mesquite and huisache.

Wildlife. Waterfowl are principal game species in rice fields and marshes. Timbered bottomlands afford good habitat for white-tailed deer and eastern gray and fox squirrels. Prairies contain suitable habitat for mourning doves and, locally, northern bobwhites and sandhill cranes. Major furbearers are raccoon, Virginia opossum, and nutria. Ring-necked pheasants have been established as game birds in some counties of the Upper Coastal Prairie.

Four species are extirpated from the Coastal Prairie, and there are 18 threatened and 4 endangered ones. The precariously endangered Attwater's greater prairie-chicken is still present in small numbers in a few localities and is being carefully managed on the Attwater Prairie

Chicken National Wildlife Refuge established for its preservation. Its existence is threatened by habitat loss.

Reduction and deterioration of wildlife habitats have been caused by tree and brush clearing, intensive agriculture, urban development, and land fragmentation. Much of the area, once protected on large ranches, is now subjected to uncontrolled development. This has resulted from the fragmentation of ranches due to increased land taxation.

5. East and West Cross Timbers and Grand and North Central Prairies

Description. This is a complex transitional area of prairie dissected by 2 parallel timbered strips extending from north to south. The region is located in North-central Texas west of the Blackland Prairies, east of the Rolling Plains, and north of the Edwards Plateau and Llano Uplift. The origin of the name "Cross Timbers" is obscure, but it may refer to the crossing through timbered areas from adjacent grasslands when the first Anglo-Americans traveled there. It may also refer to the longitudinal axes of the timbered tracts, which are crosswise to the rivers and creeks (pers. commun., Charles D. Tipton).

There are 4 plant community types, none unique, rare, threatened, or endangered. However, a rare plant, the Comanche Peak prairie clover, grows among limestone outcrops. Physiognomy is oak wood and tallgrass prairie. Dominant plants are post and blackjack oak, hickories, and tall and midgrasses, e.g., big and little bluestem, yellow indiangrass, and sideoats grama.

Land Use. Range and pasture utilize over half the West Cross Timbers, and the remaining land is used for farming. All these uses are increasing. Major land uses and future intensification in the East Cross Timbers are range, pasture, urban development, and farming. Much of the native vegetation of the region has been plowed and grazed intensively. In areas of the North Central Prairie heavily used by livestock and where prairie fires have been suppressed, native grasslands have been replaced by honey mesquite, lotebush, and grasses more tolerant of grazing, e.g., silver bluestem, Texas wintergrass, and buffalograss.

Wildlife. The white-tailed deer is the only big game animal of significance in this region. Upland game animals are the Rio Grande wild turkey, northern bobwhite, and eastern fox squirrel. Migratory game birds include the mourning dove and wintering waterfowl. Important furbearers are raccoon, Virginia opossum, coyote, striped skunk, ringtail, gray fox, and red fox (introduced European species). Two species are extirpated, 1 is unique/rare, 7 are threatened, but none are endangered. Major land-use trends affecting wildlife are intensive grazing, brush removal, and development of improved pastures, rural areas, and water impoundments.

6 and 7. Coastal Sand Plains and South Texas Brushlands

Description. The Coastal Sand Plains and South Texas Brushlands occupy a large, wide, wedge-shaped plain in South Texas below the Balcones Escarpment, east of the Rio Grande, and west of many ecotones and extensions of the Sea Oats Prairie, Coastal Marsh–Southern Cordgrass Prairie, Subhumid Coastal Prairie, and southern minor extensions of the Blackland Prairies (San Antonio and Fayette Prairies). This is the famous "Brush Country" of Texas folklore.

Physiognomy of the region is dense to rather open medium tall grassland with low to medium tall broad-leaved deciduous and needle-leaved evergreen trees and shrubs scattered singly, in groves, and in thickets, i.e., a chaparral-like savanna. Fifteen plant community types occur here, including 1 threatened (Texas ebony–snake-eyes) and 2 endangered (Texas palmetto and Texas ebony–anacua). Five species are endangered. Dominants are blackbrush acacia, seacoast bluestem, mesquite, sand live oak, and plains bristlegrass. Other components are acacias, bluestems, threeawns, gramas, signalgrass, buffalograss, sandburs, windmillgrasses, bluewood, pappusgrasses, paspalums, indiangrasses, and crinkleawn. On the basis of present-day dominants, the South Texas Brushlands and Coastal Sand Plains are a patchwork of brushland, grassland, woodland, and parkland. This vast area may be subdivided into 6 subregions: (1) Guajillo, (2) Mesquite-Acacia Savannah, (3) Mesquite–Live Oak Savannah, (4) Low Brush, (5) Freer Mixed Brush, and (6) Ceniza Shrub. This complex flora includes a high number of regional and statewide endemic species. Also, there is a high number of peripheral species reaching the northernmost limits of their range. Forested belts range from narrow to several miles wide along the Nueces, Leona, and Frio Rivers.

Land Use. This region has a history of the oldest land abuse in the state. Three centuries of continuous grazing by livestock and suppression of prairie fires have transformed the grassland into a subtropical thornbrush forest. The mesquite-chaparral vegetation now characteristic of this region is much more extensive than previously. Records of original surveys indicate that dry, gravelly soils have always supported such vegetation and that increased grazing, control of fire, and droughts suppressed the grasses to such an extent that brush has spread into adjacent level, fertile areas that were formerly covered by an abundance of grasses. Prairie relicts are still sufficiently numerous and variant to indicate stages of progressive invasion by brush species.

Dry and irrigated farming are practiced in this region. It is an important cattle-producing section of Texas and supports several of the largest cattle ranches in the world. Historically, this region was sheep country; today, sheep and Angora goats are raised in small numbers. Extensive research has demonstrated that well-planned brush management can enhance livestock production and wildlife habitat.

Wildlife. Game species in the South Texas Brushlands are more diverse and in many cases more abundant than in any other region of the state. Pronghorn were originally native but no longer occur there. White-tailed deer, Rio Grande wild turkeys, collared peccaries, northern bobwhite and scaled quail, and mourning doves are abundant in many counties. The Lower Rio Grande Valley contains principal nesting grounds in Texas for the white-winged dove, white-tipped dove, red-billed pigeon, and plain chachalaca. Major furbearers are bobcat and ringtail. Minor furbearers are striped skunk, bobcat, and gray fox. Nilgai antelope have been established on a few large ranges but are subject to mortality during unusual winter storms.

South Texas supports a rich fauna, especially birds, but the most diverse wildlife species occur in the habitats of the Rio Grande delta and along the river upstream. Included among this fauna are many tropical species, of which 3 parrot species may be extending their range northward from Mexico. Five species are extirpated; many species are unique or rare; 28 are threatened; and 4 are endangered, the best known of which are the ocelot and jaguarundi.

The Lower Rio Grande Valley is densely populated, and the subtropical climate permits intensive agriculture, especially citrus fruits and vegetables. In this area, only a small amount of critical brush habitat remains for the nesting of white-winged doves; however, they nest extensively in citrus orchards.

8 and 9. Edwards Plateau and Llano Uplift

Description. The Edwards Plateau and Llano Uplift region is the "Hill Country" of Texas—the land of limestone, granite, and numerous springs and caves. It is south of the High and Lower Plains and east of the Trans-Pecos, and it is bounded on the south and east by the Balcones Escarpment, which separates it from the South Texas Brushlands and the Blackland Prairies, respectively. The east-central portion is the Granitic Mineral, Central Mineral, or Llano "Basin," including mainly Mason, Llano, Gillespie, and Burnet Counties. Cedar brakes occur along the Balcones Escarpment. There are 13 plant community types, none threatened or endangered. Three plants are endangered.

The Edwards Plateau is a juniper-oak-bluestem savannah; the Granitic Mineral, Central Mineral, or Llano Basin is a mesquite-oak-bluestem savannah; and the Cedar Brakes is an Ashe juniper–dominant area. Important bottomland trees are oaks and pecan.

This is a region of many endemic vascular plants. In addition, spring-fed canyons along the Balcones Escarpment mark the western limit of many eastern species, while sheltered canyons on southern and eastern edges are noted for a high number of rare, peripheral Mexican species.

Land Use. Principal industries that developed in the Edwards Plateau region were cattle, sheep, and goat raising. Farming was confined to deeper soils, and feed for livestock was the main crop. Today, 98% of the land is range, primarily for wool and mohair production, although a large deer population and many exotic big game species also utilize the area.

Wildlife. Principal game animals are white-tailed deer and Rio Grande wild turkey; others are eastern fox squirrel (considered to be "vermin" by some pecan growers), mourning dove, and, in some areas, northern bobwhite. There is a relict population of Montezuma quail. Historically, black bears were common in this region. Major furbearers are ringtail, raccoon, gray fox, and striped skunk. Minor furbearers are red fox and bobcat.

Most streams in this region are clear and thus attractive to fishermen and campers. White-tailed deer and Rio Grande wild turkey are abundant (highest density in the state), and income from hunters to landowners is more important than in other sections of Texas. The growth of cedar (juniper) brush and oaks due to the stoppage of frequent burning by Indians and the extension of the livestock industry increased deer, eastern fox squirrel, and turkey populations.

Most of the exotic game mammals in Texas are located in the Edwards Plateau and exist on private lands under deer-proof fences. Important species are axis deer, blackbuck antelope, sika deer, fallow deer, mouflon sheep, and European wild boar (feral pigs). Many animals have escaped, and many pose problems for the future (e.g., axis and sika deer).

One species is extinct (San Marcos gambusia); 4 species are extirpated; many are unique or rare; 18 are threatened; and 6 are endangered. Among the best known are blindcat, Clear Creek gambusia, fountain darter, Guadalupe bass, cave salamanders, cliff chirping frog, Cagle's map turtle, golden-cheeked warbler, and black-capped vireo. The newest national wildlife refuge, the Balcones Canyonlands, has been established to the west of the Austin area. However, serious problems confront wildlife in the Edwards Plateau region. These involve continuous grazing, clearing and burning of brush, competition of wildlife with livestock and exotics, fragmentation of habitats from continued subdivision of landholdings, and expanding urbanization into adjacent canyonlands. The specialized spring- and cave-dwelling fish, amphibians, bats, and numerous invertebrates comprise the world's most diverse aquifer-associated fauna. Edwards Aquifer water is being depleted, thus threatening this unique fauna.

10. Rolling Plains

Description. The Rolling Plains region is located east of the High Plains, west of the West Cross Timbers and North Central Prairie, and north of the Edwards Plateau. It crosses the northern half of the High Plains along the breaks of the Canadian River. These plains are crossed by the Canadian, Colorado, Concho, and Red Rivers, all of which begin at the Caprock Escarpment, cut into the soft sands and clays, and produce the characteristic rolling hills and broad flats of this region. The 3 subdivisions are Mesquite Plains, Escarpment Breaks, and Canadian Breaks. Physiognomy varies from open, short to tall, scattered to dense grasslands to savannahs with bunch grasses. There are 12 plant community types, of which the cottonwood-tallgrass series is threatened. The Texas poppymallow is endangered. Until cut by early settlers, pinyon pine occurred on bluffs of both breaks. Dominant grasses are bluestems, needlegrasses, gramas, and buffalograss. Dominant upland trees are honey mesquite, junipers, and oaks. Dominant bottomland trees are cottonwoods, hackberries, elms, willows, western soapberry, and plums. Common exotics along stream courses are French saltcedar and Russian olive.

Land Use. Over ¾ of the plains is in range, but dryland and irrigated crops are important. These uses are being intensified. Sheep production has increased considerably in the southern third of the Rolling Plains that was previously devoted to cattle production. Poor range management practices increased the density of mesquite (presently the most widespread, characteristic woody plant) as well as snakeweeds, pricklypears, and sagebrushes.

Wildlife. Historically, the Rolling Plains were inhabited by an abundance of American bison, pronghorns, collared peccaries, lesser prairie-chickens, black-tailed prairie dogs, plains gray wolves, and Manitoba elk. Today, principal game animals are white-tailed deer, eastern fox squirrels (in timbered areas), Rio Grande wild turkeys, northern bobwhite and scaled quail, and mourning doves. There is local, highly restrictive hunting of pronghorns and lesser prairie-chickens along the western border of the Lower Plains. Restoration of these animals is possible in other areas but is dependent upon farming and grazing practices. Important furbearers are raccoon, Virginia opossum, coyote, striped skunk, ringtail, and red and gray foxes.

Two species are extirpated, 6 are unique or rare, 6 are threatened, and 2 are endangered. A relict species—the Palo Duro mouse, related to the piñon mouse of the Rocky Mountains—occurs only on the juniper-covered slopes of Palo Duro, Tule, and associated canyons in a few counties along the Caprock Escarpment. Most of the distribution of 2 water snakes occurs in this region: the Brazos water snake in the upper Brazos River drainage, from Haskell to Bosque Counties; and the Concho water snake in the upper Colorado River drainage, from Coke to Lampasas Counties. The Texas kangaroo rat, another relict, occurs only on hard, packed soils in the center of the mesquite plains, roughly in the area from Clay and Jack Counties west to Cottle and King Counties. The endangered interior least tern nests on river sandbars.

The Brazos and Concho water snakes and the Texas kangaroo rat are particularly vulnerable. Further damming of the upper Brazos and upper Colorado Rivers would destroy much of the habitat of the water snakes. Mesquite eradication programs are rapidly destroying the habitat of the kangaroo rat.

11. High Plains

Description. The High Plains region is a gently sloping alluvial mantle extending east of the Rocky Mountains. The eastern boundary of the area is the Caprock Escarpment. The northern portion of the plains is bisected by the Canadian River, and high escarpments border the flood plain. The High Plains are characteristically level, relatively treeless, and semiarid. There are thousands of small, shallow, seasonal lakes, or "playas."

Until converted to agriculture, physiognomy was predominantly short grasses with limited areas of shrubs and trees. There are 11 plant community types; 2 are unique (scattered sand dunes with Harvard oak, sand sagebrush, and little bluestem and tallgrass meadows along the Canadian River) and 1 is threatened (cottonwood-tallgrass). Dominant vegetation was formerly mesquite-grama-buffalograss on the plains and plum-sumac-sagewort-bluestem on the river sands. Mesquite is an invader of the High Plains, but its increase, unlike in other regions, has been slowed by lower precipitation and colder, longer winters. The numerous playa lakes on the High Plains support luxuriant growth of shallow water emergent and shoreline sedges. When dry, they support western wheatgrass. Southern salty playas support many species of salt-tolerant plants. Although cottonwood and willow trees line riverbanks and hackberries line draws, many have been replaced by French salt-cedar and Russian olive. Unique areas are vegetated sand dunes and tallgrass meadows.

Land Use. Settled late, the High Plains region was once entirely cattle country, but during the past 60 years, its economy shifted toward grain and cotton farming, which is predominant today. The building of windmills allowed westward expansion. Agriculture changed from grazing to dryland farming to irrigation. During drought periods, soils are subject to wind erosion, being a part of the familiar "dust bowl." Oil production is extensive in some localities. About 60% of the region is cropland, ½ of which is irrigated. Livestock ranching is important where terrain is sloping and urban industries are expanding. Well-irrigated and nonirrigated agriculture are intensifying; as a result, aquifers are being lowered at an alarming rate.

Wildlife. Two species are extirpated, 1 is unique, 4 are threatened, and 1 is endangered (black-footed ferret). The High and Rolling Plains were the last stronghold of the great American bison herds in Texas and their major, natural predator, the plains gray wolf. Migratory trails of bison are still evident in many places along the Caprock Escarpment. Mountain lions and black bears inhabited areas along the Caprock, and American badgers were common on the plains.

Thousands of pronghorns once inhabited this region. Local populations persist and are hunted. White-tailed and mule deer and Rio Grande wild turkeys, once locally common along wooded watercourses and canyons, have been restored. The sharp-tailed grouse may have occurred in the northern Panhandle until about 1906. An important big game animal in the area of the Palo Duro Canyon is the introduced Barbary (aoudad) sheep. Today, important furbearers are coyotes and American badgers.

The lesser prairie-chicken was once very abundant, but only a remnant remains. Their numbers have decreased because of habitat destruction due to the plow, chemical control of vegetation, and continuous livestock grazing. Today, important game birds are waterfowl (dependent upon playas), northern bobwhite (locally along the Caprock), scaled quail, sandhill cranes, and mourning doves. The ring-necked pheasant is believed to have come into the High Plains from Oklahoma, Kansas, and Colorado and is now present in huntable numbers. The playas are important stopover and breeding habitats for many species of shorebirds and waterfowl.

The black-footed ferret, the rarest North American mammal and an endangered species, once occurred in the region. It has disappeared throughout almost all of its former range as a result of near eradication of its prey, the black-tailed prairie dog. Today, although greatly reduced, the largest remaining concentrations of prairie dogs in Texas are on the High Plains. The dunes sagebrush lizard, a relict of the Great Basin desert, was stranded by climatic changes caused by a receding glacier.

12. Trans-Pecos

Description. The Trans-Pecos region is the northern Chihuahuan Desert. It occupies all of the area west of the Pecos River, which separates it from 2 other major regions, the High Plains to the northeast and the Edwards Plateau to the east. It is an area of great contrasts and much variation in topography as well as vegetation and wildlife, many species of which do not occur in other regions of the state. Topography includes basins, plateaus, mountain ranges, valleys, desert flats, bolson drainages, and sand hills. There are over 90 mountains of at least 1 mile in elevation. Major ranges (from northeast to southeast) are the Guadalupe (highest peak in Texas), Davis, and Chisos Mountains.

The Trans-Pecos contains one of the richest floras in the state, including the most endemics as well as peripheral desert species. Some authorities consider the Trans-Pecos to be the "heart" of the Chihuahuan Desert. Mountain woodlands are refugia, i.e., biological islands in an arid sea.

There are 28 plant community types, more than in any other region;

however, none are threatened or endangered. Although physiognomy is complex, there are 6 major subdivisions based upon dominant vegetation: grama-tobosa-creosotebush shrubsteppe, grama-tobosa desert grassland, saltbrush-greasebush flats, oak-juniper woodlands, tarbush-creosotebush-yucca-juniper savannah, and Mohr (shinnery) oak–bluestem sands. Pinyon and ponderosa pine communities occur at high elevations. Common invaders on continuously grazed rangeland are burrograss, fluffgrass, ear muhly, sand muhly, grassland croton, broomweeds, and cacti.

Land Use. The arid climate of the Trans-Pecos prevents extensive cultivation except in irrigated areas, the largest being the Upper Rio Grande Valley. Cattle and sheep raising are principal industries. Few areas escaped grazing damage. Among them are sparsely vegetated gypsum dunes and salt flats of little attraction to grazers. Except for spring-fed canyons, most stream courses have been damaged by livestock. Once, there was considerable mining activity for mercury and silver. Although 95% of the area is rangeland, irrigated crops contribute much to the economy of the region. Mountains, parks, wildlife management areas, and access to Mexico attract many tourists. In the future, there will be further development of rangelands, recreational facilities, and irrigation agriculture.

Wildlife. One species is extinct (bluntnose shiner), 6 are extirpated, many are unique or rare, 20 are threatened, and 8 are endangered. More rare species occur here than in any other region. Merriam elk once occurred in the Guadalupe Mountains near the Texas–New Mexico border. Rocky Mountain elk have been transplanted and are fairly well established there. Although much reduced in numbers, pronghorn occur on many large ranches and are important game animals. Bighorn sheep at one time ranged throughout most of the desert mountain ranges of the Trans-Pecos. They were fairly easy to kill and were a staple item in the diet of pioneer salt miners. Today, they are confined to the Sierra Diablo Wildlife Management Area (Hudspeth/Culberson Counties). Reintroduction of bighorns to the Black Gap Wildlife Management Area (Brewster County) failed due to their susceptibility to bluetongue disease of domestic sheep and predation by mountain lions. A few grizzly bears originally inhabited the Trans-Pecos but were exterminated in the 1890's. The few black bears remaining in Texas are in the Guadalupe Mountains and Big Bend National Parks.

Game animals native only to this part of the state are desert mule deer, Carmen Mountains white-tailed deer, and Gambel's and Montezuma quails (except for a small relict population in the Edwards Plateau). Other game animals are collared peccary, scaled quail, Rio Grande wild turkey, mourning and white-winged doves, and band-tailed pigeon. Important furbearers are coyote, gray fox, ringtail, bobcat, and muskrat.

Four fish species are endemic to the Trans-Pecos: Comanche Springs and Leon Springs pupfish (endangered), Big Bend gambusia (endangered), and Amistad gambusia (extinct). The Amistad gambusia could not survive in the Amistad Reservoir, which now covers its original habitat. Since 1947, rainbow trout have been established in McKittrick Canyon in the Guadalupe Mountains. One reptile is endemic, the gray-checkered whiptail, a lizard native to the elevated desert flats in the vicinity of the Chinati Mountains in Presidio County.

The kit fox probably deserves conservation status in Texas since it has been reduced in numbers by predator control programs. The mountain lion, though numerous and increasing in the Trans-Pecos, may be reduced if present trends continue since it is not protected.

Trends in Land Use Affecting Wildlife

Impacts and Threats

Some public and private land-use practices and activities have the potential of such extensive changes that affected areas could lose much fish and wildlife habitat. For fishes, major problems involve reservoir development, stream disturbances, aquifer depletion, introduced (exotic) species, and pollution. For amphibians, major detrimental impacts are wetland losses and pollution. For reptiles, birds, and mammals, collectively, the greatest threats are clearing and conversion of bottomland and upland vegetation. Additionally, some birds of prey and carnivorous mammals are adversely affected by predator control and agriculturally related pesticides. Among many land-use practices and activities, 8 major trends are evident.

1. Water Resource Development and Use

Most of these projects are in the eastern ⅔ of the state. Although relatively small in total area, their combined impacts on fish and wildlife habitats are disproportionately high. Examples are reservoir construction, floodwater watershed projects, stream channelization, navigation channels, levee construction, and aquifer depletion. These projects can have detrimental effects on fish and wildlife far from the construction site. For example, cumulative effects hundreds of miles inland can adversely impact bays and estuaries along the Gulf Coast.

The principal threat to bottomland forests and associated wetlands is reservoir construction and inundation. Additional losses occur from the impact of crop production and stimulated residential and commercial development around the periphery of reservoirs. Also, reservoirs change downstream flooding patterns, which adversely affect the composition and quality of bottomland forests.

2. Agricultural Practices

Agricultural activities are widespread in Texas and highly diverse. The 4 practices most detrimental to wildlife are (1) large-scale brush and riparian corridor clearing operations in the South Texas Plains, Panhandle, and Rolling Plains regions; (2) long-term, continuous, nonrotational grazing by livestock, especially but not inclusive of the Edwards Plateau and other arid and semiarid western regions; (3) conversion of bottomland forests and other riparian associations into croplands, primarily in East Texas; and (4) damage or destruction of wetlands by drainage, modification, grazing, and pollution from cattle, a major problem in the playa lakes region of the High Plains and the coastal pothole region.

Other agricultural practices cause indirect threats to wildlife. Examples are incorrect and indiscriminate use of pesticides and herbicides, predator control, and conversion of land to pastures composed of introduced grasses.

3. Forestry Practices

Commercial forestry practices in East Texas involve several practices that decrease or degrade wildlife habitats, some in the short term, others in the long term. Examples include replacement of hardwoods with pine plantations, monoculture tree farming, use of pesticides, large-acreage clear-cut harvesting, logging roads, timber-cutting debris, removal of underbrush, clearing riparian corridors, short rotation cutting, and increasing demand for hardwood products.

A major threat to both wildlife abundance and diversity is expansion of the hardwood pulp industry. This impact has the potential of major reduction of the remaining mature hardwood stands within river floodplains and tributary corridors. Over 63% of the original Texas bottomland forest has already been lost. These forests and associated wetland areas provide exceptional fish and wildlife habitat.

4. Mineral and Energy Production

Texas is a major producer of large quantities of many mineral and energy resources, e.g., brine, building stone, coal, clays, crushed stone, gravel, gypsum, lignite, limestone, natural gas, oil, salt, sand, sandstone, shell, sulfur, and uranium. Much of this industry, especially lignite production, involves large areas of surface mining. This activity, called strip-mining, can cause abrupt, total destruction of fish and wildlife habitats in the immediate area. Further degradation may spread from resulting pollution, increased industrialization, and urban growth.

Oil and gas production and refinement have damaged sensitive estuarine systems and coastal prairies by the expansion of industry and municipal development. In the West Texas Permian Basin and High Plains regions, a major problem has involved the deaths of tens of thousands of wildlife, especially waterfowl and shorebirds, that die in open-topped oilfield waste pits and tanks containing oil-contaminated processed water.

Fortunately, spent areas of surface mines are being reclaimed and revegetated with native plants to restore and enhance wildlife habitat. Also, recent regulations require oilfield pits and tanks to be covered or filled.

5. Urban/Industrial Expansion and Recreational/Leisure Developments

Conversion of rural areas adjacent to metropolitan areas threatens large areas, some of which are critical wildlife habitats. Major areas facing this problem are the coastal region, Northeast Texas, the El Paso area, and the central region, especially along the San Antonio to Dallas corridor. Development of recreational subdivisions, "ranchettes," and rural and channel-home communities contribute further to overall fragmentation of the landscape. Direct adverse effects involve fencing, land clearing, traffic, noise, lights, and free-running pets. Habitat degradation results from stream and groundwater pollution from inadequate waste treatment, erosion from construction, and general overuse of the area. These threats have affected the reservoir and forest region of East Texas, the hill country of the Edwards Plateau, and coastal bays and barrier islands.

6. Transportation

Transportation-related activities contribute to habitat destruction. Examples are construction of highways, waterways, railroads, and airports.

The Gulf Intracoastal Waterway and numerous crisscross bay channels require dredge maintenance with the resultant problem of dredged spoil material disposal in coastal bays and estuaries. Also, water salinity is changed, in turn affecting the food chain. Highway construction not only makes physical changes, but completed rights-of-way serve as corridors for the dispersal of nuisance, exotic plants. Airport complexes involve large acreages away from but accessible to metropolitan areas. Unfortunately, there is a tendency to site them in areas that are critical wildlife habitats. Although railroads are no longer being constructed, derailment and spillage of toxic materials form a major threat, especially to wetlands and streams.

7. Introduced Species

Introduction of nonnative (exotic) plants and animals has been widespread in Texas. These foreign species can be very detrimental to wildlife, both directly and indirectly. Some exotics have been established for such a long period and are so widespread that most people are unaware they are not native species (e.g., Bermudagrass, Johnsongrass, common carp, rock dove, house sparrow, house mouse, and red fox). Exotics have great potential to become pests that cannot be easily controlled, if at all.

Stewardship, Preservation, and Mitigation

Although fish and wildlife in Texas face many impacts and threats, efforts are being made to enhance their welfare. Among these are numerous private and public projects, initiatives, agreements, foundations, and land acquisition, leasing, and management programs. Many of these activities are explained in this book and so will not be discussed here. However, it cannot be overemphasized how important these contributions are. Efforts should be made to strengthen them and to emphasize the need for environmental education throughout the entire school system. A major contribution from the news media would be more emphasis on conservation issues and recognition of accomplishments made by individuals and organizations. Whether local, regional, or statewide, these efforts should be recognized for their cumulative contributions to an overall goal of preservation and enhancement of our state's natural heritage and its benefit to all citizens.

Literature Cited and Selected References

Abbott, P. L., and C. M. Woodruff, Jr., eds. 1986. The Balcones Escarpment: Geology, hydrology, ecology, and social development in Central Texas. Geol. Soc. Amer. annual meeting, San Antonio. iv+200 pp.

Amos, B. B., and F. R. Gehlbach. 1988. Edwards Plateau vegetation: Plant ecological studies in Central Texas. Waco: Baylor Univ. Press. 144 pp.

Arbingast, S. A., L. G. Kennamer, R. H. Ryan, J. R. Buchanan, W. L. Hezlep, L. T. Ellis, T. G. Jordan, C. T. Granger, and C. P. Zlatkovich. 1976. Atlas of Texas. Bur. Business Res., Univ. Tex. at Austin. 179 pp.

Baker, R. R. 1994. The biological survey of Colorado County, 1937–1939. Nesbitt Memorial Library J. (a journal of Colorado County history) 4:127–35.

———. 1995. Texas wildlife conservation—historical notes. East Texas Hist. J. 33:59–72.

Bauer, J., R. Frye, and B. Spain. 1991. A natural resource survey for proposed reservoir sites and selected stream segments in Texas. Tex. Parks and Wildl. Dep., Austin. PWD-BK-0300-06 7/91.

Bryan, K., T. Gallucci, G. Lasley, and D. H. Riskind. 1991. A checklist of Texas birds. 3rd ed. Tex. Parks and Wildl. Dep., Austin. Tech. Ser. 32. PWD-BK-4000-000M-9/91. 36 pp.

Campbell, L. 1995. Endangered and threatened animals of Texas: Their life history and management. Austin: Tex. Parks and Wildl. Press. 130 pp.

Carls, E. G., and J. Neal. 1984. Protection of Texas natural diversity: An introduction for natural resource planners and managers. Tex. Agric. Exp. Stn., Texas A&M Univ., College Station. MP-1557. iii+60 pp.

Collins, O. B., F. E. Smeins, and D. H. Riskind. 1975. Plant communities of the Blackland Prairie of Texas. Pp. 75–88 in M. K. Wali, ed., Prairie: A multiple view. Grand Rapids: Univ. North Dakota Press.

Conant, R., and J. T. Collins. 1991. A field guide to reptiles and amphibians: Eastern and central North America. 3rd ed. Boston, Mass.: Houghton Mifflin Co. 450 pp.

Davis, W. B., and D. J. Schmidly. 1994. The mammals of Texas (revised). Austin: Tex. Parks and Wildl. Press. 338 pp.

Diamond, D. D., D. H. Riskind, and S. L. Orzell. 1987. A framework for plant community classification and conservation in Texas. Tex. J. Sci. 39:203–21.

Dixon, J. R. 1987. Amphibians and reptiles of Texas: With keys, taxonomic synopses, bibliography, and distribution maps. College Station: Texas A & M Univ. 434 pp.

Doughty, R. W. 1983. Wildlife and man in Texas: Environmental change and conservation. College Station: Texas A & M Univ. Press. 246 pp.

Edwards, R. J., G. Longley, R. Moss, J. Ward, R. Matthews, and B. Stewart. 1989. A classification of Texas aquatic communities with special consideration toward the conservation of endangered and threatened taxa. Tex. J. Sci. 41:231–40.

Frentress, C. D. 1985. Wildlife habitat considerations. In letter from the Resolution Committee of the Texas Chapter of the Wildlife Society to Fred Bryant, President (March 10). Committee members: C. D. Frentress (chairman), D. W. Lay, W. J. Sheffield, and R. C. Telfair II (members).

Frye, R. G., and D. A. Curtis. 1990. Texas water and wildlife: An assessment of direct impacts to wildlife habitat from future water development projects. Tex. Parks and Wildl. Dep., Austin. PWD-BK-7100-147-5/90. 59 pp.

Godfrey, C. L., C. R. Carter, and G. S. McKee. N.d. Land resource areas of Texas. Tex. Agric. Ext. Serv., Tex. Agric. Exp. Stn., Texas A & M Univ., College Station. Bull. 1070. 24 pp.

Hatch, S. L., K. N. Gandhi, and L. E. Brown. 1990. Checklist of the vascular plants of Texas. Tex. Agric. Exp. Stn., Texas A & M Univ., College Station. MP-1655. 158 pp.

Hubbs, C., R. J. Edwards, and G. P. Garrett. 1991. An annotated checklist of the freshwater fishes of Texas, with keys to identification of species. Tex. J. Sci., Suppl. 43:1–56.

Inglis, J. M. 1964. A history of vegetation on the Rio Grande Plain. Tex. Parks and Wildl. Dep., Austin. Bull. 45. 122 pp.

Jones, J. K., Jr., and C. Jones. 1992. Revised checklist of recent land mammals of Texas, with annotations. Tex. J. Sci. 44:54–74.

Jordan, T. C., J. L. Bean, Jr., and W. M. Holmes. 1984. Texas: A geography. Boulder, Col.: Westview Press. 288 pp.

Kier, R. S., L. E. Garner, and L. F. Brown, Jr. 1977. Land resources of

Texas—a map of Texas lands classified according to natural suitability and use considerations. Bur. Econ. Geol., Univ. Tex. at Austin. Map+42 pp. suppl.

LBJ School of Public Affairs. 1978. Preserving Texas' natural heritage. LBJ School Publ. Affairs, Univ. Tex. at Austin. Pol. Res. Proj. Rep. 31:ix+1–34 pp.

McKinney, L. D. 1997. Troubled waters, part I; part II. Tex. Parks & Wildl. Mag. 55:18–27, 34–41.

McMahan, C. A., and R. G. Frye. 1987. Bottomland hardwoods in Texas: Proceedings of an interagency workshop on status and ecology. May 6–7, 1986, Nacogdoches. Tex. Parks and Wildl. Dep. PWD-RP-7100-133-3/87. v+1–170 pp.

McMahan, C. A., R. G. Frye, and K. L. Brown, eds. 1984. The vegetation types of Texas including cropland. Tex. Parks and Wildl. Dep., Austin. PWD Bull. 7000-120. Map+illus. synop. ii + 40 pp.

Mungall, E. C., and W. J. Shefield. 1994. Exotics on the range: The Texas example. College Station: Texas A&M University Press. 265 pp.

Owen, J. G., and J. R. Dixon. 1989. An ecogeographic analysis of the herpetofauna of Texas. Southwest. Nat. 34:165–80.

Page, L. M., and B. M. Burr. 1991. A field guide to freshwater fishes: North America north of Mexico. Boston, Mass.: Houghton Mifflin. 432 pp.

Phelan, R., and J. Bones. 1976. Texas wild: The land, plants, and animals of the Lone Star State. E. P. Dutton & Co. 256 pp.

Poole, J. M., and D. H. Riskind. 1987. Endangered, threatened, and protected native plants of Texas. Tex. Parks and Wildl. Dep., Austin. PWD-L-300-1A-8/87.

Renfro, H. B., D. E. Feray, and P. B. King. 1973. Geological highway map of Texas. U.S. Geol. Hwy. Map 7, Amer. Assoc. Petrol. Geol.

Rodgers, J. S. 1976. Species density and taxonomic diversity of Texas amphibians and reptiles. Syst. Zool. 25:26–40.

Shearing, D. 1991. Roadside geology of Texas. Missoula, Mont.: Mountain Press. 418 pp.

Smith, H. N., and C. A. Rechenthin. 1964. Grassland restoration: The Texas brush problem. U.S. Dep. Agric., Soil Conserv. Serv., Temple. 33 pp.

Spain, R. W., and R. C. Telfair II. 1987. The cost of strip mining. Texas Parks & Wildl. Mag. 45:2–10.

Telfair, R. C. II. 1979. Literature sources (concepts and maps) in relation to vegetational regions of Texas. Pp. 527–34 in The African Cattle Egret in Texas and its relation to the Little Blue Heron, Snowy Egret, and Louisiana Heron. Ph.D. dissertation, Texas A & M Univ., College Station. 552 pp.

———. 1983. Map of vegetational regions of Texas (based on dominants). Pp. 28–29 in The Cattle Egret: A Texas focus and world view. Kleberg Studies in Natural Resources. Tex. Agric. Exp. Stn., Texas A & M Univ., College Station.

Texas Almanac. 1996–1997. Dallas: A. H. Belo. 672 pp.

Texas Conservation Needs Committee. 1976. Conservation needs inventory—Texas 1976. U.S. Dep. Agric., Soil Conserv. Serv., Temple. 31 pp.

Texas Game, Fish and Oyster Commission. 1930. Year book on Texas conservation of wild life 1929–30. Austin: Von Boekmann-Jones Co. 110 pp.

———. 1945. Principal game birds and mammals of Texas: Their distribution and management. Austin: Von Boekmann-Jones Co. 149 pp.

Texas General Land Office and Texas Nature Conservancy. 1986. The natural heritage of Texas. 13 pp.

Texas Organization for Endangered Species. 1987. Endangered, threatened, and watchlists of plants of Texas. Tex. Org. End. Spe. Austin. Publ. 5:i+1–9 pp.

———. 1988. Endangered, threatened, and watchlist of vertebrates of Texas. Tex. Org. End. Spe. Austin. Publ. 6:i+1–16 pp.

Texas Parks and Wildlife Department. 1975. An analysis of Texas waterways: A report on the physical characteristics of rivers, streams, and bayous in Texas. Directed by R. Thuma, conducted by H. J. Belisle and R. Josselet. Tex. Parks and Wildl. Dep., Austin. 240 pp.

———. 1997. Texas threatened and endangered species: Regulations and listings. Tex. Parks and Wildl. Dep., Austin. 4 pp.

Texas Water Development Board. 1984. The Texas water plan. Austin. GP-4-1. Vol. 1 ix+1–72, vol. 2 tech. appendixes.

Thomas, J. K., C. E. Adams, and J. Thigpen. 1990. Texas hunting leases: Statewide and regional summary. Tex. Agric. Exp. Stn., Texas A & M Univ., College Station. iv+1–20 pp. + 1 map and 15 tables.

Travis, N. T., C. Hubbs, J. D. McEachran, and C. R. Smith. 1994. Freshwater and marine fishes of Texas and the northwestern Gulf of Mexico. Austin: Texas System of Natural Laboratories. 270 pp.

Truett, J. C., and D. W. Lay. 1984. Land of bears and honey: A natural history of East Texas. Austin: Univ. Tex. Press. 176 pp.

U.S. Fish and Wildlife Service. 1979. Concept plan: Unique wildlife ecosystems of Texas. U.S. Dep. Int., Region 2. 164 pp.

———. 1990 (draft). Region II wetlands. Regional concept plan. Emergency Wetlands Resources Act. U.S. Fish and Wildl. Serv., Region 2. 172 pp.

Wilson, R. E. 1990. The eastward recession of the Piney Woods of northeastern Texas, 1815 to 1989. Tex. J. Sci. 42:179–89.

I. PERSPECTIVES ON TEXAS WILDLIFE RESOURCES

Pete A. Y. Gunter and Max Oelschlaeger
Faculty for Environmental Ethics and
Department of Philosophy and
Religion Studies
University of North Texas
Denton, TX 76203-3526

1. The Need for a Texas Land Ethic

Abstract: Many factors account for the lack of a "land ethic" in Texas. The most important is the state's long frontier experience, which brought along with it strong anti-intellectualism, exaggerated individualism, and the casual expectation of unending surplus. The formulation of such an ethic is rendered especially difficult by the state's diversity, including desert; swamp forest; subtropical savannah; cool, temperate prairie; flatland, mountain, and tidal estuary; and an extreme diversity of creatures adapted to these habitats. In spite of these obstacles, a land ethic is possible, based on the writings of the American forester and game manager Aldo Leopold. Leopold proposed that a policy is good if it increases the integrity, stability, and beauty of an ecosystem, bad if it does not. We briefly explore the applications of stability, integrity, and natural beauty to questions of land use.

If two words could be chosen to sum up the character of the Lone Star State, we would urge that they be "frontier" and "diversity." Few states, if any, remained frontier as long as Texas, and few are as diverse in soils, climate, and topography. Together these 2 terms provide a striking image, suggesting hope. But they suggest problems, too: problems, and a difficult future. Of these terms, we will deal first with diversity, the less known and less recognized of the 2.

Diversity

The tendency to picture Texas as the set of an immense western movie—probably filmed in California—is slowly changing. Few have

43

grasped the profound contrasts of the state's regions as vividly as novelist Bill Brammer (1986:3–4), who protested that a place so "muddled and various is hard to conceive as one entity":

> It begins . . . in an ancient backwash of old dead seas and lambent estuaries, around which rise cypress and cedar and pine thickets hung with spiked vines and the cheerless festoons of Spanish moss. Farther on, the earth firms: stagnant pools are stirred by the rumble of living river, and the mild ferment of bottomland dissolves as the country begins to reveal itself in the vast hallucination of salt dome and cotton row, tree farm and rice field and irrigated pasture and the flawed dream of the cities. And away and beyond, even farther, the land continues to rise, as on a counterbalance with the water tables, and then the first range of the West comes into view: a great serpentine escarpment, changing colors with the hours, with the seasons, hummocky and soft-shaped at one end, rude and wind-blasted at the other, blue and green, green and gray and dune-colored, a staggered fault line extending hundreds of miles north and south. . . . The land rises steeply beyond the first escarpment and everything is changed: texture, configuration, blistered facade, all of it warped and ruptured and bruise-colored.

Geologist Darwin Spearing (1991:11) described the same panorama, drawing the same conclusions but proceeding not from east to west but from the west eastward. To envision Texas, he stated, one must see it

> sweeping from volcanic mesas and thrusted mountains in the west, to red canyons of the Panhandle, along tropical sand barriers of the Gulf Coast, and across central limestone plateaus onto hard granitic terrain in the center of the state. Rocks of all ages, from crystalline gneiss of ancient Precambrian time to the loose sand of modern beaches are found at the surface of the state, as well as every major rock type from igneous to metamorphic to sedimentary.

An area containing so many climates, soils, and topographies will probably sustain an extraordinary wealth of plants and wildlife. This is certainly true of Texas, which is home to 4,834 species of flowering plants (Hatch, Gandhi, and Brown 1990), 247 species of freshwater fishes (Hubbs, Edwards, and Garrett 1991), 204 species of amphibians and reptiles (Dixon 1987), 594 confirmed species of birds (Bryan et al. 1991), and 154 species of mammals (Jones and Jones 1992). The list can easily be lengthened. Unfortunately, so can the list of factors which undermine this cornucopia: stream channelization, overgrazing, conversion of brush and woodlands to coastal bermuda grass, the draining and filling of wetlands of every kind, clearcutting, overuse of water resources, the spread and sprawl of urban growth, increasing air and water pollution, and the mushrooming of garbage landfills. This list, too, can be lengthened at will. In every case, both the diversity and the abundance of life are undercut. The biologist has reason for dismay. So do the hunter and the birdwatcher. So, even, in the end, will the Chamber of Commerce.

Deciding how to deal with the onslaught against the land and its resources will involve many thorny problems and painful dilemmas. These are complicated by the very diversity which in other respects is such a blessing. One strains one's imagination to think of 2 locales more different than the arid, underpopulated desert mountains of the Big Bend and the swampy, junglelike bottomlands of the Big Thicket, so near to large urban populations and so interspersed with towns and villages. To sustain diversity and abundance in these areas is to confront very different problems and to consider very different strategies. The same is true for the vanishing Brush Country of the Rio Grande Valley and the Blackland Prairies of Central Texas, the flat high prairies of the Panhandle and the gnarled, streamcut limestone of the Hill Country: laws, usages, economic pressures, ethnic differences vary even more than the landscape. What might be absolutely necessary in one place might be irrelevant in another; what in one place might be folly in another might be wisdom.

Frontier

When we turn from diversity to frontier, we are on much more familiar ground. "Frontier" is more closely and much more consistently associated with Texas than "variety" or "diversity." It is easy to see why. From the first Spanish settlements (1760) through the first Anglo pioneers (1820) until nearly the end of the First World War (1918), all or part of the state was a frontier in the rawest, plainest sense: a land frontier. For over 100 years, the Lone Star State still possessed ungrazed prairie to browse, unbroken land to plow, virgin forests to cut. (Compare this with Iowa, traversed by the frontier entirely and settled in 20 years.)

It was not only the continuation of land frontiering that welded the close association between "Texas" and "frontier." It was a series of natural resource "booms," beginning with cotton, extending through cattle and timber, and ending in oil. When King Cotton was temporarily exiled at the end of the Civil War, Texans were able to round up hundreds of thousands of cattle running wild in the Brush Country and head them north to Kansas. Two decades later, they were to harvest the Post Oak Belt and the Piney Woods to make the state—a little-known fact—one of America's largest timber producers. As the cattle boom faded but before the last timber was cut, an oil boom emerged, beginning with Spindletop (1900) and extending into the 1960's.

Beyond doubt, any such simplified synopsis of Texas history as provided here omits much—much that is important. However, it does make a point. As far back as any Texan can look, the state has been engaged, generation after generation, in frontiering. There have been a number of frontiers, it is true, and these have been of different kinds and at different times. Taken in toto, however, they constitute a single virtually unbroken process. They also constitute a single little-changed mindset, a deeply ingrained expectation of frontier conditions and frontier methods. To this mindset we will now turn.

The attitudes of a frontiering people are carefully documented, e.g., one thinks of Webb's *The Great Frontier* (1953) in this respect, but there have been many similar studies, formal and informal, such as McMurtry's *In a Narrow Grave* (1968). Among its basic characteristics are an easy expectation of surplus, a casual contempt for caution, a crusty anti-intellectualism, and an exaggerated, at times fanatical individualism. Why limit the hunting of bears in the Piney Woods when there have always been bears and presumably always will be? Why limit withdrawal of underground water on the High Plains when one appears to be sitting on a veritable ocean of water? Why develop oil resources cautiously when there is a boom going, keeping Texas prosperous while the rest of the nation suffers through a Great Depression? Why listen to a bunch of college professor biologists when they warn of eroding soils and vanishing species, if one has been raised to believe that such people, besides being pretentious, don't have any common sense? And why put up with laws and regulations which, insidiously, destroy one's freedom, a freedom which, ideally, should be absolute and without exception?

Land Ethic

Why indeed? It is not that any one of these queries might not, in its context, make a good deal of sense. College professors are not by a long shot always right. Not all laws are well written, and not all restrictions of behavior are more help than hindrance. Still, taken together, these frontiering attitudes add up, most obviously where surpluses fail and destructive practices take their toll, not to a "land ethic" with its corollaries of caution and sustainability but to an antiland ethic, an approach that will in the end destroy the diversity and abundance that engendered hope and made economic optimism possible in the first place.

The simple truth is that the frontier days are long gone but not the frontier attitudes. In its modern adaptation, the frontier outlook amounts to the belief that the market, in its infinite wisdom, determines societally optimal outcomes. Utilitarian individualism is the prevailing social philosophy of the day: a view of the world as constituted by John Wayne–like, rugged, self-reliant, heroic individuals who conquer heathens and a hostile nature (raw lands and raging rivers, varmints and predators, hordes of insects and vermin, infertile soil and adverse climates), developing its resources for human purposes, thereby bringing wealth and progress to savage lands and waters. Ostensibly, the greatest good for the greatest number is served by unrestrained development.

As the recent downfall of the Soviet Union suggests, a market society is neither all good nor all bad. No doubt, there are more than contingent relations between economic and political freedom. Despite depressions, recessions, and persistent problems with distribution, the market has led to a quantitatively rich life. Texans have put the land to prosperous use—oil and gas and other extractive industries, ranching and farming, logging and associated industry, and fishing. The modern Texas economy, with its profusion of manufacture, service, insurance, and financial activities, was enabled by extractive industry and agriculture.

Yet all the outcomes of the market have not been good. Nature's economy, that is, the physical and biological processes that enable and sustain life on earth (see Georgescu-Roegen 1971; Daly and Cobb 1989), ultimately serves as a limit on economic activity. But the market exists in oblivion to nature's economy, functioning as if neither physical nor ecological constraints existed. Problems of global ecology (holes in the ozone, climate heating, the extinction or threatened extinction of thousands of species) are indications that the market is not absolute. Just as clearly, the market has led to some adverse outcomes for Texas lands with their associated flora and fauna.

John Graves (1960) detailed some of the consequences of the antiland ethic in his so-called Texas Trilogy: the damming of free-flowing rivers to provide water for urban growth and development; the get-rich-quick schemes of ranchers and farmers that degrade the land; and the displacement of native species, both plant and animal, by population growth. Graves seemed resigned to the process, suggesting that a simple law governs twentieth-century Texas: civilization advances, land suffers.

Whatever the mistakes of the past, there are at least some who believe that civilization and the land community might somehow coexist. If the market has tended to run the land to ruin, then the issue is whether or not something more than market criteria might help Texans conceptualize and ultimately determine their relations to the land. The crucial question is what this "something" might be.

Perhaps Aldo Leopold's land ethic is that something more. Make no mistake, to talk or write or think about a Texas land ethic means that considerations outside the market will influence land-use decisions. For Texans, steeped in the frontier tradition, this constitutes culture shock. At the very least, the phrase "land ethic" sounds strange, unfamiliar to Texas ears. In fact, it has been around since 1949, when it was coined by well-known American conservationist Aldo Leopold (1970).

Leopold, a professional forester and wildlife manager, began his career as a follower of Gifford Pinchot, the father of the National Forest Service. Like Pinchot, he believed that the business of the national forests was to provide board feet of timber for an expanding economy. Like Pinchot, he believed that nature exists purely and simply to serve humanity and that the application of scientific technology to nature would make possible an endless progress. Unlike Pinchot, he came to repent this view (termed "Resource Conservation Environmentalism") and develop another outlook, closer to nature and less wedded to the market—the land ethic.

Many people shudder when they hear the word "ethics." Perhaps they remember some tedious lecture inflicted on them in college. The land ethic, however, is a model of simplicity and clarity. An action or behavior or practice is good, Leopold wrote (1970:263), "when it tends to preserve the integrity, stability, and beauty of the biotic community. It is wrong when it tends otherwise." *Integrity, stability, and beauty*. These are the cornerstones of what might become a Texas land ethic, yet they take us into terra incognita, because, as Leopold noted, the tendency of society is to succumb to the fallacy of economic determinism, the belief that economics can and should determine all land use, period.

The problems with the marketplace as the sole determinant of land use are at least 2-fold (though defenders of the market ideology claim that the market can redress virtually all ills; see Nieswiadomy 1992). In the first place, embedded in this philosophy is an associated cluster of notions centering on the idea that the land is nothing more than raw material. Augmenting this notion is the idea that human beings are somehow above nature, able to control it through the power of science and its offshoot, technology. Descartes observed, near the beginning of the modern age, that through the so-called new science humankind would "render itself the master and possessor of nature." Francis Bacon put it more simply: "science is power." This philosophy propels the modern project, that is, the relentless conversion of wild lands and life into civilization. The historical and ideological aspects of this antiland ethic have been thoroughly discussed elsewhere (Merchant 1980; Oelschlaeger 1991).

The consequence has been the modern economic imperative, i.e., the conversion of *the land to standing reserve,* to raw material serving only as fuel for the economy. Holes in the ozone, the extinction of species, the destruction of natural ecosystems, and the prospect of global climate heating are the inevitable aftermath. The eminent historian of biology Ernst Mayr wrote (1982:79), "It was a tragedy both for biology and for [hu]mankind that the currently prevailing framework of our social and political ideas developed and was adopted when the thinking of Western [civilization] was largely dominated by the ideas of the scientific revolution, that is, by a set of ideas based on the principles of the physical sciences."

The second difficulty with the marketplace is its influence on societal decision making. As Mark Sagoff (1988) argued, all social preferences cannot be articulated through the market. In fact, only the preferences of economic producers and consumers are well served. The stake society has, for example, in the preservation of wild lands or in sustainability is ignored by market forces. Nowhere in the economic calculus do the stability and integrity of the land community come into consideration. In part, this is because the market radically discounts the future. Questions of intergenerational equity, e.g., the tension between the selfish interests of the present generation in cheaply produced food and those of our children and their children in a high quality environment, are not served by the market. Should subsurface water be mined (i.e., extracted at nonsustainable rates) to fuel the short-term agricultural interests of producers in profits and consumers in artificially lowered prices? Should marginal land be pressed into agriculture with federally subsidized water resource projects and price supports? The market offers no guide except to continue the process of development, with no regard for the long-term future.

Of course, there is no easy passage from Leopold's notion that an act is right when it preserves integrity, stability, and beauty to useful, effective policies. There is many a slip between theory and practice. Consider the college classroom, where tomorrow's business leaders and managers, environmental scientists and conservationists are trained. One of the leading textbooks of introductory resource conservation equates Leopold's land ethic with "basic human respect for natural resources" (Owen and Chiras 1990). This is a questionable reading of Leopold's text, since he does not use the term "natural resource" in stating the land ethic. To conceptualize the land *only as resource* is to fall into what Leopold believed was a fundamental error. He described the earth not as mere resource but as a "land community" or "biotic community." Such nomenclature goes beyond the market by including human beings as members of the land community and by not categorizing the land as merely a natural resource (a standing reserve awaiting appropriation).

If the land ethic, then, holds that something more than the market might determine our relations to the land community, the next question is specific. What would a Texas land ethic mean in terms of integrity, stability, and beauty?

Integrity

Inherent in a land ethic is a sensitivity to place, both to the concrete particulars of the land as well as to ecosystemic processes. Integrity refers not to the economic value of the land as resource (a quantity that can be measured) but to a sometimes incommensurable quality of nature, that is, wholeness. The English word "integrity" comes from the Indo-European root *tag* and, in turn, the Latin derivative *integer,* meaning whole, untouched. Even so, the scientific question of what constitutes integrity is hard to answer. Through research in the desert Southwest and later in the farmlands of the American Midwest, Leopold came to appreciate wholeness not as a characteristic restricted to totally natural, i.e., wild, landscapes but as an ideal that could also be achieved in humanized landscapes.

A "whole" ecosystem is not necessarily undeveloped but rather is uncorrupted by development, that even though used for human purposes remains unimpaired, sound. Such an ecosystem is able to sustain itself through adverse circumstances; it is healthy, vital, in a word, whole. However, when guided only by economic criteria, we characteristically make radical alterations in the land community, changes that disrupt it, fragment it, and destroy links in the web of life. Ecological dysfunction confirms the limits of exclusively economic thinking: nature does not recognize humanly imposed boundaries and categorical schemes.

Of course, the importance of integrity is not news to Texas wildlife professionals, who have long recognized that the consequences of traditional land use can be ecologically devastating. Ted Clark (1982: 129) put the issue in simple terms: "there is a need for more effective land use planning, preferably at the local level and at county or councils of government (COG) levels." Needs are one thing, satisfaction another. Joel Wooldridge (1982:64), writing in the same volume with Clark, suggested that the frontier outlook still dominates the Texas consciousness and is manifest in "the negative attitude toward land use controls" that pervade "the Texas legislature, the governor's office, and state agencies." Elected politicians and appointed officials claim, Wooldridge continued, that environmental values and economic goals are balanced. "In actuality, evidence is available all over Texas to demonstrate poor urban land use decisions made to gratify the desire for short-term economic gains at the expense of environmental quality." Which is to say, Texans today have few examples of large-scale ecosystems possessing integrity in the strongest sense of that term.

Centuries of human practice cannot be changed overnight. Neither can Texas history nor the frontier mentality. The Big Thicket of Southeast Texas, once a vast, cohesive wild community, is now crisscrossed by oil pipelines and power rights-of-way, drowned under new lake water, deeply scarred by clearcuts. It has very nearly lost its biological integrity (Gunter 1971). Similarly, the carving up and elimination of extensive "cedar" forest in the Texas Hill Country threatens the existence of one of Texas's rarest birds, the golden-cheeked warbler, while piecemeal clearcutting of the national forests of East Texas drives the red-cockaded woodpecker toward extinction. Habitat is no longer habitat when only fragments of it remain. Whatever the measure of "wholeness," every conservationist knows of vanishing species, not only in the Big Thicket but almost everywhere else in Texas. The High Plains of West Texas. The bottomlands of the Brazos. The wetlands of the Texas Coast. The once continuous forests of the Post Oak Belt. The Piney Woods of East Texas. The relentless drive toward "progress" means the loss of integrity—ecosystems simplified, biological wastelands standing as monuments to greed.

Stability

Integrity and stability are not unrelated: integrity concerns the wholeness of ecosystems, while stability pertains to the ability of eco-systems to maintain themselves. If the integrity of an ecosystem is impaired, so too is its stability. Of course, even natural (unhumanized or relatively undeveloped) ecosystems are dynamic, fluctuating. Stability does not mean invariance.

Stability is difficult to measure, and insofar as the term has been associated with the so-called balance of nature, it is controversial. Daniel Botkin (1990), for example, argued that some environmentalists have misinterpreted nature, neglecting the inherent dynamism of ecological processes in the effort to impose ideological, unecological preservationist schemes on nature. Clearly, contemporary environmental scientists cannot provide entirely adequate measures of stability, nor can they literally predict the effect of human actions upon either natural or humanized ecosystems. However, the uncertainty of scientific measurement and the conjectural nature of prediction do not negate ecological reality. Environmental science knows with certainty that human beings have repeatedly upset the stability of nature's economy.

In areas of Texas where French tamarisk (saltcedar), juniper forest ("cedar brakes"), honey mesquite, and other water-absorbing brush have overtaken former grasslands, once permanent streams now flow only in wet periods and are dry in rain-free months. The ecosystems which would have been sustained indefinitely in those streams—for bodies of water have ecosystems, too—inevitably perish. (In the case of the Concho River, removal of water-absorbing brush has allowed the water to run year-round again.) Similarly, on marginal farmlands in the western parts of the state, hard scrabble cotton farming, by dispersing and degrading thin layers of topsoil, led not only to the Dust Bowl of the 1930's but to the inability of today's grassland ecologies to ever recover their original richness and stability. Though no biotic community can last forever, it is surely folly to destabilize and degrade ecologies which can serve us indefinitely, for centuries or millennia.

Through his own pioneering research, Leopold discovered that human beings were more often than not the cause of destabilization. He found that economic criteria alone are an inadequate guide to land use since they function without regard to stability. If nothing else, land use predicated solely on economic criteria adversely affects the ability of an ecosystem to dynamically fluctuate around a historically established mean. Clearly, Leopold could not scientifically describe a stable ecosystem with the exactitude of contemporary environmental science. He was not, however, unaware of the dynamism inherent in nature itself, but his primary concern was with the effect of human action upon the land community's ability to maintain itself.

Beauty

Texas, rivaled only by California and Alaska, is unsurpassed in the diversity of its natural beauty. Yet beauty as a criterion for land use perhaps appears less plausible than either integrity or stability. To many people, beauty might seem subjective, anything but scientific. To anyone who places total faith in the market, the idea that considerations of beauty might override market-based decisions seems frightening. Beauty is simply not traded through the market—it has no use value (though states dependent upon tourists lured by scenic wonders tend to protect it).

Leopold, again, was a visionary in recognizing the importance, indeed, the centrality of beauty to the land ethic. In part, beauty was a counterbalance to the unrestrained pursuit of profit. Leopold was not a foe of capitalism, but he was opposed to land use guided only by the profit motive. Environmental historians typically seize upon the apparent opposition between beauty and utility, believing that nature can be either exploited for its instrumental value or protected for its intrinsic value, but not both.

However, as Curt Meine (1992:133–34) pointed out, beauty and utility are not contradictories for Leopold. He believed that the land ethic and economics could be reconciled, arguing that the apparent opposition between beauty and utility, or between aesthetic preservationists and utilitarian conservationists, is just that: a matter of appearance rather than reality. In the final analysis, Leopold did not believe that utility could be defined in only economic terms. Informed by the land ethic (i.e., an abiding comprehension of the land community and the relation of humankind to it), the choice between utility and beauty appears as a false dichotomy. Individuals will look at the land, Leopold wrote, "as something more than a breadbasket." They "will see the beauty, as well as the utility, of the whole, and know the two cannot be separated" (quoted in Meine 1992:137).

As a rule, a beautiful landscape indicates a healthy ecosystem. Most of us would agree that a polluted stream with its dead fish and dumped garbage is ugly, certainly in comparison with a clean stream with clear waters, untrashed borders, and abundant life. Few would argue that a prairie reduced to sparse grass, weeds, and eroded earth is as beautiful as a prairie richly covered with grass and wildflowers. To aim for natural beauty is thus often to produce a situation which is both ecologically and economically sustainable. To opt for ugliness is to choose a situation economically valuable to no one or to a few.

Environmental aesthetics is just beginning to come of age today. International conferences address the issue of the cultural significance of natural beauty (see Svobodová 1990). Scholars specialize in the subject (see Sepänmaa 1986). An environmental aesthetic would, according to Sepänmaa (1990:140), "be the investigation of the grounds for the description, interpretation, and evaluation for the environment." Given such knowledge, and societal approval, environmental aestheticians would be actively engaged in the evaluation of land use insofar as this involved beauty. Beauty might become, for example, a standard part of environmental impact assessments. Land uses that impair natural beauty might be ameliorated, lessened, curtailed, or proscribed.

Environmental aestheticians argue, among other things, that

1. the impetus to aesthetics generally is rooted in the human perception of natural beauty: art, so to speak, imitates nature;
2. built landscapes, however, also have environmental beauty, but not of the same kind as that possessed by untouched nature;
3. narrowly human criteria of beauty imposed on natural ecosystems in oblivion of the ecological dynamics of the land community are short-lived;
4. the perception of beauty is complementary to and augmented by the knowledge of natural history;
5. "deep" ecological aesthetics crosses disciplinary borders such as aesthetics, ecology, and psychology.

Conclusion

In his book *North Dallas 40*, Peter Gent (1974) described Texans as a band of thieves one step ahead of the law. Perhaps this was once true. Today, the frontier is long behind us. The pressing issue of the moment is to incorporate a land ethic into land-use decision making. Ideally, such an ethic would enable Texans to live on and relate to the land in ways that go beyond, yet are feasible within, the broad outlines of a market society. At this juncture, speculations about a postmodern age that has gone beyond the market are a separate issue. Any road from here to there will pass through the present. Whatever our goals, any present-day land ethic that ignores the reality of the market is doomed to fail.

Can we legitimately speculate about a Texas land ethic? Perhaps. A global ecocrisis unmistakably indicates that humankind is teetering on the precipice of ecocatastrophe. The slogan for the 1990's has apparently been "act locally, think globally." The international scientific community, it must be pointed out, no longer stands idly on the sidelines. The 2 most prestigious and authoritative scientific bodies in the world, the United States National Academy of Sciences and the Royal Society of London, issued a joint statement in February 1992 warning that time is running out for effective response to such problems as overpopulation, climate heating, and biodiversity (see Maddox 1992a). As Maddox (1992b), editor of the authoritative *Nature* magazine, pointed out, solutions entail international agreements. Solutions also entail actions in Texas.

Land use extends from the inner city to alpine ecosystems and everything in between—from intensely humanized landscapes to outright wilderness. A land ethic, then, entails responsible decision making over an enormous range of environments involving differing kinds of human interactions. In a sense, humans have no choice as to whether to use the land or not. As the land ethic makes clear, the conservation question is not whether but how. Leopoldian-inspired ecological ethics—whatever the ultimate goals of preservationists—is consistent with the general framework of the market.

In fact, the land ethic is the model of a balanced approach. "Leopold was impatient," Meine (1992:135–36) explained, "with those who believed that the cure-all to conservation dilemmas was negative, compulsory restriction; he constantly pressed for positive actions, for taking necessary steps to create new initiatives that engaged people in the landscape, and engaged their aesthetic sense in doing so." *The environmental problem,* as Leopold sees it, *is not the market per se; it is that the market overdetermines our relations to the land.* Market-based decision making is simply too narrow, since the "bottom line" is an artifice, a human construct, that nowhere appears in nature. The consequences of imposing a strictly and exclusively economic calculus upon the land is plain, evident in ruined landscapes all around. The crux of the issue is to learn how to live on the land without spoiling it—without upsetting its integrity, stability, and beauty.

Leopold believed that in the twentieth-century rush to civilization humankind lost sight of the ecological realities that underpin human affairs. Clearly, an exclusively economic conception of utility is truncated.

Leopold doubted, as do many, that we know precisely where to draw the line between what is and is not useful. He (1939:727) wrote, "No species can be 'rated' without the tongue in the cheek; the old categories of 'useful' and 'harmful' have validity only as conditioned by time, place, and circumstance. The only sure conclusion is that the biota as a whole is useful," and the biota includes the physical components that collectively make up the land community.

Even wilderness, construed as a form of land use, has utility. In the first place, wilderness is somehow essential, Leopold argued, to the development of human beingness. Beyond that, wilderness also has a scientific value. Writing in the inaugural issue of *Living Wilderness* (the journal of the Wilderness Society, now *Wilderness*) Leopold (1935:6) argued that "we do not yet understand and cannot yet control the long-time interrelations of animals, plants, and mother earth." Under a Texas land ethic, free nature (wilderness ecosystems) would usefully function as a baseline against which more humanized habitats might be compared. On strong scientific grounds, Leopold believed that any conception of "land health" depended upon preserving specimens of land intact where integrity and stability had not yet been degraded.

The land ethic is also pertinent to guiding the management of lands between outright wilderness and totally humanized (urban) landscapes. In *Game Management* (1986:31), the immediate forerunner to *Sand County Almanac,* Leopold wrote that the wild creatures living are "already artificialized, in that . . . [their] existence is conditioned by economic forces. Game management merely proposes that their impact shall not remain wholly fortuitous. The hope of the future lies not in curbing the influence of human occupancy—it is already too late for that—but in creating a better understanding of the extent of that influence and a new ethic for its governance."

The last chapter has yet to be written on Leopold's land ethic. However, one passage from *Sand County Almanac* always comes to mind when we reconsider his work. Too few people, he argued, appreciate the cultural value of wilderness. "Only the scholar," Leopold (1970: 279) wrote, "appreciates that all history consists of successive excursions from a single starting-point," a point of departure to which humankind "returns again and again to organize yet another search for a durable scale of values. It is only the scholar who understands why the raw wilderness gives definition and meaning to the human enterprise."

Likely this is because, even now, we succumb to the fallacy of economic determinism. But the land community has great value, far beyond the measures of economic success. We ignore its value only at the peril of failure, of collapse. In the final analysis, as Leopold (1991:212) suggested, "conservation is a protest against destructive land use. It seeks to preserve both the utility and the beauty of the landscape."

Literature Cited

Baccus, J. T., ed. 1982. Texas wildlife resources and land use. Proc. symposium on Texas Wildlife Resources and Land Use, 14–16 April. The Wildlife Society (Texas Chapter), Austin. 199 pp.

Botkin, D. B. 1990. Discordant harmonies: A new ecology for the twenty-first century. New York: Oxford Univ. Press. 241 pp.

Brammer, B. L. 1986. The gay place. New York: Vintage Books. 526 pp.

Bryan, K., T. Gallucci, G. Lasley, and D. H. Riskind. 1991. A checklist of Texas birds. 3rd ed. Tech. ser. 32. Tex. Parks and Wildl. Dep., Austin. PWD-BK-4000-000M-9/91. 36 pp.

Clark, T. L. 1982. Wildlife management programs, goals, and issues—the state perspective. Pp. 116–31 in J. T. Baccus, ed., *Texas wildlife resources and land use.*

Daly, H. E., and J. B. Cobb, Jr. 1989. For the common good: Redirecting the economy toward community, the environment and a sustainable future. Boston: Beacon Press. 482 pp.

Dixon, J. R. 1987. Amphibians and reptiles of Texas: With keys, taxonomic synopses, bibliography, and distribution maps. College Station: Texas A & M Univ. 434 pp.

Gent, P. 1974. North Dallas 40. New York: New American Library. 294 pp.

Georgescu-Roegen, N. 1971. The entropy law and the economic process. Cambridge, Mass.: Harvard Univ. Press. 457 pp.

Graves, J. 1960. Goodbye to a river. Austin: Texas Monthly Press. 306 pp.

———. 1974. Hard scrabble: Observations on a patch of land. Austin: Texas Monthly Press. 267 pp.

———. 1980. From a limestone ledge: Some essays and other ruminations about country life in Texas. Austin: Texas Monthly Press. 228 pp.

Gunter, P. 1971. The Big Thicket: A challenge for conservation. Austin: Jenkins Publ. Co. 172 pp.

Hatch, S. L., K. N. Gandhi, and L. E. Brown. 1990. Checklist of the vascular plants of Texas. Tex. Agric. Exp. Stn., Texas A & M Univ., College Station. MP-1655. 158 pp.

Hubbs, C., R. J. Edwards, and G. P. Garrett. 1991. An annotated checklist of the freshwater fishes of Texas, with keys to identification of species. Tex. J. Sci., Suppl. 43(4):1–56.

Jones, J. K., Jr., and C. Jones. 1992. Revised checklist of recent land mammals of Texas, with annotations. Tex. J. Sci. 44(1):54–74.

Leopold, A. 1935. Why the wilderness society? Living Wilderness 1:6.

———. 1939. A biotic view of the land. J. of For. 37:727. Reprinted in S. Flader and J. B. Callicott, eds., River of the mother of God. Madison: Univ. of Wisconsin Press.

———. 1970. Sand county almanac: With essays on conservation from Round River. New York: Sierra Club/Ballantine Books. Orig. publ. 1949. New York: Oxford Univ. Press. 295 pp.

———. 1986. Game management. Madison: Univ. of Wisconsin Press. Orig. publ. 1933. New York: Scribner's. 481 pp.

———. 1991. River of the mother of God and other essays, ed. S. Flader and J. B. Callicott. Madison: Univ. of Wisconsin Press. 384 pp.

Maddox, J. 1992a. National Academy/Royal Society warning on population growth. Nature 355:759.

———. 1992b. Saving the world. Nature 355:752.

Mayr, E. 1982. The growth of biological thought: Diversity, evolution, inheritance. Cambridge, Mass.: Harvard Univ. Press. 974 pp.

McMurtry, L. 1968. In a narrow grave. Austin: Encino Press. 177 pp.

Meine, C. 1992. The utility of preservation and the preservation of utility: Leopold's fine line. Pp. 131–72 in M. Oelschlaeger, ed., The wilderness condition: Essays on environment and civilization. San Francisco: Sierra Club Books.

Merchant, C. 1980. The death of nature: Women, ecology and the scientific revolution. San Francisco: Harper and Row. 348 pp.

Nieswiadomy, M. 1992. Economics and resource conservation. Pp. 113–23 in M. Oelschlaeger, ed., After earth-day: Continuing the conservation effort.

Oelschlaeger, M. 1991. The idea of wilderness: From prehistory to the age of ecology. New Haven, Conn.: Yale Univ. Press. 477 pp.

———, ed. 1992a. The wilderness condition: Essays on environment and civilization. San Francisco: Sierra Club Books. 345 pp.

———, ed. 1992b. After earth day: Continuing the conservation effort. Denton: Univ. of North Texas Press. 220 pp.

Owen, O. S., and D. D. Chiras. 1990. Natural resource conservation: An ecological approach. New York: Macmillan. 593 pp.

Sagoff, M. 1988. The economy of the earth: Philosophy, law, and the environment. Cambridge: Cambridge Univ. Press. 271 pp.

Sepänmaa, Y. 1986. The beauty of environment: A general model for environmental aesthetics. Helsinki, Finland: Suomalainen Tiedeakatemia. 184 pp.

———. 1990. The Finnish mineral substances act as a means of protecting the beauty of eskers. Pp. 85–94 in H. Svobodová, ed., *Cultural aspects of landscape.*

Spearing, D. 1991. Roadside geology of Texas. Missoula, Mont.: Mountain Press. 418 pp.

Svobodová, H., ed. 1990. Cultural aspects of landscape. Wageningen, Netherlands: Centre for Agricultural Publishing and Documentation. 179 pp.

Webb, W. P. 1953. The great frontier: An interpretation of world history since Columbus. London: Seeker and Warburg. 434 pp.

Wooldridge, J. C. 1982. Urban growth and wilderness values in Texas. Pp. 55–67 in J. T. Baccus, ed., *Texas wildlife resources and land use.*

Robin W. Doughty
Department of Geography
University of Texas
Austin, TX 78712

2. Urban Growth and Environmental Values in Texas

Abstract: Population growth and the expansion of metropolitan areas continue to exert pressure on space available for humans and indigenous flora and fauna. Emerging concerns about biodiversity, including endangered wildlife, and the quality of outdoor areas may help mitigate deleterious impacts on native species while improving the overall quality of urban-industrial environments. Increasing demands for diverse and more specialized recreational outlets and a growing interest in conservation, particularly of nongame animals, suggest that both public and private sector interest must demonstrate greater commitment to the state's heritage and its character over the long term.

In the last Chapter Report of The Wildlife Society, Joel Wooldridge (1982) emphasized the incompatibility of urban growth and wilderness values by pointing to burgeoning suburban lifestyles, a downturn in the economy, and governmental inertia or even open hostility toward the environment. Such happenings would, he noted, likely lessen concerns for nature and bring about an overall decline in environmental sensitivity and a so-called environmental ethic. Fortunately, over the past 10 years Texans have actually increased their appreciation for and understanding of land-related issues and have participated in outdoor recreation in larger numbers than ever before. The focus, however, has shifted from setting aside more and more wildlands in remote places to greater acreages for parks and preserves adjacent to metropolitan areas

60

or in urban places themselves. This chapter supplies details of recent public concerns for the environment and explains how these values have been articulated and exemplified.

Growth in the 1980's

Ranked by the 1990 U.S. census as the third most populous state (after California and New York), Texas has grown by 2.8 million people during the last decade. The official count places 16,986,510 people in the state. With California and Florida, Texas accounted for 54% of the nation's growth in the 1980's. Although it did not increase its own numbers by the whopping 27% which marked Sunbelt expansion in the 1970's, Texas grew by 19.4%, a little below the decade average since 1900 but ahead of the nation's growth rate by almost 10 percentage points (Table 2.1).

Urban areas continue to absorb most new Texans. Only 11 of 91 cities with more than 20,000 inhabitants showed numerical declines over the past 10 years. Seventy-eight experienced growth; some of the smaller ones exploded. Rowlett (23,200), Sugar Land (24,500), and Round Rock (30,900) rocketed by more than 200%, 178%, and 162%, respectively. But unlike large cities in other states, well-established Texas metropolitan areas also grew. Houston, the largest Texas city (with 1.6 million people, ranked fourth in the nation), rose a sluggish 2% in the decade. But Dallas, 1.01 million and ranked eighth, picked up 11%. San Antonio, 935,000 and tenth in the United States, expanded numerically by 19%, while El Paso (515,000, 21%), Austin (466,000, 35%), and Fort Worth (448,000, 16%) achieved very impressive increases (U.S. Department of Commerce 1993).

Not only are there more Texans than ever before, but more Texans live in urban areas. What do such trends mean for the 80% of people who live in cities in terms of accessibility to open space and environmental values?

Environmental Values

Three values achieved prominence in the 1970's. During a public opinion poll, a research firm discovered that people were basically concerned about themselves, they sought out immediate satisfaction, and they preferred doing rather than possessing things (*Outdoor Recreation* 1983). A so-called leisure ethic encapsulated these values in the 1980's. Self has remained important; however, rather than the self-indulgence of the 1980's, individuals have begun to expand personal

Table 2.1. TOTAL POPULATION OF TEXAS, 1850–1989

Total population		Change in population		
Year	Number	Decade	Number	Percent
1850	212,592			
1860	604,215	1850–1860	391,623	184.2
1870	818,579	1860–1870	214,364	35.5
1880	1,591,749	1870–1880	773,170	94.5
1890	2,235,527	1880–1890	643,778	40.4
1900	3,048,710	1890–1900	813,183	36.4
1910	3,896,542	1900–1910	847,832	27.8
1920	4,663,228	1910–1920	766,686	19.7
1930	5,824,715	1920–1930	1,161,487	24.9
1940	6,414,824	1930–1940	590,109	10.1
1950	7,711,194	1940–1950	1,296,370	20.2
1960	9,575,677	1950–1960	1,868,483	24.2
1970	11,196,730	1960–1970	1,617,053	16.9
1980	14,229,191	1970–1980	3,032,461	27.1
1989	16,986,510	1980–1989	2,757,319	19.4

Sources: Wooldridge 1982; U.S. Department of Commerce 1990.

horizons by reaching out through community involvement. Americans are less satisfied by their employment situations. They escape stress and anomie through volunteerism and a commitment to specialized interests and hobbies that include environmental issues and the challenge of outdoor pursuits such as swimming, hiking, cycling, and snow skiing. These ways of "doing things" make the natural environment an important outlet, both in the physical exercise and commitment to individual health that the public enjoys and in concerns for personal and environmental integrity and for ecosystems under pressures from development.

Public Recreation

People's activities in public recreation sites—the parks and preserves owned by city, state, and federal authorities—demonstrate changes in values. Americans have continued to show great interest in the outdoors. Ways in which people express this attachment have altered, however, and when pushed back a generation or more, it is clear that many types of outdoor activities have changed. A 1986 opinion survey sponsored by the President's Commission on Americans Outdoors reported that at least once a year, 84% of adults walked or hiked for pleasure. Half said they exercised in this fashion often or very often, while 76% of adults took part in sightseeing, picnicking, and swimming outdoors, and 43% of this latter group swam often or very often. A similar percentage exists for those who bicycle, go camping, or fish at least once annually. Slightly more than ⅓ of the public watch birds and other wildlife; 15% do so frequently. There were similar percentages for those who preferred to ride horses, sail, or windsurf (Report 1987:51).

As an index of outdoor interest, visitation to parks in Texas follows national trends, demonstrating a marked upturn in the 1980's. In fiscal year 1989–90, total visits to the more than 100 state facilities (25 more than existed in 1980) topped 21 million (Table 2.2). This represents a 43% increase over the figures for 1980–81 of close to 15 million. During the decade, the state population grew by 19.4%, so that outdoor recreation, at least in state parks, increased at slightly more than twice the rate of Texas's population growth. Approximately 87% of people who visited state parks stayed for one day; the remainder stayed at least one night. This disproportionate preference for day use remained

Table 2.2. TEXAS STATE PARK USE, 1980–1990 (in 1,000s)

Year	Overnight use	Day use	Visitor totals
1980/1981	1.9	12.9	14.8
1981/1982	2.4	14.7	17.0
1982/1983	2.5	15.8	18.3
1983/1984	2.4	16.2	18.6
1984/1985	2.4	17.3	19.7
1985/1986	2.2	18.3	20.6
1986/1987	2.1	17.8	19.9
1987/1988	2.3	18.7	21.0
1988/1989	2.3	18.5	20.8
1989/1990	2.3	18.8	21.1

Source: Texas Parks and Wildlife, Division of Comprehensive Planning 1991.

**Table 2.3. VISITOR USE OF TOP TEN STATE PARKS,
1989–90** (in 1,000s)

		Overnight use	Day use	Total visitors
1	San Jacinto	0	1,429.0	1,429.0
2	Mustang Island	44.3	918.0	962.3
3	Lake Corpus Christi	60.0	550.5	610.5
4	Martin Dies, Jr.	55.5	450.8	506.4
5	Galveston Island	90.1	414.6	504.7
6	Brazos Bend	44.6	445.1	489.7
7	Huntsville	78.6	400.0	478.6
8	Bastrop	53.1	425.0	478.1
9	Palo Duro Canyon	43.4	407.3	450.8
10	Lyndon Baines Johnson	0.0	419.1	419.1

Source: *Texas Parks and Wildlife, Division of Comprehensive Planning 1991.*

constant throughout the 1980's, whereas overnight camping declined by about 11% (Texas Parks and Wildlife 1990).

As expected, the principal Texas parks that received the most use were ones close to urban areas. The San Jacinto Battleground near Houston drew the greatest number of visitors annually due to its accessibility and historic significance (Table 2.3). Mustang Island and Galveston Island state parks are very popular because of beach access and vacation use by young adults. Lake Corpus Christi rose from sixth to third in the decade, although overnight camping in the park actually decreased by 10 million people. Day visits there, however, increased by 45%, as people took advantage of facilities for boating, swimming, and fishing.

Huntsville is another popular park in East Texas. Although its pine and oak woodlands witnessed a 14% decline in overnight use, it climbed two places, from ninth to seventh, due to a 47.4% day-visitor increase between 1980 and 1990. Among the top 10 parks, only Mustang Island State Park and Palo Duro Canyon saw increases in overnight camping for the 1980's, yet these same facilities accounted for a total of 676 million more visitors, 12% more than 10 years earlier, while overnight stays actually fell overall by 1.5%.

In short, state parks that are within easy driving distances of major urban centers such as Houston, Corpus Christi, Austin, San Antonio, and Lubbock (as reflected in Table 2.3) which also provide historic, cultural, and amenity resources geared to water-related outlets prove to be most desirable for many Texans. Water-dependent recreation is among the fastest growing outlets in the nation.

Outdoor Experiences

What are the values that guide such activities? Why do so many Americans have such a need for recreation, especially in the outdoor environment? The 1987 President's Commission answered some of these queries. Charles Jordan (Report 1987:9), director of parks and recreation, Austin, Texas, and a member of the 15-member federal commission established by President Reagan's executive order in 1985, noted that "we find that the outdoors is a wellspring of the American spirit, vital to our belief in ourselves as individuals and as a nation." He argued that Americans feel strongly about open space; it is an opinion supported and repeated again and again by individual testimony before the commission.

In one way, nature is a living museum. It retains components of wildness that provide a glimpse into a colonial or frontier past; also, it serves as a benchmark against which we can measure the pace, character, and quality of change. Outdoor recreation and the setting for leisure that natural beauty affords, according to Yale academic William Burch, also enable us to establish a connection between our private lives, our social circle, and the larger world of community. Those special places we set aside and seek out are centers in which we experience nature's rhythms and the cycles of the season. In such outdoor contacts and tranquillity, we are reminded of our own biological connections with other living things and are reassured that their lifeways are similar in many respects to our own. In experiences of nature, people discover opportunities of significance and identity; they learn about challenge and purpose and gain a sense of fulfillment in society (Report 1987:35).

Outdoor experiences also fashion basic connections between generations. Elders may pass along skills necessary for hunting or teach young people woodcraft—ways to identify and approach wildlife. Such activities supply opportunities for communication within and between members of communities and neighborhoods. Importantly, such experiences serve as an "escape." Many people feel a need to get away from the urban environment. Their reasons include a break from routine and important time for relaxation and reflection. Most go outdoors to enjoy natural beauty where noise and disturbance from crowded cities are mitigated by greater access to cleaner air and water and the inspiration that scenery, plants, and animals provide (Report 1987:40). It is no wonder, then, that among the issues that concern the public the most is protection of natural resources and open space—the basis for inspiration and affirmation of ourselves as humans. The problem lies in the losses that the public sees as occurring in this heritage, its diminution both in quantity and quality, and the conflicting uses to which open space and parklands are increasingly put.

Open Space and Wildlife

How do experts and the public in general envision solving the dilemma of keeping open space and also using it? One response is to focus on conserving their state's biological heritage while adding acreage to parks as refuges. In this way the actual environment itself and the biodiversity that enriches it are important for Texans who value the attributes of this so-called biological crossroads for North America. The politically charged topic of endangered and threatened plants and animals has been prioritized under recent Texas Parks and Wildlife Department policy, which seeks to expand research and also publicize concerns about 68 federal and 147 state-listed species.

In May 1988, Texas signed a cooperative agreement with the U.S. Fish and Wildlife Service (under the terms of the Federal Endangered Species Act of 1973) whereby funding is secured to expand research on organisms threatened by extinction. Currently, authorities are tracking some 780 species and eliciting landowner support for habitat preservation, as well as generating data about the life histories of scores of nongame organisms that may soon be in trouble (Sansom 1991).

In 1985, sales of a new nongame stamp with a decal and artwork portraying a pair of whooping cranes enabled the public to contribute directly to this type of conservation issue. Revenues from the annually printed stamp, similar to those purchased by bird hunters, assist with habitat acquisition and nongame management. In the past 5 years, upwards of $300,000 has accrued from art depicting cranes, Attwater's greater prairie-chickens, ocelots, bald eagles, and white-tailed hawks (Doughty and Parmenter 1989).

Environmental Consciousness

Expanded institutional commitment for preserving endangered wildlife fits into the trajectory of environmental concerns revealed by a survey done in summer 1990 by Rice University sociologists, who discovered that 2 of 3 Texans believe that too little money is being spent on environmental protection and improvement. A similar fraction disagreed with the proposition "jobs first and pollution second," favoring stricter laws that regulate pollution. They argued that when a plant cannot meet acceptable standards it should be shut down.

Such an intensity of concern about environmental issues does not always apply immediately to a local or community situation. Crime, drugs, and poverty come spontaneously to mind in these situations; however, when specifically asked, 20% regarded pollution as a "very serious" problem in their community. Moreover, twice as many Texans judge that environmental problems are getting worse as those who think they are getting better. And most believe that a vigorous eradication of dereliction would not hurt their own community's efforts to promote economic growth. While people characterize the critical state issues to be abatement of water and air pollution, garbage and waste disposal appear to be key issues at the local level (Klineberg 1990).

Indexes to the *Houston Post* show a similar trajectory of concerns in coverage given to environmental issues. For example, in 1987, the daily newspaper ran 166 stories on waste disposal, 47 on water pollution, 40 on parks and recreation, 37 on air pollution, 25 on endangered species, and 15 on acid rain that combined to total more coverage than was given to banks and banking and almost ⅓ of that given to the petroleum industry. At middecade waste disposal enjoyed a giant share of environmental reporting in that newspaper; it had 210 entries in 1986, while parks had 108 entries.

Such statistics point to the fact that Texans are better informed and more concerned about the environment than ever before. They value a healthy environment, qualities in nature that go beyond immediate material benefits. The campaign to reduce litter along the highways has been a success. According to a follow-up on the "Don't Mess with Texas" campaign, litter and trash along road edges declined in some places by as much as 60 percent after its inception in 1985 (Kantor 1990).

The topic of litter along the state's highways exemplifies a growing number of quality issues pertaining to the environment. Throughout the 1980's organizations and special interests committed to grass-roots support for clean water, aquifer protection, river quality, bat or lizard preservation, etc., have enlisted public support for lobbying the legislature and city councils. They represented values in action, and representatives canvassed from door to door on behalf of their particular

Table 2.4. TEXAS ENVIRONMENTAL ORGANIZATIONS

Date	Purpose	Membership
1989	Austin Releaf—facilitate tree planting	—
1982	Bat Conservation International—conservation of bats worldwide	Worldwide: 12,500 Austin: 300
1971	Clean Water Action—protect health and the environment	National: 1,000,000 Texas: 90,000
1988	Colorado River Watch Network—water quality monitoring	500
1980	Earth First!—direct action for environmental quality	membership not fixed
1967	Environmental Defense Fund—science, economics, and law to save environment	National: 200,000 Texas: c. 8,000
1971	Greenpeace Action—grassroots environmental action protection	Texas: c. 40,000
1986	Hill Country Foundation—protection of central Texas hill country	several hundred
1991	Horned Lizard Conservation Society—preserve horned lizards	500
1986	Native Prairies Association of Texas—preservation of aboriginal grasslands	400
1971	Public Citizen—consumer rights and environmental health	3,600
1977	Save Barton Creek Association—protect Edwards Aquifer	5,000
1892	Sierra Club—preservation of natural beauty	Austin: 3,600
1951	Texas Nature Conservancy—conserve biodiversity	25,000
1952	Travis Audubon Society—bird conservation and nature protection	1,900
1988	Tree Folks—tree planting	70

Source: Austin American Statesman, September 3, 1991.

concerns. Such advocacy also reflects a commitment to a healthier landscape and to a heritage that is both beautiful and diverse. The media have picked up and popularized many of these themes. Table 2.4 lists some of the better-known organizations in the state, most of which are now commonly accepted. Daily newspapers now provide weekly columns on environmental topics and proffer advice about activities and lifestyles, including recycling, that are "friendly" toward the environment.

Future Trends

The federal government controls less than 5% of the recreational sites in the Lone Star State but owns or operates 54% of actual park space, including vast acreages such as Big Bend and Forest Service lands in East Texas. State authorities provide about 30% of recreational space. With 130 sites, the Texas State Park System is able to furnish three times more parks or recreation areas than the National Park Service, for example, but falls behind when comparisons are made between state and federal holdings. The Army Corps of Engineers controls more park and recreation areas than all of the state facilities combined.

Public response to the availability of the recreational outlets has been consistently favorable as measured by increases in visitation and in the range of activities that people enjoy in the outdoors. From this perspective, additional parks and a greater range of recreational outlets appear significant, especially when $\frac{1}{3}$ of the people polled suggest that currently areas they visit are too crowded or too far away from their homes. Some folks do not find enough time to value the outdoors, others do not command sufficient funds or enough information to participate formally in outdoor pursuits (Texas Parks and Wildlife 1990).

However, time limitations from job-related duties may be tempered by outdoor experiences that are meaningful and inspiring; they permit individuals to connect with the land and find in outdoor places moments for reflection and affirmation of personal and community identity. Financial constraints to enjoying outdoor contacts may be mitigated in part by including urban and industrial areas in historic, cultural, and ecological corridors in which values may be both expressed and enjoyed. Recent efforts that identify the "city as a park" represented by "Riverspark" in the Hudson-Mohawk Urban Corridor in New England address the concept of revitalizing old business areas and waterfronts in order to inculcate greater community pride and civic consciousness. In this case public and private interests have worked together to preserve amenities and have discovered uses for existing resources in urban areas that have been neglected or degraded (Bray 1987).

An example closer to home shows how Austin residents are increasingly concerned about the integrity of the Edwards Aquifer, whose waters supply Barton Springs. Discussions about development west of the city, runoff controls, and surface water quality embroiled officials and the public in acrimonious debate that placed the integrity of the environment as central to the character and identity of the entire urban community.

Information about outdoor access and outdoor values exists as never before. It is how we use information, how we participate in the social and political settings that poses the greatest challenge. Parks are for people; that is, they are places in which the public may pursue various forms of recreational activities. Parks and the spaces that comprise them are also places in which we connect with natural things, experience our humanity, and value it in relation to the web of life of which we are a part.

Literature Cited

Bray, P. M. 1987. A new era for urban parks: The "city as a park." Pp. 394–402 in Report of the President's Commission, Americans outdoors.

Doughty, R. W., and B. M. Parmenter. 1989. Endangered species. Houston: Gulf Coast Publishing.

Kantor, S. 1990. Daredevil tactics. Austin American-Statesman, October 13.

Klineberg, S. L. 1990. The Texas environmental survey. Dep. of Sociology, Rice Univ., Houston, Tex. 13 pp.

Outdoor recreation for America. 1983. Washington, D.C.: Resources for the Future.

Report of the President's Commission. 1987. Americans outdoors: The legacy, the challenge. Washington, D.C.: Island Press.

Sansom, A. 1991. State requirements regarding threatened and endangered species. Endangered Species Forum, October 9, Austin, Tex.

Texas Parks and Wildlife, Comprehensive Planning Branch. 1990. TORP—assessment and policy plan. Austin. 340 pp.

U.S. Department of Commerce, Bureau of the Census. 1993. 1990 census of population and housing. Washington, D.C.: GPO.

Wooldridge, J. 1982. Urban growth and wilderness values in Texas. Pp. 55–66 in J. T. Baccus, ed., Texas wildlife resources and land use. Austin: Wildlife Society.

James G. Teer
Welder Wildlife Foundation
Sinton, Texas 78387

3. Texas Wildlife— Fourteen Years Later

Abstract: This chapter examines events and philosophic tenets of Texans 14 years after the 1982 symposium "Texas Wildlife Resources and Land Use," sponsored by the Texas Chapter of The Wildlife Society. The 1980's and early 1990's were a time of conservation unrest made so by increased involvement of the state's citizenry. Texas's citizenry demanded more participation and transparency in government conservation activities. The results of societal interest were greater appreciation for nongame and endangered species and habitats, promotion of biological diversity, management at ecosystem and landscape levels, development of the animal rights movement, and application of the strategy for marrying conservation interests with human needs. Sustainable use became institutionalized in the World Conservation Strategy with applications to local uses of wildlife. Privatization of wildlife resources and the increase in translocations and introductions of exotic animals by the private sector were key issues in the decade of the 1980's and continue to this date. Conflicts between user groups and societal values for preserving all life on lands given over to agricultural and industrial development joined with privatization and exotic animals as key issues. An explosion in fencing of private land to contain large mammals occurred, and regulations were passed by the Texas Parks and Wildlife Department to permit private property owners to take as many deer as needed to properly manage their ranch herds. Private landowners waged a heated battle to preserve property rights by opposition to most conservation legislation passed in the previous 25 years. Their battle cry was that future generations cannot be the major focus of conservation efforts and that conservation cannot be achieved by denying the rights, responsibilities, and cultural norms of present generations.

In 1982, I presented the keynote address in wildlife values, uses, and issues at the symposium "Texas Wildlife Resources and Land Use" (Teer 1982), which was sponsored by the Texas Chapter of The Wildlife Society. I briefly described the great natural resources of Texas and problems that affected them, and I discussed problems that would attend them in the future. Burgeoning human numbers, intensification of agricultural practices, and poor public relations of conservation agencies were addressed. Specific issues were funding of nongame conservation efforts, losses of streams to dams and decreasing water releases to estuaries, increasing costs of hunting lease fees, trophy deer management, restoration of mined lands, and translocations of nonnative wildlife. My goal in this chapter is to discuss conservation and management of wildlife resources by examining 4 principal events and philosophic tenets that have developed and been adopted by conservation agencies and our citizenry since 1982.

Sensitive and Scarce Life

The 1980's were a time of unrest in the conservation community, with citizen interests reaching an all-time high. Never had society taken a larger interest in environmental and conservation concerns as they did in that decade. The effect was to join conservation and environmental issues with economic and social ills of the nation. When we examine the record over the past 3 or 4 decades, it becomes clear just how far society has ventured into conservation affairs, territory in which it rarely entered, or reluctantly so, in the past and then usually in issues surrounding consumptive uses of wildlife.

Citizen conservationists became preoccupied with the Endangered Species Act. Conservation agencies reoriented some of their efforts to protect scarce and sensitive life. Citizens, now much more aware of threatened habitats and life therein, demanded it. The professional conservation community added biodiversity to its lexicon of conservation interests. The scale of effort increased from species and habitats to larger dimensions of guilds, landscapes, and ecosystems. Federal and state conservation agencies rushed to incorporate these larger contexts in their programs while at the same time providing leadership and support for endangered and threatened species. Declines in continental populations of waterfowl in wetlands, extinction rates of plant and animal life in species-rich tropical forests, and the northern spotted owl in the Pacific Northwest symbolized threats to landscape-level systems. In all cases, humans were at the center of the picture, and their numbers were and remain the specter that orchestrates conservation efforts.

Along with these changes came a great push by animal rights advocates to disenfranchise uses of animals for almost any purpose. Hunting and fishing, medical research, food and fiber production, and recreational uses of animals for such activities as rodeos, racing, and even nature study were targets of the animal rights movement. Energies and economies of organizations were mustered on both sides of the question of rights of animals with the issue still debated and unsettled. Funded with enormous budgets, animal rights organizations mounted a campaign to undermine traditional values and uses of the natural world.

Promotion of biodiversity by the conservation community has many unsolved problems, not the least of which are conflicts with production systems in which specific animals are produced for utilitarian purposes. How does management of such a species utilized by humans impact other life in habitats given over to its welfare? Do deer and other species coexist under intensive deer management? This question is vital to management where habitat is managed for large mammals and game birds (Teer in press; Hobbs 1996). It is equally or even more important to the agricultural community whose members work the land to produce goods and services needed by an ever-increasing human population.

Strategies for protecting biodiversity are still untested. Many are short-term fixes which will not succeed in the context of today's human populations using a finite resource base. For example, parks and sanctuaries are inadequate to protect all endangered and threatened species on a worldwide basis. About 97% of the land area in Texas is privately owned. In the first place, many parks fail to protect even those species they were established to protect. Gap analyses have demonstrated this failure (Scott, Csuti, and Caicco 1991; Scott et al. 1993). Many sanctuaries are little more than parks on paper, made so by governments with few or no resources, staff, and money to protect them from incursions by the public. Of the 3,500 major sanctuaries in the world (World Resources Institute 1986), less than half are considered secure. Quality of management and degree of protection vary widely.

The conservation strategy of protecting life through setting aside lands is often flawed because people are not considered. Nonetheless, sanctuaries are necessary and needed in all lands, but people's needs have not always been considered in conservation plans. Further, adequate staff and budgets have not been provided to give protected areas a reasonable chance to succeed. The Man and the Biosphere Program includes human needs in its systems of sanctuaries and prescribes buffer and use areas for local people.

Partnerships between government conservation agencies and the private sector are being promoted to protect scarce species and their habitats. Because of widespread misunderstanding and insensitivity of government agencies in protecting threatened and endangered species, partnership arrangements are at risk. An outright estrangement occurred between the conservation community and those who own or control the land. The agricultural community and other businesses have declared firm opposition to more lands being taken from the private sector. Landowners in Texas and elsewhere in the nation are extremely suspicious and uneasy over government agencies' regulations and statutes. Many believe that government can and will condemn their property to save wetlands and threatened and endangered species and will provide open and free access to their property for recreational pursuits. Suspicion is a major cause of unrest in the agricultural industries despite efforts on the part of conservation agencies to assure them that precipitous incursions on property rights are vastly overstated and almost never used.

How far have we progressed in protecting our environment and its creatures? Perhaps the most telling evidence is industry's efforts to convince stockholders and society in general of its commitment to be "good environmental citizens." Many reports to stockholders are now accompanied by environmental and conservation reports outlining a company's commitments to protect wildlife and improve environmental quality. Some are a little overdone, and others are outright propaganda. However, we should not condemn them or even question their motives. The fact is that agriculture and industry are catching up with societal values, and action is replacing lip service in a great many corporate and government projects.

Nonetheless, on the whole, conflicts between conservation efforts and the desires and needs of people have increased in the last decade. Economic problems and recessions during the 1980's resulted in a backlash to conservation issues. Communities that are affected by conservation issues when jobs and community welfare are at stake are vocal advocates of "jobs 1st." Aided by the U.S. government, spotted owls and ancient forests are giving way to forestry and lumbering interests in the Pacific Northwest.

Environmental concerns among Texans are slightly lower today than they were in 1992 and 1990, but their commitment to environmental protection remains strong (Klineberg 1994). By a margin of 70–24%, Texans overwhelmingly disagree with the suggestion that we are not harming the environment when we do normal things like driving cars and running air conditioners. The media, which have much to do with citizen awareness of environmental problems, are no longer leading Americans toward a greater awareness of them. Articles on environmental problems in 2 leading news magazines, *Time* and *Newsweek*, declined dramatically between 1990 and 1994. Texans see crime and the economy as more pressing.

In Texas, an example of a major conflict between the conservation community and other interests occurred in the Balcones Canyonlands west of Austin. Several species of plants, vertebrates, and cave-dwelling invertebrates were threatened there by expansion of housing and businesses. The conservation community, businesses, and landowners were polarized in their positions on protecting the scarce species. Many landowners do not wish to sell or give over their properties through conservation easements to either the business community or the government for refuges and sanctuaries. The city of Austin, Travis County, real estate developers, ranch owners, and several conservation agencies of government and nongovernment agencies hammered out a compromise. Concessions to development and to conservation interests were made. The U.S. Fish and Wildlife Service and the Texas Parks and Wildlife Department created an extensive sanctuary system. Sanctuaries (refuges) were carved out and placed among an increasing human population in one of the great scenic areas of Texas.

Water is the great conservation issue now and will be increasingly so in the future. Scarce water and who owns it are epitomized by the debate over the Edwards Aquifer in San Antonio and the continuing exhaustion of the Ogallala Aquifer in the Panhandle and High Plains. Many agricultural areas, cities, and industries are scrambling and vying for water.

Another example of polarization of opinions and interests among the citizenry is exemplified by the increase and spread of mountain lions in West and West-central Texas. Lions are being seen for the first time in many years in the East Texas timberlands. They are increasing in the Rio Grande Plains and Edwards Plateau where some are killed as vermin or opportunistically killed by deer hunters. They have no legal protection; they can be taken by any means at any time of the year in any numbers. For years conservationists have attempted to provide some measure of protection to them. Efforts have been made to place them on the "game list," which would provide seasons and bag limits, protective measures which they currently do not have. Others want them to be completely protected, i.e., no sport hunting and no depredation permits. The livestock lobby has largely been responsible for preventing any legislation to protect them. Landowners, especially those in the Trans-Pecos region, do not want any interference or management of "their lions on their lands by any public agency."

These examples typify the various constituencies that have conflicting interests in conservation of the natural world. Much to its credit, the Texas Parks and Wildlife Department has in the last several years instituted a public review process to accommodate and resolve conflicts among user and protectionist groups. It has organized advisory committees on private lands, wetlands, and endangered and sensitive life. Participation rather than regulation is the new approach to conservation in Texas and worldwide.

Sustainable Use of Wildlife Resources

Despite the dogmatic expressions against utilization of wildlife by protectionists and animal rightists in recent years, sustainable use has become an extremely important strategy for conserving wildlife and its habitats. Not new, the concept began to take hold with international agencies advising conservation of wildlife resources in developing and Third World nations. It has application to the developed, affluent nations as well.

The concept of sustainable development was institutionalized with the World Conservation Strategy. Simply stated, the strategy is defined as "development that meets the needs of the present without compromising the ability of future generations to meet their own needs" (World Commission on Environment and Development 1987). The strategy usually translates to meeting human needs. Aside from the elemental needs of basic requirements for survival, priorities of all nations and peoples are social justice (human rights), national sovereignty (freedom), economic strength (stability and enough for all), and political partnership (equality among nations and ethnic or racial groups). If it is to succeed, conservation of the world's resources must be practiced in the context of these essential human values.

Privatization of Wildlife Resources

Landownership and tenure systems are major influences on wildlife management in Texas. About 4 million acres of land (2%) of this large state are in public property. Thus, wildlife management is practiced almost universally on private lands. The state is charged with administering wildlife resources and equitably distributing opportunities to take and use wildlife resources to the people.

Texas is vastly different from other states, especially the 17 western states where at least half the region is in public lands managed by a few large government agencies and bureaus. The Texas system is disavowed if not despised in many regions because of the commercialization of hunting and fishing recreation. Landowners and resource managers of most agencies in Texas have endorsed and promoted this system because of its powerful influence on protection of habitat and wildlife resources.

However, an insidious development of the commercial system has been the gradual but inexorable transfer of wildlife from public to private ownership. Owners of land, i.e., owners of wildlife habitat, have strict control of access to the land and of land management on their property. Ownership prerogatives have evolved from a quasi-partnership arrangement with the Texas Parks and Wildlife Department to one in which private property owners are now asking for more control of how wildlife resources are managed and distributed to users. These translate to rights for setting bag limits, seasons, means, and methods of taking. Requests may not be spelled out in these explicit rights, but they do predict them in operational management.

Over a period of about 40 years, more and more authority has been transferred to private property owners for wildlife management. Deer management in the state has evolved from very strict bucks-only regulations that were changed with the first antlerless deer season in Mason County in 1954. Surveys were used to establish surplus numbers, and a strict permit system was used to control the harvest. The number of deer harvested under the system was always less than the number of permits issued, often in a ratio of 10 permits to each deer harvested. Either sex deer seasons were a great departure from the bucks-only season that had been espoused for 50 years in the state.

As time passed and as landowners and managers found that deer herds could withstand greater offtakes than had been the case, restrictions were slowly relaxed to increase the harvest over a wider range of counties to the point where permits and quotas were no longer required in many counties. Seasons were lengthened and bag limits liberalized. Landowners were expected to police themselves, simply because deer meant money, and none would be obliged to overharvest their basic resource.

Next came the obsession by many landowners to produce trophy deer. Permits were given to some landowners to pen deer for breeding experiments in an effort to produce "superbucks." The superbucks were to be released back into wild stocks or sold on the hoof to hunters and other breeders. "Deer breeding" still occurs, especially in the Edwards Plateau and Rio Grande Plains. In the last few years, interest has increased in this expensive long-term effort.

More important to deer management attitudes and activities have been efforts to produce trophy deer on extensive rangelands and timberlands in the state. Briefly stated, trophy deer management requires adequate nutrition, which means reduction in herd numbers on many ranges, and allowing deer to achieve physical maturity, which usually means allowing deer to reach ages of largest body and antler growth.

To assist in this goal, many landowners fenced their properties with 8- and 9-foot-high fences. An incomplete survey made by the author and a representative of the Texas Parks and Wildlife Department, Leroy "Butch" Young, revealed that over 4 million acres had been fenced by the early 1990's. Fencing with "deer-proof" fences has greatly increased in the last 15 years. Impediments to free-ranging deer and genetic variability, adequate harvest of herds under fences, and simply another bite into a public resource are issues surrounding high fencing of private property. Landowners have the right to fence their property in any manner they desire. In doing so, however, they fence in wildlife and take it from use by the public to which it belongs under existing laws.

Texas courts will likely adjudicate this issue in future years, for there is sound merit on both sides. An 8-foot, 60-mile fence enclosing the Chama Land and Cattle Company in northern New Mexico, for example, was lowered to 42 inches as a result of a New Mexico State District Court action in August 1991. The reason: to permit "free movement of the public's game animals along traditional migration routes."

Of importance in the state is a move to permit owners of land to manage deer numbers through harvest by their own methods and means. The reason is clear. Ownership provides larger options for management by the private sector. It has been difficult for some large ownerships to reduce deer numbers under current regulations. Landowners seek more management rights because of hunting liability risks and because many large landowners do not wish to have an "army" of hunters traipsing over their property to reduce surplus animals. Many declare that landowners with proprietary rights can better manage wildlife than government. Thus, the proposal has been made to permit landowners themselves to harvest surplus deer.

Wildlife biologists are somewhat ambivalent in their reaction to a permit system for allowing landowners to harvest deer outside the usual hunting systems. For years, they have recommended reduction of deer numbers to improve the quality of deer harvested. On the one hand, many overpopulated deer herds need reduction kills by one system or another. On the other, some conservationists argue that hunters should harvest surplus deer if the landowner will permit access to them. Offtakes as high as 1 deer to 10 acres have been documented where hunter numbers and effort are carefully managed.

Only a few hunters have objected strenuously to permits given to landowners to reduce deer herds under management permits. They feel that the sport is being taken away from them. Sportswriters have been important allies to biological reasons for removing surplus deer for herd improvement, and, by and large, they have championed equitable distribution of wildlife through sport hunting. It is quite paradoxical that, as of this writing, few have objected to deer being removed from herds by property owners.

Control of deer management continues to pass from the state to private property owners. In the opinion of many wildlife managers, sportsmen, and others, the transfer of management and harvest control of wildlife from the state to private property owners will be complete when landowners and land managers are given rights to determine numbers (bag), composition (sex and age classes), and means and methods of taking.

The commercial or fee hunting system is the progenitor of privatization of wildlife and, undoubtedly, has been the largest impetus for conservation of game species especially. It has been responsible for restoring wildlife to many ranges in Texas where it had been almost completely extirpated. It has been important in restoring habitat and in changing land-use practices to favor wildlife. Despite their objections, other states are increasing their involvement in such systems.

However, most hunters and conservationists believe the commercial system must not evolve to the point where abuses of public rights are compromised. Many hunters believe they are being priced out of opportunities to hunt and that hunting and fishing recreation is ultimately going to the European elitist system. Under the most careful permitting system for removing surplus deer, hunting opportunities for the public are at risk. The state administers wildlife for the people, and most Texans believe that is where it should remain.

Translocations of Exotic Animals

Without question, Texas is among the leaders in introductions and translocations of exotic animals. Only Florida and California rival the state in the numbers and kinds of exotic releases. With tropical to subtropical climates, these 3 states are primary targets for releases of many species originating in similar habitats and climates around the world.

Surveys by personnel of the Texas Parks and Wildlife Department at about 5-year intervals have shown steady increases in the kinds and numbers of exotic animals in Texas. The last survey made in 1994 showed that 124 species or races totaling 195,483 individuals were present on 637 ranches in 155 of the 254 counties in Texas (Traweek 1995). Of the total, 77,218 were free-ranging in unhusbanded populations, mostly in Central and South-central Texas. The 5 most numerous were axis deer, nilgai antelope, aoudad or barbary sheep, fallow deer, and sika deer. All are escapes or were deliberately released into wild habitats. Some have experienced enormous increases. The nilgai antelope, for example, has increased from 3,334 in 1963 to 28,728 in 1994. While these data may vary by several percentage points, they do reflect the growing uses of wildlife habitat by exotic animals and the potential for serious problems in wildlife habitats.

Exotic animals have a very strong lobby in public affairs. Several organizations champion their use. Changes in laws affecting them are extremely difficult to pass. The Texas Exotics Association and the Texas Wildlife Association are primarily made up of landowners whose interests are largely economic. Hunter organizations and professional conservation groups have been rather passive in this matter.

By and large, most conservation agencies and organizations in other states strenuously object to introductions and releases of exotics in wild habitats. Many states are reviewing and strengthening laws governing nonnative species (Teer 1991). Texas, on the other hand, while not endorsing the translocation and uses of exotics, has no laws that restrict introductions and translocations. Exotics are simply treated as domestic animals in statutes and regulations.

Ranching of exotic animals for meat and other products is rapidly becoming an important agricultural enterprise in North America. Game farms are experiencing explosive growth and becoming a serious issue in Canada and the United States. Problems with diseases being spread to native ungulates are at the forefront of objections. Brucellosis, tuberculosis, and meningeal worms are but 3 of the pathogens and parasites that have been implicated in transfers of diseases from "domestic wildlife" to wild stocks.

Several game farms have been established in Texas, and cropping of exotic wildlife for special markets is being practiced on many ranches. One such ranch, the Heart-Bar Ranch near Yancey, Texas, is perhaps the most advanced game farm in Texas, if not in the United States. There, some 3,000 adult and juvenile fallow deer are intensively farmed on about 400 acres of center-pivot irrigated pastures. Its operations are a textbook example of game farming. Heart-Bar Ranch sells fallow deer and equipment to handle exotics to all who are interested.

Most wildlife biologists know the objections to uses of exotics and their history and potential for harm to native wildlife and domestic animals. Uses of exotics for any purpose pose potential problems for native wildlife and domestic animals. However, most biologists agree that exotics are here and that the question surrounding their use is now more rhetorical than real.

There are few "croppers" of exotic animals, but the number of ranches with surplus animals is large. Venison is a specialty item at the present time in markets in the New World. The size of the world market for venison is not known. African, Australian, and now North American sources are growing rapidly. After the industry has developed through sales of brood stock, some authorities predict a major retrenchment and retroflection in the industry. The heyday of the sale of broodstock of several species for sport hunting, including axis deer and blackbuck antelope, has passed. Now, the exotic wildlife industry is looking at meat and animal by-products for their major source of income. Fallow deer seems to be the animal of choice in North America, with Eurasian red deer a close second. Game farms with large ratite birds, i.e., ostriches and rheas, once a hot item in Texas and elsewhere, have now declined sharply due to oversupply and lack of development of markets for meat, hides, and feathers.

State agencies, including the Texas Parks and Wildlife Department, the Texas Department of Agriculture, and the Texas Department of Health, should review the exotic animal issue with the goal of strengthening statutes and regulations for protecting native stocks, domestic animals, and even human health.

Epilogue

Despite the conservation problems and conflicts wildlife resources face in Texas, the beauty and wealth of the natural world remain with us. Probably at no time in our history has it been more at risk. For that matter, at no time in our history have numbers and demands on our resources been so great. Whatever values are assigned to wildlife by various elements of society, all agree that we would be poorer if wildlife resources were lost. Our responsibility and our legacy to those that follow us will be what we do to manage ourselves—our own numbers—from here into the future.

Literature Cited

Hobbs, N. Thompson. 1996. Modification of ecosystems by ungulates. J. Wildl. 60(4):695–713.

Klineberg, S. L. 1994. The Texas environmental survey (1990, 1992, 1994). Department of Sociology, Rice University, Houston. 14 pp.

Scott, J. M., B. Csuti, and S. Caicco. 1991. Gap analysis: Assessing protection needs. Pp. 15–26 in W. E. Hudson, ed., Landscape linkages and biodiversity. Washington, D.C.: Defenders of Wildlife.

Scott, J. M., F. Davis, B. Csuti, R. Noss, B. Butterfield, C. Groves, J. Anderson, S. Caicco, F. D'Erchia, T. C. Edwards, J. Ulliman, and R. G. Wright. 1993. Gap analysis: A geographical approach to protection of biological diversity. Wildl. Monog. 123:1–41.

Teer, James G. 1982. Texas wildlife: Now and for the future. Pp. 9–20 in J. T. Baccus, ed., Texas wildlife resources and land use. Proc. symposium on Texas Wildlife Resources and Land Use, 14–16 April. The Wildlife Society (Texas Chapter), Austin. 199 pp.

———. 1991. Non-native large ungulates in North America. Pp. 55–66 in L. A. Renecker and R. J. Hudson, eds., Wildlife production: Conservation and sustainable development. Agric. For. Exp. Stn., Univ. of Alaska, Fairbanks. 601 pp.

———. In press. Management of ungulates and the conservation of biodiversity. In Curtis Freese, ed., Harvesting wild species. Baltimore: Johns Hopkins University Press.

Traweek, M. S. 1995. Statewide census of exotic big game animals.

Tex. Parks and Wildl. Dep., Austin, Fed. Aid Proj. No. W-127-R-3, Project No. 21. 53 pp.

World Commission on Environment and Development. 1987. Our common future. Oxford and New York: Oxford University Press. 400 pp.

World Resources Institute. 1986. A report by the World Resources Institute and the International Institute for Environment and Development. New York: Basic Books. 353 pp.

II. FUTURE EXPECTATIONS IN LAND USE

Bruce R. Miles
Texas Forest Service
College Station, TX 77843

4. Status of the Forest Resource in Texas

Abstract: Texas's timber resources are being squeezed by the opposing forces of increased demand for wood products and increasing environmental constraints to harvesting. Texas timber harvesting is at record levels, and the pine harvest has exceeded growth for the last seven years. Reforestation on nonindustrial private lands is inadequate. At the same time, environmental concerns have the potential to restrict harvesting in the South. More intensive multiple-use management of nonindustrial private lands would help mitigate these trends. Wildlife could hold the key to encouraging a stewardship ethic and improving management on these lands.

The forests of Texas are diverse and scattered across the state. They include the oak-juniper mountain forests of the Davis Mountains in West Texas, the hardwood and juniper woodlands of Central Texas, and the pine/hardwood timberlands of East Texas. While the forest land area in Texas approaches 23 million acres, an area larger than the state of Indiana, it is the East Texas timberlands that are commercially most important (Fig. 4.1).

East Texas Forest Facts

Located in 43 East Texas counties, the state's 11.8 million acres of timberland comprise the western edge of the southern pine region. The East Texas timberlands include tall, dense stands of loblolly and short-leaf pine; rolling hills covered with a mix of pine and a variety of hardwoods such as sweetgum, hickory, and southern red oak; and wet,

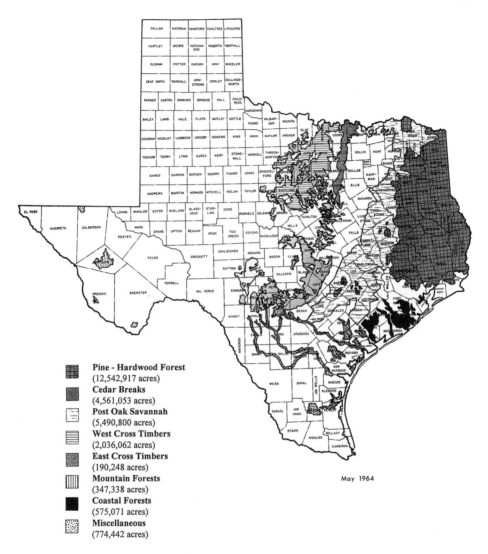

Pine - Hardwood Forest
(12,542,917 acres)
Cedar Breaks
(4,561,053 acres)
Post Oak Savannah
(5,490,800 acres)
West Cross Timbers
(2,036,062 acres)
East Cross Timbers
(190,248 acres)
Mountain Forests
(347,338 acres)
Coastal Forests
(575,071 acres)
Miscellaneous
(774,442 acres)

May 1964

Fig 4.1. *Tree regions of Texas and forested area of each.*

bottomland areas containing water oak, baldcypress, water tupelo, and ash (Fig. 4.2).

In East Texas, 93% of timberland is under private ownership. Sixty percent of timberland, 7.0 million acres, is held by nonindustrial private forest (NIPF) landowners. This group includes private individuals, families, partnerships, and corporations not involved in the manufacture of wood products. Forest industry owns another 33%, or 3.8 mil-

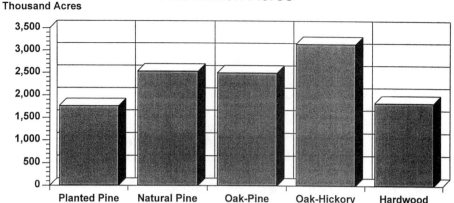

Fig. 4.2. *Timberland acreage by forest type.*

lion acres. The remaining 7% (0.8 million acres) is publicly owned, consisting primarily of the Davy Crockett, Sabine, Angelina, and Sam Houston National Forests (Fig. 4.3). Texas's 8.5-billion-dollar forest products industry, the ninth largest manufacturing employer in the state, depends on this forest resource. The wood industry directly employs over 60,000 workers and annually pays out $1.6 billion in wages and salaries. In 31 of the 43 East Texas counties (72%), it is the first or second largest manufacturing employer.

Among all states, Texas ranks ninth nationally in value added by manufacturing within the wood-based industry. It is the third largest wood panel producer, seventh largest pulpwood consumer, and twelfth largest lumber producer. In 1992, Texas produced 2.6 billion square feet of plywood and waferboard, 2.8 million tons of paper products, and 1.3 billion board feet of lumber. Texas's lumber production alone would build over 120,000 homes each year.

The South's Fourth Forest

It is important to note that the current crop of stately pines has not always been with us. In the early 1900's East Texas was severely cut over, burned, and left for Mother Nature and a few foresters to heal. It was replanted and regenerated, cut again, replanted and regenerated again, and is now being cut for the third time. Texas's

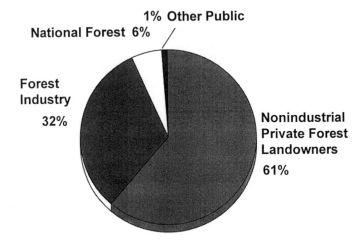

11.8 Million Acres

1% Other Public
National Forest 6%

Forest Industry 32%

Nonindustrial Private Forest Landowners 61%

Source: Miller and Hartsell, Forest Statistics for East Texas Counties-1992.

Fig. 4.3. *Timberland ownership.*

"fourth forest" is now being established, and it is this with which we must concern ourselves.

The Nation's Wood Basket

The southern pine region is rapidly becoming the "wood basket" of the nation. Environmental concerns over old growth harvesting and protection of the endangered northern spotted owl, among other factors, have permanently reduced the timber sale volume from the northwestern national forests. One study estimated that to offset even the minimum predicted 13% harvest decline in the western national forests, southern lumber production would need to increase by more than 1 billion board feet. Recent developments indicate that western harvest declines will likely be much larger and will include state and private timberlands as well.

At the same time, the environmental forces at work in the Northwest are becoming increasingly strong in Texas and across the South. Timber harvests from the national forests in Texas will almost certainly be curtailed due to the endangered status of the red-cockaded woodpecker. Although this does not represent a large share of the total Texas harvest, it is critical to the economies of localized areas of the state and is the source of much of the large-diameter sawlogs on which many mills depend for the high quality lumber in their product mix. Environmental constraints will also affect private lands as the nationwide trend spreads to the South. The public tolerance of the continued use of even-aged management, on which high yield plantation management depends, is a key issue.

The forest products industry is becoming increasingly responsive to these public concerns and has implemented programs to address management of environmentally sensitive areas. An example is Temple-Inland's bottomland hardwood management program. Temple-Inland is the largest forest landowner in the state, with holdings in Texas and Southwest Louisiana of 1.3 million acres. Of that, approximately 135,000 acres are bottomland hardwood forests, with an additional 40,000 acres of coastal flatwoods. These stands have undergone only a limited amount of harvesting over the past 30 years, mostly consisting of pine removal. However, these stands will become a more important source of hardwood fiber for the company's mills in the future. Outside experts along with company foresters and biologists have recently developed a comprehensive management plan for these areas which provides for wood fiber production as well as protection and enhancement of wildlife habitat, biodiversity, and water quality. As a result, approximately 55,000 acres will be managed under uneven-aged single-tree and group selection methods as streamside management zones, wildlife corridors, and sensitive areas. The remainder will be managed under even-aged management with clearcuts limited to 30 acres, natural regeneration to maintain species and genetic diversity, and interconnecting wildlife corridors to discourage habitat fragmentation.

Increased exports are also exerting pressure on Texas timber resources. Overseas exports of chips, logs, and finished products are increasing. From 1986 to 1989 exports of wood products from Texas increased from $46 million to $194 million.

Troubling Trends

The 1994 Forest Survey of East Texas, conducted by the U.S. Forest Service with the cooperation of the Texas Forest Service and forest industry, assessed the condition of the resource in 43 East Texas counties. Among the most important findings were that

1. hardwood timber harvests increased 21% between 1986 and 1992 while softwood harvest increased 9%,

2. removals of pine continued to exceed growth by about 1% a year between 1986 and 1992 (although this is an improvement over the 3% overcut between 1975 and 1986, it still represents a long-term situation that must be reversed),

3. as a result of removals exceeding growth, pine inventory has begun to decline,

4. on the positive side, growth of pine was up 10% while hardwood growth increased 21%.

Since the 1992 survey, pressures on the forest resource have accelerated, and several new mills have been added or announced. These include 2 large oriented strand board facilities, 2 large chip mills, and several sawmills. Annual pine timber harvests exceeded growth by 9% in 1992 as a result of continued expansion of mill capacity (Fig. 4.4). As production of lumber, paper, and panel products all achieved record levels, the harvest of timber in the state was the highest ever recorded.

Signs of growing timber resource scarcity have been predicted throughout the South over the next few decades. The 1990 U.S. Forest Service long-range timber study, "The South's Fourth Forest," indicated that continuation of recent trends may lead to a loss of 85,000 jobs within the lumber and wood products and paper industries across the South by 2030. Indirect job losses could exceed 200,000. The study projected continuing increases in demand for southern timber products, further reductions in timber growth, and declining inventories.

However, the trends can be mitigated through increased management of timberlands. Intensified forest management on industrial and public forest lands has already brought these lands close to their productive capacity. However, the NIPFs, comprising 60% of the timberland base in the state, remain largely understocked and undermanaged. According to the 1992 forest survey, 2.1 million acres on NIPF timberlands are inadequately stocked with trees and need active management to increase productivity to acceptable levels.

The potential for increasing timber production varies by ownership. Generally, Texas timberlands are growing at only about 50% of their productive potential. Opportunities do exist if owners would take advantage of them. In Texas, the fourth forest study identified economic opportunities for investment on 4.4 million acres of timberland as well as reforestation of over 1.0 million acres of mar-

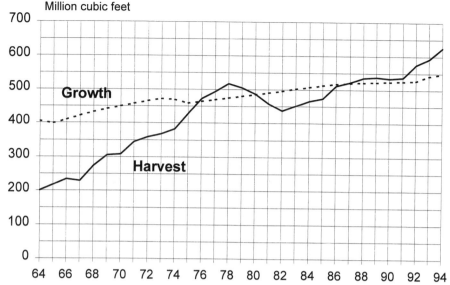

Fig. 4.4. *Pine growth and harvest in East Texas, 1964–1994 (Source: Texas Forest Service, harvest trends).*

ginal pasture and highly erodible cropland. The result could be an additional 207.0 million cubic feet of annual growth, about a 50% increase.

Solutions

Reforestation: The First Step

The forest products industry has been responding to this challenge and systematically replanting its own lands as they are harvested. An average of 140,000 acres are planted annually on industry lands. Reforestation on NIPF lands has been poor; only 20,000–25,000 acres are planted annually (Fig. 4.5). Generally speaking, for every 100 acres cut in Texas NIPF holdings, only 6 acres are being replanted. Even considering natural regeneration, only about ½ of pine and mixed pine-hardwood stands which receive heavy cutting regenerate with good pine stocking. The average landowner, the majority of whom are over 60 years of age, is not willing to invest in a product that will not reach maturity for 35–40 years. Historically, NIPF owners have been reluctant to make an investment in reforestation and have only actively practiced tree planting when financial incentives programs were available. In the late 1950's and early 1960's, the Soil Bank Program resulted in

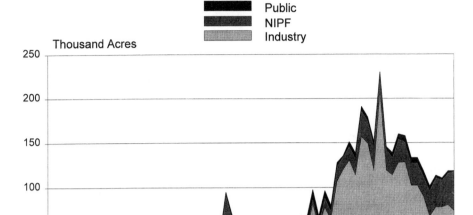

Thousand Acres

Fig. 4.5. *Historical reforestation in East Texas. NIPF = Nonindustrial private forests (Source: Texas Forest Service, harvest trends).*

the planting of as many as 60,000 acres per year. At the termination of this conservation program, tree planting on NIPF lands dropped to 4,000 acres per year. In 1974, a federal Forest Incentives Program (FIP) was initiated. Texas currently receives about $525,000 per year in this program, which reimburses the landowner for 50 percent of the costs of site preparation, tree planting, and timber stand improvement. Annual demand for FIP dollars exceeds supply by 2 to 1, and the program is responsible for reforestation of about 12,000–14,000 East Texas NIPF acres each year.

The forest products industry recognized its responsibility to *and dependency upon* the NIPF landowner by establishing the Texas Reforestation Foundation (TRe) in 1981. A unique and successful program, TRe provides cost share assistance to nonindustrial landowners for site preparation, tree planting, and timber stand improvement. The program is similar to the federal FIP program but is unique in that it is funded by voluntary contributions from the state's forest industry. Since 1981, the industry has contributed $3 million to assist landowners and has helped plant trees on 7,000–9,000 acres annually across East Texas.

Stewardship: The Ultimate Goal

Tree planting is not the total answer. There simply must be better forest management of the small private ownership to protect and enhance the forest-related environmental values. In other words, *stewardship*.

Stewardship embodies a responsibility of landowners for the care and wise use of their land, not only pursuing personal goals but at the same time respecting the rights of others, recognizing the interdependence of all elements of the environment, and preserving the ability of the land to meet society's future needs. Good stewardship of forest lands will provide this country's need for clean water and air, healthy populations of fish and wildlife, quality outdoor recreation, and ample forest products. Forest stewardship contributes to the natural beauty of Texas while guarding against soil erosion and protecting wetlands.

Wildlife: The Catalyst for Change

Texas landowners have changed. Most Texans' views of the state come not from wide open spaces or vast majestic forests but from fluorescent-lit offices and congested city streets. We are an urbanized state, and owners of our private woodlands are no exception. Increasing numbers of NIPF owners only occasionally visit or become actively involved with the management of their lands. If stewardship, with all its lofty goals, is to succeed, something must be injected into the system to draw these folks back to the land. Wildlife is the catalyst capable of doing just that.

This "new breed" of Texas landowners has not been raised in a rural environment and is not comfortable seeing trees planted or harvested. He or she is enthusiastic, however, about knowing wildlife could be found on his or her property and thrilled as the prospect of seeing them. Therefore, interest in improving wildlife habitat often is the key to reconnecting the landowner with his or her land.

Same Species, Different Names

Excluding the use of high fences, the most effective means of manipulating wildlife is to manage their habitat. Foresters call it *silvicultural treatments of forest stands*. Biologists refer to it as *wildlife habitat management*. Regardless of the label, it is occurring on the same acre, and wildlife call it *home*.

Without a doubt, the key to good habitat is diversity. Closely associated with diversity is interspersion of habitat types. The dilemma often facing landowners and managers in the East Texas Piney Woods is the *perceived* choice between timber and wildlife. Again, the solution lies in good stewardship through active management of their entire forest resources. Forest management and wildlife management are perfectly compatible. Examples include the use of prescribed fire; thinning overcrowded stands of timber to both increase wood fiber production and the amount of grasses, forbs, and understory tree species for wildlife; and creating forest openings to be used as logging sets (central loading areas where logs are temporarily stockpiled before being trucked to the mill) during timber harvests and planted in supplemental food and cover crops in interim periods. Incorporating "Best Management Practices" (BMPs) such as protecting wide areas around streams and drainages, called streamside management zones (SMZs), and seeding in roads and skidder trails increases diversity, insures water quality, and provides travel corridors between habitat types.

Texas landowners must begin to take stewardship responsibility seriously, but they do not have to make the journey alone. Foresters and biologists stand ready to give technical assistance and guidance to those willing to get involved in managing Texas's forest and wildlife resources.

The Challenge Ahead

As Texas rushes towards the twenty-first century, its forests are facing greater pressures than ever for both commodity and noncommodity uses. Demand for wood products has steadily increased, and projections show that this trend will continue for the next several decades. Meanwhile, reforestation and timber management, particularly on NIPF lands, have been inadequate. Opportunities to improve productivity are being lost. At the same time, demands for other benefits, including wildlife, wilderness, recreation, and biodiversity, continue to exert pressures on the resource, as does increasing urbanization. In sum, these issues are forcing a reduction in the land base available for timber production. In order to meet these increasing demands, it will be essential for the forestry community to find ways to more intensively manage forests for greater timber productivity while incorporating greater emphasis on nontimber values.

Literature Cited

Lang, L. L., and D. F. Bertelson. 1987. Forest statistics for East Texas counties—1986. Resource Bull. SO-118. USDA For. Serv., Southern For. Exper. Stn. New Orleans, La. 66 pp.

Lord, R. G. 1986–1992. Texas timber harvest trends. Publications 142, 143, 144, 145, 147, 150, 151. Texas A & M Univ. System, Tex. For. Serv., College Station, Tex.

McWilliams, W. H., and R. G. Lord. 1987. Regenerating the nonindustrial pine forests of Texas: How are we doing? TFNews 66(3,4): 16–19.

———. 1988. Forest resources of East Texas. Resource Bull. SO-136. USDA For. Serv., Southern For. Exper. Stn., New Orleans, La. 61 pp.

Miller, P. E., and A. J. Hartsell. 1992. Forest statistics for East Texas counties—1992. Resource Bull. SO-173. USDA For. Serv., Southern For. Exper. Stn., New Orleans, La. 55 pp.

O'Laughlin, J., and R. A. Williams. 1988. Forests and the Texas economy. Texas A & M Univ. System, Tex. Agric. Exper. Stn., College Station, Tex. 64 pp.

USDA Forest Service. 1988. The South's fourth forest: Alternatives for the future. For. Resource Rep. No. 24. Washington, D.C.: USDA For. Serv. 512 pp.

Don E. Albrecht
Associate Professor
Department of Rural Sociology
Special Services Building
College Station, Texas 77843-2125

5. Agricultural Development and Sustainability

Abstract: Agricultural development and change have long had important implications for wildlife resources. Agriculture results in dramatic habitat changes, making the environment more favorable for some wildlife species and less favorable for others. Technology, environmental concerns, farm policy, and other changes in agriculture greatly affect the way that farmers operate and thus have an important influence on wildlife resources. This chapter provides an overview of some of the more important changes occurring in agriculture that may have wildlife implications. The changes discussed include decreases in the number of farms, with corresponding increases in the size of the average farm, a recent financial crisis that forced many producers out of agriculture, uncertainty about the quality or quantity of future water supplies, new public farm conservation programs, and the emergence of new types of technology.

From the time that European settlers first arrived in the New World and began establishing their form of agriculture, there has been a close and important relationship between agriculture and wildlife resources. As with many other types of human activities, agriculture results in changes in the habitat of wildlife species. As forests are cleared, swamps drained, and grassland plowed, farming dramatically changes the areas in which wildlife grow, breed, seek shelter, and find food. To a large extent, agriculture increases human habitat while decreasing the habitat for other species. Further, changes in habitat occurring as a result of agriculture create environments more favorable to some species and less favorable to others.

Obviously, when land is initially transformed into farmland, habitat changes are dramatic. In addition, however, changes occurring in the use of farmland or in farming practices over time will also have major implications for wildlife. At the present time, there are about 1 billion acres of farmland in the United States. With such a close relationship between agriculture and wildlife and with so much land involved, it is critical for professionals and others interested in wildlife to be aware of the changes occurring in agriculture and the implications of these changes. The purpose of this chapter is to examine some of the major changes occurring in agriculture that affect wildlife. Also, an attempt is made to discuss some of the issues in agriculture likely to impact wildlife during the 1990's.

Transformations in Agriculture

To even the most casual observer, it is readily apparent that agriculture in this country has changed dramatically during the past few decades. During the 1930s, for example, farms in the United States numbered more than 6 million and averaged 150 acres each. At that time, the farm population exceeded 30 million people, which meant that about 1 in every 4 Americans was living on a farm. Typically, the farmer and his or her family provided the majority of the labor on their farm, and the farm was generally the sole or primary source of the family's livelihood.

By 1987, the number of farms had declined to about 2.1 million, and the farm population was 5.5 million, only 2.4% of the total U.S. population. The average farm in 1987 was 461 acres, about 3 times as large as during the 1930's. Further, nearly ½ of the farm operators reported that their primary occupation was something other than farming. In addition, agricultural production had become increasingly concentrated on a few very large, commercial farms. By 1987, only about 1.2% of the farms had gross farm sales of $500,000 or more, but these farms accounted for over ⅓ of the nation's gross farm sales.

The changes occurring in Texas agriculture have been similar in scope to those in the rest of the country. In 1930, there were nearly 500,000 farms in the state of Texas; by 1987, this number had declined to 188,788. During this time, the size of the average farm had increased from 252 acres to 691 acres. In 1987, 53.6% of the Texas producers stated that their primary occupation was something other than farming. On 47.6% of the Texas farms in 1987, the gross farm sales were less than $5,000. In contrast, only 1.2% of the farms had gross sales of $500,000 or more, but these farms had over 50% of the gross farm sales in the states.

Economic Importance

The 1987 census of agriculture reported that the gross sales of agricultural products in Texas for the year exceeded $10.5 billion. At that time, Texas ranked second of the 50 states in farm sales, trailing only California, which had farm sales of over $13.9 billion. A decade earlier, Texas was third in farm sales behind both California and Iowa.

Of the total agricultural sales in Texas, 71% ($7.5 billion) were from the sale of livestock and livestock products, while the remaining 29% were from crop sales ($3.0 billion). In 1987, Texas was the nation's leading state in terms of livestock sales, while Iowa was second. There were 4 states where the crop sales exceeded those in Texas: California, Illinois, Iowa, and Florida. The sale of cattle and calves is the single most important agricultural enterprise in the state of Texas.

Obviously, agriculture is a critically important economic endeavor to the state. However, the economic importance of agriculture in Texas varies tremendously from one part of the state to another. The most important agricultural regions in the state include the Panhandle and South Plains areas. The most important agricultural counties include Deaf Smith (gross sales $578 million), Parmer ($343 million), Hansford ($311 million), and Castro ($281 million).

Over a decade ago, John Hutchinson, writing in the 1982 report, predicted widespread economic problems in agriculture in the 1980's. These predictions were prophetic, as economic issues in agriculture gained widespread attention as many producers experienced a severe financial crisis during that decade. As a result of declining farm prices, high interest rates, and the increased cost of farm inputs, many farmers experienced extensive financial stress as their debt-to-asset ratios climbed. In fact, many farm operators were forced to leave agriculture for economic reasons. Persons most likely to leave agriculture for financial reasons during the 1980's tended to be younger, well-educated, operating medium- to large-sized farms, and using farming techniques that were recommended by experts. While the severity of the farm crisis declined during the last years of the 1980's, concern about the financial situation in agriculture continues in the 1990's and beyond. Obviously, for agriculture to remain a viable and sustainable enterprise, it must remain financially stable so that producers are able to make a reasonable living. Continued attention to developing farm exports and controlling domestic production are essential.

Number of Farms and Farm Size

For decades, the number of farms in both Texas and the rest of the United States has declined rapidly. Despite these declines, throughout the decades Texas has had more farms than any other state. The primary reasons for these declines were a series of major labor-saving technological developments. These technologies greatly increased the amount of land that an individual farmer could operate, and, as a result, there was a steady decline in the number of farms. A very surprising trend emerging from the 1980's was that this long-established movement toward fewer and larger farms was reversed. In 1978, there were 175,395 farms in Texas, with an average size of 773 acres. Since then, there has been a steady increase in the number of farms and a decline in the size of the average farm.

Historically, the primary reason for decline in the number of farms was rapid decrease in the number of very small farms. Technological developments resulted in changing economies of size where the small farms were at a major economic disadvantage. As a result, between 1930 and 1978, the number of farms with at least 50 acres in Texas declined from 166,768 to 30,478, a decrease of 82%. Since 1978, there has been a complete turnaround with a rapid increase in the number of very small farms. By 1987, there were 49,833 Texas farms with 49 or fewer acres, an increase of 64% from just 9 years earlier. Thus, it is recent growth in the number of small farms that is the main reason for increase in the number of Texas farms during the past decade. During the 1980's, there was little change in the number of farms in other farm size categories.

As opposed to previous eras, small farms of today are generally not limited resource, subsistence farms. Rather, most of these farms are part-time or retirement farms located on the urban fringe. Thus, many of the counties with a high proportion of very small farms are part of the Dallas, Houston, or San Antonio metropolitan areas. For example, in 1987, 57% of the 927 Dallas County farms had less than 49 acres, 54% of the 1,936 Harris County farms had less than 49 acres, and 48% of the 1,950 farms in Bexar County had less than 49 acres. Often, these very small farms are more concerned with amenities than with agricultural production which could greatly impact wildlife habitat. Another concern with agriculture on the urban fringe is the continuing expansion of the city and the subsequent loss of farmland.

There is much diversity in the size of the average farm from one part of Texas to another. Generally speaking, there is an increase in the size of the average farm as one moves from east to west. There were 4 counties in the state in 1987 (Kenedy, Loving, Culberson, and Brewster) where the average farm was more than 20,000 acres. These were all counties with very large cattle ranches. At the opposite extreme, there were 27 counties in the state where the average farm was less than 200 acres in size. All of these counties were in East Texas or on the fringe of a large city.

During the 1990's, concern about the number and size of farms in Texas has continued. Major changes in the number of farms, or in the number of farms in certain size categories, provide important clues about the economic and social climate of agriculture. During the 1980's, the number of farms in the medium-sized categories appeared to stabilize, ending decades of decline. However, current economic conditions indicate that many of these farms are in a precarious financial situation. Most likely, the number of very small and very large farms will continue to increase. Small farms will be operated by persons not dependent on agriculture, and large farms will produce an increasingly greater share of the state's agricultural commodities. However, the future of the midsized, family-operated farm is less certain.

Water Availability and Quality

Through the decades, Texas agriculture has faced a number of critical issues. Forecasting such issues in advance is always a risky and inexact business. However, it is a near certainty that problems related to the availability and quality of water for agricultural purposes will be near the top of the list. Since agriculture is the most prominent user of water in Texas, and since agriculture and wildlife often compete for water resources, trends in water use in agriculture are critical.

For decades, irrigation of crops has played a vital role in Texas agriculture. Whenever it is used, irrigation greatly increases crop yield. In many areas of the state, natural rainfall is insufficient for dependable crop production. In other parts of the state, irrigation greatly increases diversity of crops and also provides insurance that some crops can be produced even during drought years. Importance of irrigation to Texas agriculture is obvious when an examination is made of areas of the state where irrigation is most important. These are generally areas where sale of agricultural products is most extensive. For the most part, counties with the highest amounts of irrigation have the highest sales of agricultural products. Irrigation is the most extensive in the High Plains region, with other important pockets in the Rio Grande Valley, the Gulf Coast rice-producing areas, and the area overlying the Edwards Aquifer.

The future of irrigation in Texas is an issue of major concern. Most of the water used for irrigation purposes in Texas is drawn from underground aquifers. The most important of these is the Ogallala Aquifer located in the Texas High Plains. Pumpage from the Ogallala Aquifer is considerably greater than the estimated natural recharge and, consequently, will not be able to support irrigation of crops at current levels for the long term. As a result of intense irrigation over the past few decades, water levels in the Ogallala Aquifer have declined considerably. Because of these declining water tables and increasing energy costs associated with irrigation, there has been a substantial decline in irrigated acreage in the High Plains in recent years. As a result, the number of acres irrigated in Texas declined from over 7 million in 1978 to less than 4.3 million in 1987. During the 1990's, there has been a continued decline in irrigated acreage in the High Plains. This will affect agricultural production in that region and is also likely to have important regional demographic and socioeconomic implications.

In addition, water problems are also likely to emerge in other parts of the state as well. At the present time, there is concern about the future of irrigated agriculture in the Edwards Aquifer area. Unlike the Ogallala, depletion and recharge are not the major concerns with the Edwards Aquifer. With the Edwards, recharge is primarily by percolation from stream flow and by direct infiltration of precipitation. Water entering the aquifer then generally flows eastward toward natural discharge points, including Comal and San Marcos Springs. In a typical year, the Edwards Aquifer receives and dispenses about 700,000 acre-feet of water. However, in years when rainfall is below normal, the amount of water entering the aquifer is reduced, and, consequently, the amount of water that can be discharged at the springs is also reduced.

Concern with availability of Edwards Aquifer water for irrigated agriculture is a result of greatly increased demands for its use of water for other purposes. The primary reason for the increased demand is the burgeoning population of the region, especially the city of San Antonio, which is now one of the 10 largest cities in the United States. The

Edwards Aquifer is the main and in some cases sole source of water for household, commercial, recreational, aesthetic, and industrial purposes for these growing urban areas. During years of drought, the amount of Edwards Aquifer water available for irrigation is questionable, especially since agriculture typically cannot pay as much for water as some of these other users.

In addition to the availability or quantity of water resources in Texas, there is also much concern about the quality of such resources. Agriculture is one of the major contributors to water quality problems as a result of runoff from cattle feedlots, leaching of farm pesticides into both groundwater and surface water supplies, erosion of soil from cropland, and other similar problems. Obviously, contamination of water supplies is of major importance to wildlife resources, and it is important that this issue be monitored in the future.

Farm Conservation Programs

Recent farm bills have resulted in changes in agriculture that have positively affected wildlife resources in the United States. The 1985 Farm Act had several significant conservation provisions. The Swampbuster provision prohibited drainage and cultivation of wetlands; the Sodbuster provision restricted producers from plowing fragile grasslands; while the Conservation Reserve Program (CRP) gave producers an incentive to retire highly erodible cropland and other fragile land from production for a period of 10 years. By 1988, the CRP program included 34.4 million acres. The 1990 Farm Act expanded the conservation provisions of the 1985 Farm Act by providing several new programs. These programs have dramatically improved wildlife habitat in several areas of the country.

New Technologies

Perhaps the greatest potential source for change in agriculture in the 1990's is from development of new technologies and, in particular, generation of new biotechnologies. For decades, technological breakthroughs have been the major impetus for changes in agriculture, and developments in biotechnology have the potential to bring about equally rapid and massive changes. Potential biotechnology products, including pest- and herbicide-resistant plants, bovine somatotropin, and ice-minus bacteria, may have tremendous impacts in both Texas and the rest of the United States on the number or sizes of farms and their productivity, geographic location, and economic status.

Conclusions

The history of agriculture in both Texas and the rest of the country has been a history of massive social change. This nation has transformed from a country where farmers were the most numerous occupational group to a country where they are only a small minority of the population. The nature of life on the farm and farm work has changed dramatically as well. A result of these changes is that the American farmer is the most productive on earth, and a small number of farmers are able to produce enough food and fiber for our needs, in addition to allowing for massive exports. American agriculture allows for the cheapest, safest, and most nutritious diet of any people on earth. Also critical is an improvement of farming practices so that the negative effects it has on wildlife resources are reduced.

Tommy R. Knowles
Texas Water Development Board
P.O. Box 13231
1700 N. Congress Avenue
Austin, Texas 78711-3231

6. Water for Texas: An Overview of Future Needs

Abstract: Water is a precious natural resource and basic economic com-modity. It is distinct from other natural resources and has no substitute. Humans and the environment, on which their existence depends, must have water to survive and prosper. Water interrelates with and affects almost every aspect of human and natural existence and thus becomes an extremely complex subject of planning and management.

How much water does Texas have? Is there enough for the people, the economy, and the environment? Will there be enough for future gen-erations? Where are the supplies? Can they be made available for use at affordable costs? Will they be safe to drink and to use in other ways?

To address these fundamental questions, vast amounts of data must be gathered and evaluated, and sound planning principles and assess-ment techniques must be applied. In turn, alternatives, conclusions, and recommendations must be coordinated with the state legislature; federal, state, and local agencies; and the general public. In 1990, the Texas Water Development Board adopted the 1990 Texas Water Plan titled *Water for Texas, Today and Tomorrow.* Most of the following information was obtained from that document.

In a number of areas of the state today, available yield in existing surface water or groundwater supplies will barely be sufficient to meet water demands during a critical drought period. Intense groundwater use for a variety of purposes around the state has significantly reduced aquifer levels and pumping yields in many areas, impacting ground-water quality and causing, in some locations, other undesirable effects such as land subsidence or severe reduction or cessation of springflow.

New surface water development has also become increasingly con-strained by regulatory and, in some cases, physiographic limitations. Many favorable sites for reservoir projects are already developed, and the remaining sites must be addressed considering factors such as dis-tance from demand centers, potential yields, costs, and higher environ-mental values. Efficient use of available water through water conserva-tion or reuse is essential to extend existing supplies limited by these factors.

Many of the problems affecting surface water and groundwater quality in Texas originate from stormwater runoff and wastewater dis-charges from agricultural and highly populated urban areas. In some areas the quality of water available is affected by naturally occurring contaminants such as chlorides or nitrates. Human activities which re-duce natural streamflows can also impact water quality. The continuing expansion of water quality regulations will require more costly and higher-level treatment of point source wastewater discharges, as well as increased educational efforts, demonstration of best management ap-proaches and control techniques, and expanded technical and financial assistance to address nonpoint source pollution problems.

While stronger water quality standards, with resulting changes in wastewater effluent limitations, should improve the quality of raw wa-ter, new standards established under the federal Safe Drinking Water Act will affect an array of standards for quality and will impact all pub-lic water supply systems with higher costs of service. A large number of small community systems, many dependent on groundwater, will face formidable expense to install new water treatment systems to meet cur-rent and forthcoming drinking water regulations, thus potentially plac-ing increased demands on surface water availability.

In many cases, more nontraditional management practices, includ-ing water conservation, reuse, desalinization, watershed yield augmen-tation, reservoir operations optimization, and other methods, can be employed to more efficiently use and extend available water supplies. These techniques are gaining increased attention and use as competing demands for water have heightened the difficulty and cost of providing new conventional water supply sources.

The potential impact of upstream development on the availability and quality of water necessary for instream environmental needs and freshwater inflows to the bays and estuaries is a major concern to the state. Use of rivers and bays for navigation, commercial dredging, commercial/sport fishing, oil and gas production, maintenance and propagation of aquatic life, and diverse recreational activities is extensive and must be included in comprehensive water planning.

Serious flood conditions, ranging from hurricane/tropical storm flooding of flat coastal areas along the Texas Gulf to high velocity flash flooding in the narrow ravines and gorges of Central and West Texas to the lower velocity but high volume riverine flooding in North-central, Northeast, and East Texas, affect more than a quarter of the state. Flood protection can be costly, involve environmental impacts, provide direct relief to limited beneficiaries in an area, and involve problems with funding, political decision making, and infrastructure management. Nonstructural flood control measures can, in many instances, be viable, cost-effective alternatives or complementary measures to costly structural flood control measures.

Groundwater Resources and Use

More than 81% of Texas is underlain by 9 major and 20 minor aquifers (Figs. 6.1 and 6.2). These aquifers receive an average annual natural recharge of about 5.3 million acre-feet and contain about 3–4 billion acre-feet of usable quality water in storage, of which only a portion is recoverable using conventional water well technology.

More than 70% of the 6.4 million acre-feet of recent annual groundwater pumpage was for irrigated agriculture, with municipal use accounting for about ⅕ of the total pumpage. Due to widespread availability and relatively low cost of supply, groundwater accounts for about 63% of total water used for irrigation and about 45% of water used by municipalities. Groundwater use in 1987 by category was as follows: irrigation, 71.7%; municipal, 21.3%; manufacturing, 30%; livestock, 1.9%; mining, 1.3%; and steam-electric, 0.8%.

In many areas, the quantity of groundwater withdrawn has exceeded the natural recharge of aquifers, resulting in declining groundwater levels, which can cause both supply and quality problems. Declining aquifer levels can also reduce springflows and result in reduced surface water supplies for uses by humans and the environment. In Texas, groundwater is private property that may be conveyed with the sale of the land.

Surface Water Resources and Use

Texas has 15 major river basins and 8 coastal basins (Fig. 6.3). The 23 river and coastal basins have approximately 3,700 streams and

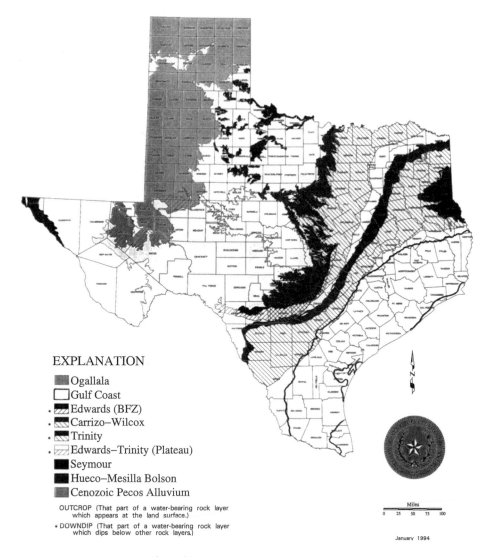

EXPLANATION

![Ogallala] Ogallala
![Gulf Coast] Gulf Coast
. ![Edwards (BFZ)] Edwards (BFZ)
. ![Carrizo–Wilcox] Carrizo–Wilcox
. ![Trinity] Trinity
. ![Edwards–Trinity (Plateau)] Edwards–Trinity (Plateau)
![Seymour] Seymour
![Hueco–Mesilla Bolson] Hueco–Mesilla Bolson
![Cenozoic Pecos Alluvium] Cenozoic Pecos Alluvium

OUTCROP (That part of a water-bearing rock layer
which appears at the land surface.)
. DOWNDIP (That part of a water-bearing rock layer
which dips below other rock layers.)

Miles
0   25   50   75   100

January 1994

Fig. 6.1. *Major aquifers of Texas.*

tributaries and 80,000 linear miles of streambed. Physiographic and climatological features may vary dramatically from the headwaters to outlets into other rivers or at the Gulf of Mexico. For instance, long-term average annual precipitation contributing to rainfall runoff and surface water supplies varies dramatically across the state, ranging from 56 inches near Beaumont in East Texas to 8 inches in far West Texas near El Paso.

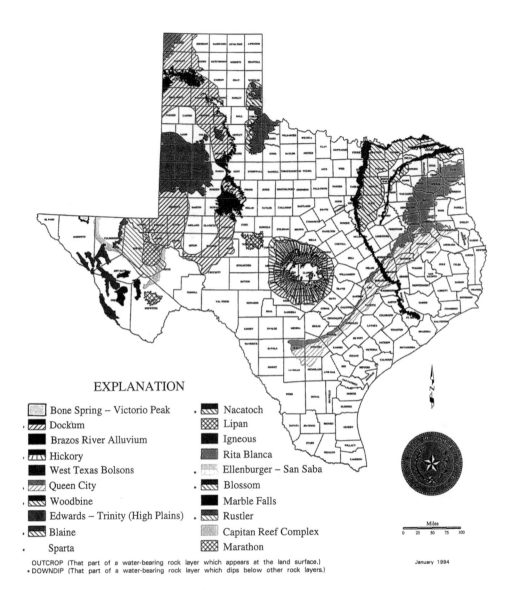

EXPLANATION

- Bone Spring – Victorio Peak
- Dockum
- Brazos River Alluvium
- Hickory
- West Texas Bolsons
- Queen City
- Woodbine
- Edwards – Trinity (High Plains)
- Blaine
- Sparta

- Nacatoch
- Lipan
- Igneous
- Rita Blanca
- Ellenburger – San Saba
- Blossom
- Marble Falls
- Rustler
- Capitan Reef Complex
- Marathon

OUTCROP (That part of a water-bearing rock layer which appears at the land surface.)
• DOWNDIP (That part of a water-bearing rock layer which dips below other rock layers.)

January 1994

Miles
0 25 50 75 100

Fig. 6.2. *Minor aquifers of Texas.*

Average annual runoff (streamflow) is about 49 million acre-feet, ranging from about 1,100 acre-feet per square mile at the Texas-Louisiana border to practically zero in parts of the Trans-Pecos Region of West Texas. Between 1940 and 1970, statewide runoff varied from an average 57 million acre-feet per year during the wettest period

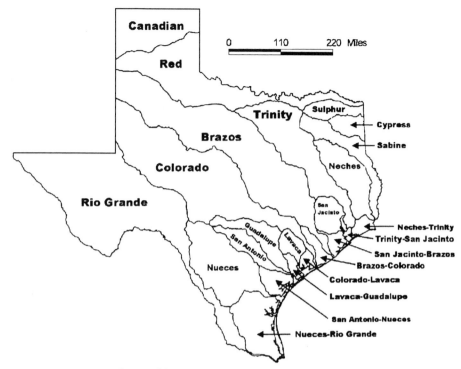

Fig. 6.3. *River and coastal basins of Texas.*

(1940–1950) to as little as 23 million acre-feet per year during the most severe recorded statewide drought of the early and mid-1950's.

There are currently 188 (38 federal and 150 nonfederal) major reservoirs with 5,000 acre-feet or greater storage capacity in Texas (Fig. 6.4). In addition, 1 federal and 2 nonfederal reservoirs are currently under construction. The 191 major reservoirs have a total conservation storage capacity of about 37.1 million acre-feet. Storage capacity for flood protection totals about 17.9 million acre-feet in these reservoirs.

The dependable firm surface water supply (i.e., the uniform yield that can be withdrawn annually from total storage through extended drought periods, dependable run-of-the-river supplies, and dependable supplies in certain reservoirs that are operated in other than a firm yield mode) is about 11 million acre-feet, or 30% of total conservation storage. Of the 11 million acre-feet of dependable supply from the state's major reservoirs and rivers, current withdrawals total about 6 million acre-feet, or about 55% of the firm dependable surface water supply.

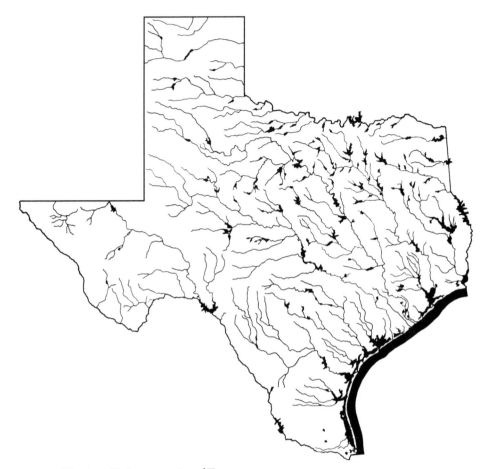

Fig. 6.4. *Major reservoirs of Texas.*

Approximately 83% of the remaining 5 million acre-feet of dependable surface water supply is committed through existing contractual agreements or reserved to meet future projected needs. However, over half of the remaining 17% of uncommitted supply is in the Sam Rayburn Reservoir.

Irrigated agriculture accounts for more than 40% of statewide surface water diversions. The amount and share of use of surface water for irrigation is noticeably less than groundwater use due to surface water's more distant location from agricultural demand centers and generally higher costs of supply. In addition to the diversions for consumptive uses, the nonconsumptive use of surface water plays a critical role in the biological productivity of instream and bay and estuarine environments. Surface water use in 1987 by category was as follows: irrigation, 44.1%; municipal, 27.9%; manufacturing, 19.5%; steam-electric, 4.6%; livestock, 2.6%; and mining, 1.3%.

The quantity of water used for a variety of purposes by various regions and urban/rural areas of the state of Texas is highly dependent on the demographic, economic, climatological, and water availability features. These factors distinguish each city and region from one another and when combined provide a summation and overview of the state's total water use and supply.

Projected statewide water demand and supply forecasts were made by the board for the 50-year planning period, 1990–2040 (Table 6.1). With increasing water demand, additional water supplies will be necessary to meet projected needs. The board projected that water conservation can be achieved in all water-using sectors. For municipal use, it was estimated that per person water use could be reduced 15% by the year 2020.

With the potential conservation savings forecast in the plan and the provision of new surface water projects, limited reallocation of existing surface water storage, additional groundwater pumping in selected localized areas, and wastewater reuse and return flow projects, future state water supplies would be sufficient to meet the projected water needs of the state in the next 50 years. If projected conservation savings are not realized, further supply sources and other water-related facilities beyond those already identified can be developed, but at significant additional costs.

While recent historical trends of the 1980's have indicated either absolute decline or noticeable reductions in the growth rate of major Texas water use sectors, total water use requirements in Texas are projected to increase over the 50-year planning horizon but to a level lower than previous Water Plan forecasts. Because of better information on declining trends in the amount of irrigated acreage and irrigation water use, lowered base population and economic levels and growth rates actually realized in the 1980's, the board's most recent water use projections reflect less growth in future water requirements than those projections made in the 1984 Water Plan.

The board estimated that the population of Texas would increase from some 17.56 million persons in 1990 to over 35.62 million in 2040. That is a doubling within 50 years. Associated with this growth is a projected increase in water demand of from 3.719 million acre-feet

Table 6.1. PROJECTED STATEWIDE WATER DEMAND AND SUPPLY

Item	Year		
	1990	2000	2040
Population (millions)	17.56	20.99	35.62
WATER DEMAND (MILLION ACRE-FEET)			
Municipal	3.7	4.2	6.5
Manufacturing	1.6	2.0	3.4
Steam-electric	0.5	0.6	1.1
Mining	0.2	0.2	0.4
Irrigation	8.5	7.3	6.6
Livestock	0.3	0.3	0.3
Total	14.8	14.6	18.3
PROJECTED SUPPLIES (MILLION ACRE-FEET)			
Surface water	10.7	10.7	10.5
Groundwater	6.7	6.3	5.7
Local surface water	0.7	0.7	0.8
Reuse	0.2	0.2	0.5
Return flows	0.1	0.1	0.1
New surface water	0.1	0.5	1.3
Total	18.5	18.5	19.0

in 1990 to over 6.49 million acre-feet in 2040 with conservation savings. Manufacturing water demand is also expected to double, from 1.62 to 3.44 million acre-feet. Water demand for steam-electric power generation should increase from 0.46 to 1.1 million acre-feet. Irrigation is the one demand category that is not expected to increase. Due to several factors, including increased conservation, water demand for irrigation is projected to decrease from 8.5 to 6.6 million acre-feet by 2040. Total demand for water should increase from 14.8 million acre-feet in 1990 to 18.3 acre-feet in 2040. The major reason this increase is not larger is the 2 million acre-feet decrease for irrigation.

As indicated, future annual water supplies of over 19 million acre-feet would be required by the year 2040 to meet the high case water demands if projected conservation savings are obtained. Of the total statewide supply needed by the year 2040 for the with-conservation case, about 17 million acre-feet, or 90%, would come from existing regional surface water, local surface water, and groundwater supplies with an additional 2 million acre-feet, or 10% of total needed supplies, coming from new surface water reservoirs, reuse, or use of return flows.

New surface water reservoirs would account for about 1.4 million acre-feet, while expanded water reuse and use of return flows would provide about 630,000 acre-feet of the year 2040 total supplies. Groundwater use is projected to decline statewide, although additional groundwater supplies will continue to be developed in localized areas such as portions of East Texas.

Therefore, while the net remaining surface water supplies in the year 2040, as a percentage of total surface water capacity, are approximately 13%, there can be additional future supplies developed from other new surface water supply projects and potentially from groundwater, reuse, and return flow sources as well. Additional conservation savings, beyond those projected by the board, would help extend whatever available supplies exist.

If the board's projected water conservation savings cannot be realized by the year 2040, then, in addition to the total water supplies referenced previously, another 747,000 acre-feet of supplies would be required from 6 additional new surface water reservoirs, groundwater usage would rise by about 740,000 acre-feet, and reuse and the use of return flows could increase by another 93,000 acre-feet in this situation.

Environmental Importance of Water in Texas

Riverine, wetland, bay, and estuarine water resources are important to wildlife in the state. Streamflows and waters passed through reservoirs provide "life needs" to these ecosystems; however, their requirements temporarily and quantitatively are very different. Determining these needs has been the focus of Texas studies for over 2 decades. If an ecologically sound environment is provided through maintenance of habitats in these ecosystems, it will help protect the associated wildlife.

The coastal ecosystems of Texas are inhabited by one of the most diverse waterfowl populations in the world because of the tremendous productivity and complex wetland habitats inherent to our coast.

These species depend on these coastal environments during at least some portion of their lives. In fact, Texas Water Development Board studies in cooperation with the Texas Parks and Wildlife Department have identified 13 different functions of freshwater inflows to our coastal bays and estuaries.

Reservoir operations are also important for maintaining overbanking flows below dams to maintain bottomland forest composition and fish and wildlife in our state's diverse river systems. Ecological considerations are assessed for all water development projects in the 50-year planning horizon that affect the habitats of flow-dependent species, which include several species of fish, water snakes, river turtles, and waterfowl. Many species of wildlife are enhanced by the still waters of lakes, and Texas is now famous for its outstanding bass fishing in these lakes. Deer, raccoons, and many other wildlife also use lakes, and their populations have increased as a result of these developments.

Future water needs will result in impacts of wildlife resources. While recognizing this fact it is also necessary to realize that we can usually reduce impacts through mitigation, avoidance of important water resource habitats, and conservation, planning, and operations that enhance environmental resources. The board is committed to the feasibility assessment of sharing water resources across river basins, which we refer to as the Trans-Texas Water Program. By pursuing this program, it may be possible to avoid many of the inevitable reservoir developments in the drier areas of the state.

Reservoirs inundate terrestrial habitats, often important bottomland hardwoods that are required by many species of wildlife, and segments of flow rivers. These habitats will be lost forever, so we need to avoid reservoirs when possible. The Trans-Texas Water Program proposes to evaluate interbasin transfers and system operating agreements to move water from water-rich areas to water-short areas of the state. A more comprehensive method for managing a region's water resources is possible through a "system" concept, whereby the need for and delivery of water are coordinated across several or all of the water basins involved. Such a system has 4 basic advantages: (1) it increases the overall availability of water, (2) it provides more certainty and flexibility in meeting instream flow needs, (3) it provides more certainty and flexibility in meeting bay and estuary needs, and (4) it reduces the impacts of drought. Water for wildlife can be provided with more certainty through this program, and therefore the enhancement of fish and wildlife productivity is expected in some areas.

The quality and quantity of wastewater discharges are also important to the state's estuarine wildlife. Demonstration projects using highly treated wastewaters have shown increased net primary production in deltas of 2 Texas estuaries. The Rincon Bayou–Nueces Marsh Demonstration Initiative between the board and the U.S. Bureau of Reclamation has shown enhancement benefits to the marshes of the Nueces Delta which complement the Gulf Coast Joint Venture under the North American Waterfowl Management Plan, the Partners in Flight Program under the Neotropical Migratory Bird Conservation Plan, and the National Estuary Protection Act of 1970.

The management of groundwater for maintenance of irrigation and municipal water needs as well as spring flows is an important water resource issue that must be dealt with. Major springs of concern are those associated with the Edwards Aquifer in the Austin–San Antonio region. These spring systems have important functions that make protection consideration necessary. The spring flow supports critical habitats for several threatened and endangered species, provides instream flow for an important fishery in the Colorado and Guadalupe Rivers, supports major recreational uses, supplies water needed for downstream water rights, maintains water quality, and provides vital inflows to coastal environments.

Facility Needs

The board anticipates that if its projected water conservation savings are realized, new water and wastewater facilities in Texas in the next 50 years are expected to cost a minimum of $37 billion dollars. Over $\frac{1}{4}$ of these expenditures have to be incurred in the 1990's. Should the board's projected water conservation savings not be obtained by Texas municipalities, it is estimated that roughly a 10% increase (+$3.4 billion) in water and wastewater facilities costs, above the with-conservation forecasts, would be realized. Under this scenario, the expected costs of meeting minimum water and wastewater infrastructure requirements for Texas in the next 50 years would total over $40.5 million.

Spending for wastewater improvements is projected to place the largest demand upon statewide water-related public water infrastructure financing over the next 50 years. About 53% of identified facilities needs are attributable to wastewater improvements, while 47% are estimated for water improvements.

The board examined a variety of supply and demand management and development alternatives that could address these potential water supply shortages, including both structural and nonstructural measures. In considering structural methods, the board has identified an array of different types of new supply projects that could economically address these deficits.

Overall, the estimated costs for 14 new reservoirs, 5 new chloride control projects, 4 existing project modifications, and 29 cross-country conveyances that provide for water supply account for only about $4.8 billion, or 13% of the cost of total identified water and wastewater infrastructure needs. Other utility infrastructure such as water treatment, storage, pumping, transmission, wastewater treatment, and collection (i.e., typical municipal facilities) is projected to total over $32 billion, or 87% of the state's total $37 billion in identified water and wastewater facility needs.

In addition to these requirements, about $1.9 billion in flood protection needs have also been identified from various studies completed by the U.S. Army Corps of Engineers, board-sponsored, and other federal and local studies. These costs do not represent total statewide needs but are simply costs identified by the studies available to the board.

From the board's analysis of projected water demands, existing supplies and facilities of individual utilities, and an assessment of projected regional-level water demands and supplies, supply deficits of surface and groundwater were projected in various portions of the state of Texas. Overall, 14 new major surface water supply reservoirs are projected to be needed in the 50-year planning horizon if the board's projected water conservation savings are attained. Various other potential reservoir sites that have been previously studied by various federal, state, and local entities are also considered as alternative sources of new surface water supply. One or more of these alternative reservoir sites may be developed to meet identified needs should it ultimately be determined that a recommended or prime alternative supply project is infeasible. Additionally, some of these supply projects will be developed to help meet the water needs of Texas beyond the board's 50-year planning horizon.

In addition to the construction of new surface water supply reservoirs, the board also examined other alternatives for providing future water supply and is recommending several new projects that would increase or improve existing, available surface water supplies. Because of high chloride (salinity) levels in various riverine waters due to passage over certain geologic formations, manmade brine contamination, or seawater intrusion, the board is recommending 5 chloride control projects to improve water quality and/or reduce costs of treatment to potable water standards. A brine injection project is recommended to reduce the salinity of Canadian River water in Texas. In the upper Red and Brazos river basins, small impoundment reservoirs are proposed to retain and evaporate saline waters and lessen the effects on downstream water quality.

Saltwater barrier projects are also proposed for the Lower Neches and Trinity river basins to minimize the impacts of seawater intrusion on higher quality riverine supplies. Further surface water supplies could also be made available by the reallocation and/or modification of total reservoir storage in federal projects to increase the amount of water storage allocated to water supply storage. The board recommends reallocations for the existing Bardwell, Whitney, and Waco reservoir projects. The Corps of Engineers has also been requested to perform a reallocation study for Lake O' the Pines in Northeast Texas. The board in addition recommends a major diversion project that would move water from the Trinity River into the existing Richland-Chambers and Cedar Creek Reservoirs. This would increase the yield of those existing water supply sources and defer additional new major supply projects until later in time. In many cases, major water conveyance pipelines and other facilities would be needed to transport surface water supplies from both new and existing reservoirs to the general locations of the major water demand centers. In some instances, proposed new reservoirs would provide releases upriver of the water demand center(s), and much of the conveyance costs could be avoided.

Concluding Comment

Population and economic growth with additional significant regulatory requirements will exert great pressure on local governments to provide needed water service. Actions are needed now to ensure that Texas has clean, reliable, and affordable water for all Texans, their environment, and their economy.

Melvin B. Hodgkiss, Director
Railroad Commission of Texas
Surface Mining
and Reclamation Division
P.O. Drawer 12967, Capitol Station
Austin, TX 78711

William S. Chovanec, Chief
Technical Services
Railroad Commission of Texas
Surface Mining
and Reclamation Division
P.O. Drawer 12967, Capitol Station
Austin, TX 78711

7. Extraction of Coal and Uranium Resources

Abstract: In 1975, the Railroad Commission of Texas (RCT) began to regulate coal, lignite, and uranium mining. Later in 1980, Texas became the first state in the nation to operate a federally approved state regulation program for coal mining. Each coal mine application is made available to 11 state and federal agencies for their review. Consideration is given to threatened or endangered species, minimization of mine disturbance, reclamation standards, and fish and wildlife protection and enhancement. While coal mining has steadily increased from 2.2 million tons in 1971 to 55.6 million tons in 1990, uranium mining has declined from a high of over 3 million tons in 1980 to only 0.25 million tons in 1991. Between 1983 and 1991, the number of acres surface mined for lignite has remained steady—between 3,010 and 3,777. Upon completion of mining, the land is returned to premine land contours and revegetated. While early reclamation plans featured coastal bermudagrass to a large extent, more recent plans place greater emphasis on the establishment of wildlife corridors and plant species beneficial to wildlife. To assist mine companies, the Texas Parks and Wildlife Department recommends criteria to select reclamation species for erosion control and wildlife use. Continued cooperation between the RCT and the state and federal fish and wildlife agencies will enhance wildlife on mine properties.

Regulation

Prior to 1975, surface mining reclamation was not directly regulated by a governmental agency. The lack of regulation led to the disturbance of many acres of land without reclamation being performed to place the land back into a productive condition.

On June 21, 1975, the Texas legislature passed the Surface Mining Control and Reclamation Act. This act placed a set of environmental standards on coal and uranium mining and provided for the Surface Mining and Reclamation Division of the Railroad Commission of Texas (RCT) as the regulatory agency to enforce this law. The act became effective on January 1, 1976, and was binding on all land mined after June 21, 1975.

The Texas Surface Mining Control and Reclamation Act subsequently led to the creation of regulations to serve as a set of minimum standards to be met in obtaining a permit to mine lignite, coal, or uranium in the state. These regulations required comprehensive environmental evaluations, mine plans, and reclamation plans to be submitted as part of any mining permit application. These regulations also included provisions for commission personnel to monitor and enforce mining and reclamation requirements of approved permits.

In 1977, the 9th Congress of the United States adopted the Federal Surface Mining Control and Reclamation Act of 1977 (SMCRA) (P.L. 95-87) to be enforced by the Office of Surface Mining (OSM) of the Department of the Interior. This law affords states the opportunity to assume "primacy" over federally regulated coal-mining operations. To obtain state primacy over coal mining, the Texas legislature passed the Texas Surface Coal Mining and Reclamation Act in 1979. Subsequently promulgated rules were submitted to OSM for program approval. In 1980, Texas became the first state nationally to obtain state regulatory program approval and obtain primacy in regulating coal mining under SMCRA.

Current regulations for both coal and uranium require applicants to address potential impacts to fish, wildlife, and related environmental resources. Specifically for coal, requirements are (1) the reporting of critical habitat for threatened or endangered species listed by the secretary of the interior, or any plant or animal listed as threatened or endangered by the state, or any bald or golden eagle; (2) specific design and construction of electrical power lines and other transmission facilities used for or incidental to the surface mining activities on the permit area; (3) plans to minimize disturbance to and to provide enhancement for fish and wildlife in the area; (4) specific reclamation standards if fish and wildlife habitat is to be a primary postmining land use; (5) specific reclamation standards where cropland is to be the alternative postmining land use on lands diverted from a fish and wildlife premining land use, where appropriate for wildlife and crop management practices; and (6) the provision of greenbelts where the primary land use is to be residential, public service, or industrial land use.

Upon completion of review of an application to mine coal the regulations require that the commission make specific findings "in consultation with State and Federal fish and wildlife management and Conservation agencies" regarding the adequacy of the fish and wildlife reclamation plans. To accomplish this, notice of each permit application is sent to 11 state and federal agencies for review and comment. These agencies include:

1. Department of Water Resources (now Texas Natural Resource Conservation Commission, TNRCC)
2. Department of Health
3. Air Control Board (now TNRCC)
4. Historical Commission
5. Bureau of Economic Geology
6. Texas State Soil and Water Conservation Board
7. Texas Parks and Wildlife Department
8. U.S. Fish and Wildlife Service
9. General Land Office
10. U.S. Soil Conservation Service
11. Office of Surface Mining (Regional Office)

These agencies are given an opportunity to comment on the application within the areas of their expertise or jurisdiction.

Production and Affected Acreage

Production records have been maintained by the Surface Mining and Reclamation Division since 1976 for coal and 1978 for uranium. Prior to this time, only estimates of production levels could be obtained. Coal production (Table 7.1) has steadily risen from an estimated 2.2 million tons in 1971 to a record production of 55.6 million

Table 7.1. COAL PRODUCTION IN TEXAS

Year	Tons
1971 (estimated)	2,200,000
1972 (estimated)	4,545,000
1973 (estimated)	6,944,000
1974 (estimated)	8,000,000
1975 (estimated)	11,002,000
1976	14,290,980
1977	16,899,441
1978	20,518,435
1979	26,960,570
1980	30,178,220
1981	32,763,935
1982	34,750,787
1983	38,925,397
1984	41,283,698
1985	45,387,479
1986	48,491,612
1987	50,673,093
1988	52,321,750
1989	54,064,834
1990	55,559,753
1991	54,414,003

tons in 1990. At the current time, Texas is ranked as the sixth largest producer of coal/lignite in the United States. As a fuel source, Texas lignite accounts for approximately 27% of the electrical power generated in the state.

Currently, there are approximately 167,575 acres within 23 mining permit areas in Texas. A diagram depicting the general locations of permitted coal, lignite, and uranium mines in Texas is presented in Figure 7.1.

Uranium production (Table 7.2) increased significantly in 1980 but began to decline in 1981. This decline is the result of a decreased

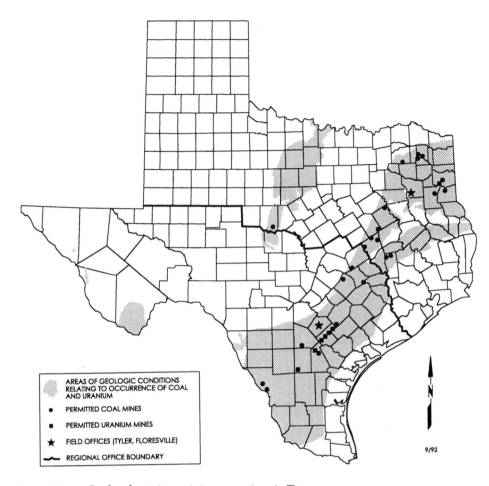

Fig. 7.1. *Coal and uranium mining operations in Texas.*

demand for uranium oxide (U_3O_8) which has caused a significant drop
in the price of this fuel source. The current spot market price is lower
than the cost of producing the oxide. This has led to a subsequent reduction in mining and the associated labor force. Since 1976, approximately 31,100 acres of land were permitted for uranium-mining activities at 31 locations in 6 different South Texas counties. Although
approximately 18,000 acres remain permitted for mining, there are no
active uranium surface mines in Texas at the current time. The majority
of the remaining permitted acres have never been disturbed by mining
activities or are being reclaimed at this time. Therefore, remaining comments will primarily address coal and lignite surface mining activities.

Table 7.2. URANIUM PRODUCTION IN TEXAS

Year	Pounds of oxide
1976 (estimated)	695,000
1977 (estimated)	1,529,000
1978	1,160,067
1979	2,879,310
1980	3,160,199
1981	1,893,154
1982	1,289,184
1983	800,000
1984	600,000
1985	160,000
1986	0
1987	0
1988	261,428
1989	245,363
1990	279,227
1991	254,532

Although not at the same rate, the acreage disturbed by coal mining (Table 7.3) has increased as production has climbed. The amount of land that is disturbed will change as the coal seams which are encountered fluctuate in thickness and as the relative progress of reclamation activities varies. Other factors which contribute to the variance are activities such as the construction of maintenance facilities, haul roads, sedimentation ponds, and storage facilities which are generally not reclaimed as quickly as mined areas.

Upon completion of mining, the land is graded to the approximate original contour and revegetated. The use of temporary or permanent vegetation is dictated by the season in which the regrading activities are completed. Temporary vegetation is replaced by permanent vegetation at the beginning of the next growing season. Table 7.4 is based upon permanent vegetation plantings, which must be established and demonstrated to be successful over a 5- or 10-year extended responsibility period (ERP) prior to final release of bond. The ERP is 5 years in areas

Table 7.3. AMOUNT OF LAND DISTURBED BY COAL MINING IN TEXAS

Year	Acres/year	Cumulative total
1976	1,174	1,174
1977	1,463	2,636
1978	1,870	4,506
1979	2,763	7,269
1980	2,458	9,737
1981	3,349	13,087
1982	2,612	15,699
1983	3,010	18,709
1984	3,671	22,380
1985	3,251	25,631
1986	3,602	29,233
1987	3,673	32,870
1988	3,777	36,647
1989	3,454	40,101
1990	3,410	43,511
1991	3,387	46,898
1992 (estimated)	3,738	50,636

where the average annual rainfall rate is greater than 26 inches and 10 years in more arid regions.

All land disturbed by mining activities must be within the confines of a mining permit boundary. Mining permits are generally issued for terms of 5 years. Permitted acreage, however, often reflects areas that cover a life-of-mine plan (20–40 years).

Wildlife, Mining, and Reclamation

The key to developing and maintaining wildlife communities that are abundant and healthy in the state of Texas is to provide habitats which encourage the return of wildlife species to areas which have been disturbed and reclaimed. In order to accomplish this, revegetation species selection must include types of vegetation that provide both cover and a source of food.

**Table 7.4. AMOUNT OF LAND
DISTURBED BY COAL MINING WHICH
IS PERMANENTLY REVEGETATED**

Year	Acres/year	Cumulative total
1976	1,651	1,651
1977	5,726	2,222
1978	1,950	4,172
1979	2,198	6,370
1980	2,521	8,891
1981	2,050	10,941
1982	2,662	13,603
1983	2,527	16,130
1984	3,696	19,826
1985	3,696	23,522
1986	3,913	27,435
1987	4,581	32,061
1988	5,967	37,983
1989	4,119	42,102
1990	4,794	46,896
1991	4,782	51,678

In the past, the primary species used for reclamation purposes has been coastal bermudagrass. This particular species spreads quickly and is very efficient in binding the soil to prevent erosion, especially on slopes. This species is also especially well suited for mine reclamation areas where the postmine land use will be pastureland for livestock production. It is favored by many landowners. During mining and subsequent reclamation, acceptable runoff and water quality standards must be met. This encourages the use of species which will bind the soil and decrease the amount of suspended solids eroded from the area.

In conjunction with the coastal bermudagrass, leguminous species have been used as a temporary cover and to help reestablish the nitrogen cycle of the soil. The use of legumes has also stimulated a certain amount of migration into these areas by wildlife species.

More recently, greater emphasis has been placed on developing the establishment of wildlife corridors and cover areas. Many of the more

recent reclamation areas are being reclaimed with native and introduced grass and woody plant species that provide an excellent source
of seed and cover. Table 7.5 lists some of the plant species which have
been used in reclamation.

Some mine areas are reclaimed with primarily native species. Observations indicate a significant increase in bird activity in reclaimed areas
of this type. The selection of plant species used in reclaimed areas plays
an important part in the degree of success attained in the reestablishment of a self-sustaining wildlife community. To assist the mining companies in the selection of native plants for erosion control and wildlife
use, the Texas Parks and Wildlife Department provides a mining permit
applicant with a recommended list of about 250 species, criteria for
their selection, and desirable characteristics of plants and plant associations. These species should possess as many of the following characteristics as possible:

1. selected plants should be of the same local climatic and ecological
   region, topography, and soil conditions,
2. selected plants should be noncompetitive, i.e., compatible,
3. the association should cover as much area as possible (overlapping
   canopies),
4. the association should form at least 2 canopy layers above the soil
   surface,
5. selected plants should include a mixture of physical and habit
   forms, e.g., deciduous, evergreen, tree, shrub, vine, forb, grass,
6. the association should provide annual, all-season fruits,
7. the association should provide areas of adequate cover,
8. some components of the association should establish quickly and
   provide rapid growth,
9. selected plants should include at least 1 nitrogen-fixing species, if
   feasible,
10. plantings should be arranged in irregular groups rather than uni-
    form rows so that the association will produce a more natural
    form.

Mining companies have been devoting greater attention to developing areas that are not being mined and areas between mine sites as wildlife corridors. They are also interspersing constructed wildlife enhancement areas within reclamation areas which are connected by developed
wildlife corridors. The field inspectors have reported an increasing
number of forbs in the areas that were first sprigged with coastal ber-

Table 7.5. PERMANENT VEGETATION PRESENTLY BEING PLANTED FOR SURFACE-MINING RECLAMATION IN TEXAS

Perennial grasses	Legumes and forbs	Shrubs and vines	Trees	Aquatics
*Bahiagrass	*Alfalfa	*Arborvitae	Ashes	American lotus
*Bermuda-grasses	Bundle-flowers	Beautyberry	Baldcypress	
Bluestems	*Clovers	Buttonbush	Blackgum	Arrowhead
Bristlegrass	*Cowpea	Coralberry	*Catalpa	Bulrush
Brome	Englemann daisy	Dewberry/ blackberry	Cottonwood	Bur reed
Buffalograss		Elderberry	Dogwood	Cattail
*Buffelgrass	*Lespedezas	*Eleagnus	Elms	Chufa
Carpetgrass	Partridge pea	Grape	Hawthorns	Cordgrass
*Dallisgrass	*Singletary pea	*Honeysuckle	Hickories/ pecan	Duck potato
Deertongue		*Indigo	Hollies	*Elodea
*Fescue	Sunflowers	Peppervine	Junipers	*Japanese millet
Gamagrass	*Sweet-clovers	*Pyracantha	*Kentucky coffee tree	*Pearl millet
Grama		Trumpet-Creeper	*Locust	Pickerelweed
Green spangletop	*Vetches	Viburnum	Maples	Pondweed
Indiangrass	Western indigo	Virginia creeper	Mulberry	*Reed canarygrass
*Kleingrass	*Winterpea	Wax-myrtle	Oaks	Sedges
*Lovegrasses			Osage orange	Sesbania
Panicgrass			Persimmons	Smartweed
*Ryegrass			Pines	Waterlily
Sand dropseed			Plums	Wild celery
Sideoats grama			Redbud	*Wild rice
Switchgrass			River birch	
Wheatgrass				

* Introduced plants (nonnatives, i.e., exotics).

mudagrass and have also observed increasing numbers of quail and dove on reclaimed sites which include wildlife enhancement areas.

Most reclamation areas now have permanent water impoundments and developed wetlands interspersed throughout the area. These impoundments are being stocked with fish and have shown good development. The primary species being stocked are area largemouth bass, channel catfish, and sunfish. Some of these fish have been harvested and tested for high concentrations of potentially toxic elements. No high concentrations have been detected in the fish that were tested from reclaimed mine areas, and they appear to be healthy and increasing their populations. Appropriate wetland and wildlife forage vegetative species are being planted in association with these impoundments to allow them to function both as livestock watering locations and as wildlife enhancement areas.

The commission also continues to coordinate its review of mining permit applications with state and federal fish and wildlife management and conservation agencies in an effort to develop sound reclamation plans that will continue to enhance the development of wildlife communities far into the future.

William F. Hood
Wildlife Biologist
Texas Department of Transportation
125 E. 11th Street
Austin, Texas 78701-2483

8. Transportation and the Environment

Abstract: The increasing emphasis on environmental protection in both public and private sectors has been an impetus for the Texas Department of Transportation (TxDOT) to seek new and diverse ways to design, construct, and maintain needed transportation systems that are environmentally sound. This chapter looks at changes at TxDOT brought about by heightened environmental concerns.

The chapter describes the department's organization, which consists of divisions, districts, and area offices, with the organization and functions of the Environmental Affairs Division receiving a majority of the attention. As the result of the increased level of environmental expertise at the division and district levels and of the increased consideration afforded environmental issues, examples of projects involving individual Section 404 permits and the resulting mitigation have been provided. Examples of both informal and formal Section 7 consultations under the Endangered Species Act have been included. Also addressed are some of the department's efforts in off-site wetland mitigation, habitat protection, protection of rare plant populations located within TxDOT right of way, and threatened and endangered species research.

This chapter was written to update a paper entitled "Texas Highways and the Natural Environment," written in 1982 by R. L. Lewis, P.E., a former state design engineer for the then State Department of Highways and Public Transportation. In the brief span of 15 years between 1982 and 1997, the Texas Department of Transportation (TxDOT) has undergone changes far more dramatic than indicated by the name change. These changes in attitude, policy, and actions, as they relate to environmental issues, will be discussed.

In 1982, the primary mandate of TxDOT was to provide safe, efficient, and effective transportation of people and goods in the state of Texas. This mandate was met, providing the people and travelers of Texas with a high quality transportation system throughout a vast geographic area.

One change that occurred during the last 15 years is in the area of environmental concerns. The preservation of our state's natural resources is receiving a higher degree of attention than at any time in the past. This priority is based on shifting public attitudes toward the environment, a stricter regulatory structure, and a general desire for more environmentally appropriate and sensitive public projects. However, this increase in environmental awareness is juxtaposed with an increasing need for improved transportation facilities for an expanding population which, in turn, provide an impetus for economic development. Inevitably, arenas of the environment and transportation collide, challenging TxDOT to find the balance: safe, efficient, and effective transportation systems that reflect sound environmental strategy.

This challenge is reflected both in the TxDOT mission statement and its vision statement. TxDOT's mission "is to work cooperatively to provide safe, effective, and efficient movement of people and goods." The TxDOT vision statement reads, in part, that TxDOT will provide "environmentally sensitive transportation systems that work together."

TxDOT Organization

TxDOT is organized into 25 geographic areas or districts. Each district has a district office that provides primary transportation project development for the area within its jurisdiction. Each district is further decentralized into 1 or more suboffices or area offices. Area offices typically provide construction and maintenance services, as well as construction oversight.

TxDOT has a number of divisions that deal with the specific elements of transportation development such as design, construction, and maintenance. TxDOT's Division of Environmental Affairs began operations in January 1992 and was responsible for the overall development of departmental environmental policy, encompassing all aspects of TxDOT's environmental activities and training. This division and the Environmental Section of the Division of Highway Design were merged in October 1993, creating the Environmental Affairs Division

(ENV). At the time of the merger, the duties of the Environmental Section were related primarily to the review of environmental documentation for proposed highway projects, including surveys resulting in compliance with appropriate regulations and laws.

In addition to these duties, the current ENV also supplies technical support to district and division staffs as requested. ENV is currently allotted 65 full-time positions representing a broad and diverse interdisciplinary level of education and skills, with many years of experience in environmental sciences and related issues, including cultural resources management.

The division is divided into various areas of expertise and function. The administrative portion of the division is primarily responsible for personnel issues and project management. The policy, planning, and technical services sections of the division include the (1) Pollution Prevention and Abatement Section, which addresses air quality, noise abatement, and solid waste/hazardous materials issues; (2) Natural Resources Management Section, with responsibilities including animal and plant ecology (including threatened or endangered species), water resources (including wetland issues), and all permits associated with these issues; and (3) Cultural Resources Management Section, which deals with archaeology, historic buildings and structures, and the socioeconomic aspects of projects.

The personnel of these sections conduct field surveys, review environmental documents, and coordinate environmental issues with state and federal resource and regulatory agencies. In addition, the staff works closely with district personnel to identify potential adverse environmental impacts that might be avoided or minimized and to develop mitigation plans where adverse environmental impacts are unavoidable. These mitigation plans are developed in response to impacts to resources such as wetlands, threatened or endangered species, wildlife habitats, and cultural resources.

The Environment in Project Development

During the preliminary planning phase of a transportation project, an assessment is made to identify potential environmental impacts. This assessment can result in a relatively short environmental assessment for simple projects to more complex and lengthy environmental impact statements for larger projects. Currently, TxDOT is moving from an era of highway construction to one more concerned with the operation and maintenance of the existing transportation system.

However, there is still the need to provide additional capacity in urban areas and new highway facilities in suburban areas and some rural areas. All projects, ranging from simple to complex, are planned, designed, constructed, and maintained in compliance with environmental laws and regulations. Monitoring and enforcement of these laws and regulations have been strengthened in the past 15 years to reflect growing concerns about diminishing natural and cultural resources and changing public attitudes toward environmental preservation and the state's heritage.

In response to changes in public attitudes about environmental issues and the Sunset Commission's review of TxDOT, it was determined that TxDOT should execute memoranda of understanding (MOU) with a number of resource and regulatory agencies, such as the Texas Historical Commission (THC), Texas Parks and Wildlife Department (TPWD), and Texas Natural Resource Conservation Commission (TNRCC). These MOU detail coordination procedures with these agencies and contain criteria that help determine whether the environmental documentation for a given project is to be coordinated with the respective agency. The MOU have allowed agencies such as TPWD to provide comments based on their knowledge and expertise that may not be readily available to ENV staff. In addition, review of environmental documents by outside agencies has given TxDOT the opportunity to upgrade and improve the quality of environmental documentation.

As TxDOT works closer with outside agencies and with the heightened concerns on various issues, individual laws are being observed with a higher level of consideration and response than in the past. For example, concerns about ever-decreasing wetland acreage in Texas have resulted in the stepped-up monitoring and enforcement of rules and regulations associated with Section 404 of the Clean Water Act by the U.S. Army Corps of Engineers (USACE). In response to this need, the staff of the Natural Resources Management Section of ENV and some district personnel have received professional training in the delineation of wetlands, as well as resource negotiation and conflict management. This has enabled TxDOT to draft effective Section 404 permits that include sound, acceptable mitigation plans.

Examples of projects that have required individual Section 404 permits include (1) construction of the U.S. 181 causeway across Corpus Christi Bay from Corpus Christi to Portland; (2) upgrading of State Highway (SH) 100, which serves South Padre Island in Cameron County; and (3) construction of a bridge at the Trinity River on

Farm-to-Market (FM) 3278 in Polk and San Jacinto Counties. The mitigation plans associated with these permits included the construction of dredge containment areas and expansion of an existing bird rookery (U.S. 181), the construction of shallow, tidally influenced wetlands (SH 100), and the creation of a shallow-water, bottomland hardwood wetland (FM 3278).

Initially, TxDOT dealt with wetland creation on a project-by-project basis, usually located within the highway facility right of way. This resulted in small, scattered wetlands with less than desirable wetland functions. The passage of state legislation in 1991 allowed TxDOT to acquire mitigation properties that were not adjacent to highway rights of way, i.e., off-site. This allows the acquisition or creation of larger and more functional wetland tracts. This effort is supported by both TPWD and the U.S. Fish and Wildlife Service (USFWS).

As these possibilities were explored, TxDOT moved into the establishment of off-site wetland mitigation areas. The first experimental effort was conducted in concert with TPWD when TxDOT aided that agency in the purchase of approximately 100 acres of cypress-tupelo swamp associated with Caddo Lake and Caddo Lake State Park. This acquisition eventually allowed TxDOT, through the Section 404 process, to gain environmental clearance for 4 projects located in the department's Atlanta District.

In the fall of 1994, TxDOT completed the required coordination procedures, resulting in a memorandum of agreement (MOA) with the Fort Worth District of USACE, the U.S. Environmental Protection Agency (EPA), TPWD, USFWS, and TNRCC for the acquisition and establishment of an off-site, 2,200-acre wetland mitigation area on the Sabine River in Smith County, north of Tyler, Texas. This mitigation area, known as the Anderson Tract, is owned and managed by TPWD.

In the fall of 1995, another MOA was executed with the same state and federal agencies for the acquisition and establishment of a second major off-site wetland mitigation area. This 3,300-acre project is known as the Blue Elbow Swamp and is in deep Southeast Texas between the Sabine River and Orange, Texas, along Interstate Highway (IH) 10. As with the Anderson tract, the Blue Elbow Swamp is owned and managed by TPWD.

Another environmental issue which now receives more attention than in the past involves wildlife habitat and threatened or endangered species. Prior to the mid-1980's, TxDOT was involved in only 1 formal Section 7 consultation and very few informal consultations. ENV's biological resources staff has expanded to include 4 biologists. A number of district offices also now have biologists or environmentally educated members on staff to handle the increased number of projects coordinated with both TPWD and USFWS. Early in the planning process, district staffs are encouraged to coordinate projects with the Texas Biological and Conservation Data System of TPWD. This allows ENV staff to analyze potential project impacts better while project alternatives are still available, which in turn allows TxDOT to design projects that can avoid and minimize impacts to protected species and their habitats.

The following represents examples of recent formal Section 7 consultations initiated by TxDOT. The earliest formal consultation, initiated in the early 1980's, involved impacts to the Navasota ladies' tresses, a rare orchid, associated with upgrading SH 6 in the Bryan/College Station area in Brazos County. This consultation resulted in surveys for individual members of the species in the project area, as well as in other likely areas in both Brazos and Grimes Counties. In addition, an 8-acre refugium was established adjacent to SH 6 to protect the species and for USFWS, TPWD, and TxDOT to conduct research.

In the past 4 or 5 years, TxDOT has participated in a number of formal and informal consultations. In Travis County, Section 7 consultations have been completed on a number of highway improvement projects, including upgrading Ranch-to-Market (RM) 2222; improvements to RM 620, including a new bridge structure at the Colorado River; and SH 45, the Austin Outer Loop. These consultations involved either the black-capped vireo or the golden-cheeked warbler or both, as well as 5 cave invertebrates. As a result of the consultations on the migratory bird impacts, TxDOT was required to time construction of projects to coincide with the absence of the species. The consultations resulted in the ongoing survey of 2,000–4,000 acres of land within Travis County for the presence and reproductive success of the birds over a period of 3–4 years. The amount of land surveyed has varied depending on acquisition of right of entry from private property owners. In addition, TxDOT completed research involving the study of factors contributing to nest predation within the habitat of golden-cheeked warblers; the use of insects as a food source by golden-cheeked warblers in their nesting habitat; and the effect of traffic noise on territory selection by golden-cheeked warblers.

A Section 7 consultation was required to complete a safety project on SH 21 in Bastrop County involving the Houston toad. Research conducted under contract with TPWD indicated that the toads were attempting to cross the highway facility during the breeding season, resulting in a relatively high percentage of toad fatalities. The consultation process resulted in mitigation to construct devices within the right of way designed to funnel the toads to existing highway culverts.

Unfortunately, not all consultations have occurred prior to initiation of project construction. TxDOT is in the process of completing consultation requirements associated with impacts on black-capped vireos during the upgrade of U.S. 277 in Val Verde County. Due to a lack of communication within TxDOT and between TxDOT and TPWD, the project went to construction without knowledge about potential impacts to the black-capped vireo and the Tobusch fishhook cactus. Construction was stopped while the consultation process was completed. As a result of the consultation, TxDOT agreed to conduct annual vireo surveys within the right of way for a period of 5 years, ending in the summer of 1997. In addition, individual Tobusch fishhook cactus plants would be removed from the right of way and be propagated at a botanical garden. As the result of the project displacing suitable vireo habitat, TxDOT would attempt to protect approximately 400 additional acres exhibiting suitable habitat for the vireo.

The construction of a bridge over the Trinity River in Polk and San Jacinto Counties in East Texas on FM 3278 resulted in a Section 7 consultation due to the presence of a bald eagle nest approximately 1,100 feet from the proposed right of way. As the result of the consultation process, a mitigation plan was developed that included timed construction, limiting access on the right of way near the nest, and tree plantings to form a sight barrier. Even though a weather system blew the nest tree down, additional consultations with USFWS resulted in keeping the proposed mitigation plan in place in case the eagles attempted to rebuild a nest in the area sometime in the future.

TxDOT has consulted with USFWS informally on several projects. The construction of a county road bridge over the Colorado River in Runnels County was completed with informal consultation due to the potential presence of the Concho water snake. The construction plans were amended to include curbs on the bridge and retention structures at the end of the bridge to prevent runoff from directly entering the river.

TxDOT is currently working informally with USFWS to address several problems relating to protected species in the Rio Grande Valley. TxDOT has constructed several "cat walks" in an attempt to provide protected highway undercrossings for the ocelot. In addition, TxDOT is initiating contract research to determine the use of these cat walks by ocelots and for the presence of ocelots south of George West, Texas, along U.S. 281 in Live Oak and Jim Wells Counties. TxDOT is also working with USFWS to reduce fatalities to the brown pelican on the Queen Isabella Causeway during winter weather systems. A number of ideas have been developed, including electronic message boards, improved lighting, warning signs, and reduced speed limits. The work with ocelots and pelicans is ongoing.

Another issue receiving a greater degree of attention relates to displacement of wildlife habitat not regulated by either the Endangered Species Act or the Clean Water Act, Section 404. Working with TPWD, TxDOT is attempting to identify and quantify forested areas disturbed by project construction. These areas can be riparian or upland in nature. TxDOT and TPWD coordinate on potential mitigation for these habitats based on the quality and quantity of the areas impacted.

Another ongoing initiative involves maintenance of new and existing highway facilities were rare and protected plants are found within TxDOT's rights of way. TxDOT and TPWD are developing individual management plans to protect rare or protected plant species where they occur within the right of way. Each of these plans is being developed on a species-by-species and site-specific basis. Components of the plans may include timing of required mowing, regulating mowing heights, and the use or exclusion of herbicides. TxDOT is also proposing creation of a signing system to protect rare plant populations from possible disturbances resulting from maintenance and other activities. The signs will be designed to decrease risks to the species posed by poaching.

In addition, TxDOT districts are establishing some areas that will not be mowed routinely. This will allow vegetation that is conducive habitat for ground-nesting birds and small mammals to grow within the right of way. In some areas of intense agricultural or cultivation practices, this could represent the only suitable nesting habitat for such birds and mammals in the immediate area.

Summary

As discussed in this paper, TxDOT has begun a number of initiatives within the past 10–15 years which, when fully implemented, will go a long way toward allowing the department to meet its mission as it pertains to transportation systems and natural resource protection. In order to fully implement all these initiatives, TxDOT must continue to train personnel, particularly at the district level. The proper training in environmental issues and ethics will result in a level of knowledge that will allow environmental issues to be addressed properly early during the planning process. Early initiation of environmental procedures and coordination with resource and regulatory agencies will result in an environmentally friendly transportation system in which the citizens of Texas can take pride.

III. THE PUBLIC
AND FUTURE DEMANDS
FOR WILDLIFE

John Herron
Texas Parks and Wildlife Department
4200 Smith School Rd.
Austin, TX 78744

9. Wildlife Diversity Issues

Abstract: The importance of wildlife diversity is growing within wild-life agencies. While public demand for outdoor recreation is increasing, public awareness of the outdoors and outdoor issues appears to be on the decline. State wildlife agencies are finding that they need new ways to protect a larger array of wildlife resources, as well as including new groups of outdoor constituents in the decision-making process. Solu-tions should be developed using approaches which address people and politics as well as wildlife. By addressing wildlife diversity issues, biolo-gists and the agencies they work for will be better able to fulfill their mandate of conserving *all* wildlife, as well as meeting the needs of a diversifying public.

Background

"Wildlife diversity" is the current, politically correct term for what we once called nongame wildlife and includes urban wildlife issues as well. The importance of wildlife diversity to both constituents and state wildlife agencies is growing. Public demand for a wider variety of out-door recreational pursuits is increasing. Recent studies indicate that 32% of Texans actively pursue wildlife watching as a hobby, and this is expected to increase 16% by the year 2000 (Texas Parks and Wildlife 1995). However, even though more Texans are seeking outdoor activi-ties, public awareness of the outdoors and outdoor issues appears to be on the decline. State wildlife agencies are finding that they must change and work toward finding ways to protect a larger set of wildlife re-sources, as well as include new groups of outdoor constituents in the decision-making process.

Part of this change relates to the urbanization of American society. In terms of land use, Texas is still a rural state, with over 80% of the state in cropland, rangeland, or forest. But in terms of human populations, Texas is one of the most urbanized states in the country, containing 3 of the 10 largest cities in the United States and an urban population that comprises 80% of the total state population. The conversion of native habitat to human habitat continues at a rapid pace, matching a state population that has nearly doubled, from 9.5 million in 1960 to 18.5 million today. Agriculture has changed as well, with more acres farmed more intensively. Farm fields are much "cleaner" now than they were 50 years ago; cotton fields which were once covered with scattered weeds are now monotypic stands of pure cotton, weed-free thanks to the development of herbicides.

The effects of humans on the landscape, as well as corresponding changes in attitudes toward wildlife and the land, are forcing wildlife agencies to deal with a broader array of wildlife species. Part of this change is summarized well by Adams (1994:xi), who noted:

> Historical interest in wildlife conservation and management in North America has focused on game species in rural and wilderness environments. Indeed, the foundation of the wildlife management profession is so rooted. The first wildlife textbook, written by pioneer conservationist Aldo Leopold in 1933, was titled *Game Management*. The logic of this emphasis rests on the fact that game species were of primary importance to people as a source of food during early settlement of the continent and that the human population was small and scattered across the countryside. With advances in agriculture, most North Americans today are no longer dependent on wildlife game for food, and most of us now live in the city rather than the country.

This trend has been noted by other wildlife professionals as well. Dasmann noted in 1966 that the wildlife profession "was too closely identified with game animals and hunters and was too narrow-minded" (Adams 1994:xii). Dasmann recommended that wildlife biologists

> get out of the woods and into the cities. They must work with city and metropolitan regional planners, with landscape architects and all others concerned with the urban environment to make the cities and metropolitan regions, the places where people live, into environments where each person's daily life will be enriched to the maximum extent possible by contact with living things and natural beauty.

But even today, many wildlife biologists would be shocked to be told this is their job. Dasmann's proposal has little to do with managing wildlife populations; in fact, its purpose is not directed at wildlife but at changing human attitudes. This isn't exactly what most of us were trained for in college. But the fact remains, changing times require wildlife professionals and agencies to reconsider how they can best accomplish their mission of conserving wildlife populations for future generations.

Although much of this emphasis on nongame, urban wildlife and wildlife diversity is new, early conservationists were also interested in more than just game management. Aldo Leopold (1949:xvii), considered by many to be the founder of game management, said,

> There are some who can live without wild things, and some who cannot. . . . Like winds and sunsets, wild things were taken for granted until progress began to do away with them. Now we face the question whether a still higher "standard of living" is worth its cost in things natural, wild, and free. For us of the minority, the opportunity to see geese is more important than television, and chance to find a pasque-flower is a right as inalienable as free speech.

One of the first conservation acts in this country was the establishment of Yellowstone National Park in 1872, an action designed to preserve the diversity of a unique area, along with its wildlife, for the enjoyment of future generations. The first wildlife refuges were established in 1903 and 1904, designed to offer haven to waterfowl and other animals as well. The Migratory Bird Treaty Act was passed in 1916, offering protection to migratory birds, some of which were considered game, others that were valued for their feathers, and many that had no specific value (Swanson 1979).

In the 1930's, hunters successfully promoted license and tax systems to support wildlife management. At the time, their interests went well beyond a desire for more animals "for the pot" or as trophies to hang on the wall. They were reacting to the Dust Bowl days and conditions which were critically affecting all wildlife in the country. Many species of wildlife were on the brink of extinction, including ducks, turkey, and deer. Most of the leading conservationists of the day were hunters (e.g., Aldo Leopold, John Muir, Ding Darling), but their interests went well beyond hunting.

The efforts of these hunters worked. We now have deer, turkeys, and wood ducks in astonishing numbers, and along with those animals we've saved thousands of acres of habitat. In the process, hunters unintentionally "bought" influence with state wildlife agencies. Anglers followed suit nearly 20 years later with their own tax on fishing.

With these new funding sources, fish and wildlife agencies began to focus more and more on game management. In the process, wildlife managers created the adage that "what's good for game animals will benefit all wildlife." And it was true . . . mostly. Thousands of acres of wildlife areas were set aside, preserving wetlands, grasslands, and forests that benefit many wildlife species, both hunted and nonhunted.

During the next 50 years, people realized that even this monumental effort wasn't enough. Not all wildlife species benefited. As Rachel Carson noted in her landmark book *Silent Spring* (1963), many developed countries were on the verge of losing a number of common species due to a headlong rush to improve conditions for humans. We came close to sacrificing the integrity and health of entire ecosystems, as well as endangering robins and other songbirds with the indiscriminate use of pesticides. Fortunately, Carson's warning was heard, and we stepped back from the brink of ecological disaster.

But wildlife still wasn't "saved." During the 1960's, biologists discovered the peregrine falcons, bald eagles, and brown pelicans were in trouble due to pesticide residues. The Endangered Species Act and National Environmental Policy Act were passed in the early 1970's to fill additional gaps. Both measures did much good, yet we still see nongame species at risk due to the current emphasis on rare and unique species and a corresponding disdain for anything "common." As noted in a recent publicity campaign for wildlife diversity, "about the only way to save a species is to drive it to extinction" (IAFWA 1994: Sec. 1:3). This narrative continues: "if animals aren't hunted or fished or endangered, they simply don't get attention. For example, endangered and game animals—only about 250 species—get more than 95% of our wildlife money, while over 1,800 other vertebrate species share the remaining 5%." In order to conserve nongame wildlife, wildlife agencies will have to eventually address this problem of funding and its corresponding "attention deficit" for nongame species.

Today's Issues

The issues facing nongame fish and wildlife management today are not much different from the issues facing wildlife management in general (Wilkins and Peterson 1979). These issues fall into 4 basic categories.

- The **lack of data** and information on the distribution and status of most nongame and urban species.
- **Resource issues** concerning managing nongame and urban wildlife and their habitats.

- **People issues** concerning the public's lack of awareness of wildlife (and nongame species in particular) as well as human impacts due to recreational demand.
- **Political issues** concerning laws, protection, and funding for nongame and urban wildlife.

Data Needs

Proper management of any resource requires information concerning current status of that resource. Whether one deals with budgets, machine parts, or wildlife, effective management requires an inventory of resources on hand. Unfortunately, there still isn't any effective way to monitor the status of the approximately 900 species of vertebrate wildlife that are not game or threatened and endangered (Table 9.1). Do we know whether robins are less common now than in the 1960's? What about snakes and butterflies?

We have very limited data concerning the abundance and distribution of most nongame species. State wildlife agencies do have access to limited data collected by volunteers, such as Christmas Bird Counts and Breeding Bird Surveys done by birders. Similarly, most states have data concerning the historic range of many species but with little quantification of numbers, density, or trends.

A good example in Texas is the horned lizard. "Horny toads" were so common in the 1960's that nearly every child in the Southwest seemed to have one as a pet. Now they are a state-listed endangered species. Why? The reasons are still unclear in spite of the visibility of this example. Without some sort of statewide monitoring, it is difficult to assess the factors that are affecting different species.

Table 9.1. TEXAS WILDLIFE DIVERSITY— VERTEBRATE WILDLIFE SPECIES BY CATEGORY

Nongame species	966	81%
Game species	98	8%
Threatened or endangered species	107	9%
Species formerly present, now extinct	21	2%
Total	1192	100%
Species unique to Texas	126	11%

Source: Graham 1992.

Unfortunately, the size of the undertaking (improving our knowledge of the distribution, abundance, and management needs of nongame species) can require tremendous resources. If Texas is spending $10 million a year to monitor and manage game species, how much more will be needed to manage all wildlife? Realistically, we can't expect a 400% increase in staffing and funds. Instead, we must "work smarter" by focusing on species groups and ecosystems or defining conservation priorities.

Priority systems can help managers decide where to commit limited resources, but these "ranking systems" can also result in overlooking the status and needs of most common species. For example, in Midwest Breeding Bird Surveys, biologists have noted drastic declines in the numbers of meadowlark and mourning doves during the past 20 years. Yet these species are still the most common species encountered. Does this indicate a need for special attention or an issue that is less critical than focusing on rarer species? While it is important to know what affects rare or endangered species, a "triage" approach does little to monitor and understand what works well. Instead of focusing on emergencies and "patients in critical need," wildlife agencies should follow the example set by health care organizations and focus on "health maintenance" (i.e., maintaining healthy ecosystems). Without an understanding of functional ecosystems, as well as problems, it's easy to let common species slip from our grasp.

Resource Management

Habitat loss and change is the single most important issue facing nongame and urban wildlife in Texas. A few wildlife species actually benefit from habitat changes, e.g., cowbirds, cormorants, opossums, starlings, and house sparrows. Other species are facing riskier times; Texas has lost over 95% of its native prairies, wetlands, and bottomland hardwoods. Coastal wetlands have been drastically altered with the Intercoastal Waterway changing the balance of freshwater and saltwater flows in coastal marshes. Wildlife that depend on these unique habitats are in decline. Without proper planning and management, we risk losing part of the natural heritage that is uniquely Texas, the animals and habitats that our great-grandparents enjoyed.

Who manages for nongame animals like robins and milk snakes? Who was "on watch" while horned lizard numbers plummeted? Relatively little is being done in Texas that directly targets nongame or urban wildlife. Many nongame species undoubtedly benefit from game management, but few biologists have quantified or tested the effectiveness of game management techniques on nongame wildlife. A great deal has been learned over the past 30 years concerning managing forests for birds (Hagan and Johnston 1992) but not for other nongame species. There is also a good body of work concerning wetland management and the associated effects on wildlife. Many biologists have studied prairie and rangeland management but with much less effort directed at managing for grassland species of nongame wildlife. In terms of urban habitat management, professionals have produced a great number of papers concerning the effects of corridors, core preserves, and habitat fragmentation, but much of this work is theoretical and remains unproven in terms of effective management techniques.

Similarly, most biologists recognize that we need to move away from single-species management toward the identification and management of key habitats and ecosystems. But again, we have very little information available on the habitats that nongame and urban species depend upon or where these habitats are increasing or decreasing. We need to increase our knowledge of the factors that affect abundance and health of these nongame populations.

Many biologists suggest we move to an "ecosystem management" approach, measuring "diversity." However, there is little definition of how to measure success. What is diverse enough? On what scale? Managing for edge effect maximizes species diversity on a local scale but can hurt species that require large blocks of contiguous habitat by fragmenting the habitats they depend upon. As biologists, we are just beginning to develop the knowledge base needed to make management recommendations for most nongame and urban species.

People

Many of our management concerns relate more to people than to wildlife. Human population growth, urban development, and agricultural changes are factors that greatly affect wildlife populations and habitat. If we are going to anticipate these trends, we need to understand "people trends" such as demographics, economics, and attitudes. Unfortunately, as biologists we often take these "people factors" for granted or hope someone else will deal with them.

The good news is that many people are interested in nongame animals (Tables 9.2, 9.3). Everyone knows a nongame animal, even though they may not understand the term "nongame" or "wildlife diversity" (Duda 1994). Recent surveys show that over 30% of adult Tex-

Table 9.2. WILDLIFE-RELATED RECREATION IN TEXAS—
NUMBERS OF PARTICIPANTS AND EXPENDITURES

Hunters	1.1 million	8%	$1.1 billion
Anglers	2.8 million	21%	$1.6 billion
Wildlife watchers	4.0 million	32%	$0.9 billion

Source: U.S. Fish & Wildl. Serv. 1993.

ans actively involve themselves with wildlife. In 1991, 16% of all adult Americans reported taking a trip away from home *for the primary purpose* of observing wildlife (Duda 1994; USFWS 1993). Nationwide, nature photographers almost equal the number of hunters and exceed the number of golfers.

The bad news is that we're losing a number of people who used to participate in nature-related activities. There are more alternate forms of recreation available today than there were 30 years ago. The number of hunters in Texas is down 12% from 1983. Hunting, fishing, and wildlife watching must now compete with tennis, golf, boating, skiing, and video games. People are turning to other forms of outdoor recreation such as backpacking, canoeing, kayaking, rock climbing, and mountain biking. Many of these new outdoor users see little direct connection between their activities and wildlife, even though their experience would be much poorer without wildlife and the wild areas these recreationists prefer. In addition, people have less free time and are more selective about what they do with their time. It appears that people prefer "quick" activities that take only a few hours, compared to a whole day or several days.

With less participation in activities that are directly wildlife-related, fewer members of the public understand wildlife or environmental issues. Many members of the public dislike some nongame species, and others are only interested in "charismatic megafauna" like wolves, cougars, dolphins, and whales. With increased urbanization and human population growth, public concern over "nuisance" wildlife has increased to the point that providing advice concerning nuisance wildlife is now a major part of any wildlife biologist's job. The end result is that we have the opportunity to connect with a large segment of the public that likes wildlife but a challenge in maintaining this interest and in informing the public of the needs of wildlife.

Table 9.3. WILDLIFE-RELATED RECREATION IN TEXAS

26%	feed wildlife	4%	photograph wildlife
22%	watch wildlife	3%	plant for wildlife
5%	visit park areas		

Source: U.S. Fish & Wildl. Serv. 1993.

A growing facet of wildlife diversity management concerns urban wildlife management. Urban areas generally contain wildlife species which cohabit well with humans. These areas typically have low species diversities and a wide variety of degraded habitats. In addition to habitat destruction, most wildlife mortality is human-related, whether by predation from cats and dogs, automobile/wildlife collisions, mowing, or chemical spills and pollutants. Aquatic wildlife face the additional threat of siltation, water lever fluctuations, and poor water quality.

In addition to working with wildlife resources, urban biologists have an important role in assisting and educating the public. Urban residents generally know less about wildlife than do residents of rural and suburban areas. Due to the nature of the habitat and attitudes of its human residents, urban biologists, even more than their rural counterparts, must be well versed in "human dimensions" as well as ecology (VanDruff et al. 1994). These biologists find themselves involved in land-use planning and environmental issues. Since nearly all urban land is privately owned by a huge number of different landowners, urban biologists seldom have much management control over habitat. Instead, they must focus their efforts on influencing people through education, information, and technical assistance efforts.

Since nongame and urban wildlife appeal to a variety of Texans, outreach programs must also appeal to a diverse clientele. While it is important to reach children, minority, and urban populations, it is also important to realize that many people develop interests in nongame and urban wildlife as adults or even as senior citizens. Wildlife watching appeals to both sexes, to families, to individuals, and to rural constituents. The potential target audience is more than just individuals, communities, and businesses; units of local government are often interested in nongame and urban wildlife as well. Working with this diverse set of constituents means that urban biologists must be able to use a diverse set of approaches and tools.

Politics

Unfortunately for many of us who thought we'd be able to spend our careers in a remote cabin like "Grizzly Adams," today's wildlife biologists must learn how to work within political and social realms if they hope to succeed in conserving wildlife.

One of the most pressing political issues facing wildlife management today is the controversy concerning endangered species. It affects everything most wildlife biologists do, from fielding public questions to gaining access to private land in order to survey game animals.

Much of the opposition to endangered species protection has solidified in the "wise use" movement. The wise use movement has rallied around the issue of "private property rights" as well as a general philosophy opposing "big government." The approach has been quite effective in getting the attention of the public as well as government officials. There are some valid points brought up by wise-use proponents, that some agencies rely too heavily on regulation and too little on other approaches to conserve habitats. So far, wildlife agencies and conservation groups have been ineffective in dealing with this vocal minority, in spite of the philosophical inconsistencies many wise-use groups express.

To "environmentalists" (now a politically value-laden term in itself), the wise-use movement appears to define "wise" use as "unrestrained," free from oversight, restriction, or accountability. On the surface, the "private property rights" philosophy implies that property owners have a right to do whatever they wish with their property, whereas environmentalists quickly point out that there have always been constraints placed on landowners, at least in 200 years of U.S. history (Pope 1995). Wise-use groups promote private property rights but seldom address public property rights, the role government has to conserve certain resources (air, water, wildlife, soil) for the common good. In spite of the rhetoric, few property owners seem willing to allow their neighbors to do whatever they want with their property. What is clear is that at this point in time, property rights issues are so highly polarized that it is difficult for wildlife agencies to assess public needs and desires in this area.

An issue at the other end of the spectrum that concerns many wildlife biologists, hunters, and anglers are the "antihunting" and "animal rights" movements. On the surface, antihunting wouldn't seem to be an issue affecting nongame or urban wildlife management. Unfortunately, though, the public's distrust and concern over antihunting issues often create suspicion that nongame and urban programs are designed to cater to these "opponents," since some antihunters are bird watchers, nature photographers, or wildlife enthusiasts. Arguments are sometimes made that strengthening nongame programs represents "giving in" to these members of the public. Similarly, many members of the public view proposals for "biodiversity," "ecosystem management," and wilderness preservation with suspicion, since some antihunting organizations promote these diversity issues as ways of opposing hunting and game management. Wildlife biologists need to be aware of these concerns and point out that antihunting groups represent a minority of nongame enthusiasts as well as demonstrate the real need for managing all wildlife species, not just a few.

The common theme among these political issues is that state wildlife agencies need better processes for dealing with differing public opinions. Agencies must be serious about the fact that they are, after all, public employees using public dollars to manage public resources. By using effective public involvement processes, wildlife agencies can determine who has how much say in the fate of wolves in Alaska, warblers in Central Texas, or water in a stream.

Finally, a major political issue facing wildlife diversity management is funding. Nongame and urban wildlife programs affect more species and more members of the public than any other wildlife program but can only address a very limited number of issues at current funding levels. Solving wildlife diversity issues will require additional effort, and these efforts require funding. Where disagreement occurs is how to provide funding, mostly concerning who should pay.

Since wildlife belongs to the public, most funding discussions relate to finding ways to get the public at large to pay for the management and protection of "their" wildlife, just as they fund programs directed at clean air and clean water. Another common approach is to advocate "user pay" approaches, but it's difficult to identify who is using nongame wildlife and whether many of these activities are actually "use" in the sense of using up any nongame resources. (This is one reason for avoiding use of the term "nonconsumptive use," since we all are wildlife "consumers" by our constant impact and consumption of wildlife habitat. Each time a house is built or a highway constructed, each of us contributes to a reduction in wildlife habitat and species.) A third user pay approach is to charge for activities that "use up" habitat, through real estate fees, auto-related fees, and the like. Finally, many states rely on voluntary programs, such as "check-offs" on state income tax forms or special license plates. Ultimately, the ability of any nongame and urban wildlife program to serve the public as well as conserve the majority of wildlife species will depend upon finding new ways to fund these programs.

Strategies and Solutions

The issues and problems facing wildlife diversity are difficult but can be overcome if wildlife agencies can distribute their efforts in several areas.

Inventory and Monitoring. Establish monitoring programs, at least for key species and habitats, so that we can be aware of changes in distribution, numbers, and population health or nongame and urban wildlife. This will allow biologists and wildlife agencies to react before a species is in serious jeopardy.

Research and Management. Study factors that affect the health and distribution of nongame and urban wildlife. Based on this information, develop and validate management techniques for nongame and urban species, improving our science as we implement it.

Habitat and Wildlife Conservation. Increase the protection of nongame and urban wildlife habitat. Since 97% of the state is privately owned, the only effective habitat-protection techniques will be those that work for private property owners. Incentive programs, cooperative projects, and voluntary easements all need to be explored. Incentives must be developed that encourage long-term conservation of natural resources instead of exploitation for short-term financial gain. Different programs should be developed to appeal to urban property owners and developers, rural landowners, communities, businesses, and units of local government. Land acquisition and conservation easements should be used in those unique situations where other means of habitat protection don't work. Avoid single-species emphasis; instead, emphasize the needs of wildlife and habitats as a whole. Single-species management should be viewed as an approach that undermines successful conservation.

An Integrated Approach. As nongame and urban wildlife management techniques are developed, these techniques should be integrated into traditional fisheries and wildlife management practices. Training should be provided to biologists to make them aware of these techniques. In turn, wildlife agencies should provide technical assistance and management information to the public.

Outreach/Education. Work with the public to improve their awareness of wildlife: that it exists, what habitat is, and the value of wildlife as part of functioning ecosystems. Efforts cannot be limited to any single demographic group. Some programs should be directed at schoolchildren, particularly by giving them the opportunity for "hands on" experiences. Outreach efforts directed at children represent a long-term strategy and are probably best handled by education specialists rather than biologists. This will require a major commitment by wildlife agencies, not just the desire and commitment of a few biologists.

There is a strong need for wildlife diversity outreach directed at adults. Research and experience indicate that adults are very open and interested in nongame. Most birdwatchers and nature photographers start as adults. These adults affect the attitudes of children as well. In addition, adults are the segment of the population that currently makes the resource decisions that affect nongame and urban wildlife.

Reaching urban populations presents a special challenge, since research indicates that inner city residents have little contact with nature and generally will not travel to outlying natural areas. The only solution is to take the message to them. Wildlife agencies should increase their presence where constituents live. Mobile education centers and outreach teams are approaches that show promise. Nature centers can be effective but are expensive to build as well as to operate. Any educational effort works best when done as a team approach with local sponsors and community groups. When dealing with minority groups, seek the assistance of members of that minority group. However, the need to increase urban outreach efforts must not come at the expense of rural programs. Wildlife agencies should continue outreach efforts that encourage rural landowners and communities to conserve wildlife and habitat.

Information. Increase efforts to provide good wildlife information to the public so that citizens are able to educate themselves. Providing information is a different process than education; information dissemination is a much simpler and more passive undertaking. Informational efforts should focus on using the media, providing information through printed publications, news articles, magazines, radio, and TV. Printed publications such as informational flyers, brochures, and pictures about nongame animals are in great demand. Increase the use of high-tech approaches to providing information; modern technology is providing many new ways of distributing information to schools and citizens through satellite links, computer networks, interactive TV, and other multimedia approaches. In addition to improving public awareness, these electronic media will also improve information transfer between department employees. These new technologies hold great promise but must be used in conjunction with the more traditional outlets in order to get the message out to a broad cross-section of the public.

Wildlife-Related Recreation. Increase opportunities for wildlife recreation and encourage public participation in outdoor recreation activities. People need places where they can see wildlife. Without viewing opportunities, the public has little opportunity to experience and learn to appreciate the outdoors. Studies show that the lack of time is the most important factor limiting people's participation in the outdoors (Duda 1994); the best way to counter this is to offer the public ample opportunity close to home (such as near cities and towns). Agencies also should better develop viewing facilities on existing properties as well as acquire additional properties where needed. In addition, agencies should work with communities and private landowners to help them develop nature tourism opportunities for the public. As access plans are implemented, it is important to include conservation measures to limit overuse of the resource.

Better Government. Improve agency public-policy processes, since most wildlife conservation is accomplished through political processes. Agencies must implement effective procedures for assessing and responding to public interests. Biologists should become familiar with constituents and become trained in public-policy processes. Agencies must strive to reduce bureaucracy, regulate only where necessary, and seek other means to affect public actions, such as through education and public participation. Better governmental processes will allow agencies to more readily deal with vocal minorities who push issues such as private property rights and antihunting.

Funding. Work toward increasing the funding available to wildlife diversity programs. However, these funding efforts should not be at the expense of current funding programs. Every state wildlife agency in the United States has a legal mandate to monitor, manage, and conserve all wildlife, but only about $1/2$ of these agencies receive funding other than hunting and fishing fees to fund these programs. Options other states have used include general tax revenue, special bonds, income tax check-offs, specialty license plates, real estate fees, and special automobile registration fees. Currently, a coalition of conservation groups, spearheaded by the International Association of Fish and Wildlife agencies, is proposing a national wildlife diversity funding program, referred to as "Teaming with Wildlife" or the "Fish and Wildlife Diversity Funding Initiative." This initiative proposes to mirror the very successful programs already in place for game management (Pittman-Robertson and Wallop-Breaux). The Fish and Wildlife Diversity Funding Initiative would direct income from small surcharges on outdoor equipment, bird feeders, and binoculars back to the states for wildlife diversity and recreation programs. It's too early to tell whether this proposal will succeed where others, such as the 1980 Fish and Wildlife Conservation Act, have failed.

Wildlife programs should also actively seek funding partners, donations, and grants. However, state agencies generally have limited success in fund raising, probably due to public resistance toward donating to agencies that already receive tax dollars. Wildlife agencies must use caution in any fund-raising approach, since funding efforts put these agencies in competition with many supporting conservation organizations. Once funding is obtained, it is important that agencies provide people with information on wildlife diversity programs that are in place and show that funds are being used for worthwhile projects.

Emphasize Common Values. Most citizens encounter nongame or urban wildlife on a daily basis, and most people value wildlife for its beauty and uniqueness. Watching wildlife appeals to folks for a variety of reasons, from an individual's desire for privacy and reflection, as part of the aesthetic experience of being outdoors, or as a family. Hunters, anglers, campers, homeowners, ranchers, and farmers value wildlife watching as part of the total outdoor experience. Nongame species are also part of the natural heritage of the state and so appeal to traditional values as well. While the study of wildlife also has scientific value, most constituents value wildlife for these other reasons; the lesson we should keep in mind is that the public may value wildlife in a different way than agency administrators and biologists.

Summary

Wildlife diversity issues are complex. Solutions should be developed using a wide array of approaches which address people and politics as well as wildlife. Society has changed greatly during the past 50 years. By addressing wildlife diversity issues, biologists and the agencies they work for will be better able to meet the challenge of this change.

Literature Cited

Adams, L. W. 1994. Urban wildlife habitats. Minneapolis: Univ. of Minn. Press. 186 pp.

Carson, R. 1962. Silent spring. Boston: Houghton-Mifflin Co.

Duda, M. D., and K. C. Young. 1994. Americans and wildlife diversity: Public opinion, interest, and participation in wildlife viewing and wildlife diversity programs. Harrisonburg, Va.: Responsive Management. 155 pp.

Graham, G. 1992. Texas wildlife viewing guide. Helena, Mont.: Falcon Press. 160 pp.

Hagan, J. M., and D. W. Johnston. 1994. Ecology and management of neotropical migrant landbirds. Washington, D.C.: Smithsonian Institution Press. 609 pp.

International Assoc. of Fish and Wildl. Agencies (IAFWA). 1994. Source book: Fish and wildlife diversity funding initiative. Washington, D.C.

Leopold, A. 1949. A Sand County almanac. New York: Oxford University Press. 228 pp.

Pope, C. 1995. The new politics. Speech presented to the Commonwealth Club, San Francisco, Calif., June 31. Reprinted by Sierra Club, 730 Polk St., San Francisco, CA 94109.

Swanson, G. A. 1979. Historical highlights in American conservation. Pp. 3–6 in R. D. Teague and E. Decker, eds., Wildlife conservation: Principles and practice. Washington, D.C.: The Wildlife Soc. 280 pp.

Texas Parks and Wildlife Dept. and Texas Dept. of Commerce. 1995. Nature tourism in the Lone Star State: Economic opportunities in nature. Austin: Tex. Parks and Wildl. 24 pp.

Tylka, D. L., J. M. Schaefer, and L. W. Adams. 1987. Guidelines for implementing urban wildlife programs under state conservation agency administration. Pp. 199–205 in L. W. Adams and D. L. Leedy, eds., Integrating man and nature in the metropolitan environment. Columbia, Md.: Natl. Inst. for Urban Wildl.

U.S. Dept. of Interior, Fish and Wildlife Service and U.S. Dept. of Commerce, Bureau of Census. 1993a. 1991 national survey of fishing, hunting and wildlife-associated recreation. Washington, D.C.: U.S. Govt. Printing Office. 178 pp.

———. 1993b. 1991 national survey of fishing, hunting and wildlife-associated recreation—Texas. Washington, D.C.: U.S. Govt. Printing Office. 74 pp.

VanDruff, L. W., E. G. Bolen, and G. J. San Julian. 1994. Management of urban wildlife. Pp. 507–30 in T. A. Bookhout, ed., Research and management techniques for wildlife and habitat. Bethesda, Md.: Wildlife Soc. 740 pp.

Wilkins, B. J., and S. R. Peterson. 1979. Nongame wildlife. Pp. 178–83 in R. D. Teague and E. Decker, eds., Wildlife conservation: Principles and practice. Washington, D.C.: The Wildlife Soc. 280 pp.

Clark E. Adams
Department of Wildlife
and Fisheries Sciences

John K. Thomas
Department of Rural Sociology
Texas A & M University
College Station, TX 77843

10. Human Dimensions Research in Texas: Past Efforts and Future Needs

Abstract: This chapter summarizes the results of 10 years of human dimensions in wildlife management research by describing several statewide studies that were conducted and how wildlife management policies and practices were impacted by these studies. It also identifies emerging wildlife-related issues revealed from study results. Three studies focused on hunters, the general public, and private landowners who leased their land for hunting. Two studies examined the commercial trade of Texas nongame wildlife and rattlesnake roundups. The results of these 5 studies provided some valuable insights into the Texas public's attitudes, activities, and expectations concerning Texas wildlife and natural areas. Responsive management actions motivated by study results are discussed. Future recommendations are given related to hunters and hunting, expanding public use of wildlife and natural areas, and preventing a tragedy of the commons.

The human dimensions initiative in wildlife management research began in the spring of 1982 and was discussed by Adams and Thomas (1982:100–101). Although their questions regarding future needs emphasized hunter studies, all questions were transferable to the entire Texas public's attitudes, activities, and expectations concerning wildlife. These researchers adopted a comprehensive approach to the study of human dimensions (e.g., hunters, the general public, landowners, special wildlife user groups) and developed a 10-year research agenda. This chapter summarizes the results of 10 years of human dimensions in wildlife management research by describing several statewide studies that were conducted and their impact on wildlife management policies and practices. It also identifies emerging wildlife-related issues revealed from study results.

Past Efforts

Texas Hunter Study

Prior to the 1980's, only a few regional or game-specific studies about hunters were available (e.g., Berger 1974; Mazzaccaro 1980). In 1982, a telephone survey of 3,080 Texas hunters assessed their attitudes, preferences, and practices concerning Texas wildlife and existing wildlife regulatory policies. We published the results in a contract report, several journals, and a conference proceedings. Here we summarize highlights of the results with particular emphasis on those findings that expanded available information about the licensed Texas hunter.

The statewide assessment answered several critical questions about Texas hunters: who they are, where they hunt, why they hunt, what economic impact hunting has on the Texas economy, what concerns they have for wildlife and natural areas that may go beyond hunting, and why they would discontinue hunting.

The majority of licensed Texas hunters surveyed in 1982 were Anglo, male, and urban and came from the upper socioeconomic strata of the state's population in terms of income, occupation, and education. Most hunters hunted on land owned by friends or relatives, their own land, public land, or company-owned/leased land compared to about ⅓ who hunted on land leased from private landowners. Nearly 75% went hunting to escape their urban environments and to experience the outdoors, compared to 2% who sought trophies. They hunted white-tailed deer more than any other game species. The total market value of white-tailed deer hunting was estimated to contribute approximately $210 million to the Texas economy. Overall, hunters were aware of factors contributing to the deterioration and loss of wildlife habitat and supported (over 75%) several proposals, including land-use planning, acquisition of private land by the Texas Parks and Wildlife Department (TPWD) for public use, and protection of coastal wetlands to mitigate these conditions. Additionally, hunters highly supported increased public education on wildlife and natural habitats. Time (e.g., job responsibilities) and money (e.g., lease cost) were the two most frequently mentioned factors that would contribute to hunter attrition.

Texas hunters were also asked to give their opinions on existing wildlife regulatory statutes that pertained to the County Commissioners Courts having veto power over TPWD management recommendations in their county and whether the TPWD should have full regulatory authority over all wildlife in Texas. Over 60% did not feel that the County Commissioners Courts should have the power to veto TPWD regulations, and over 80% favored full authority of the TPWD.

After the Texas hunter study became public, 2 events took place that may have been precipitated by these results. Wildlife professionals had to change their preconceived notions about the focus of Texas hunters. Although not documented, discussions at state and regional wildlife management training workshops in the early 1980's centered on methods of producing trophy bucks. This focus was justified by the misconception that Texas hunters wanted to hunt more trophy bucks. This undocumented belief was so strong among wildlife managers that some refused to accept the 1982 study results. One manager, upon hearing that only 2% of the Texas hunters were seeking trophy bucks as their first most important reason for going hunting, said flatly, "That is wrong!" This type of comment reflected an attitude among some wildlife professionals that they know better than the public what the public's wants and needs were concerning the state's wildlife resources.

Another event that took place after the 1982 Texas hunter study was the passage of the Wildlife Conservation Act of 1983 by the 68th Legislature. This act gave the TPWD full regulatory authority over all wildlife in Texas, thus eliminating the veto power of the County Commissioners Courts. It is unknown how the reported opinions of Texas hunters on this issue affected the Conservation Act legislation, but the result was a more centralized regulatory authority and less confusing TPWD code book.

The Texas hunters' desire to expand the domain of public hunting areas was addressed by the Type II Wildlife Management Area Program initiated in 1987 (Thomas and Adams 1991). The primary purposes of the provision of Type II lands were to provide low cost hunting but also fishing, camping, hiking, and nature photography opportunities to the public. In 1994, the TPWD public hunting program was consolidated into one public hunting program, i.e., no longer Type I and Type II programs.

As early as 1982, Texas hunters were aware of the need to increase public education on Texas wildlife. Adams et al. (1987) documented an extremely low level of knowledge by urban high school students concerning the identification, natural history, and availability of selected wildlife species. In 1986, $0.14 per capita of the TPWD operating budget was for public education compared to $0.50 each for wildlife and fisheries management and $1.39 per capita for law enforcement (Stone 1987). Increased public education on wildlife was provided, in part, by the adoption of Project WILD by the Information and Education Division of the TPWD in 1985. Success of this public education initiative can be attributed to the dedicated efforts of Ilo Hiller, Project WILD coordinator, TPWD. Since November 1991, she has orchestrated the training of 262 active facilitators who have conducted 900 workshops in which nearly 19,000 public and community educators were trained.

Public Uses of Texas Wildlife and Natural Areas

In 1988 we conducted a study that provided base-line data on real and latent public ($n = 2,050$ respondents) demands for wildlife resources and access to natural areas (Adams and Thomas 1989). The Texas public study examined (1) the demographic characteristics of consumptive and nonconsumptive users of Texas wildlife resources; (2) public demand for wildlife-related activities and access to natural areas and factors that limit participation; (3) the attitudes of the public toward the environment, conservation of natural resources, hunting, and wildlife ownership and management; (4) the level of public support for existing and future wildlife-related programs provided through the TPWD wildlife division and alternative means of financing these programs; (5) the public's primary sources of information on wildlife and types of information desired; and (6) factors affecting landowners' willingness to provide public access to their land for wildlife-related recreation.

Study findings indicated that the Texas public can be categorized into 4 distinct groups (nonactivists, appreciatives, utilitarians, and enthusiasts) based on their level of participation in selected wildlife-related activities. Most (58%) were categorized as "enthusiasts," indicating that within the last 3 years they took trips to participate in both consumptive and nonconsumptive activities. Real demand for hunting by respondents was the lowest when compared to other wildlife-related activities. The public had sincere concerns about the state of the natural environment and wildlife resources. Few respondents (19%) knew which agency was responsible for managing the state's wildlife resources and were unsure of its legal ownership. Information most desired by respondents was on the state's environmental problems, wildlife, and recreational areas. Their information on these topics was least likely to come from wildlife-related organizations or personalities. Rather than lack of interest, time and money were the factors that most prevented public participation in hunting and nonconsumptive activities. Respondents were supportive of hunting for food, game management, and predator control but opposed hunting for recreation, making a profit, and trophies. The Texas public has the greatest interest in visiting natural areas containing deer, then songbirds. A majority of the small number of landowners contacted in the study did not want to allow public access to their property even if additional income could be earned. Their greatest concerns were property damage followed by lack of interest and conflicting land use.

Study results revealed that the TPWD and other wildlife-related agencies need to (1) increase their profile among the Texas public and expand their constituency base, (2) diversify information types and delivery strategies, (3) incorporate nonhunting recreational opportunities on Type II land located near urban centers, (4) examine competition between hunting and other forms of outdoor recreation for public time and dollars, and (5) determine levels of public access to private lands. This study also revealed that there is a measurable level of antihunting sentiment among the Texas public that indicates a need for increased implementation of hunting education programs by wildlife professionals (Adams and Thomas 1990). These strategies would include putting public education on a parity level with other components of the wildlife management process, training hunters in ethics and public relations, and attempting to tell the "real story" about hunting.

The results of this study were used, in part, to support several changes in the TPWD's direction and internal structure of programs. The Texas Conservation Passport was first issued in 1991 by the TPWD to provide an opportunity for residents to participate in many of the wildlife-related activities they said were important. The passport is a form of nonhunting license that allows the holder to visit any state-run natural area to participate in a variety of nonconsumptive activities. This action by the TPWD was to provide for the wildlife-related needs of a larger constituency group among the Texas public. Further, the old Information and Education (I&E) Department was expanded to divisional status under the name of Conservation and Communication Division in 1990 to enhance public information and education on Texas wildlife and natural areas and to heighten the public's awareness of the TPWD as the agency responsible for the management of the state's wildlife resources. This change gave this division a higher level of autonomy from other divisions and the opportunity to set its own program agenda. Finally, study results indicated that the public was greatly concerned about wetland protection and felt that the state was not doing enough to protect the natural environment. These results were used by the TPWD executive branch to convince the Texas Legislature to increase the budget of the Resource Protection Division by 68% in 1990 (A. Sansom, executive director, TPWD, personal communication).

Lessors and Hunting Leases

The Texas-lease-hunting system has evolved in response to the mutual interests of hunters, the state, and landowners (Steinbach and Ramsey 1988) and has become one of the most extensive systems in North America (Burger and Teer 1981). Although the landowner's role and influence on the lease system has been substantial, only limited, regionally specific information about landowners who lease hunting rights has been gathered (Teer and Forrest 1968; Steinbach et al. 1987). A 1989 study of lessors characterized Texas private lands ($n = 7,399$) leased for hunting in terms of (1) years of operation, facilities and services provided, operational expenses, and income; (2) predominant habitat and wildlife; (3) agricultural and recreational uses; (4) wildlife management practices; (5) lease sizes; and (6) types of game present and hunted.

Detailed results of this study were reported as a statewide summary (Thigpen et al. 1991), by ecological regions (Thomas et al. 1990), and by comparisons of lessors and nonlessors (Adams et al. 1992). Overall, hunting lease operations cannot be perceived as a business enterprise in the same sense as ranching and farming. Few records were kept by lessors on operating expenses, perhaps because their investments in facilities and services for hunters and wildlife management techniques were minimal. Few lessors offered alternative wildlife-related activities to the public or nonresidents as a means of deriving additional income and expanding lease operations to full income-generating potential. With a few exceptions, hunting leases in Texas were informal agreements between landowners/managers and hunters, limited to state resident hunters, and focused on, although not limited to, white-tailed deer. The decision priorities to lease private land for hunting were, in descending order, to obtain additional income, control trespass, and operate a business enterprise. Many landowners who sold leases also granted free access for hunting.

As one should expect, habitat characteristics, agricultural use, and game animals present and hunted distinguished lease operations among ecological regions. The Edwards Plateau has the oldest and most land-owner-managed hunting-lease operations when compared to the other 9 regions. Comparatively, lease hunting was in the early stages of de-velopment in the Rolling and High Plains and Blackland Prairies eco-logical regions where the youngest and smallest lease operations were located. Median operating expenses ranged from $200 to $700 by eco-logical region and was $200 statewide. Statewide, $33,331,805 of lease income was reported by surveyed licensees. The median income per lease was $1,100. At least ⅔ of the operations in each region earned lease income, except for operations in the Piney Woods and High Plains regions, where 52% and 42% reported no income. Median total in-comes were highest in the Trans-Pecos and Gulf Prairies regions. Feed-ing wildlife was the wildlife management technique used most on leased acres statewide, particularly in the Edwards Plateau and Piney Woods regions. Constructing tanks/ponds, planting food plots, and controlling game harvest were most popular in the Rolling Plains, Piney Woods, and Trans-Pecos regions, respectively. Less than ⅓ of the operators in any ecological region conducted wildlife census and sex/age counts, operated a check station, fallow plowed, controlled brush, or erected high fences. More than 65% of the operations in all regions of the state had gun hunts, except in the High Plains (34%). Bow hunts were conducted mostly in the Piney Woods and Blackland Prairies re-gions, where nearly half of the lease operations also offered fishing op-portunities. No single region could be distinguished by trapping, field trials, or nonhunt recreation.

Respondents to the hunting lease study were divided into nonlessors (e.g., those respondents who purchased a hunting lease license but did not operate a lease during the 1989–90 season, $n = 840$) and lessors (e.g., those who did lease land to hunters, $n = 6,559$). Lessors were significantly ($P \leq = 0.05$) different from nonlessors in terms of land-ownership; years in operation; in operating a hunting lease as a busi-ness enterprise, for additional income, and to prevent trespass; number of game animals hunted; and location of lease operation by ecological region. However, these two groups could not be distinguished from one another in terms of numbers of acres leased, management practices conducted, types of recreation provided, or game animals present. Only 20–36% of the white-tailed deer range was under a legal hunting lease license during the 1989–90 hunting season. Only 18–30% of the total white-tailed deer hunters paid for a lease to hunt.

The results of this study have not been in the public domain long enough to evaluate their impact on the wildlife management process. However, some results might be used by wildlife professionals to provide programs that would help lessors better manage their wildlife resources and habitats and hunting lease businesses. Wildlife management recommendations will need to be given in the context of different levels of management effort and investment in order to convince landowners to expand public hunting on private lands.

Commercial Trade of Texas Nongame Wildlife

The only Texas nongame commercialization issue addressed in the literature has been the bobcat pelt harvest, which is regulated by the CITES treaty (Bluett et al. 1989). Prior to 1989, statewide studies concerning the commercial use of nonendangered, nongame vertebrate species in Texas had not been conducted, and the species that might be at risk due to commercial activity were unknown. To assess this situation, a 1989 investigation into the nongame trade was conducted using telephone interviews, written inquiries, and personal interviews. The investigation was supplemented by examination of catalogs, price lists, classified advertisements, and material provided by state and federal agencies. Persons contacted included state and federal agency personnel, special interest groups, businesses, wildlife rehabilitators, taxidermists, university and zoo personnel, and veterinarians (Jester et al. 1990). The study documented public demand in the rattlesnake market, pet industry, food industry, apparel and decoration industry, opportunistic markets, and the Oriental folk medicine market. The pet industry utilized all species of legally collectible wildlife. The apparel, decoration, and food markets utilized selected species. The opportunistic markets specialized in the use of live coyotes, mountain lions, black-tailed jackrabbits, and feral pigeons. The Oriental folk medicine market utilized venomous snakes and their parts.

The commercial use of Texas nongame can be characterized as an opportunistic and fragmented collection and distribution network. Yet this network has national and international ramifications through a multiple market system and entry into the illegal trade of wildlife and, therefore, lacks a definable structure for analysis. Overall, the trade in Texas wildlife may be substantial. Markets for nongame wildlife are diverse, native nongame wildlife is readily accessible to commercial exploitation by nonresidents, and businesses involved in nongame commercialization are more concerned about animal rights and animal welfare groups than regulation by the state. The commercial trade of Texas nongame wildlife, regardless of magnitude, results in a few people realizing profits without putting anything back into this resource, which is owned by all citizens. All that is required to collect nongame wildlife in Texas is a hunting license. However, the license is not incorporated into the same management strategies (e.g., seasons, bag limits, and animal census techniques) used for game animals. There are no regulatory requirements on the commercial trade of nongame wildlife in the state.

To mitigate trade practices and the lack of regulatory management, 2 future studies were recommended, including the impact of rattlesnake roundups on the collection and trade of rattlesnakes and a national assessment of state departments of natural resources regarding their efforts in regulating the trade of nongame. Development of a dealer/broker permit with mandatory reporting of animals used in trade was also recommended.

Texas Rattlesnake Roundups

The commercial trade study indicated that the western diamondback rattlesnake is a commercialized species. Part of that commercial activity can be attributed to rattlesnake roundups, which have been in existence almost 70 years in Texas. The first examination of rattlesnake roundups focused on the potential effects of gassing dens of rattlesnakes and other den occupants (Campbell et al. 1989). Unfortunately, no comprehensive information existed about the participants in these roundups or the potential impacts of roundup activities on rattlesnake populations. Consequently, a study was conducted by Adams et al. (1991) to (1) assess the extent of commercial trade of Texas rattlesnakes; (2) describe hunters and hunting methods; (3) provide historical, biological, and sociological data on rattlesnake roundups; and (4) assess regulations regarding the collection and commercialization of rattlesnakes. Data were collected through personal interviews with spectators ($n = 1,336$) and hunters ($n = 212$) attending rattlesnake roundups held in Taylor, Sweetwater, Brownwood, Big Spring, and Freer—5 of the 16 roundups conducted in 1991. Findings revealed how many spectators attended roundups, where they came from, their beliefs about rattlesnakes, and demographic characteristics. In addition, data were obtained from hunters on how long, where, why, and when they hunt; their demographic characteristics; their knowledge of rattlesnakes; and weight of rattlesnakes brought to a roundup.

Interviewed spectators were primarily Anglo, male, 25 to 44 years of age, accompanied by other family members, and area residents. The majority of rattlesnake hunters were Anglo, male, 25 to 44 years of age, and resided in the country or small rural communities. Compared to hunters, spectators held many more misconceptions concerning rattlesnakes. Large majorities of hunters and spectators did not perceive roundups to have a major impact on rattlesnake populations. Den hunting was common in North Texas, compared to road hunting in South Texas. Rattlesnake hunting for roundups occurred most frequently in the county of the roundup or contiguous counties. A large majority of the trade in rattlesnakes was conducted away from roundups. Only 19,427 pounds of rattlesnakes were sold by hunters to dealers at the 16 roundups in 1991. Price per pound varied from $4.00 to $5.50. When compared to other states, Texas ranks low in the regulatory control of rattlesnake collection and commercialization.

The management implications based on these and other results suggest that the TPWD consider collecting rattlesnake-related field data from willing landowners, establish check-station strategies at roundups, promote educational programs at roundups, and pursue obtaining annual inventory information from businesses involved in the trade of rattlesnakes. Moreover, the TPWD may need to strengthen its regulatory posture concerning collection and commercialization of rattlesnakes and other nonendangered nongame vertebrates.

Future Needs

Hunters and Hunting

The future of hunting in Texas is dependent on the resolution of a double dilemma: a declining hunter population on the demand side and a declining landbase to accommodate the existing hunter population on the supply side. Decreases in the hunter population can be attributed to low youth recruitment and attrition of urban adult hunters. The increase in single-parent (mother) families probably intensifies low youth recruitment since the father was the traditional linkage with hunting. The number of special resident hunting licenses (sold to individuals under 17 years of age and 65+ years old) declined at double the rate of other hunting licenses between 1988 and 1989. Over the past 10 years there have been large decreases in small game hunters. These trends may be indicative of and will perpetuate continued low youth recruitment into hunting. Wildlife agencies need to develop initiatives to encourage sport hunting commensurate with healthy game populations. Programs that introduce young people to hunting through hunter mentors or guides need to be developed. The experience will need to go beyond merely shooting to include training in hunting skills, including stalking, reading game animal signs, hunter safety and ethics, and game animal habits and natural history. There may be exceptional opportunities to introduce youth to hunting through pursuit of doves or small and upland game on private lands and TPWD public hunting lands.

There also have been large losses of urban hunters in the 18- to 25-year age group over the past 10 years, and adult hunters in Texas are becoming an aging population. The attrition of adult hunters could be for the same reasons given in both the Texas hunter and general public studies discussed above, i.e., time and money. There have been dramatic downturns in the Texas economy since the 1982 Texas hunter study, and the economy remains depressed. A follow-up statewide study of Texas hunters is needed to determine how the hunter population has changed in the past 10 years and what factors have made them quit hunting. The worst case scenario may be that the pursuit of hunting as a recreational alternative for Texas residents is constrained by increased expense and decreased availability of places to hunt and/or has been replaced by other recreational pursuits.

Expanding Public Use of Wildlife and Natural Areas

The natural resource orientations and concerns about the environment by Texas residents have undergone fundamental changes in the last 10 years. There is a clear pattern of increasing nonhunting rather than hunting interest in the state's wildlife resources. The wildlife profession must develop programs that increase public knowledge and use of wildlife and natural areas that go beyond hunter education and hunting. The 1988 public study discussed above provided ample information on public desires in this regard. For example, the majority of respondents wanted programs on wildlife in urban areas, environmental problems in Texas, wildlife ecology, and Texas wildlife. They also desired field trips to view wildlife, programs to help developers plan for wildlife, and grants to communities to conduct wildlife conservation projects. All of these educational needs could be met through expanded programming in the Texas Agricultural Extension Service, TPWD, and the many wildlife-related societies and organizations based throughout Texas.

The wildlife profession now has two opportunities to implement resource ecology education into Texas public schools that goes beyond Project WILD. One window of opportunity has been in existence since 1988 through agriscience teachers and a curriculum called Wildlife Recreation and Management. Agriscience teachers have a curriculum without an activity-based laboratory component (Adams and Eudy 1990). They have sought direction and help from many wildlife-related groups, but our assistance has been meager at best by some, and others have rebuffed their requests for help. Passage of Senate Bill 1340 during the 1991 legislative session mandated the inclusion of environmental education in all Texas public schools and offers a second opportunity for the wildlife profession to infuse resource ecology education into public schools. Presently, there are no funds, personnel, or curricula to expedite this mandate. Texas Wildlife Forever, Inc., is becoming involved, through a major capital campaign, in the informal and formal wildlife educational needs of the Texas public. As far as meeting the wildlife educational needs of the whole campus and community, wildlife professionals throughout the state are either sitting on their hands or wringing them in despair with worries about maintaining the status quo. Wildlife professionals should get into the mainstream of these changes and become part of the process that will set the stage for formal and informal wildlife education for the future.

The Future of Hunting in Texas

The future of hunting in Texas will be dependent upon the supply of hunters in general and, more specifically, those who have ready access to viable hunting areas. For hunters who purchase leases, they must consider what the lease offers in terms of price, geographic location, available and huntable game, and services and facilities. For others, access to hunting areas may involve locating private land owned by friends or relatives or use of TPWD public hunting lands. These factors will be increasingly weighed against alternative recreational pursuits that provide an equal or greater level of enjoyment and exercise. For example, many urban hunters are faced with the decision to spend $550 on a hunting lease in the Texas Hill Country which they might use 2 or 3 times a year or to spend their $550 on a golf club membership that can be used year-round and provides considerably more personal challenge and exercise.

The future of lease hunting will depend on the number of landowners who are willing to become lease operators. Land access is a problem in Texas since most (97%) of the land is privately owned. The state and the hunters rely on the private landowner as the sole-source provider of both game and land access. Landowners enter into hunting lease negotiations with personal preferences regarding who will hunt on their land and for how long and what game animals can be hunted. The decision to sell hunting leases also is based on how compatible this temporary activity will be with existing land uses. Adams et al. (1991) found that only 18–36% of the white-tailed deer range in Texas was under a legal hunting lease license during the 1989–90 season. Trend data are not presently available that would determine whether a land closure mentality has developed or is in the process of developing among private landowners. Kaiser and Wright (1985) suggested that land closure is now a broad-based trend caused by real and perceived misconduct of users, exclusivity of resource use by owners, insufficient economic incentives for owners, and potential injury liability problems.

Preventing a Tragedy of the Commons

The studies on the commercial trade of nonendangered nongame vertebrates and rattlesnake roundups in Texas revealed contemporary examples of the classic tragedy of the commons due to commercial exploitation of a part of the state's wildlife heritage. All reptiles and amphibians represent the commons. The tragedy begins when these animals receive a market value. This first step in the tragedy has already been taken, and the market is highly diversified (Jester et al. 1990; Adams et al. 1991). As outsiders in the process, wildlife professionals can only monitor the population stability of each nongame species by watching how its market value rises or falls. High prices usually mean high demand for limited supplies, resulting in intensified harvest of the species. At this point, the tragedy is nearly played out. The commons have been harvested to the point where they finally gain some regulatory protection as endangered or threatened species. The western diamondback rattlesnake is a specific example of a Texas nongame vertebrate that has market value. However, the absence of regulatory management places no constraints on human utilization of this resource. There are no limits on the numbers of western diamondback rattlesnakes that may be taken by Texas residents and nonresidents or commercial deals within and outside the state.

The absence of regulatory management leads to lack of public records to monitor harvest pressure on species targeted for commercial trade. Few roundup organizers keep annual logs of the weight of rattlesnakes turned in by hunters. The TPWD has never used the roundup supply of rattlesnakes to obtain biological and hunter information that would provide baseline and longitudinal data on the status of rattlesnake populations. Commercial dealers do not perceive the need to provide information on the "market competitive" aspects of their business such as where they buy rattlesnakes, how many pounds per year they process, and their business clientele.

Finally, the residents of Texas own all endemic wildlife and expect, by legislative mandate, the TPWD to look out for their interests when particular species are utilized by another subset of the public. If economic benefits are being derived from a public resource, then the public should realize some compensation for these benefits. Generally, those who use the wildlife resource provide this compensation for its management. This rationale has been applied to all game fish, game, and fur-bearing animals.

Adams et al. (1991) provided some management recommendations that considered the similarities and differences between rattlesnake roundups and other community events that involve wildlife. For example, deer hunting evokes the same level of enthusiastic support by hunters and community residents as do rattlesnake roundups. Deer hunting and rattlesnake roundup communities rely on each event to generate additional income, the majority of which results from the multiplier effect from goods and services purchased by participants in both types of events. Both events are seasonal and long-standing Texas traditions, result in the harvest of a portion of the wildlife resource, involve many social activities in addition to resource consumption, and require that hunters have a hunting license.

The difference between deer hunting and rattlesnake roundups is less TPWD involvement in the management tasks concerning rattlesnake populations, including monitoring population status, running check stations, assessing hunter success and geographic differences in hunting pressure, and conducting hunter safety programs. There are many management opportunities regarding rattlesnakes and roundups.

First, ranchers could be identified who would allow field studies on their land to determine the impact of roundup hunting on natural populations of rattlesnakes. Second, the numbers of rattlesnakes brought to a central location such as roundups offer a "check station" opportunity to obtain quantities of biological and hunter information on rattlesnakes on an annual basis. A third opportunity relates to much needed public education on rattlesnakes. Although education is attempted in different ways at roundups, the public is still largely uninformed concerning the elementary aspects of rattlesnake natural history, anatomy, behavior, value, and mythology. There is an education niche that needs to be filled at roundups.

Other management implications were realized based on the involvement of commercial dealers with rattlesnakes before, during, and after roundups. The activities of dealers in the rattlesnake trade are quite similar to fur buyers. The only similarity between them is that both types of businesses trade in large volumes of a Texas wildlife resource. However, unlike fur buyers, the rattlesnake trade is presently unregulated by the TPWD. Management opportunities exist in identifying all commercial dealers in and out of state that utilize Texas rattlesnakes, obtaining annual records of the volume and nature of their trading activity (e.g., how much, from whom, and prices paid). Pursuit of these management actions would provide regulatory consistency regarding the commercial trade of Texas wildlife, allow the citizens of the state to derive some financial return from the commercial use of their wildlife resource, and comply with similar recommendations made by commercial dealers.

Finally, the state needs to reconsider its regulatory posture regarding the collection and commercialization of nongame vertebrates. The western diamondback rattlesnake is only one of many species affected by the present situation. The results of the commercial trade and rattlesnake roundup studies demonstrated that a strengthened regulatory posture is required not so much for roundups but more to avert extended commercial utilization of nongame vertebrates (particularly reptiles) by commercial interests.

Literature Cited

Adams, C. E., and J. L. Eudy. 1990. Trends and opportunities in natural resource education. Trans. North Am. Wildl. and Natur. Resour. Conf. 55:94–100.

Adams, C. E., K. J. Strnadel, S. L. Jester, and J. K. Thomas. 1991. Texas rattlesnake roundups. Tex. Agric. Exp. Stn. and Texas A & M Univ. System, College Station, 74 pp.

Adams, C. E., and J. K. Thomas. 1982. Hunter surveys: Past efforts and future needs. Pp. 92–103 in J. T. Baccus, ed., Texas wildlife resources and land use. The Wildlife Society (Texas Chapter), Austin. 199 pp.

———. 1983. Characteristics and opinions of Texas hunters. Proc. Ann. Conf. Southeast Assoc. Fish and Wildl. Agencies 37:244–51.

———. 1989. Public uses of Texas wildlife and natural areas in Texas. Tex. Agric. Exp. Stn. College Station. 82 pp.

———. 1990. Identifying and responding to antihunting sentiment. Proc. Ann. Conf. Southeast Assoc. Fish and Wildl. Agencies 44: 401–07.

Adams, C. E., J. K. Thomas, P. Lin, and B. Weiser. 1987. Urban high school students' knowledge of wildlife. Proc. of the National Symposium on Urban Wildlife. Chevy Chase, Md., pp. 83–86.

Adams, C. E., J. K. Thomas, and C. Ramsey. 1991. A synopsis of Texas hunting leases. Wildl. Soc. Bull. (submitted).

Berger, M. E. 1974. Texas hunters: Characteristics, opinions, and facility preferences. Ph.D. diss., Texas A & M Univ., College Station. 131 pp.

Bluett, R. D., M. E. Tewes, and B. C. Thompson. 1989. Geographic distribution of commercial bobcat harvest in Texas 1978–1986. Tex. J. Sci. 41:379–94.

Burger, G. V., and J. G. Teer. 1981. Economic and socioeconomic issues influencing wildlife management on private lands. Pp. 252–78 in R. T. Dumke, G. V. Burger, and J. R. March, eds., Wildlife management on private lands. The Wildlife Society (Wisconsin Chapter). La Crosse, Wis.: La Crosse Print Co. 568 pp.

Campbell, J. A., D. R. Formanowicz, Jr., and E. D. Brodie, Jr. 1989. Potential impact of rattlesnake roundups on natural populations. Tex. J. Sci. 41:301–17.

Jester, S. L., C. E. Adams, and J. K. Thomas. 1990. Commercial trade in Texas nongame wildlife. Tex. Agric. Exp. Stn. and Texas A & M Univ. System, College Station. 22 pp.

Kaiser, R. A., and B. A. Wright. 1985. Recreational access to private land: Beyond the liability hurdle. J. Soil and Water Conserv. 40: 478–81.

Mazzaccaro, A. P. 1980. A study of whitewing dove hunters in South Texas and the Republic of Mexico. Ph.D. diss., Tex. A & M Univ., College Station. 191 pp.

Pope II, C. A., C. E. Adams, and J. K. Thomas. 1984. The recreational and aesthetic value of wildlife. J. Leisure Res. 16:51–60.

Steinbach, D. W., M. K. Glover, J. R. Conner, and J. M. Inglis. 1987. Economic and operational characteristics of recreational leasing in the Edwards Plateau and Rio Grande plains of Texas. Trans. North Am. Wildl. and Nat. Resour. Conf. 52:496–515.

Steinbach, D. W., and C. W. Ramsey. 1988. The Texas "lease system": History and future. Pp. 54–68 in D. Rollins, ed., Recreation and rangelands: Promise, problems, projections. Soc. Range Manage., Corpus Christi. 82 pp.

Stone, R. A. 1987. Wildlife conservation education efforts by information and education (I & E) divisions. M.S. thesis, Texas A & M Univ., College Station. 53 pp.

Teer, J. G., and N. K. Forrest. 1968. Binomial and ethical implications of commercial game harvest programs. Trans. North Am. Wildl. Conf. 33:192–203.

Thigpen, J., C. E. Adams, and J. K. Thomas. 1991. Statewide summary: Texas hunting leases. Tex. Agric. Ext. Serv. Publ. L-2441. 4 pp.

Thomas, J. K., and C. E. Adams. 1982. An assessment of hunters' attitudes and preferences concerning Texas wildlife and wildlife regulatory policies. Tex. Agric. Exp. Stn., College Station. 415 pp.

———. 1985. Socioeconomic factors affecting land access to hunt white-tailed deer. Wildl. Soc. Bull. 13:388–94.

———. 1991. Type II wildlife management areas in Texas. J. Environ. Systems 20:147–155.

Thomas, J. K., C. E. Adams, and D. Gill. 1984. White-tail deer hunting in Texas: Socioeconomic factors affecting access to land. Tech. Rpt. No. 84-1. Dept. Rural Sociology, Texas A & M Univ., College Station. 79 pp.

Thomas, J. K., C. E. Adams, and J. Thigpen. 1990. Texas hunting leases: Statewide and regional summary. Tech. Rpt. No. 90-4. Dept. Rural Sociology, Texas A & M Univ., College Station. 48 pp.

Deborah Slator Gillan, D.V.M.
Bart J. Gillan, III
Slator Ranch
H.C. 10, Box 62
Llano, Texas 78643

11. Landowners' View of Wildlife and Wildlife Users

Abstract: Fee-lease hunting was born in Texas out of economic necessity and in turn is the major factor sustaining healthy wildlife populations and habitat in modern times. The value attributed to wildlife encourages ranchers to deal with problems associated with wildlife and wildlife users. Domestic cattle are compatible with and enhance wildlife habitat when properly grazed. Increased federal control of private property through regulations or purchase are primary concerns of ranchers for the future. Ranchers feel they are best suited to manage wildlife and natural resources on private rangeland.

Of all segments of the population and agribusiness community, ranchers as inhabitants and caretakers of our native rangeland exert the greatest impact on wildlife in Texas today. Over 50% of Texas land remains as rangeland, almost exclusively owned by private individuals. Thus, the ranchers' perspective is vital to the existence and future of Texas wildlife.

Historical View

Since the early days of Texas, the numbers and species of wildlife present perhaps indicated the quality of rangeland and assisted the rancher in determining where to locate his family. Subsistence hunting was commonplace as wild game was used to supplement the ranch family diet. Frequently, the livestock produced was the cash crop utilized to pay bills and purchase supplies. Venison (both white-tailed and mule deer), rabbits, squirrels, fish, and feral pigs found their way to the ranchers' tables. Other meals came from game birds such as wild turkeys, ducks, doves, and quail.

Hunting and observation of these game animals gave the rancher an in-depth knowledge of their behavior. Wildlife travel patterns, feeding habits, and breeding and nesting requirements noted by the rancher could be associated with climatic changes. The early arrival of scissor-tailed flycatcher pairs signaled an early spring. A red-eared slider crawling uphill away from water gave promise of rain. A raccoon shot while raiding the corn crib in early fall that had a "primed out" pelt might mean an early cold winter. The instant southward migration of the "buzzard," or turkey vulture, was a sure bet that the first cold snap was on its way. Severe weather changes often decimated wildlife populations, venting the same wrath on the rancher and his livestock. Sharing equal vulnerability with wildlife, ranchers developed a bond with and respect for some native species that continue today.

Drought conditions of the 1930's coupled with the Depression era forced nonranchers and rural townspeople alike to hunt wildlife for survival. Neighboring ranchers were tolerant to the needs of others, often supplying impoverished families with game. More than one ranch family was saved from financial ruin by rounding up and selling feral pigs on their property during this time.

These severe economic conditions gave birth to fee-lease hunting as practiced today in Texas. One of the early pioneers was Mark A. Moss of Llano, who first "posted" his ranch property to trespassers in the mid-1930's and prohibited the hunting of wild game for 5 years. (Mark Moss also is credited with introducing exotic wildlife [blackbuck, mouflon sheep, and barasingha] to the Texas Hill Country. In conjunction with Charles Schreiner III of Kerrville, Harry Jersey of San Antonio, and others, he founded the Exotic Wildlife Association in 1967.) After his deer population had sufficiently increased, Moss began leasing hunting rights to other local people for money under a strict set of rules. Over the next 10 years, adjoining ranchers observed the financial bonus from leasing and adopted the fee-lease practice. By the 1950's, hunting income was considered an important secondary cash crop to most Central Texas ranchers, often paying property taxes and sometimes winter feed bills.

Native Deer Herds Increase

The eradication of the screwworm fly in the early 1960's had an immense effect on domestic livestock as well as native wildlife populations. For decades, the presence of screwworms and their larval infestation of living tissue was a nightmare for ranchers. Any raw or open wound on any animal could serve as the site for adult screwworms to lay eggs. After hatching, the fly larvae devoured adjacent living tissue, causing catastrophic damage to hides and carcasses and often resulting in death. Native wildlife populations were equally susceptible to screwworm invasion in the umbilicus of newborns, birthing and fighting wounds, or raw antlers as the velvet was rubbed off. With the success of the sterile fly release program and eventual eradication of screwworms in Texas, the primary parasite of the native deer population was also eliminated. The resultant explosion in native deer numbers was tempered only by weather.

Unknowingly, ranchers' livestock and range practices were creating habitat more conducive to deer and quail populations than the grassland prairies of early Texas. Three land practices in particular were instrumental in molding the landscape for future wildlife populations.

The development of barbed wire and the ensuing fencing of the open range changed the grazing practices of livestock from the free-roaming, cyclical grazing of their bison predecessors. Confined to grazing within the bounds of a specific pasture or ranch, livestock selectively ate choice grasses and forbs (weeds), causing a proliferation of less palatable woody plants (browse). Suppression of wildfires and "modern" fire control methods also promoted the development of woody browse plants that had been routinely purged when wildfires were common. The development of water sources by ranchers for livestock under fence simultaneously provided wildlife greater access to more feeding and nesting areas. All 3 forces gradually changed the tall grass prairie into a land filled with mosaic patterns of brush, hardwood trees, and meadows of prairie grasses. This landscape was ideally suited to a myriad of birds and mammals, most notably the white-tailed deer, quail, and the Rio Grande wild turkey.

Soaring white-tailed deer populations in Central Texas gave rise to early attempts to manage and control wildlife populations by harvesting antlerless deer. The Mark Moss Bar-O Ranch in Llano again pioneered doe-only hunts in the 1950's as a means of removing surplus deer that exceeded the carrying capacity of the rangeland. Teer,

Thomas, and Walker (1965) reported that in 1955, 607 deer of both sexes were taken from the 8,763-acre Bar-O Ranch. Another 71 deer were unretrieved—shot, crippled, and dead. This practice was more the exception; ranchers generally protected their female deer, allowing hunters to shoot only bucks with branched antlers. Although spike-antlered deer harvest was legalized in 1960, ranchers and hunters alike did not begin harvesting spike bucks with any regularity until the mid-1970's.

Economic Factors

As more and more ranchers began leasing their land to paying hunters, the economic benefit of wildlife to landowners and their communities became apparent to all. By the late 1960's, fee hunting in Texas had become "big business." This new industry was responsible for the economic viability of many small rural towns that previously had been dependent exclusively on livestock and agricultural commodities.

The recreational uses of native ranchland had a tremendous impact on land prices in the 1970's and 1980's, especially in Central Texas. Wealthy urban investors and city dwellers who yearned for "a little piece of land" or their own "ranchette" caused rural land prices to sky-rocket. The presence of wildlife for aesthetic appeal as well as recreational hunting increased sales prices to levels unsurpassed in Texas real estate history. Fair market prices were paid up to 200–250 times the annual agricultural income per acre. Hill Country land that was leasing for $8–$10 per acre (grazing and hunting rights included) in 1984 might sell in excess of $2,000 per acre on the open market. A speculative land frenzy ensued when real estate investors expected (and received) significant profits from rapid land turnover.

Rural land sales, even though speculative and soon invalidated by bankruptcy or reversion to the seller for nonpayment, were the basis for estate comparable valuations. Ranching families surviving a death by the landowner during this period were saddled with federal inheritance taxes levied on family ranchland based on these speculative comparable sales. Many deceased ranchers' beneficiaries were forced to liquidate part or all of the entire operation to pay inheritance taxes.

Modern Developments

Droughts periodically plague the rangelands of Texas, causing stress to rancher, livestock, and wildlife indiscriminately. Soaring white-tailed deer populations were especially vulnerable to drought, and many deer die-offs were noted by ranchers and wildlife professionals. Alarmed by the senseless waste of animals, many ranchers and hunters requested professional assistance; thus, wildlife management spread to the private sector.

Professional wildlife biologists employed by state agencies or hired as independent private consultants have been instrumental in disseminating information and assisting the landowner in managing the wildlife on his property. Plans for developing healthy deer and wildlife populations were individually tailored to the goals established by the landowner for his particular ranch property.

Ranchers may receive management guidance from any of several sources. Since 1973, the Technical Guidance Program, Wildlife Branch, of the Texas Parks and Wildlife Department has provided professional on-site assistance to cooperating ranchers. U.S. Natural Resource Conservation Service personnel assist ranchers in developing wildlife management plans and have helped establish cooperative associations of small, neighboring ranchers to effectively manage wildlife populations on combined rangeland. County Agricultural Extension offices of Texas A & M University provide seminars and information on wildlife management techniques to ranchers. All spread the latest research and practical applications to interested ranchers and landowners.

Funding for these state-supported research projects, wildlife management, and law enforcement activities are generated directly from the Texas hunter. All revenue received from hunting license sales and related game stamps such as the archery stamp, turkey stamp, white-winged dove stamp, and federal and state duck stamps fund state wildlife management activities. Similarly, marine motor fuel taxes, fishing license and corresponding saltwater fishing stamp sales support sport-fishing management within Texas. The Pittman-Robertson Act levies a federal excise tax on firearm and ammunition sales. This "federal aid" generated within the Pittman-Robertson Act via the sportsman's tax dollar reimburses the state 75% on all wildlife expenditures.

Private research endowments such as the Welder Wildlife Foundation and the Caesar Kleberg Wildlife Research Institute provide vital research models and information. Notwithstanding these nonprofit organizations and other charitable contributions, it is the American hunter's willingness to pay for an outdoor experience on private land in Texas that is the dominant force behind the thriving wildlife populations on Texas rangeland today. The demand for a quality hunt and outdoor experience has helped spur most of modern research. Genetics and nutrition studies coupled with other scientific research provide the basis for modern white-tailed deer management programs. Soon, research on deer and other wildlife will rival in volume the work done on cattle.

Ranchers themselves are becoming involved in promoting wildlife education. Many livestock organizations have formed subgroups promoting modern wildlife management information and techniques among their membership. The Wildlife Division of the Texas Farm Bureau and its related branch of the Texas and Southwestern Cattle Raisers Association are 2 of the larger organizations to recognize and promote wildlife concerns within their membership.

The U.S. Natural Resource Conservation Service, the Texas Parks and Wildlife Department, the Texas Chapter of The Wildlife Society, the Fort Worth *Star Telegram,* and other agencies and organizations have developed various awards recognizing ranchers' achievements in wildlife management and habitat restoration. The growing public awareness and demand for nonconsumptive wildlife experiences could provide new economic opportunities for owners of some ranchland. Many urbanites have expressed a willingness to compensate the landowner for use of his property for birdwatching, nature walks, wildlife photography, etc. This form of leasing might appeal to some ranchers; others would have no interest in public access regardless of the profit.

Rancher-User Relationships and Risks

Ranchers as a whole tend to prefer a solitary lifestyle. Many individuals choose the peace, quiet, and seclusion of rural life even though greater income and conveniences would be available if they lived in town. These personalities would not welcome public intrusion into their private world and values regardless of payment provided. Although these same ranchers must personally deal with their hunters, the ranchers' dependence on the hunting-lease income as a vital cushion against cyclical livestock prices and weather conditions allows them to accept their presence. Most ranchers, however, welcome the beginning of deer season and the opportunity to visit with their hunters just as eagerly as they yearn for the *end* of the hunting season and a return to "normal" conditions.

The average rancher leases to city dwellers searching for an opportunity to do some hunting and escape from urban life. Historically, the term of lease was for the entire year or restricted just to the hunting season. Often, long-lasting relationships, even friendships, developed between the rancher and hunter. Day-hunting enterprises developed as a means of providing the large number of hunters necessary to harvest adequate numbers of deer in overpopulated regions.

Ranchers tend to be possessive of their lease clientele, often referring to them as "my hunters" when either bragging or complaining about them to other ranchers. Although "lease hopping" and bargain hunts have always appealed to some, most hunters remain loyal to their lessor if the arrangements and conditions are mutually agreeable. It is still common to hear of ranchers that have retained the same group of lease hunters for 30 or more years.

Although ranchers are extremely dependent on income from wildlife resources, most demand that their lessee hunters abide by some rules or code of ethics toward wildlife. Hunters caught by the landowner in unacceptable behavior toward either humans or animals are generally not tolerated. Turkey hunters found shooting into a roost might be evicted for no other reason. And nothing disgusts ranchers and their paying hunters more than to find a poacher's "road kill" or decapitated carcass in a pasture, the meat left unharvested and spoiled.

Any rancher or rural landowner who deals with the public should be acutely aware of the potential liability as a property owner. The increased incidences of litigation associated with landownership make all ranchers fearful of public access to their land. The possibility that any person could conceivably sue for "alleged negligence" or "attractive nuisance" and collect enormous settlements from the landowner is frightening. Texas juries have awarded awesome sums even when the landowner had not consented to or had prior knowledge of the individual's presence on his property. A rancher's fear of losing the ranch just because he owns the ranch is significant.

In view of the current legal climate in Texas, most ranchers who allow public access to their property carry liability insurance policies. If hunting is allowed on the property, many insurance carriers require additional premium surcharges in order to include the hunting exposure. During the mid-1980's, an increasing number of carriers completely withdrew from the farm and ranch owner market. Those remaining underwriters frequently demanded additional insurance premiums based on total gross income, not just hunting-related proceeds, if they would insure the operation at all. One major farm/ranch insurance carrier will cover hunting exposure only if it consists of less than 50% of the gross ranching income. Skyrocketing insurance premiums secondary to out-of-control jury awards make liability insurance unaffordable for some ranchers. For these individuals, "going bare" (no insurance) is their only alternative.

Not all landowners immediately became involved in commercial hunting. As ranch families sold out or were forced to move from the land, absentee ranchers residing in urban areas purchased rangeland as a secondary venture. Many properties were purchased as hunting preserves. These owners restricted the hunting to family members and guests.

During the Texas economic crisis of the 1980's, state and most local governments began assessing new recreational income valuations as part of the ad valorem taxes. The few ranchers who were not yet commercially hunting quickly began leasing their hunting rights, since they were already taxed on income they were not receiving.

Problems Common to Livestock and Wildlife

Cattle ranching and certain wildlife enterprises are ideally suited to exist simultaneously on the same rangeland and in fact complement one another. Consequently, it is not surprising that wildlife species and domestic livestock would share some similar problems.

Newborn offspring of cattle, sheep, and goats are as vulnerable as newborn fawns to predation by coyotes and mountain lions. In the absence of an ample wildlife population, kid goats and lambs often fall victim to opportunistic carnivores. The economic impact of predation losses to ranchers is well documented. In 1990, $7.5 million in losses among Texas sheep and Angora goat producers alone were reported (Texas Agricultural Statistical Service 1991). Local livestock associations were created to cost-share trappers' expenses in reducing coyote populations.

Ranches situated near towns and urban areas may be victimized by unwanted domestic dogs and cats dumped on rural roads and streams. Those pets that do survive become predators of newborn deer, quail, turkey, and ground-nesting birds, as well as domestic livestock and poultry.

Although cattle at reasonable stocking rates pose little threat to deer populations for available forage, the diet of sheep and goats consists primarily of the same forbs and browse consumed by native and exotic deer. Producers of sheep, goats, and exotics must carefully inventory and ration available forage if they are to have successful wildlife enterprises.

Uncontrolled red imported fire ant proliferation threatens the newborn of all domestic and wildlife populations nesting or giving birth on the ground. Southeast Texas ranchers report losses of calves, fawns, and other animals as fire ant stings on eyes, nose, and mouth become fatal before the newborn is old enough to escape. The explosive northward invasion of fire ants in Texas will severely reduce native wildlife populations as well as cost ranchers millions in livestock deaths.

Transmissible Diseases

Several diseases that are constantly present in the native wildlife population can be transmitted to domestic livestock. Leptospirosis (now considered endemic within domestic cattle) was maintained and spread through contaminated water sources by healthy white-tailed deer and other wildlife species acting as reservoirs. Bluetongue, a viral disease principally affecting sheep, exists in healthy deer as a source of infection and may cause abortion in cattle.

Pseudorabies, a reportable disease (confirmed cases must be reported to state regulatory officials) of swine, was found to occur in approximately 15% of the wild pig population of parts of Southeast Texas in the late 1980's (pers. commun., Howard Whitford, D.V.M., Texas Veterinary Diagnostic Laboratory, Texas A & M University, College Station). Each year, the Texas A & M University Veterinary Diagnostic Laboratory confirms 2–3 cases of rabies in domestic livestock. Raccoons, foxes, skunks, and bats are the primary carriers of rabies in native wildlife populations.

The deadly Anthrax bacteria is perpetuated in wildlife populations of parts of Southwest Texas (San Angelo to Uvalde) and occasionally breaks out in epidemic proportions in domestic cattle. One group of Val Verde County hunters helped initiate an experimental oral vaccination program of the local white-tailed deer population during an anthrax outbreak in 1979, continuing the vaccination process until 1986 (pers. commun., Tommy Hailey, technical guidance biologist [retired], Texas Parks and Wildlife Department).

Several other diseases and parasites of lesser significance are perpetuated in wildlife populations and occur occasionally in domestic livestock.

Range Management Philosophy

More and more professional biologists and resource managers are touting the beneficial and vital role that grazing livestock play in certain ecosystems. Properly planned grazing allows cattle to efficiently remove grass cover, thus enabling sunlight to penetrate the bitten plant's base and stimulate the production of more growth. Manure and urine are deposited on the range surface, spontaneously fertilizing the land and returning valuable minerals and nutrients to the soil. Hoof action of excited livestock naturally breaks and aerates the soil surface, allowing water and minerals to penetrate more effectively without mechanical intervention.

Proper grazing technique allows for sufficient recovery time or "rest" for the bitten plant to replenish its energy stores and continue above-ground growth. Several methods of rotating livestock from pasture to pasture have been developed; each ensures some degree of rest from grazing domestic livestock. We employ a flexible form of high intensity, low frequency grazing whereby large numbers of beef cattle are concentrated in pastures for a short period of time during the growing season, thereby maximizing the recovery period for bitten plants.

Planned grazing techniques act as a natural stimulus to the environment, promoting greater diversity and stability in soil and plant communities. Biologists at the Kerr Wildlife Management Area, Hunt, Texas, have noted a spontaneous pasture rotation of the native deer herd which coincides with maximum forb production 1 to 3 months following cattle grazing the same pastures. This symbiotic relationship between properly grazing livestock, wildlife populations, and a healthy environment shows great promise for improving future rangelands. (For more detailed information on this relationship, see Savory 1988.)

Studies at the Kerr WMA on the effect of removing grazing animals from native grassland indicated a substantial reduction in numbers and species of native vegetation over a period of 30 years. Correspondingly, the removal of livestock from the Aransas National Refuge and Matagorda Island resulted in a decline in biodiversity that was hindering the Whooping Crane Recovery Plan.

In a similar vein, native deer populations require hunting pressure to keep the habitat from being destroyed. In the absence of sufficient natural predators (screwworms, carnivores, hunters, etc.), uncontrolled white-tailed deer populations threaten the welfare of many native forbs, shrubs, and browse plants. Especially at risk are quasi-residential areas of Central Texas where soaring "tame" and "pet" deer populations exhibit abnormal behavior patterns toward humans and native vegetation.

Ranchers' Future Concerns

The rapidly expanding listing of threatened and endangered species is viewed by many ranchers as an excuse for big government to seize control of private property and encroach on traditional private property rights of landowners. Perceived misinformation and inclusion of species on "threatened" lists that are known to flourish in certain regions create distrust and fear of the motives driving the Endangered Species Act (ESA).

Single species management as practiced under the ESA is impractical and contradictory from a biological approach as well as prohibitive financially to private landowners and all taxpayers. If the habitat is not sufficient to sustain a particular species, no amount of artificial intervention will support that species over the long term unless the whole ecosystem is managed and capable of responding.

The liberalized definition of wetlands under the Clean Water Act is equally alarming to ranchers. Stock ponds, standing water runoff, or other transient sources of wildlife water will cease to be developed by ranchers if their very existence invites federal regulation and control. The wildlife habitat that needs cross-fencing and water development will decline.

Ranchers are distressed that overzealous interpretations of these laws by the courts and through U.S. Fish and Wildlife Service regulations prohibit and restrict the landowner's ability to operate and improve his land as he sees fit. The Davis Mountain–Trans-Pecos Heritage Association, which amassed 12 million acres among its membership within the first 3 years of existence, promotes "conservation served through private ownership" instead of what its members view as inefficient and abusive governmental regulation.

In recent years, large acreages in Texas have been purchased, either outright by the state or federal government or through several nonprofit organizations, in the name of conservation. When a park designation is achieved, the revenue lost to local governments from these properties removed from the tax rolls must be made up by neighboring private taxpayers, not the general public.

Ranchers watch in dismay as large tracts of native range, once sparsely populated by humans, become "stocked" with minivans and people in sneakers. As the great naturalist Aldo Leopold (1949) explained, "All conservation of wildness is self defeating, for to cherish we must see and fondle, and when enough have seen and fondled, there is no wilderness left to cherish."

At the time of this publication, ranchers and hunters are subjected to increasing attack from extreme environmental groups and antihunting, animal rights activists. Segments of the news media are all too eager to present biased, one-sided distortions of the true rancher-hunter-conservationist image. It is the ranchers' hope that, in time, dissemination of the complete rangeland scenario, backed by undisputed facts and statistics, will receive the accuracy and respect it deserves.

Conclusion

Ranchers as a group have a deep reverence and respect for the land on which they live, work, and play as well as nature's wildlife with which they share the land. Despite fluctuating market prices, unpredictable weather, governmental regulation, inheritance taxes, and encroaching urbanization, many ranch families have remained on the same property for over 100 years and are committed to remaining there for 100 years more. Every day they are outdoors, working on the land and watching the interaction between themselves, the soil, and the wildlife upon it. Ranchers believe that the landowner is the best qualified, most concerned, and most capable person to efficiently manage and conserve the wildlife and renewable natural resources on his property.

Literature Cited

Leopold, A. 1949. A Sand County almanac. New York: Oxford University Press. 295 pp.

Savory, A. 1988. Holistic resource management. Washington, D.C.: Island Press. 564 pp.

Teer, J. G., J. W. Thomas, and E. A. Walker. 1965. Ecology and management of white-tailed deer in the Llano Basin of Texas. Wildl. Monogr., The Wildl. Soc. 15:52.

Texas Agricultural Statistical Service. 1991. Predator losses totaled $7.5 million to Texas farmers and ranchers. Tex. Agric. Stat. Serv., Austin. SM-10-91:3.

James A. DeLoney
Consumer Research Program Area
Texas Parks and Wildlife Department
Austin, Texas 78744

12. The Implications of the 1995 Texas Outdoor Recreation Plan on Wildlife Use and Demand

Abstract: The 1995 Texas Outdoor Recreation Plan (TORP) has many links to wildlife resource use. Many of its recommendations directly address measures to acquire, protect, and/or provide access to natural areas, wildlife, and wildlife habitat. Special studies conducted as part of the TORP process show that citizens have strong feelings about environmental and wildlife issues in Texas. The TORP covers recreation issues directly and indirectly related to wildlife resource management, such as demand for variety in opportunity, budget reductions, liability, and legal issues. A comparison of consumptive and nonconsumptive uses of wildlife statistics from the TORP present interesting findings. More in-depth studies could improve the data's value. Specifically, a better understanding of the relationships between consumptive and nonconsumptive uses of wildlife and other recreation activities would be valuable to decision makers. Future studies should investigate these relationships to broaden the use of the results at the Texas Parks and Wildlife Department.

The 1995 Texas Outdoor Recreation Plan (TORP), the seventh edition of the state's plan, has 1 goal: increase and improve the quality of outdoor recreation opportunities in Texas. Since almost all noncommercial wildlife resource use (consumptive and nonconsumptive) necessarily implies recreational use, the research, planning, and public input required to produce the state recreation plan have many applications in wildlife resource planning. This chapter highlights the most significant of these applications. It also illustrates the strong concern Texans have to protect natural resources and the environment, to promote the role of the 1995 TORP as a viable wildlife resource planning tool, and to inculcate a greater appreciation for the need to improve coordination and cooperation between wildlife and recreation interests.

Components of the TORP, updated every 5 years to satisfy federal Land and Water Conservation Fund requirements, apply directly to wildlife resource issues. The Assessment and Policy Plan (APP), the main document, is based on statewide research and public input. It presents recreation issues, needs, and recommended actions in a statewide format. It provides statewide information on outdoor recreation supply and demand. The Open Project Selection Process addendum introduces sponsors to project evaluation criteria for matching grants from the Land and Water Conservation Fund. Priority scoring varies from project to project, with points awarded for the conservation and purchase of natural areas, open space areas, and wetlands. Finally, the Texas Wetlands Plan, which must be developed in consultation with the state agency responsible for fish and wildlife resources, directly addresses the resources and recreational use of wetlands.

Key TORP Recommendations

The Assessment and Policy Plan highlights the top 5 issues facing Texans and our visitors, along with the top 10 actions needed to address each issue. Issues and actions were identified and prioritized through an extensive public input process. If implemented, these actions would have the most significant impacts toward meeting outdoor recreation needs in Texas. Implementation of these actions could have major impacts on the management and protection of wildlife resources in Texas.

Public Opinion Affecting Wildlife

Research conducted in previous TORP planning cycles has implications for those interested in wildlife research and management, particularly in the area of establishing public opinion on issues which impact wildlife and wildlife resources. TORP research documents that Texans have strongly favored the protection of resources valuable for recreation and wildlife purposes for many years. Texans' opinions on state park and environmental issues and their preferences for the types of natural resources they would most like to visit have implications for the conservation and management of wildlife resources.

In 1986, the Texas Parks and Wildlife Department (1987) asked Texas residents to cite reasons why they enjoy outdoor recreation. Seventy percent said "to enjoy nature and the outdoors," followed by "to be with family or friends" (53%) and "it's quiet and peaceful" (52%). Respondents cited these 3 reasons the most often. This report, titled *Recreational Issues in Texas: A Citizen Survey—The Technical Report*, shows that Texans have very strong concerns for environmental protection, concerns which have major implications for the conservation and management of wildlife resources.

When asked "Do you agree or disagree with the following statements about TEXAS STATE PARKS?" Texans responded as follows:

	Percent agree	Percent disagree	Percent undecided
• State parks should have areas left in a natural condition for preservation purposes	92	3	4
• Oil exploration and drilling should be allowed in state parks	15	75	10
• State parks should have areas where limited hunting is allowed	33	61	6

When asked who the general public thinks should "do more to protect the environment," they responded:

	Percent agree	Percent disagree	Percent undecided
• Citizens	96	2	2
• Private industry	87	5	8
• Local government	84	7	9
• State government	74	10	16
• Federal government	74	15	12

Responses by the public to other statements on the survey further illustrate the public's strong concerns for the environment.

	Percent agree	Percent disagree	Percent undecided
• Destruction of outstanding natural resources is a significant problem in Texas	51	18	31
• Conserving wildlife habitat is more important than developing land for population and economic growth	56	22	21
• Protection of rivers and streams is a problem in Texas	74	9	17
• Gulf Coast waters in Texas are too polluted	49	15	36

The high percentages of the population agreeing compared to those disagreeing are significant. The large number of undecided respondents indicates that the public does not necessarily take a position to agree or disagree on statements they feel uncertain about.

Public attitudes strongly favor the provision of greater access to areas associated with wildlife resources and use.

	Percent agree	Percent disagree	Percent undecided
• More public recreation areas will be needed along rivers and streams	67	16	17
• More public recreation areas are needed along lakes	66	18	16
• More wilderness areas open to the public are needed in Texas	56	18	26
• Automobiles should be allowed on the beaches of the Texas Gulf Coast	15	72	13

Results show that the majority agree that more public recreation areas are needed along rivers and streams and lakes but that automobiles should not be allowed on the Texas Gulf Coast beaches. By a 3–1 margin, the public agrees that more wilderness areas open to the public are needed in Texas. Responses to the question "Which three of these areas would you most like to visit in Texas?" reveal the types of natural resources most popular with the general public for outdoor recreation purposes.

1. Mountains   62%
2. River or stream   61
3. Lake or reservoir   58
4. Gulf Coast   48
5. Forest   42
6. Open ranchland   9
7. Desert   7
8. Swamp or marsh   2
9. Other   1

Public preferences and opinions, such as those identified above, tie inextricably to the 5 statewide outdoor recreation issues and the 50 recommended actions cited in the 1995 TORP Assessment and Policy Plan and to many related wildlife resource issues. The top-ranked action identified by participants in the public input process to address the second-ranked statewide issue, "Conserving Natural Resources for Recreational Uses," illustrates this tie: "create and promote incentives (other than government acquisition), such as tax breaks and liability waivers, for the private sector, particularly private landowners, to preserve natural resources and to make these preserved resources available for recreation use by the public as parks, recreational areas, and open spaces" (DeLoney et al. 1996).

Actions from the fourth- and fifth-ranked statewide issues, "Meeting Recreational Open Space Needs" and "Tourism and Outdoor Recreation," respectively, further illustrate how the resolution of outdoor recreation issues may resolve wildlife resource management issues by proxy: "use floodplains and other non-developable lands for open space, greenbelts, and recreational areas, and provide linkages of trails with parks, historical sites, and open space"; "package and promote tourism in Texas emphasizing ecotourism, nature tourism, natural and cultural heritage, trails, and other forms of outdoor recreation" (DeLoney et al. 1996).

Public desires for greater access to high quality natural resources, such as mountains, water bodies, forests, and the Gulf Coast, and for a wider variety and higher quality of outdoor recreation opportunities call for greater access to existing public lands and the renovation, upgrading, and maintenance of existing sites, all at a time when budgets for public resources have been severely strained in recent years. Resolution of outdoor recreation and wildlife issues may require actions of a complementary nature. For example, setting aside parklands in their natural state also preserves wildlife habitat. Setting aside lands for wildlife preservation can create opportunities for outdoor recreationists to engage in wildlife observation, nature study, walking for pleasure, or hiking. With limited budgets (and all budgets are limited), policies may need to be tailored to balance recreation and wildlife use of new areas. Gaining access to privately owned lands, 90–98% of the lands in Texas, will impact wildlife issues such as landowner attitudes toward governmental agencies, hunters, hunting leases, liability concerns, etc., all of which affect the provision of outdoor recreation and wildlife opportunities by the public and private sectors.

Providers of both public and private outdoor recreation and wildlife opportunities should find information in the 1995 TORP of particular value since it is based on original research, amplified and refined by extensive public input throughout the 5-year plan development process. However, research conducted to develop the TORP and special studies need to be followed by more in-depth work to generate a better understanding of the relationships between outdoor recreation and wildlife. If outdoor recreationists are given greater access to publicly administered wildlife management areas, how will improved access impact wildlife populations? How are expenditures made by public agencies, such as the Texas Parks and Wildlife Department, when meeting its mandates for both the provision of outdoor recreation opportunities and wildlife management? Using information found in the 1995 TORP and special reports to compare hunting and wildlife-related activities with other outdoor recreational activities illustrates the more detailed information available in these documents and the need for further research.

Hunting and Other Recreational Activities

How does hunting compare to other outdoor recreation activities presented in the 1995 TORP Assessment and Policy Plan? Tables 12.1–12.6 show the percentage of the population participating in outdoor recreation activities for the year 1994, including hunting, nonconsumptive uses of wildlife, and other recreational activities recreationists may participate in along with wildlife-related activities. Data are presented for persons in Texas and the Texas market region (Texas, Arkansas, Louisiana, Oklahoma, and New Mexico) ages 16 years and older

Table 12.1. PARTICIPATION IN OUTDOOR RECREATION ACTIVITIES BY TEXAS RESIDENTS, AGE 16 AND OLDER, IN 1994

Rank	Activity	Percentage of population participating	Millions of participants
1	Walking	65	8.9
2	Visit the beach	61	8.4
3	Family gathering	60	8.2
4	Sightseeing	55	7.5
5	Visit outdoor nature museums or zoos	47	6.4
6	Picnicking	45	6.2
7	Swimming in nonpool	37	5.1
8	Visit visitors centers	35	4.8
9	Camping	30	4.1
10	Viewing/photographing other wildlife	30	4.1
11	Freshwater fishing	28	3.8
12	Boating	28	3.8
13	Running/jogging	27	3.7
14	Watching or photographing birds	25	3.4
15	Bicycling	25	3.4
16	View nature in a water-based surrounding	24	3.3
17	Hiking	18	2.5
18	Off-road riding	17	2.3
19	Fish viewing or photographing	13	1.8
20	Hunting	12	1.6
21	Saltwater fishing	12	1.6
22	Horseback riding	8	1.1

Sources: Adapted by DeLoney and Eley, Consumer Research, TPWD 1996 from K. Cordell et al., 1995, Texas and the Texas Market Region: A Special Report Based on the Data from the National Survey on Recreation and the Environment 1994–95, USDA Forest Service, Outdoor Recreation and Wilderness Assessment Group, Southern Research Station, Athens, Ga., 132 pp.; Texas State Data Center 1995. Database submitted by Texas A & M University, Department of Rural Sociology, College Station, Texas.

Note: To calculate millions of participants, Texas State Data Center population figures for population age 16 and older, 13,691,083, were used (74.5% of total 1994 population, which was 18,378,185). Millions of participants = % of population participating × 13,691,083.

Table 12.2. PARTICIPATION IN OUTDOOR RECREATION ACTIVITIES BY TEXAS RESIDENTS, AGE 16 AND OLDER, IN 1994, BY AGE GROUP

Activity	Percentage of population participating by age group			
	16 & over	16–29	30–49	50 & over
Walking	65	75	68	54
Visit the beach	61	68	67	47
Family gathering	60	66	66	48
Sightseeing	55	57	60	48
Visit outdoor nature museums or zoos	47	49	54	36
Picnicking	45	44	53	35
Swimming in nonpool	37	45	41	24
Visit visitors centers	35	36	40	28
Camping	30	37	35	18
Viewing/photographing other wildlife	30	26	35	26
Freshwater fishing	28	25	36	21
Boating	28	34	31	20
Running/jogging	27	51	23	10
Watching or photographing birds	25	17	27	30
Bicycling	25	34	28	12
View nature in a water-based surrounding	24	20	32	17
Hiking	18	29	19	7
Off-road driving	17	21	16	12
Viewing or photographing fish	13	8	18	12
Hunting	12	17	12	9
Saltwater fishing	12	14	13	8
Horseback riding	8	16	8	1

Source: Adapted by DeLoney, Consumer Research, TPWD 1996 from K. Cordell et al., 1995, Texas and the Texas Market Region: A Special Report Based on the Data from the National Survey on Recreation and the Environment 1994–95, USDA Forest Service, Outdoor Recreation and Wilderness Assessment Group, Southern Research Station, Athens, Ga., 132 pp.

Table 12.3. PARTICIPATION IN OUTDOOR RECREATION ACTIVITIES BY TEXAS RESIDENTS, AGE 16 AND OLDER, IN 1994, BY LEVEL OF EDUCATION

Activity	College grad	High school, technical school, or some college	Some high school
Walking	72	65	49
Visit the beach	66	59	54
Family gathering	64	61	49
Sightseeing	67	56	23
Visit outdoor nature museums or zoos	55	46	31
Picnicking	52	45	28
Swimming in nonpool	42	34	34
Visit visitors centers	44	35	17
Camping	22	34	35
Viewing/photographing other wildlife	33	30	19
Freshwater fishing	24	37	39
Boating	30	29	25
Running/jogging	26	24	36
Watching or photographing birds	32	23	16
Bicycling	23	25	29
View nature in a water-based surrounding	31	23	10
Hiking	17	20	15
Off-road driving	12	18	23
Viewing or photographing fish	13	14	7
Hunting	8	14	18
Saltwater fishing	12	12	9
Horseback riding	7	8	14

Source: Adapted by DeLoney, Consumer Research, TPWD 1996 from K. Cordell et al., 1995, Texas and the Texas Market Region: A Special Report Based on the Data from the National Survey on Recreation and the Environment 1994–95, USDA Forest Service, Outdoor Recreation and Wilderness Assessment Group, Southern Research Station, Athens, Ga., 132 pp.

Table 12.4. PARTICIPATION IN OUTDOOR RECREATION ACTIVITIES BY TEXAS RESIDENTS, AGE 16 AND OLDER, IN 1994, BY GENDER AND RACE

Activity	Percentage of population participating by			
	Gender		Race	
	Male	Female	Caucasian	Non-Caucasian
Walking	65	66	67	54
Visit the beach	65	57	62	55
Family gathering	64	57	62	51
Sightseeing	56	54	57	42
Visit outdoor nature museums or zoos	46	48	49	33
Picnicking	42	48	47	38
Swimming in nonpool	43	32	40	20
Visit visitors centers	36	35	37	23
Camping	36	25	33	17
Viewing/photographing other wildlife	27	32	32	16
Freshwater fishing	35	22	30	17
Boating	33	24	31	12
Running/jogging	32	22	25	42
Watching or photographing birds	21	29	25	24
Bicycling	29	22	26	21
View nature in a water-based surrounding	22	25	25	15
Hiking	22	15	21	2
Off-road driving	21	12	18	7
Viewing or photographing fish	14	12	12	15
Hunting	21	5	13	5
Saltwater fishing	18	6	12	8
Horseback riding	9	8	9	1

Source: Adapted by DeLoney, Consumer Research, TPWD 1996 from K. Cordell et al., 1995, Texas and the Texas Market Region: A Special Report Based on the Data from the National Survey on Recreation and the Environment 1994–95, USDA Forest Service, Outdoor Recreation and Wilderness Assessment Group, Southern Research Station, Athens, Ga., 132 pp.

Table 12.5. PARTICIPATION IN OUTDOOR RECREATION ACTIVITIES BY TEXAS RESIDENTS, AGE 16 AND OLDER, IN 1994, BY ANNUAL FAMILY INCOME

Activity	Percentage of population participating by annual family income		
	Under $25,000	$25,000–$50,000	Over $50,000
Walking	58	72	65
Visit the beach	49	66	63
Family gathering	48	64	64
Sightseeing	45	59	57
Visit outdoor nature museums or zoos	32	59	52
Picnicking	38	51	45
Swimming in nonpool	28	36	41
Visit visitors centers	*	*	*
Camping	28	37	28
Viewing/photographing other wildlife	20	34	31
Freshwater fishing	24	34	27
Boating	17	29	33
Running/jogging	21	27	29
Watching or photographing birds	24	23	26
Bicycling	12	30	27
View nature in a water-based surrounding	15	29	24
Hiking	17	21	17
Off-road driving	13	16	18
Viewing or photographing fish	8	14	14
Hunting	8	15	12
Saltwater fishing	5	13	14
Horseback riding	7	5	11

Source: Adapted by DeLoney, Consumer Research, TPWD 1996 from K. Cordell et al., 1995, Texas and the Texas Market Region: A Special Report Based on the Data from the National Survey on Recreation and the Environment 1994–95, USDA Forest Service, Outdoor Recreation and Wilderness Assessment Group, Southern Research Station, Athens, Ga., 132 pp.

* Figures for this activity are not available.

**Table 12.6. PARTICIPATION IN OUTDOOR RECREATION
ACTIVITIES BY TEXAS RESIDENTS, AGE 16 AND
OLDER, IN 1994, BY NUMBER OF PEOPLE
IN HOUSEHOLD**

Activity	Percentage of population participating by number of people in household			
	One	Two	Three	Four & over
Walking	61	64	69	67
Visit the beach	46	56	70	70
Family gathering	47	60	64	66
Sightseeing	44	55	60	59
Visit outdoor nature museums or zoos	35	37	62	57
Picnicking	38	43	47	52
Swimming in nonpool	25	31	52	42
Visit visitors centers	26	32	35	46
Camping	23	25	34	39
Viewing/photographing other wildlife	21	29	35	31
Freshwater fishing	17	24	38	35
Boating	23	27	35	30
Running/jogging	25	18	35	33
Watching or photographing birds	19	32	24	20
Bicycling	15	20	33	32
View nature in a water-based surrounding	18	24	24	27
Hiking	18	12	19	24
Off-road driving	14	15	16	21
Viewing or photographing fish	10	12	16	13
Hunting	9	11	16	13
Saltwater fishing	7	12	14	13
Horseback riding	10	5	9	10

*Source: Adapted by DeLoney, Consumer Research, TPWD 1996 from K. Cordell et al., 1995, Texas
and the Texas Market Region: A Special Report Based on the Data from the National Survey on
Recreation and the Environment 1994–95, USDA Forest Service, Outdoor Recreation and Wilderness Assessment Group, Southern Research Station, Athens, Ga., 132 pp.*

for the entire population, by age group, by level of education, by race and gender, by family income, and by number of people in the household.

Hunting ranks below all nonconsumptive wildlife activities measured. For example, 30% of the population aged 16 years and older report participation in viewing/photographing other wildlife compared to 12% for hunting. Further, nonconsumptive uses of wildlife may occur while outdoor recreationists are participating in other recreational activities such as walking, visiting the beach, and sightseeing. Duda et al. (1996) report that "the percentage of hunters in the U.S. has remained stable between 1980 and 1990." Recent statistics on hunting show its growth to be rather stable in Texas while the nonconsumptive wildlife activities are increasing in popularity.

When the popularity of recreational activities is measured by the average number of trips and the average number of days of participation, nonconsumptive wildlife activities are even more significant. Of the 23 activities shown in Table 12.7, 2 nonconsumptive wildlife activities are ranked second and third by the average number of days of participation per year—watching/photographing birds and viewing/photographing wildlife, respectively. Differences between hunting and nonconsumptive uses of wildlife may be attributed to the higher proportion of the population participating in the nonconsumptive activities and the limited number of hunting days available during the hunting seasons.

Participation in wildlife recreation activities, other than fishing or hunting, while participating in other outdoor recreation activities is shown in Table 12.8 for persons who did not participate in either fishing or hunting. Recreationists participate in wildlife recreation activities in significant numbers while participating in other activities. This finding has implications for the providers of picnicking, hiking, camping or backpacking, scenic driving or sightseeing, and water-related activities. Clearly, providers of these opportunities, particularly at public parks with large natural resource bases, should note this relationship.

Wildlife Management Issues

A chapter in the 1995 TORP APP titled "Public Opinions on Land Management Issues, Wildlife Values, and Wilderness Values" was written by this author to present information which could be used by the Texas Parks and Wildlife Department staff in their effort to make "wildlife management areas" managed by the department more acces-

Table 12.7. PARTICIPATION IN OUTDOOR RECREATION ACTIVITIES BY PEOPLE IN THE TEXAS MARKET REGION IN 1994, AVERAGE NUMBER OF TRIPS AND AVERAGE NUMBER OF DAYS BY ACTIVITY

(per total number of respondents)

Activity	Average number of days	Average number of trips
Walking	63.5	N/A
Watching/photographing birds	29.2	3.6
Viewing/photographing wildlife	14.0	3.2
Visit the beach	10.4	4.8
Sightseeing	9.9	4.3
Bicycling	8.4	2.1
Freshwater fishing	6.2	4.1
Family gathering	5.4	3.8
Motorboating	4.5	1.7
View nature/water-based surrounding	4.2	0.9
Picnicking	4.0	2.4
Swimming in nonpool	3.5	1.4
Hiking	3.2	1.3
Off-road driving	3.0	1.7
Camping (developed area)	2.0	1.0
Camping (primitive area)	1.7	1.0
Hunting small game	1.1	0.8
Hunting big game	1.1	0.7
Rafting/tubing/floating	0.3	0.2
Hunting migratory birds	0.3	0.3
Saltwater fishing	0.2	0.2
Sailing	0.1	0.1
Canoeing	0.1	0.1

Source: Adapted by DeLoney, Consumer Research, TPWD 1996 from K. Cordell et al., 1995, Texas and the Texas Market Region: A Special Report Based on the Data from the National Survey on Recreation and the Environment 1994–95, USDA Forest Service, Outdoor Recreation and Wilderness Assessment Group, Southern Research Station, Athens, Ga., 132 pp.

Note: Sample size for certain activities for Texas residents was too small; therefore, Texas market region respondents were analyzed. Some activities included in Tables 1–6 are excluded from this table because data were not collected.

Table 12.8. PARTICIPATION IN WILDLIFE RECREATION ACTIVITIES (OTHER THAN FISHING OR HUNTING) WHILE PARTICIPATING IN OUTDOOR RECREATION ACTIVITIES (percentage of respondents)

Other outdoor recreation activities	Response	
	Yes	No
Scenic driving or sightseeing	92	8
Picnicking	68	30
Backyard activities	65	35
Day hiking	59	41
Camping or backpacking	59	41
Water activities	46	51
Other	14	84

Source: Adapted by DeLoney, Consumer Research, TPWD 1996 from K. Cordell et al., 1995, Texas and the Texas Market Region: A Special Report Based on the Data from the National Survey on Recreation and the Environment 1994–95, USDA Forest Service, Outdoor Recreation and Wilderness Assessment Group, Southern Research Station, Athens, Ga., 132 pp.

Note: Percentage totals may not equal 100 due to missing responses and rounding to whole numbers.

sible to nonconsumptive users. Information in that chapter is based on the National Survey on Recreation and the Environment conducted by the USDA Forest Service. This information has important implications for decision makers addressing the issue of making departmental wildlife management areas more accessible and illustrates the importance of the TORP as a resource for information on wildlife issues. Examples which follow illustrate the usefulness of data found in the 1995 TORP.

Citizens in the Texas market region were asked their opinions on 4 wildlife management issues shown in Table 12.9. Eighty-eight percent agreed that encountering wildlife during an outdoor recreation trip made them more satisfied with the trip. Eighty-one percent agreed that "the opportunity to view wildlife and/or fish in a natural setting is important in my selection of outdoor recreation sites." Almost 71% agreed that they would contribute time, money, or both to an organization that works to improve the quality of wetlands, streams, and lakes, even if the results of this activity may not be observed for 5–10 years. Another 64% preferred to have interpretive signs or other infor-

Table 12.9. CITIZENS IN THE TEXAS MARKET REGION OPINIONS ON WILDLIFE MANAGEMENT ISSUES IN 1994 (percentage of respondents)

Wildlife management issue	SA	A	D	SD	Totals A	Totals D
When I encounter wildlife during an outdoor recreation trip, it always makes me more satisfied with the trip.	27	61	6	1	88	7
The opportunity to view wildlife and/or fish in a natural setting is important in my selection of outdoor recreation sites.	20	61	14	1	81	16
If asked, I would contribute time, money, or both to an organization that works to improve the quality of wetlands, streams, and lakes, even if the results of this activity may not be observed for 5–10 years.	11	59	19	3	71	22
I prefer to look for wildlife where there are interpretive signs or other information sources to answer any questions I may have.	10	54	27	3	64	30

SA = Strongly Agree   A = Agree   D = Disagree   SD = Strongly Disagree

Source: Adapted by DeLoney, Consumer Research, TPWD 1996 from K. Cordell et al., 1995, Texas and the Texas Market Region: A Special Report Based on the Data from the National Survey on Recreation and the Environment 1994–95, USDA Forest Service, Outdoor Recreation and Wilderness Assessment Group, Southern Research Station, Athens, Ga., 132 pp.

Note: Percentage totals may not equal 100 due to missing responses and rounding to whole numbers.

mation sources to enhance their experience, while a surprising 30% disagreed with this statement. This finding may have implications for market segmentation of visitors to public wildlife management areas in Texas and provisions to meet their needs when visiting these areas (DeLoney et al. 1996).

Tables 12.10 and 12.11 deal with present opinions of citizens in the Texas market regions on resource management and wilderness issues. Ninety-three percent agreed that "public outdoor recreation areas must continue to be maintained in order to better serve the public." Ninety percent agreed that they use on-site signs and maps to get the most out of a visit to an outdoor recreation area, while 78% use off-site signs. Contrary, 51% disagreed that the government should allow more pri-

Table 12.10. CITIZENS IN THE TEXAS MARKET REGION OPINIONS ON RESOURCE MANAGEMENT ISSUES IN 1994 (percentage of respondents)

Resource management issue	Strongly agree	Agree	Disagree	Strongly disagree
Public outdoor recreation areas must continue to be maintained in order to better serve the public.	31	62	6	1
I typically use on-site signs and maps to get the most out of a visit to an outdoor recreation area.	22	68	5	6
I typically use off-site signs and maps to get the most out of a visit to an outdoor recreation area.	13	65	12	10
The United States has a responsibility to share its scientific knowledge in resource management practices with developing countries.	18	58	11	14
Management of the nation's natural resources is well balanced between resource use and resource protection.	6	58	18	18
Government agencies are constantly improving natural resource management practices through application of scientific research findings.	4	51	18	27
The government should allow more privately operated commercial recreation development such as ski resorts, boat rentals, or food concessions on public lands.	8	41	18	33

Source: Adapted by DeLoney, Consumer Research, TPWD 1996 from K. Cordell et al., 1995, Texas and the Texas Market Region: A Special Report Based on the Data from the National Survey on Recreation and the Environment 1994–95, USDA Forest Service, Outdoor Recreation and Wilderness Assessment Group, Southern Research Station, Athens, Ga., 132 pp.

Note: Percentage totals may not equal 100 due to missing responses and rounding to whole numbers.

Table 12.11. RELATIVE IMPORTANCE OF THE VALUES OF WILDERNESS ISSUES TO CITIZENS IN THE TEXAS MARKET REGION IN 1994

Wilderness issue value statement	Percentage of respondents rating each value				
	EI	VI	I	SI	NI
Protecting water quality	52	21	22	2	0
Knowing future generations will have wilderness areas	48	26	20	3	<1
Providing recreation opportunities	23	26	41	5	1
Protecting wildlife habitat	47	23	23	2	1
Providing spiritual inspiration	26	17	37	9	7
Preservation of natural areas for scientific study	19	24	43	6	5
Preserving unique plants, animal ecosystems, and genetic strains	31	19	34	7	3
Knowing that the option exists in the future to visit a wilderness area of my choice	35	23	28	3	6
Protecting air quality	49	23	23	<1	3
Providing income for the tourist industry	9	19	35	17	15
Protecting rare and endangered species	37	29	22	3	4
Providing scenic beauty	33	19	37	7	2
Just knowing that wilderness and primitive areas exist	35	23	40	3	<1

EI = Extremely Important   VI = Very Important   I = Important
SI = Slightly Important   NI = Not At All Important

Source: Adapted by DeLoney, Consumer Research, TPWD 1996 from K. Cordell et al., 1995, Texas and the Texas Market Region: A Special Report Based on the Data from the National Survey on Recreation and the Environment 1994–95, USDA Forest Service, Outdoor Recreation and Wilderness Assessment Group, Southern Research Station, Athens, Ga., 132 pp.

Note: Percentage totals may not equal 100 due to missing responses and rounding to whole numbers.

Table 12.12. POSSIBLE FEATURES WHICH WOULD ENHANCE WILDLIFE-RELATED RECREATION ACTIVITY PARTICIPATION
(percentage of respondents)

Feature	Yes	No
Brochures or maps	86	11
Maintained trails	84	14
Signs or displays	81	16
Visitors center	70	27
Guided tours	57	41

Source: Adapted by DeLoney, Consumer Research, TPWD 1996 from K. Cordell et al., 1995, Texas and the Texas Market Region: A Special Report Based on the Data from the National Survey on Recreation and the Environment 1994–95, USDA Forest Service, Outdoor Recreation and Wilderness Assessment Group, Southern Research Station, Athens, Ga., 132 pp.

Note: Percentage totals may not equal 100 due to missing responses and rounding to whole numbers.

vately operated commercial recreation development on public lands. While these and other findings in themselves should not be the sole basis for decisions made by the department on the issue of accessibility to wildlife management areas managed by the department, the department should certainly take the citizens' opinions into account. Since the policy decision has been made to make the wildlife management areas more accessible to the public, the most important question to the department now may be how the department provides this access, given citizens' opinions on these issues.

Table 12.12 lists the features reported by citizens which would enhance their participation in wildlife-related recreation activities. Features less intrusive to the environment when provided (brochures or maps, 86%; maintained trails, 84%; signs or displays, 81%) were more popular with citizens than visitors centers (70%). Guided tours (57%) were the feature least desired of the five features listed.

Would recreationists engage in travel to visit wildlife management areas in Texas? Forty-one percent report that they do plan trips specifically to participate in outdoor recreation activities in primitive areas, and 40% reported that they had visited a primitive area in the last 12 months. Of those who visited a primitive area in the last 12 months,

Table 12.13. COST RESPONSIBILITY FOR THE PROVISION OF SERVICES PROVIDED ON PUBLIC LANDS (percentage of respondents)

Service	User fees	Taxes	Both user fees & taxes	Don't provide service
Boat ramps	52	18	23	0
Special exhibits and presentations	45	14	34	0
Campgrounds	42	14	41	0
Visitors centers	38	24	38	0
Trails	36	24	34	<1
Picnic areas	32	33	32	<1
Parking areas	31	34	32	0
Historical sites	25	35	34	1
Other facilities	23	16	40	1
Rest rooms	18	42	35	0

Source: Adapted by DeLoney, Consumer Research, TPWD 1996 from K. Cordell et al., 1995, Texas and the Texas Market Region: A Special Report Based on the Data from the National Survey on Recreation and the Environment 1994–95, USDA Forest Service, Outdoor Recreation and Wilderness Assessment Group, Southern Research Station, Athens, Ga., 132 pp.

Note: Percentage totals may not equal 100 due to missing responses and rounding to whole numbers.

61% spent 10 days or less, while 32% spent 11 days or more (DeLoney et al. 1996). These findings present statistical evidence that people would visit wildlife management areas made accessible to the general public.

Perhaps the ultimate question for a public agency such as the Texas Parks and Wildlife Department is what services citizens want on public lands and how they view the cost responsibility for these services. Table 12.13 records citizens' views on costs for services which may be typically provided on wildlife management areas. Sources of costs assessed were user fees, taxes, or both user fees and taxes. Almost no one felt that these services should not be provided. A follow-up on these findings with more in-depth research, such as focus groups, could amplify citizens' preferences, giving the department even more justification for important decisions.

Conclusions

Although the 1995 Texas Outdoor Recreation Plan and related research documents address outdoor recreation, findings presented in the documents serve as a valuable resource for those responsible for wildlife management planning and decision making. Given the trend toward increased participation in the nonconsumptive wildlife uses as recreational activities, wildlife resource and recreation planners should cooperate on future research. Studying research findings in the 1995 TORP and related documents could provide valuable directions for more in-depth research. If conducted cooperatively among wildlife resource and recreation planners, research resources could be better utilized to conserve Texas's valuable natural resources to meet the needs of all Texans and our visitors.

Literature Cited

Cordell, K., et al. 1995. Texas and the Texas market region: A special report based on the data from the national survey on recreation and the environment 1994–95. USDA Forest Service, Outdoor Recreation and Wilderness Assessment Group, Southern Research Station, Athens, Ga. 132 pp.

DeLoney, J. A., et al. 1996. 1995 TORP assessment and policy plan. Consumer Research, Tex. Parks and Wildl. Dep., Austin. 194 pp.

Eley, R. E., et al. 1996. 1995 TORP open project selection process—an addendum to the assessment and policy plan. Consumer Research, Tex. Parks and Wildl. Dep., Austin. 14 pp.

Texas Parks and Wildlife Department. 1987. Recreational issues in Texas: A citizen survey—the technical report. Comprehensive Planning Branch, Tex. Parks and Wildl. Dep., Austin. 19 pp.

Texas State Data Center. 1995. Database submitted by Texas A & M Univ., Dep. of Rural Sociology, College Station.

IV. WILDLIFE MANAGEMENT AND RESEARCH

Ted L. Clark (retired)
Wildlife Division, Texas Parks
and Wildlife Department
Austin, TX 78744

13. Wildlife Management Programs, Goals, and Issues: The State Perspective, 1990

Abstract: In discharging its responsibility for the conservation of wildlife resources, the Wildlife Division, Texas Parks and Wildlife Department, utilizes the species management concept. The species concept provides for the comprehensive needs of the resources from a statewide perspective according to predetermined management goals and objectives. The management concept is administered through a category program director and several species program leaders, operational regional directors, and field biologists. Individual species programs and pertinent conservation issues are discussed.

This chapter is a companion to a paper prepared by the author which addressed the status of wildlife resources and their management from the state perspective as of 1980. I have updated the original by presenting similar data relative to the period 1981–90 (a contribution of Texas Federal Aid in Wildlife Restoration Project W-129-M). The information presented is my perspective as of the spring of 1990 and was taken from various federal aid and administrative reports, planning documents, resource data sets, and personal communications supplied by the staff of the Wildlife Division, Texas Parks and Wildlife Department (TPWD).

The opinions expressed and the conclusions drawn from analysis of these data are solely those of the author based on extensive experience and knowledge gained during more than 35 years' service with the TPWD as a researcher/manager/administrator of the wildlife resources of Texas.

The TPWD is the agency of state government delegated specific responsibility and authority for the conservation of statutory wildlife resources. The Wildlife Division is responsible for the department's regulatory, management, and research activities of the terrestrial vertebrate wildlife resources. The goal of the Wildlife Division is the conservation of all wildlife resources along sound biological lines for the public's common benefit. To accomplish this goal, the objectives of the division are (1) to conduct a program of applied research directed at the solution of wildlife problems, (2) to promote a sound program of wildlife conservation based upon prior research, and (3) to maximize recreational opportunity through improved methods of wildlife production and conservation.

The programmatic method is embodied in the species management concept. This concept is perceived to have several distinct advantages over the area concept of management, which it replaced. The species concept has its greatest advantage in more adequately providing for the comprehensive needs of the resource. It also results in the singular pursuit of established management goals and objectives. Furthermore, the concept looks at all wildlife programs from a statewide perspective and attempts to meet resource needs on a priority basis. The species management concept is administered through a category program director and several species program leaders who coordinate activities for a species or group of species, through operational regional directors, and subsequently field biologists. It is through this administrative chain that our field personnel work on the various species programs. All of the work is aimed at accomplishing a species project objective within a specified time period as detailed in annual operation plans.

Programs

Big Game

The Big Game Program encompasses management of 7 species of mammals designated by statute as game animals. These species are white-tailed deer, mule deer, pronghorn, collared peccary, aoudad sheep, bighorn sheep, and elk. The black bear, previously included in this program, was transferred to the Nongame Program in 1987 when this species was removed from game status. In 1981 elk were classified as game animals only in those counties west of the Pecos River; however, this was expanded to include 6 counties in the northwestern Panhandle in 1987. Big game species are quite diverse in terms of numbers, distribution, habitat requirements, and public esteem, necessitating a variety of management philosophies and approaches.

White-tailed Deer. The white-tailed deer continues to be the leading game species in the state in terms of hunting recreation and is the most widely distributed and numerous of the big game species. The 1981 estimate placed the population at approximately 3 million animals with the species being most abundant, in order, in the Edwards Plateau, South Texas Brush Country, Post Oak Savannah, East Texas Forests, and Cross Timbers and Prairies ecological regions, which collectively accounted for almost 93% of the total. The population had increased to about 3.3 million by 1990 with these same ecological regions collectively harboring over 94% of the total population. For the 10-year period 1981–90, the population increased by 66 and 42% in the East Texas Forests and Cross Timbers and Prairies, respectively, while the population declined by 3% in the South Texas Plains. In 1990, the Edwards Plateau continued to be the dominant area for white-tailed deer, supporting approximately ½ of the herd. With respect to white-tail numbers, the Edwards Plateau was followed, in order of importance, by the South Texas Brush Country, East Texas Forests, Cross Timbers and Prairies, and Post Oak Savannah. In 1981 and 1990, respectively, 533,130 and 562,477 hunters harvested 300,052 and 429,532 whitetails, expending 3.7 and 5.2 million days of hunting effort. It is noteworthy that both the harvest and number of hunters achieved all-time highs of 504,953 and 567,344 during the hunting season of 1987–88.

Since 1981, the white-tail population, annual harvest, and total hunter days have all shown a significant increase. There were highly significant increases in the populations in the East Texas Forests and Cross Timbers and Prairies ecological regions. Concomitantly, in these two regions there has been a substantial increase in the harvest (107 and 66%) and hunter days (49 and 38%) while the number of hunters has increased only slightly (12 and 13%), respectively.

Statewide total harvest increased from 300,052, composed of 76% bucks and 24% antlerless in 1981 to 429,532, composed of 56% bucks and 44% antlerless in 1990. Between the referenced periods total harvest increased 43%, with approximately 90% of the increase occurring in the antlerless segment.

Deer management on a statewide level continues to be accomplished largely through regulations governing length of hunting seasons, bag limits, and harvest methods. With such a large deer population and the relatively moderate hunting pressure applied to it, these regulations can be rather liberal. In 1981, a gun hunting season of 51 days and an archery only season of 30 days, with a bag limit of 3 deer, was considered the standard by department biologists. Antlerless deer were available for harvest under an antlerless deer permit system in 96 counties and by hunter choice (either-sex) system in 15 counties. Hunting regulations continued to be liberalized during the decade of the 1980's, and by 1990 the standard gun hunting season was 65 days and archery only was 30 days in duration, with a bag limit of 4 white-tails. Antlerless deer were now available for harvest under an antlerless deer permit system in 38 counties and by either-sex regulations in 138 counties.

The goal of the white-tailed deer project is to improve the quality of the resource and to increase the public's deer-hunting opportunities. The department continued to supply the tools to accomplish this goal by progressively liberalizing hunting regulations but until the decade of the 1980's was largely unsuccessful in achieving it, due primarily to Texas landowners' control of access to the resource and their reluctance to apply management practices that would significantly alter population levels, their composition, and their condition.

In 1981, it was felt that for the department to achieve its goal there would have to be a significant change in deer harvest systems on privately owned land which would allow more hunters access to the resource. Additionally, most of the increased hunting pressure would have to be directed at the antlerless segment of the population, which was and is greatly underutilized. At the same time the landowner would have to become more knowledgeable of deer habitat requirements and the necessity of providing ample forage and cover on a year-round basis.

By 1990 the department had made a quantum leap in achieving the goals of the white-tailed deer program. During the 1980's there was indeed a significant change in harvest systems on private and public lands of the state. Although the number of white-tail hunters has increased only 5.5%, from 533,130 in 1981 to 562,477 in 1990, hunter days have increased 40.3%, from 3,713,942 (6.97 per hunter) to 5,211,184 (9.26 per hunter).

The annual harvest rate relative to the deer population increased from about 10% in 1981 to 13% in 1990. Most of this increase can be attributed to the increase in the take of antlerless deer. The taking of antlerless deer was first authorized in 1953 when 946 were taken in Kerr and Mason Counties. The annual antlerless harvest increased very slowly and did not exceed 100,000 until 1984 but reached more than 200,000 only 3 years later. For the period 1981–90 the annual buck harvest has ranged from 227,400 in 1981 to 294,100 in 1987 and has averaged about 255,000 annually.

By the mid-1980's there was a dramatic change in landowner attitudes toward deer management, especially as related to population control. Landowners finally embraced what wildlife biologists had been espousing for more than 50 years: the welfare of the deer on their land is a direct product of proper habitat management.

In 1981, the department spent about $643,000 annually on white-tailed deer, not including technical guidance and law enforcement. Of this, $513,000 was spent on management-oriented activities. The remaining $130,000 was spent on applied research, which is directed at improving the department's management capability. By 1990 the Wildlife Division had actually reduced its expenditures on white-tails to approximately $440,000, of which about $68,900 was spent on research and the remainder expended on management activities.

In 1981 I stated, "The long-term future of the white-tailed deer in Texas is not bright, although present population levels will probably persist through this decade. It is apparent, however, that habitat degradation and urban encroachment have begun to take their toll." Obviously my assessment of the white-tailed deer situation was overly pessimistic, born of 25 years of frustrating efforts at bringing about improvements of the public resource which was dependent upon habitat quality controlled by the private sector. Never in my 35-year professional career have I seen the public in general and private landowners in particular more receptive to the principles of sound wildlife management. This bodes well for the future.

Mule Deer. Although the range of the Rocky Mountain mule deer may extend into the northwestern Panhandle, virtually all mule deer in Texas are of the smaller desert subspecies. Desert mule deer are found in a semiarid environment comprised of a mosaic of habitat types from desert shrub at the lowest elevations, through semidesert shrub/grasslands, chaparral, mountain shrub, woodland, and some forest at the highest elevations. Habitats generally receive 20 inches or less of precipitation annually. Much of this erratic precipitation occurs in the form of brief thundershowers falling on bare ground, resulting in rapid runoff with little moisture retained in the soil.

Mule deer currently occupy approximately 23 million acres in the Trans-Pecos, Edwards Plateau, High Plains, and Rolling Plains ecological regions. The population in the Trans-Pecos is largely continuous and is contiguous with mule deer in the western Edwards Plateau which are largely confined to the Pecos River drainage. In the Panhandle they occur in disjunct populations in conjunction with the rolling hills and canyons associated with the breaks and tributaries of the Brazos, Canadian, and Red Rivers and the Caprock Escarpment. The Trans-Pecos populations are largely endemic, those in the western Edwards Plateau emigrated from the Trans-Pecos, and the department's transplanting of mule deer from the Trans-Pecos is largely responsible for the established Panhandle populations.

Most of the occupied range is thought to be at carrying capacity. Populations during the period 1981–90 have fluctuated between 150,000 and 250,000, of which approximately 90% occur in the Trans-Pecos and western Edwards Plateau, with the remainder occurring in the High and Rolling Plains of the Texas Panhandle. There is significant potential mule deer habitat that is either deficient in broodstock or on which habitat improvement and/or predator control would result in substantially higher populations. Lack of water is a major limiting factor on much of this potential range.

Demand for mule deer hunting is high, and the resource could sustain a significantly greater harvest; however, access to the resource is limited by its occurrence on privately owned land. The annual harvest in recent years represents only 2% of the mule deer population and is composed almost entirely of bucks. The annual buck kill by hunters represents an average harvest rate of about 9% of this segment of the population. This conservative harvest is possibly due to the decision of many landowners to accommodate a limited number of hunters to harvest only mature bucks, thereby maximizing economic return per deer harvested.

During the period 1981–90 the annual harvest of mule deer ranged from a low of 3,100 in 1983 to a high of 7,300 in 1988 and averaged 5,460. Hunter numbers ranged between 13,000 and 20,500. In 1988 the traditional 9-day hunting season was increased to 16 days at the urging of some landowners, outfitters, and hunters in the Trans-Pecos desiring more time to implement their harvest strategies. There was widespread opposition to the longer season coming primarily from Trans-Pecos landowners, who contended that the mule deer harvest would be substantially increased during the longer season, which they deemed detrimental. Although inconclusive, there has been an increasing trend in the numbers of hunters and hunter days as well as the percentage of bucks harvested since the season was lengthened by 1 week. There are no solid data to indicate this trend is adversely impacting the mule deer population as a whole.

Hybridization and competition with white-tailed deer, high predator populations, drought, nutrition problems, and possible competition with domestic and other wild ungulates have been implicated as negatively impacting mule deer populations in the Trans-Pecos. Current census data indicate high fawn mortality, the causes of which are not documented. Mortality and survivorship information on the adult segment of the population is equally lacking. Relevant data are needed on population dynamics and habitat preferences of desert mule deer in the Trans-Pecos region to establish models which can be used to project population trends for use in making sound management decisions. Historically, habitat use and preference of desert mule deer have not been investigated with the accuracy and precision afforded by current technology in radio telemetry and computer applications. The need for sound harvest regulations and flexible herd and habitat management that is responsive to changing ecological conditions is paramount to the sustained use of the resource.

The department's management activities for mule deer are similar to those for white-tails and accounted for an annual expenditure of $64,000 in 1981 compared to $208,000 in 1990, of which more than $122,000 was attributed to research of population dynamics and habitat preference of desert mule deer in the Trans-Pecos region.

Pronghorn. Historically, 2 subspecies of pronghorn are reported to be endemic to Texas: *Antilocapra americana americana* and *A. a. mexicana.* The subspecies *americana* occurred in the Texas Panhandle with *mexicana* occupying the remainder of the range in the state. Pronghorn occurred as far east as the 97th meridian, and their numbers probably exceeded 1 million. By 1903 the occupied range had diminished to the western ⅓ of the state, and the Texas Legislature closed the hunting season. The state's pronghorn population was estimated at only 2,400 in 1924, most of which occurred in the Trans-Pecos ecological region.

As a result of protection, the population decline was halted, and herds gradually began to increase. In 1939, the department initiated a restocking program which through 1980 had resulted in the trapping and transplanting of 5,548 pronghorns to suitable habitat in Texas. For the 10-year period 1981–90 an additional 736 pronghorns were transplanted within the state.

During 1980–90, pronghorn occupied about 13.5 million acres in the Trans-Pecos, High Plains, Rolling Plains, and Edwards Plateau ecological regions. During this period, the population ranged between 12,000 and 26,000 and averaged 19,460, with about 70% occurring in the Trans-Pecos and 10% in each of the other 3 ecological regions.

Pronghorn hunting regulations are rather restrictive; the hunting season is limited to 9 days, with a bag limit of 1 by special permit issued by the department. Virtually all pronghorn occur on private property. Although hunter access is closely controlled, approximately 90% of the huntable population is open to hunting annually.

For the period 1981–90 between 918 and 2,588 hunting permits were issued annually. Harvests have been as low as 538 in 1983 and as high as 1,017 in 1987. Virtually all of the annual harvest is comprised of bucks. An average of only 42% of the permits issued were used with an average hunter success of 93%. Permit utilization is relatively low, possibly due to the decision of many landowners to harvest only mature bucks, escalation of access fees charged by landowners, and the distance of the pronghorn range from major population centers.

Restocking has been an important management activity for pronghorns for over 50 years but will be substantially reduced in the future. This change in management philosophy has been brought about by (1) poor success of restoration efforts outside the Trans-Pecos, (2) difficulty in obtaining sufficient suitable broodstock, (3) difficulty in capturing broodstock, which is very labor intensive and expensive, and (4) a paucity of suitable restoration sites which can support viable populations. Virtually all of the Trans-Pecos range is fully stocked. Restoration efforts in the Permian Basin and Panhandle have been largely unsuccessful in meeting restoration objectives. Normally a single stocking of 40 pronghorn (preferably in a ratio of 3 : 1 does to bucks) have been released on a restoration site, but due to trapping and natural mortality, this appears to be insufficient. Even the release into Gray County in 1990 of 94 animals obtained from Utah has been judged a failure. Currently, the only acceptable capture technique is the hazing of animals by aircraft into a portable corral, which is labor intensive and therefore efficient only for the capture of 20 or more animals at a time.

Management activities involve an annual aerial survey of approximately ½ of the pronghorn range. Harvest quotas are calculated for each herd and are designed to maintain a post–hunting season sex ratio of 4 females per male. Age and horn development data are collected to monitor the effect of harvest strategies on these parameters.

In the Trans-Pecos net wire fences, a legacy of past large-scale grazing of sheep, continue to present a serious problem to the free movement of pronghorns. Although they do not have movement patterns that extend over great distances, the movement from summer-fall range to winter-spring range and from dry to wet areas is of great importance. Restrictions of these movements by net wire fences during critical periods results in periodic die-offs of the herds. Providing access for pronghorns through net wire or closely spaced barbed wire fences will allow movement of the animals to seasonal grazing areas and watering sites. Unfortunately, most landowners continue to be unwilling to modify their fences to permit such movement.

The biggest threat to pronghorn habitat in the Panhandle is the conversion of rangeland to cropland. There is some evidence that oil and gas development with the attendant increase in human disturbance and associated poaching can seriously impact the many small scattered herds.

Predation by coyotes is a serious limiting factor in pronghorn production throughout their range. The most serious predation occurs during the fawning season and within 4–6 weeks after birth. Small isolated herds are especially vulnerable to coyote predation because of the relatively few fawns birthed compared to predator densities.

The pronghorn has been subjected to unusual stresses which have affected its well-being since European man's first encroachment into its habitat. Probably no other big game species in Texas has been so reduced in number and existed under such adverse circumstances as pronghorns and yet recovered to the point of being fairly abundant in local areas. The successful attainment of the pronghorn program goal will largely depend upon the department's ability to increase recreational opportunities of this resource on private land in a cost-effective manner.

Collared Peccary. Collared peccary or javelina, the only member of the peccary family that occurs in the United States, originally ranged from the Rio Grande to the Red River; however, for the past 50 years the species has been restricted to the southern ⅓ of Texas from the lower Gulf Coast to the Trans-Pecos. Probable causes for their decline in numbers and distribution are habitat destruction and a generally unfavorable attitude toward javelina by farmers and ranchers because of purported depredations on agricultural crops and livestock. Javelina are most abundant in the South Texas Plains and are also common throughout most of the Edwards Plateau and Trans-Pecos. In the South Texas Plains and Edwards Plateau the species is closely associated with dense brushy thickets, which are used for cover. Brushy draws and canyons are also heavily utilized for cover in the Trans-Pecos. Pricklypear cactus is the dominant food item throughout its Texas range. Efforts to reestablish the species in the northern part of its historic range have been few and unsuccessful.

Population trends are monitored through observations of javelina during deer census activities; however, these observations do not provide sufficient data to make population estimates. Although the annual population index as measured by acres per javelina fluctuates, javelina are believed to be at carrying capacity in relation to range condition of the occupied habitat.

Javelina are hunted throughout their range, with no closed season in the primary range and a 5-month hunting season (October through February) along the northern periphery. The bag limit is 2 javelina per season. Javelina rank eighth out of nineteen game species in terms of hunting pressure received and second among big game species. The reported harvest has been remarkably stable during the period 1981–90, ranging from 19,000 to 24,000, averaging 20,570 annually. Hunter numbers have ranged from 36,000 to 46,000, averaging 41,425 annually.

Bighorn Sheep. Desert bighorn sheep formerly occupied most of the arid mountain ranges west of the Pecos River. Probably never very abundant due to the scarcity of water and forage in this region, a noticeable decline in numbers was apparent by the late 1800's. Causes of the decline are believed to be a combination of factors associated with the movement of civilization into the region, unrestricted market and subsistence hunting, competition with domestic livestock for forage, transmission of diseases introduced with domestic livestock, and denial of access to critical habitats by net wire fences.

The last native bighorns were sighted in the Sierra Diablo Mountains in 1960. In 1954, the department initiated a bighorn restoration program consisting of a 427-acre brood pasture on the Black Gap Wildlife Management Area (WMA) into which 16 bighorns from the Kofa Game Range in Arizona were introduced. With desert bighorn broodstock in short supply throughout its range, the program strategy consists of propagating broodstock in captivity from which surplus animals are released into suitable vacant habitats or used to stock other brood pastures. Subsequently, other brood facilities were constructed at the Sierra Diablo WMA and on the Chilicote Range in Presidio County. The initial broodstock has been supplemented with bighorns from Mexico, Utah, Nevada, Arizona, and wild trapped sheep from prior releases in Texas. Only the Sierra Diablo and the Chilicote Ranch brood pastures contain sheep, the Black Gap facility having been abandoned in 1977 after the broodstock was decimated by disease (bluetongue) and mountain lion predation.

There have been numerous releases of bighorns from the referenced brood facilities with varying degrees of success. The first "soft" release of 20 bighorns in 1971 from the Black Gap facility into the wild on the area failed. Other subsequent releases of pen-reared bighorns have fared better. Population estimates of captive and free-ranging bighorns as of April 1990 are presented in Table 13.1.

In 1988 the first legal hunts for Texas bighorn sheep since 1903 took place in the Sierra Diablo Mountains. Two permits were authorized,

Table 13.1. POPULATIONS OF BIGHORN SHEEP IN TEXAS, 1990

Location	Status	Estimated numbers
Sierra Diablo WMA	Captive	69
Sierra Diablo Mtns.	Free-ranging	127
Chilicote Ranch	Captive	18
Chilicote Ranch	Free-ranging	6
Elephant Mtn. WMA	Free-ranging	31
Van Horn Mtns.	Free-ranging	25
Glaze Veterinary Clinic	Captive	1
Baylor Mountains	Free-ranging	18
Total		295

and although no mature rams were taken a total of 72 bighorns was observed on the 2 hunts, attesting to established huntable populations in the area. One additional permit was authorized in each of 1989 and 1990, resulting in a 12-year-old ram with horns of 29 inches in length and just over 14 inches in basal circumference being taken in December 1990.

The future of desert bighorn sheep in Texas will depend on TPWD actions and land-use practices employed by landowners in existing and potential habitats. From the standpoints of topography and vegetation, there is an abundance of unoccupied potential bighorn habitat in the Trans-Pecos; however, many of these habitats are degraded or unsuitable for bighorns due to long-term overgrazing with domestic livestock, lack of water, fences that would restrict access to critical habitat, uncontrolled free-ranging exotic wildlife, high predator populations, and diseases carried by domestic livestock and exotic wildlife. On department-owned lands habitat improvements, primarily water development and control of predators and exotic wildlife, are needed to enhance their ability to support desert bighorn sheep.

Aoudad Sheep. Aoudad sheep, a native of North Africa, was introduced into the Palo Duro Canyon by the TPWD in 1957 and 1958. The 2 releases consisted of a total of 44 animals obtained from a game ranch in New Mexico. Aoudads are designated as game animals only in the Panhandle counties of Armstrong, Briscoe, Donley, Floyd, Hall, Motley, Randall, and Swisher, where they occur as a result of the department's introduction. Elsewhere they are not regulated and are considered the property of the landowner.

By 1963, the population had become firmly established, and a limited hunting season was established. From 1963–81 the harvest was regulated by permit, and until 1974 all aoudads taken were required to be examined at a department check station, where biologists collected information on horn measurements, body weights, food habits, and hunter success. The highest harvest was 189 recorded in 1980; however, harvest has steadily declined since that time, with an estimated harvest of only 18 in 1990.

The decline in the harvest is strongly correlated with a decline in the aoudad population in the 8 counties where it is a game animal. Estimated at 1,200 animals in 1977, aoudad numbers are currently estimated at 500 head. The cause of the decline is believed to be a nematode (*Elaeophora*) which travels to the brain through the carotid artery. The parasite has also been recorded in mule deer in the Palo Duro Canyon, and apparently it was transmitted to aoudad on feeding grounds shared by aoudads and deer. Mule deer do not exhibit any overt symptoms to *Elaeophora;* however, in aoudads it causes facial lesions and blindness.

In addition to the Palo Duro Canyon introduction, aoudads have been released in many areas by the private sector. Currently, the statewide population is estimated at 20,402 and ranked fourth in numbers among 80 exotic species surveyed by the department in 1988. They are most numerous in the Edwards Plateau and Trans-Pecos ecological regions but also occur in the Post Oak Savannah, South Texas Brush Country, and the Cross Timbers and Prairies.

In the Palo Duro Canyon their status as a game trophy has largely been supplanted by mule deer, and in other parts of Texas their popularity has diminished as increases in their numbers and distribution have removed the "exotic" aura they once enjoyed. In the Trans-Pecos, aoudad inhabit many areas that could support desert bighorn sheep, and in these areas their presence could adversely impact establishment of huntable bighorn populations.

Small Game

This program is designed to provide research and management data necessary to assure the maintenance of small game populations and essential habitats to meet increasing sport demands. Species included in this program are wild turkey, quail, prairie-chicken, squirrel, pheasant, rabbits and hares, chachalaca, and furbearers.

Wild Turkey. Three subspecies of turkeys—the Rio Grande, eastern, and Merriam's—occur in Texas. The Rio Grande is the most numerous and is found in 9 of the 12 ecological regions in Texas. The East Texas Forests is home to all extant eastern turkey. Texas continues to support approximately 30% of the nation's wild turkey population. Turkey population trends are estimated from spring gobbler counts, roost counts, landowner interviews, summer hen-poult counts, and postcard surveys of rural postal route holders. The annual population in Texas through 1980 fluctuated between 250,000 and 500,000 birds. The decade of the 1980's saw a tremendous increase in the numbers and distribution of turkeys, especially the Rio Grande subspecies. Indeed, the period 1981–90 could be labeled the "decade of the turkey" in Texas. Estimates of the turkey population during the 1980's exceeded 600,000, which I consider to be conservative. Range expansions into what were considered marginal habitats were noted in the East Texas, Panhandle, and Trans-Pecos regions.

Hunter kill of turkeys is derived from 2 annual statewide surveys: the big game survey captures the fall-winter harvest, and the small game survey records the take during the spring gobbler season. The annual turkey harvest through 1980 was approximately 29,500 birds, of which 25,000 were taken in the fall and 4,500 gobblers were harvested during the spring season. During the 1980's the annual harvest was approximately 81,000. Just as noteworthy is the increase in the spring harvest of gobblers, which averaged 38,600 annually. In 1980 spring gobbler hunting seasons were provided in 69 counties. This type season was available in 163 counties in 1990.

Beginning in 1979 the department initiated a program to reestablish the eastern turkey in the East Texas Forests using wild-trapped broodstock obtained from other states in trade for wildlife species indigenous to Texas. Through 1986, fewer than 200 birds were stocked. A breakthrough occurred in 1987, when the department, with the National Wild Turkey Federation (NWTF) playing a key role in the negotiations, was able to purchase eastern turkey broodstock from out of state rather than having to trade for them. Since 1987 over 2,400 wild-trapped eastern turkeys have been purchased by Texas. The price established for each turkey was approximately $500, which reflects the time and effort required to trap wild turkeys and transport them to new areas. Broodstock were obtained from Alabama, Florida, Georgia, Iowa, Louisiana, Mississippi, Oklahoma, South Carolina, and Wisconsin. Funding for the purchase of turkeys has come from a variety of sources. The department has provided appropriated funds generated from the sale of hunting and fishing licenses. The corporate timber companies in East Texas contributed by donating back to the department a portion of the revenue generated on lands each had enrolled in the Type II public hunting lands program. The U.S. Forest Service shared in the costs of turkeys stocked on National Forest lands. The NWTF has contributed funds, as have numerous private individuals. The eastern turkey restoration plan targeted suitable habitat in 58 counties for stocking. Stocking is complete in 20 counties and in progress in 12 others. It is anticipated that the objectives of this restoration effort will be realized in 1995.

The TPWD has had an active restoration program for Rio Grande turkey which dates back to 1933. Through 1980 13,573 wild-trapped Rio Grande turkey were transplanted in areas of suitable habitat. During the period 1981–90, 12,104 additional birds were stocked. The Rio

Grande turkey restoration program was winding down by 1990 as virtually all suitable habitat was occupied. As a measure of the success of this program I estimate that approximately ⅔ of the annual wild turkey harvest is derived from restoration populations.

The outlook for the wild turkey continues to look promising. The eastern population is increasing, and the department expects to start trapping eastern birds in-state in the near future. The loss of turkey habitat will continue and will be significant in some counties. The major cause of this loss is encroachment of subdivision developments with the accompanying human disturbance.

Quail. Four species of quail occur in Texas: the Montezuma, Gamble's, scaled, and northern bobwhite. There is no open season on Montezuma quail, and only the bobwhite and scaled quail are important as game birds. The bobwhite is the most widely distributed, occurring in all regions of the state except the western Trans-Pecos. The best bobwhite populations occur on the rangelands in the western half of the state.

The objectives of the department's quail program continue to be maintenance and enhancement of quail habitat through advice to landowners and sportsmen and implementation of harvest regulations that optimize utilization of this very cyclic wildlife resource.

Annual population trends are determined from data collected on more than 100 randomly distributed 20-mile roadside count lines conducted in August. Annual quail harvest and hunter activity is determined from the statewide small game survey. These data are used to monitor quail population and harvest trends as a basis for adjustments in season lengths and bag and possession limits.

During the period 1980–83 the standard season length was 90 days, which was increased to the current 114 days in 1984. Based upon the population levels as determined by annual surveys, the quail bag limit was set at 12, 16, or 20 regionally during the 1980–87 seasons. Finally, the staff convinced the Parks and Wildlife Commission that bag limits have virtually no impact on subsequent quail population levels as the harvest is self-limiting. In 1988 a liberal season of 114 days with a bag limit of 15 was established statewide which remains in effect at this time.

Quail rank third in importance as a game species in Texas, behind white-tailed deer and mourning doves. Based upon the statewide small game harvest survey for the period 1981–90, an annual average of 275,000 hunters expended 881,000 hunter days to harvest 2,104,000 quail, of which 81% were bobwhites. The Rio Grande and Prairies, Rolling Plains, and Cross Timbers Brush Country ecological regions account for approximately 60% of the harvest. Some of the highest quail harvests ever recorded in the United States have occurred in the Rio Grande Plains. As an example, in 1987 quail hunters harvested 5,000 quail during the first 2 days and 12,000 for the season on the 15,200-acre Chaparral WMA, located in Dimmit and La Salle Counties.

Maintenance of quality habitat continues to be of primary importance to the future of the quail resources. Fortunately, there is an increasing interest in quail management in Texas which has been triggered by information provided to landowners and sportsmen by the department and other conservation agencies.

Prairie-Chicken. The lesser prairie-chicken once occupied most of the Texas Panhandle and Rolling Plains of North Texas. In 1980 populations were limited to only 12 counties but are now known to occur in 16 counties. The population fluctuates between 6,000 and 14,000 in response to range condition but has averaged about 10,000 over the last 20 years. The annual harvest of lesser prairie-chickens continues to range from 600 to 1,200 birds per year. A 2-day hunting season with a bag limit of 2 and a possession limit of 4 is unchanged from what it was in 1980.

A prairie-chicken restoration program was initiated in 1982. Prairie-chicken hens and their broods were trapped and transplanted to new habitats judged to be suitable range. This program proved to be very labor-intensive, and establishment of viable populations was disappointing. This restoration effort was terminated in favor of attempts to achieve habitat improvement on occupied range.

Squirrels. The eastern fox squirrel is widely distributed in Texas, occurring in all areas except extreme West and South Texas. Eastern gray squirrels are largely restricted to bottomland habitats of East Texas. Squirrels are the fourth most hunted species in Texas; however, the number of squirrel hunters has been declining since 1981. In 1981 there were 231,299 hunters compared to 135,801 for 1989. Harvest of squirrels during this period declined 71% from 1,119,000 to 321,000, although the kill per day was essentially unchanged. The decline in squirrel hunting activity is concomitant with the increase in numbers and distribution of white-tailed deer in East Texas. Outside the eastern forest belt, interest in squirrel hunting declines westwardly until it becomes almost nonexistent in the western Edwards Plateau.

The most serious problem facing squirrels is the loss of habitat as a result of forestry and agricultural practices, reservoir construction, and urbanization. The objective of the squirrel program is the retention and/or increase in hardwood habitats.

Pheasant. The pheasant was first released in Texas along the Gulf Coast in 1933–34, but these birds had virtually disappeared by 1939. Subsequently, pheasants emigrated from Oklahoma, although land-owners also released additional birds in the Panhandle. These releases probably explain how pheasants crossed the Canadian River breaks, thought to be a barrier to the southward expansion of the population. Currently, viable pheasant populations occur in 37 Panhandle and 7 coastal counties.

A pheasant propagation program, initiated in 1964 by the department, has resulted in the release of over 150,000 pheasants of 5 subspecies in 8 of the 12 ecological regions. Pheasants were established in 7 Gulf Coast counties as a result of these stocking efforts. The pheasant release program, primarily utilizing pen-reared birds augmented by several thousand wild-trapped birds from other states, was terminated in 1987 due to the limited success in establishing a viable breeding population on most of the release sites and the reluctance of land-owners to open their lands to hunting.

Pheasants have been hunted since 1958 in the Texas Panhandle and since 1976 in 7 coastal counties. Pheasants rank eleventh out of 19 game species in Texas in hunting pressure received. A 16-day season is provided for 37 counties in the Panhandle and an 83-day season in the 7 Gulf Coast counties. Pheasant hunter numbers, harvest, and hunter days for the period 1986–90 averaged 42,600, 88,500, and 66,300, respectively.

The future of the pheasant is keyed to department actions and agricultural practices on private lands. Agricultural changes will impact the quantity, quality, and diversity of pheasant habitat. The Conservation Reserve Program offers unique opportunities to enhance pheasant populations by increasing roosting, nesting, and winter cover.

Migratory Game

The Wildlife Division's Migratory Game Bird Program is designed to provide research and management data necessary to maintain migratory game populations and their essential habitats. It also provides for equitable use of migratory game birds by the hunting and nonhunting public. The migratory nature of these species as well as treaty obligations require coordination of regulations and management plans between all Central Flyway states, the U.S. Fish and Wildlife Service, and several foreign governments. Migratory game birds in this program include ducks, geese, coots, doves, pigeons, rails, gallinules, snipe, woodcock, and sandhill cranes.

The future of migratory species dependent upon wetland habitats continues to be far from bright. Drainage and filling will continue to erode the habitat base for these resources. The population trend for upland migratory species should remain relatively static through the remainder of this century.

Waterfowl. Most waterfowl populations are migratory resources that are shared by people of many geographical regions. Therefore, the management of these birds through harvest regulations is a cooperative effort between state and federal agencies with the final responsibility resting with the U.S. Department of the Interior. This, however, does not relieve the states of the responsibility of applying other management techniques and gathering data to support Flyway harvest regulations and to support proposed harvest regulations within their own boundaries.

In Texas, waterfowl are found statewide, but major wintering concentrations are found along the Gulf Coast, in North-central and East Texas, and in the High Plains. Numbers of wintering waterfowl vary annually from 3 to 5 million. During the 1980's, the number of waterfowl hunters in Texas averaged 72,000 annually, and the average annual waterfowl harvest was slightly over 767,000, with 80% being ducks. Nevertheless, a recent survey indicates significant reductions in the numbers of waterfowl hunting stamps sold, waterfowl hunters, and waterfowl harvested, especially ducks. From 1982 through 1990, an annual average of over 103,000 Texas duck stamps has been sold.

The habitat base for waterfowl in North America continues its long-term decline. Increased concerns for waterfowl abundance in North America have led to cooperative programs to address their needs in a systematic and efficient manner such as the North American Waterfowl Management Plan and associated joint ventures. Texas, as a partner in this plan, can contribute more than most states. Most waterfowl winter or migrate through Texas, which is situated at the southern terminus of the Central Flyway. Harvest by Texas hunters accounts for $1/3$–$1/2$ of the Central Flyway harvest, and, in turn, about half the wintering waterfowl remaining within the Flyway are in Texas.

One of the most important and controversial issues ever to face sportsmen and the conservation community was the reduction of waterfowl losses to lead poisoning resulting from their ingestion of toxic lead shot. Although a suitable substitute for lead shot had been developed and made available to the hunting public and the mandatory use of nontoxic ammunition has been required in specific areas, strong resentment against its use remained among some hunters. This issue was largely resolved in 1986 with the mandatory implementation of a phased schedule for total conversion to nontoxic shot nationwide by 1991. Personnel of the Wildlife Division played a leading role in the resolution of this critical resource issue.

In 1981, a state waterfowl stamp was enacted by the Texas Legislature. Revenue from the stamp is dedicated to waterfowl management, research, and habitat acquisition. Through 1990, seven tracts totaling approximately 23,000 acres of wetland habitat had been acquired at a cost of $8.9 million using revenues generated by the stamp. An additional 4,100 acres were acquired through donation.

Migratory Shore and Upland Game Birds. This category refers to all migratory game except waterfowl and includes doves, pigeons, sandhill cranes, snipe, gallinules, rails, and woodcock. In Texas there is a significant harvest of only doves and sandhill cranes.

Doves. The mourning dove is the most important game bird in the United States and in Texas relative to the numbers of birds harvested and man-days of recreation provided. Approximately 400,000 Texas dove hunters annually hunt more than 1.4 million days and harvest 5–7 million mourning doves. Through 1982 Texas was traditionally divided into a north and a south hunting zone with bag limits varying between 10 and 15. In 1983 a third hunting zone was added, with a bag limit of 12 in each zone. Texas is both a major breeding and wintering area for mourning doves in the Central Management Unit.

Mourning dove research and management activities have included spring breeding, fall migration, and winter population surveys; statewide harvest surveys; nesting and production studies; mortality investigations; and harvest regulations. These studies indicate the mourning dove population in Texas experienced a downward trend from the mid-1960's to the mid-1970's but has been relatively stable since that time.

The white-winged dove has long been a favored game bird in Texas, especially in the Lower Rio Grande Valley (LRGV), where 80% of the population has historically occurred. During the 1970's the annual white-wing breeding population averaged about 530,000, with 40% using native brush nesting habitat. During the 1980's the breeding population averaged 436,000, with 65% using native brush habitat. The LRGV experienced two major freezes in 1983 and 1989 which devastated the native brush and especially mature citrus favored by nesting white-wings. This loss of nesting habitat was followed by a major shift northward in the white-wing breeding population. By 1990 more than 50% of the white-wings nesting in Texas did so outside the LRGV, with the greatest density reported in the San Antonio area. Significant white-wing breeding populations now occur as far north as Austin, Kerrville, and Abilene.

White-winged dove activities are concerned primarily with population dynamics and habitat preservation. White-wings are a very gregarious species, and nesting densities occasionally exceed 400 pairs per acre. Due to their gregarious nature, whitewings are also extremely vulnerable to hunting pressure, and the hunting season is usually limited to only 4 half-days in early September. Approximately 40,000 hunters annually harvest 200,000 to 400,000 whitewings.

Loss of nesting habitat due to agricultural development and periodic freezes has adversely impacted white-wing populations in the LRGV. During 1975–80, the department purchased 8 native brush tracts totaling 770 acres. An additional 3,072 acres in 8 tracts have been acquired between 1981–90. Some recently purchased agricultural land will be managed as white-wing food plots or reforested with native brush. Funds for white-wing habitat acquisition and development are derived from the sale of white-winged dove hunting stamps.

Sandhill Crane. Three subspecies of sandhill cranes are winter residents in Texas. The majority of the cranes that winter in the Panhandle are lesser sandhills. Greater sandhill cranes and Canadian sandhill cranes winter primarily along the middle and lower coast and prairie areas inland. The lesser subspecies is by far the most common. Sandhill crane hunting was first permitted in the Texas Panhandle in 1961 and in South Texas in 1983. About 3,000 Texas crane hunters hunt over 5,000 days and harvest 6,000–9,000 cranes annually.

Furbearers

The Fur-bearing Animal Program encompasses the management of 20 species of mammals that are designated as furbearers by state statute. These species are quite diverse in numbers, distribution, habitat requirements, and commercial values, thus necessitating a variety of management philosophies and approaches.

The raccoon is the leading fur-bearing animal, followed in order by opossum, foxes, and skunks based on number of pelts sold. It is important to note that coyotes and bobcats are not legally classified as fur-bearing animals but are commonly tabulated in furbearer population and harvest surveys because of the commercial value of their pelts. Revisions of state law in 1981 and 1983 and subsequent regulatory implementation has substantially consolidated furbearer management activities into a statewide process.

During the 1973–74 fur season, approximately 7,000 licensed furtakers harvested an estimated 600,000 fur-bearing animal pelts with an estimated value of $3.8 million. During the succeeding seasons the number of licensed furtakers and the annual harvest continued to increase. At the close of the 1979–80 Texas fur season, 46,227 licensees had harvested approximately 1,272,000 animals with the value of the pelts being estimated at $19 million. The number of licensed trappers had declined to approximately 14,000 by 1990. This decline is attributed primarily to the low pelt prices on the international markets.

Objections from the nonhunting public to the management of furbearers on a sustained harvest basis are increasing. The use of steel leghold traps to harvest fur-bearing animals is generating considerable emotional concern. The TPWD has the authority to regulate sport hunting and trapping of fur-bearing animals; however, the number taken annually is influenced more by fur prices paid for pelts than by any other factor.

Nongame and Endangered Species

Texas, with its diverse habitat types, has 1,134 vertebrate species. These include 132 mammals, 582 birds, 213 freshwater fishes, 145 reptiles, and 62 amphibians. Additionally, there are innumerable species of invertebrate animals that are included in the nongame category for department management responsibility.

Drastic modification of the environment has placed many of these species in a precarious situation. Their plight has generated a concern for all forms of nonhuman life and resulted in passage of the state's Endangered Species Act of 1973. This was recodified in 1975 as chapters 67 and 68 of the Parks and Wildlife Code, which provides primary management and regulatory authority for vertebrate and invertebrate nongame wildlife statewide. In April 1989, overall responsibility for coordinating endangered resources conservation was administratively placed in the Resource Protection Division of the TPWD, but substantial responsibility remains in the Nongame Resources Program of the Wildlife Division for implementation of threatened and endangered animal conservation actions.

In 1980 45 animals indigenous to Texas were listed as endangered, including 14 mammals, 11 birds, 6 reptiles, 3 amphibians, and 11 fishes. The number of endangered species increased to 55 by 1990 and included 15 mammals, 11 birds, 10 reptiles, 6 amphibians, and 13 fishes. Although on the list in 1990, the black-footed ferret, jaguar, margay, and red and Mexican gray wolves are thought to be extirpated from the state. The Attwater's prairie-chicken census indicated only 458 left on the coastal prairies, and it is thought this species will be extinct in the wild by the turn of the century. On a more positive note, black bear, brown pelicans, whooping cranes, and bald eagles seem to be making a comeback in Texas. The mountain lion, which has been proposed for endangered listing, remains unprotected; however, the department has initiated studies to better evaluate its status.

The Wildlife Division continues to play a significant role in research and management activities involving certain endangered wildlife, including ocelots, jaguarundi, bald eagles, brown pelicans, red-cockaded woodpeckers, whooping cranes, black-capped vireos, aplomado and peregrine falcons, Attwater's prairie-chickens, black bears, Houston toads, American alligators, and Eskimo curlews. As a result of the research and management effort directed at the American alligator, this species was removed from the endangered list, and an annual controlled harvest was initiated in 1984. Through 1990 9,083 alligators were legally taken in Texas.

Although past program efforts have focused heavily on threatened or endangered species for obvious reasons, the majority of nongame species are not so restricted or sensitive. Many species are encountered commonly by Texans and are subject to great curiosity. This interest annually generates thousands of diverse public inquiries which have been processed by telephone and in writing by Nongame Resources Program staff. To help meet this demand the Wildlife Division has investigations under way to address the status, ecology, and management of bobcats, mountain lions, colonial waterbirds, cavity-nesting birds, cormorants, swallow-tailed kites, rattlesnakes, feral pigs, and Texas diamondback terrapins. The progressive urbanization of Texans is expected to generate increased future demand for nongame information.

Each year, millions of dollars are spent by Texas residents and tourists on appreciative uses of wildlife resources, including bird watching, nature photography, bird feeding, hiking, and camping. Winter tourism is a particularly important economic industry in Texas. Maintaining the integrity of the native wildlife resources of the state and their habitats is vital in light of the avid interest manifested by the public, with nongame resources being the focus of much of that interest.

The department's Nongame Program has come a long way since its inception in 1973, despite the restricted and unpredictable nature of funding for nongame conservation. A stable funding source is essential for appropriate program development to meet the department's responsibilities for nongame resources. Public financial support for the Special Nongame and Endangered Species Conservation Fund has been disappointing and inadequate, necessitating the identification of additional, annually reliable funding sources to defray costs of the program.

The first nongame wildlife management area, the 207-acre Candy Abshier in Chambers County, was acquired in 1990 through a gift/sale arrangement with Sun Oil Company. Two additional nongame tracts, the 152-acre Atkinson Island in Harris County and 4-acre Kiskadee Area in Hidalgo County, were also acquired in 1990 through donations.

Techniques suitable for use in habitat management applications are limited or lacking for many nongame species. Quantitative estimates of populations, habitat requirements, and information on effects of land-use changes, agricultural practices, and urban development are inadequate. Because of their behavioral patterns and scarcity, many nongame species are difficult to census and monitor. Demands for utilization of nongame species have increased; consequently, the need for data has increased. Without these data, potential management practices cannot be evaluated and implemented.

The Nongame Program has matured from its infancy into adolescence. It is now accepted as a viable component of the department's comprehensive wildlife stewardship. I feel that in the future the nongame program will grow, out of necessity, at a faster rate than conservation programs directed at consumptive wildlife.

Public Hunting

The Public Hunting Program provides for maximum public recreational use of various department-owned, -leased, or -licensed areas which are compatible with other uses of these areas. Provisions for public use addresses the needs of both consumptive and nonconsumptive users.

Prior to 1986 public hunting was restricted to certain of the department's wildlife management areas. Hunting was permitted on selected state parks beginning in 1986. A significant increase in public hunting opportunity was achieved in 1987 with the initiation of the Type II hunting program.

Under the Type II system, public users are required to purchase an annual permit which allows them to participate in a variety of authorized activities on multiple areas located throughout the state. Departmental staffing is generally not required of most Type II activities, and public use is not restricted other than by permit requirements and limitations on the number of permits available. Adequate protection of wildlife resources is provided through establishment and enforcement of appropriate hunting seasons, bag limits, and means and methods of taking. In addition, participants in hunts for very limited species (mule deer, pronghorn, etc.) are selected by drawing from among Type II permittees who apply for these restricted hunts. In most instances, nonconsumptive users are also required to possess a Type II permit.

During the 1980–81 hunting season, 6,645 hunters expended 9,139 days participating in the harvest of surplus game animals on 14 WMAs comprising some 258,560 acres. In 1990–91, 40,427 hunters expended 182,662 days hunting on 118 areas containing 1,008,239 acres which included 7 state parks (41,716 acres), 26 WMAs (221,749 acres), and 85 Type II areas (744,774 acres). In addition, Type II permittees were provided an additional 48,367 days of nonconsumptive wildlife-oriented recreation.

While the Type II hunting program was responsible for most of the increased public hunting opportunity, tremendous strides were made in this respect on department-owned areas. Between 1981 and 1990 the number of hunters participating on department lands increased 171%, hunter days increased 137%, the number of areas used increased by 136%, while the hunted acreage was essentially unchanged.

It is anticipated that the Wildlife Division will continue to expand public use of both a consumptive and nonconsumptive nature on all lands it controls. Public demand for this type of recreation is high and expected to increase. The challenge to the division is to keep pace with this demand in an acceptable cost-benefit manner.

Technical Guidance

The theme of the Wildlife Private Lands Enhancement Program (Technical Guidance) is wildlife habitat preservation and development. The program evolved in 1973 to send experienced biologists directly to the interested public for the purpose of dispensing information on wildlife and habitat management. Through 1990, technical assistance has been provided to more than 4,000 land managers controlling approximately 29.5 million acres.

The program is accomplished through 3 fundamental activities designed to give a balanced approach to the operation. These include wildlife habitat preservation and development, demonstration of wildlife management practices, and information transfer on wildlife and wildlife management practices.

The task of wildlife habitat preservation and development involves working with landowners or land managers on an individual or cooperative group basis. Written site-specific management plans are prepared as guidelines. The other 2 activities are geared for mass distribution or contacts. These deal with the public through group contacts and development and dissemination of information of a more generalized nature down to site specific advice not requiring a written comprehensive management plan.

Issues

Although most of Texas is still habitat for native wildlife, these habitats are generally degraded as a result of chronic overgrazing. Moreover, dramatic decreases in wildlife habitat appear imminent from impacts of rapid population growth associated with the Sunbelt phenomenon and decentralization of metropolitan areas accompanied by urban sprawl, from rural industrialization, and from energy exploration and production.

Other ongoing activities having particularly deleterious impacts derive from monoculture forestry, reservoir construction in the humid and subhumid regions of the state, and inundation of bottomland hardwood forests. Large-scale and complete clearing of brush and tree cover from the South Texas Brush Country for grass and row crop production is also very destructive of wildlife habitat. All of these impacts place an increasing ecological burden on remaining adjacent habitats which are already below potential carrying capacity for wildlife as a result of abusive land uses.

Texas ranked third in population among the 50 states with almost 17 million in 1990. Historical records show the hunting population has ranged from 4.7% of the total population in 1956 to 8.8% in 1975 to 6.5% in 1990. A more meaningful analysis awaits trends over a longer time; however, data for the last 15 years indicate a noticeable decline in the number of hunters relative to population. It is anticipated that the number of sport hunters will remain relatively constant, while their percentage of the total population continues to decline. Lease (trespass) costs of hunting, lack of time to devote to hunting, competition with other forms of recreation, lack of interest, and slowed recruitment to hunting appear as causal factors. Animal rights and antihunting groups are becoming more active and militant in Texas, possibly becoming a detriment to wildlife conservation in the future. The implications of a continued decline in hunters and license fee revenue generated by them could be a precursor of diminution or elimination of activities relating to conservation of wildlife and their habitats.

In terms of participation, the demand for all wildlife recreation is grossly estimated to be 35 million recreation days. About 1.2 million hunters are afield for 25 million hunter days annually, while nonconsumptive users number 8 million and expand about 10 million recreation days annually. In equivalent terms the present theoretically available supply of all wildlife is estimated to be 41 million recreational days. It must be recognized, however, that while the supply of wildlife exceeds demand, this supply occurs on private lands and becomes available only at the discretion of the landowners. In this sense, the demand for wildlife probably exceeds real available supply. It is clear that well-planned and definitive activities which promote increased availability of wildlife and the conservation and enhancement of habitats will be required for the department to help meet public demand for wildlife-oriented recreation on a shrinking resource base. Increased fees for licenses and permits are a basic need.

In 1980 the required mitigation of losses of wildlife and their habitats due to publicly funded development projects was only beginning to be recognized by governmental agencies. Now mitigation of these losses is generally accepted as an appropriate expense of these projects. Perhaps the most common form of mitigation has been the purchase of quality wildlife habitat for transfer in fee title for management by the TPWD. The Wildlife Division received 20,708 acres between 1982–90 in this manner. Additionally, funds have been provided to defray the costs of mitigation activities incurred by the department.

Milo Shult and Don Steinbach
Texas Agricultural Extension Service
Texas A & M University
College Station, Texas 77843

14. Wildlife Extension and Technical Assistance: Programs, Goals, and Issues

Abstract: Current extension and technical assistance programs of the Texas Parks and Wildlife Department, U.S. Natural Resource Conservation Service, and Texas Agricultural Extension Service are summarized. Landownership and population trends are described which dictate future extension considerations. Needs for more effective extension programs and better audience targeting are discussed.

The purpose of this chapter is to review the various wildlife extension programs currently operating in Texas and to discuss their effectiveness in view of future land-use trends. For discussion purposes, the term "extension" will be used to include both technical assistance and education programs by public agencies.

It would be inappropriate to suggest that extension activities are conducted solely by a handful of agencies. In reality, most universities, colleges, and organizations in the private sector with wildlife interests have outreach programs designed to transfer information on wildlife resources to various audiences. It is not our intent to neglect those efforts.

However, as a practical approach in the space permitted, an appraisal of extension programs must be limited. For that reason, comments will be restricted to activities of the Texas Parks and Wildlife Department, the Natural Resources Conservation Service, and the Texas Agricultural Extension Service. These agencies will be used as examples of current programs in Texas and will serve as the "yardstick" to measure extension needs in the future.

Current Programs

Texas Parks and Wildlife Department

As the primary state regulatory agency for wildlife and fisheries, the Texas Parks and Wildlife Department has a role in the conduct of extension programs. There are 2 entities within the Texas Parks and Wildlife Department which have as primary objectives information delivery for various publics across the state of Texas.

As in most state fish and wildlife agencies, the Communications Division of the Texas Parks and Wildlife Department serves as a source of information on wildlife and fisheries for many Texans. The division performs that role in a variety of ways. The division is responsible for publishing the monthly *Texas Parks & Wildlife* magazine and serves as a major distribution point for various brochures available from the department. Staff specialists are responsible for responding to incoming calls from Texans on a variety of wildlife issues through 2 toll-free telephone lines maintained for that purpose. The staff of the Conservation Communications Division also works very closely with the Texas Outdoor Writers Association to provide information on departmental activities through that outlet.

Video production has been expanded to produce regular releases for public television, and these are used within the school systems. In addition, staff members within the division work with schools to provide other programs on wildlife. Regular radio spots and talk programs are produced and available also. The thrust, then, of the Communications Division of the Texas Parks and Wildlife Department could perhaps best be summed up as a major distribution point for a variety of pieces of information on wildlife and fisheries within the state of Texas to a diverse group of audiences.

The Texas Parks and Wildlife Department has an Education Division in which the Hunter Education and Aquatic Education Programs are administered. Other programs involved are Project WILD and Angler Education. A new program called Becoming an Outdoor Woman is also conducted in this division.

The Texas Parks and Wildlife Department also has a unit responsible for the delivery of technical assistance information. The Private Lands Enhancement Program of the Wildlife Division of the Texas Parks and Wildlife Department was established on September 1, 1973, as a primary vehicle to combat loss and misuse of wildlife habitats in the state (Anonymous 1981). This program was established in direct response to increased requests for assistance on the management of wildlife species during the 1960's. As requests for assistance increased throughout the 1960's and into the early 1970's, 5 biologist positions were created to serve the 5 major wildlife regions in the state. The number of positions has fluctuated slightly since 1973 and is now at 10, providing a technical guidance biologist in each of the wildlife regulatory districts. The remaining staff of the Wildlife Division also work with private landowners and managers in addition to their other duties, and this program is receiving additional emphasis.

The methodology used in the program is that of direct assistance by qualified technical personnel to individuals controlling the land resource across the state. This direct assistance is supported by other activities including field days, seminars, mass media presentations, and published papers, brochures, bulletins, and leaflets. A quarterly newsletter was initiated November 1990 and is mailed directly to participating landowners, providing additional timely management information, techniques, and notes.

Direct assistance is generally provided on site and may vary from oral information to a complex, written wildlife management plan that focuses on a properly functioning, diverse ecosystem. The process incorporates planning that benefits a wide variety of wildlife in concert with land-use goals and management of featured species identified by the land manager. The service is strictly advisory and is provided without charge to cooperating land managers. Recent legislation directed that wildlife management plans were to be strictly confidential between the biologist and the landowner and not subject to the open records, unless written permission was granted by the landowner. In a brief summary of the accomplishments of this program from 1973 through 1980, over 4,000 land managers received assistance on over 25 million acres of land. In 1995, over 10 million acres were actively enrolled in wildlife management plans.

In addition to this direct technical assistance to private landowners, the Private Lands Enhancement Program though the entire Wildlife staff in 1995 provided over 900 programs to more than 75,000 sportsmen, landowners, land managers, educators, and the public through seminars, field days, and workshops. These activities, coupled with the use of mass media, have served as a primary mechanism of providing general information and creating interest in the assistance program.

Natural Resource Conservation Service

The Natural Resource Conservation Service (NRSC), formerly the Soil Conservation Service (SCS), has changed significantly in its capability to provide technical assistance in wildlife management to Texas landowners since the first publication of these proceedings in 1982.

Fifteen years ago NRCS operated offices in 234 of the 254 counties in Texas, and the remaining 20 counties could expect assistance from neighboring counties. County offices, or field offices, were staffed by personnel trained in many management disciplines, including soil science, agricultural engineering, forestry, agronomy, range management, wildlife management, and fisheries management.

In the intervening 15 years the capacity of NRCS to deliver technical assistance has diminished. The agency still operates about the same number of field offices, but staff sizes have declined in many offices. Field offices where forestry and range are the major vegetative cover types have been the hardest hit by these reductions. Unfortunately, these offices have traditionally received the most requests from landowners for wildlife management assistance.

Two of the primary reasons for this declining service are budget reductions, which translate into staff reductions, and the Farm Bills of both 1985 and 1990. In 1981 the NRCS budget in Texas was $54.5 million. Ten years later the budget had declined to $52.5 million. In 1981 NRCS in Texas employed 1,189 personnel; by 1991 employment had been reduced to 889.

The 1985 Food Security Act and 1990 Food, Agriculture, Conservation and Trade Act—both more commonly known as the 1985 and 1990 Farm Bills—changed the primary role of the soil Conservation Service from an agency that provides technical assistance upon request to an agency that insures compliance by participants in USDA programs with conservation provisions of the 2 Farm Bills.

Protection of highly erodible croplands and cropped wetlands by agricultural producers is required by the Farm Bills. Staffs in counties where these fragile resources are significant have been increased at the expense of field offices with large acreage of forests or range.

NRCS will continue to do its best to deliver technical assistance in wildlife management upon request. In 1991 the agency staffed 6 area biologists, the same number as in 1981, to assist personnel in field offices. Although these biologists are involved in Farm Bill activities, they continue to devote as much time as possible to training field office personnel in wildlife and fisheries management and assisting landowners with developing conservation plans.

Wildlife management in Texas has traditionally been directed toward game species. Landowner interest in a broader array of species has been spearheaded by declining farm and ranch income from traditional sources, fewer hunters, and the Endangered Species Act (ESA) of 1973. Interest by private landowners in endangered and threatened species is usually negatively motivated. Specifically, Section 9 of the ESA threatens landowners who adversely affect species or their habitats with criminal or civil penalties. NRCS in Texas has begun an initiative to assist landowners during conservation planning in determining the probable presence of federally endangered and threatened species and selecting farm and ranch activities that will not adversely affect the resource.

Although the form of technical assistance delivered by NRCS to landowners has changed over the past 10 years, the agency's goal will continue toward ensuring a private lands resource base that generates income for current landowners while protecting natural resources, including wildlife, for future landowners.

Texas Agricultural Extension Service

The Texas Agricultural Extension Service (TAEX) is a part of the Texas A & M University System and functions as the extension education arm of the land-grant university. TAEX has 4 major program emphasis areas: Agriculture and Natural Resources, Home Economics, 4-H and Youth, and Community Resource Development. Although wildlife and fisheries personnel within TAEX are administratively located in the agriculture and natural resources area, the diverse nature of the wildlife programs cuts across the other major program components.

TAEX uses a delivery system somewhat akin to that of the NRCS but with some rather noticeable differences. The major thrust of TAEX is to conduct educational programs through the offices of county extension agents across the state. County extension agents function in the role of generalists who are supported by a wide variety of specialists in various subject-matter areas.

The local structure of TAEX's programs is based on planning by local citizens working with the county extension agent. In each county there is a group of citizens identified as the Program Development Council (PDC), which serves as a focal point for the identification of needs for educational programs within the county. Under the PDC are a variety of subcommittees in which wildlife and fisheries may or may not be identified by name as a specific subject-matter area. In some instances, wildlife work may be planned, conducted, and evaluated under the auspices of another PDC subcommittee such as beef, range management, sheep and goats, etc. Based on the needs perceived at the county level, specialists in wildlife and fisheries are responsible for developing materials to be used in educational programs across the state.

Educational programs of TAEX rely on many of the same techniques described for those of TPWD and the NRCS. These include the use of video, satellite, meetings, seminars, short courses, symposia, mass media, and a wide variety of publications.

Many of the commodity-based decisions affect broader issues such as water quality and conservation of natural resources, etc. At the county level TAEX asks broadly based committees to identify issues that are of concern to the citizens to guide long-range extension programs. One other educational technique utilized by the county extension agent is the result demonstration.

The result demonstration is a concept which has been used since the inception of the cooperative extension effort across the United States at the turn of the century. It has proven to be the most successful educational technique dealing with private landowners relative to adoption of agricultural practices. The basic premise behind the result demonstration is that actual adoption of practices on a given farm or ranch will have a greater influence on other members of the community than will recommended but unobservable management practices coming from outside resources. Each year county extension agents report a wide variety of result demonstrations to all agriculture producers in their counties through Result Demonstration Handbooks. These demonstrations actually represent application of research findings applied at the local level. In any given county, the demonstrations conducted may be on a wide variety of subjects such as pecan production, swine management, beef cattle production, and white-tailed deer management. The extension program serves as a link between counties and efforts of the Texas Agricultural Experiment Station. This coordinated effort is designed to insure an open line of communication between producers and users of research data.

In TAEX, there are 10 specialists in wildlife and fisheries who support the programs at the county level—2 wildlife specialists and 3 fisheries specialists are headquartered at Texas A & M University, and 2 wildlife specialists and 3 fisheries specialists are headquartered around the state. The programs conducted by the specialists can be summarized as providing information in the following areas: (1) fisheries management, (2) aquaculture, (3) terrestrial wildlife management, (4) wildlife damage control, (5) 4-H and youth programs, and (6) conservation education. The conservation education category covers a wide variety of programs, including hunter short courses and response to requests for information on numerous wildlife issues.

Future Trends in Land Use

It would be redundant to attempt to categorize all the changes in land-use practices and resultant effects on wildlife resources which are being discussed. However, certain statistics should be identified which are of particular importance to technical assistance and extension education programs. The questions of who will control wildlife resources in the future and where the impacts on wildlife resources will originate are of critical importance in a discussion of targeting programs in the coming years.

We know that Texas is presently a state primarily held in private ownership. Estimates from real estate economists indicate that over 98% of the more than 263,000 square miles of land is under the direct ownership of private individuals and corporations (pers. commun., Ivan Schmedemann, professor, Texas A & M University). Texas ranks number 1 in the nation in the number of farms and ranches with over 159,000 management units on 138.7 million acres. The magnitude of this resource clearly indicates that future technical assistance and extension education programs must continue to be directed toward private landowners.

Despite the fact that the vast majority of land in Texas is held in private ownership, the population in Texas is rapidly increasing and shifting from rural to urban areas. The report from the Texas 2000 Committee, Office of the Governor, provided a wide array of statistics indicating these population shifts (Anonymous 1980). For example, in 1950, the population had increased to 13.4 million. Perhaps more astounding is that nearly 20% of that population increase occurred in the decade of the 1970's.

The distribution of these population increases also affects the types of extension programs to be conducted. In 1850, only about 4% of Texans lived in urban areas, and approximately 96% lived in rural communities. One hundred years later, in 1950, 63% of the people were in urban areas and slightly over 37% in rural communities. In just 20 years (1970), nearly 80% of the population in Texas was urban. The implication of the impacts of rapidly expanding urban populations on wildlife and fisheries resources of the state are clearly apparent.

Another important characteristic of Texas populations which will affect the way that extension programs must be conducted is the source of these new people. In the decade 1940–50, nearly 95% of the increase in the population came from "natural" increase (natality minus mortality) and only slightly over 6% from migration into the state. In the decade of the 1970's, nearly ½ of the population increase was from migration into the state. The Sunbelt migration is bringing a wide variety of new audiences into the state of Texas whose perceptions of wildlife resources are potentially markedly different from those third- and fourth-generation rural natives of the state. Unlike the population shift from natural increase, ingress brings in instant users and impacts on the resources. Thus, the need to respond to these shifts is more acute.

Sprague and Hailey (1980) summarized the critical nature of land as a limiting factor for agriculture production and wildlife habitat in Texas. The decade 1958–68 saw the loss of 0.5 million acres of land to development. In the following decade, 1968–78, the loss increased to 2.5 million acres. In view of the population statistics indicated above, there can be very little reason to assume that development and conversion of land use away from agriculture and wildlife habitat will diminish. In many instances, the decisions relative to these developments are being made by people who are unaware of the impacts on wildlife.

At the same time, a variety of groups is becoming more acutely aware of the need for wildlife management in the state of Texas. In 1979 a survey of the Association of Texas Soil and Water Conservation Districts indicated wildlife management ranked ahead of such problems as loss of agricultural land, wind erosion, and reclamation of surface mining as a major concern (Sprague 1979). In that same survey, 74% of the districts indicated a need for increased education efforts to solve problems of improper wildlife management. Overgrazing ranked as the number one need and, interestingly enough, is also a serious problem affecting the wildlife resources in Texas today.

Areas of Concern in Extension

What are some of the problems facing the implementation of effective extension programs in the state? Probably the foremost problem with respect to the delivery systems of the 3 agencies used as examples in this chapter would be diminishing resources in the face of expanding demand.

Conservation education programs are not being implemented in schools in an ever-increasing urbanized society; thus, understanding of our natural resources is decreasing. The Texas Parks and Wildlife Department's Conservation Communications Division has considerably reduced its use of localized and regional communications in the face of manpower reductions and concentrates on statewide mass media approaches that are more general in nature.

Prior to 1982, the biologist staff of the NRCS in Texas consisted of 14 full-time positions but has been reduced to 9 positions which they have been able to maintain (pers. commun., Frank Sprague, biologist, NRCS). The biologist's responsibility also has changed to a greater regulatory role. This brings the total of wildlife biologists with the Texas Parks and Wildlife Department, the Texas Agricultural Extension Service, and the NRCS with direct responsibility for extension-type programs to 22 full-time positions.

Another example of limited resources is in the travel capabilities of the specialists in TAEX. Since 1972, the operating budgets have been, in effect, level funded when one takes inflation into account. This problem is magnified by the fact that the primary cost in travel has been one of the major increases in costs during the last decade. Lack of travel funds can severely limit wildlife extension programs. The technical assistance and education programs are vitally dependent upon on-the-ground contacts to be effective.

Faced with the diminishing resources available to those agencies (and others who have responsibilities for extension type programs), the prognosis is that we must do better with less. Probably the most effective way to accomplish this is for the involved agencies to greatly enhance coordination and cooperation among their professional staff members. It is in the best interests of the state of Texas and also the wildlife resources for TPWD, NRCS, TAEX, and all other groups that have any type of extension outreach programs to improve greatly the lines of communication between the agencies and organizations.

Another way that we need to be doing a better job with fewer resources is to target our educational efforts more effectively. Perhaps one of the most poorly used terms in the discussion of technical assistance and extension education programs is the phrase "the general public." We cannot simply say that we are designing extension programs for the general public and expect the products of those programs to be targeted to the specific needs and desires of the wide diversity of audiences in our state. Ramsey and Shult (1982) discussed the educational approaches to wildlife management on private lands. A summary of their discussion on targeting programs for individuals follows.

First, the general characteristics of adult audiences clearly differentiate them from youth audiences. These characteristics are directly affected by wildlife management education programs. Most adult audiences seek problem-centered information.

Second, accurate and precise audience identification is critical to the success of extension activities. For example, the term "private individual landowner" is too broad when the objective is implementation of management practices. The type of ownership and/or agricultural enterprise, coupled with the motivation of the individual and resource constraints, must be identified and accounted for in program planning.

Third, delivery system techniques must be matched with receptivity of the audience. The media blitz may be appropriate to elicit responses from some audiences. However, experience has shown that interpersonal contact from credible sources is essential in working with private individual landowners. This includes not only contact with the wildlifer but support from opinion leaders in peer groups as well.

Fourth, management programs for wildlife must be integrated into the total land-use program as envisioned by the landowner. Economic and/or social costs and benefits of wildlife must be available to facilitate the decision-making process if wildlife is to be considered in the farm/ranch/woodlot scheme.

Fifth, the wildlife profession must, if education is a viable method for implementing management practices, do a better job of interpreting costs and benefits of wildlife management practices in terms of value to the landowner.

Another very recent example of the impact of audience identification and targeting of information is brought out by Trent (1982). In a study in North Carolina, a set of 6 pamphlets were identical in preparation with the exception of 2 different titles used for each one. For example, type 1, which was a "how to" title, might be "How to Build a Great Body," while type 2, which would indicate subject content, might be

"Milk in the Diet." In the course of the study it was discovered that 75% of the test population, when offered these publications on a no-charge basis, selected those titles which were directly aimed at solving their problem (i.e., the "how to" type). Only 25% selected the titles based on subject content. It would behoove each of us to examine the titles of extension type publications on our shelves to determine which ones are directed at problem solving and which ones indicate only sub-ject-matter content.

Therefore, future needs for wildlife extension programs lie in (1) greater utilization of the human resources on hand (for there is little evidence of expansion in this area), (2) more refined audience identifi-cation and analysis techniques, and (3) better targeting of extension programs using the most efficient approaches possible. And finally, the wildlife profession in general must accept the fact that decisions will be made on a daily basis which directly affect wildlife resources. The mag-nitude and direction of these decisions can probably be impacted most dramatically not through regulation but through effective education and technical assistance.

Literature Cited

Anonymous. 1980. Texas trends. Texas 2000 Project. Austin. 247 pp.
————. 1981. The technical guidance program of the Wildlife Divi-sion. Tex. Parks and Wildl. Dep., Austin. 35 pp.
Henson, J., F. Sprague, and G. Valentine. 1977. Soil Conservation Ser-vice assistance in managing wildlife on private lands in Texas. Trans. N. Am. Nat. Resour. Conf. 42:264–70.
Ramsey, C., and J. Shult. 1982. Educational approaches to wildlife management on private lands. Proc. Symp. Wildl. Manage. on Pri-vate Lands, Milwaukee, Wis.
Sprague, F. 1979. NRCS assistance to private landowners. Paper pre-sented at Texas and Southwest Cattle Raisers Assoc., Houston. 8 pp.
Sprague, F., and T. Hailey. 1980. Wildlife management and the private landowner. Paper presented at Wildlife Society (Texas chapter), 10–12 April.

We gratefully acknowledge the contributions of Kirby Brown, Texas Parks and Wildlife, and Gary Valentine, NRCS, to the preparation of this manuscript.

Kirby L. Brown
Program Director
Private Lands Enhancement
and Public Hunting
Wildlife Division,
Texas Parks and Wildlife Department
4200 Smith School Road
Austin, TX 78744

15. Texas—
A Private Lands State

Abstract: Texas is a private property state with 97% of the land in private ownership. The diverse landscape and history of settlement have had a great influence on the landowner ethic and the strong private property rights orientation of landowners. Wildlife management was little recognized until the 1960's, when leases for hunting rights became big business. Incorporating wildlife considerations into agricultural operations remains a low priority for most landowners. However, new programs encourage conservation, landowner organizations are becoming proactive toward conservation, and landownership patterns are changing, with recreational use receiving greater emphasis. With an urban public demanding integrated land-use considerations for wildlife, rural landowners should take a proactive approach with locally developed, community-based, voluntary actions to address landscapes, ecosystems, and wildlife.

The vast Texas landscape is composed of about 170 million acres of land and spans 10 diverse ecological areas (Gould 1975). Unlike the western states, the bulk of the land is not in government ownership. In fact, 97% of Texas landscapes are privately owned. This makes Texas one of the leading private property states. Private landowners are the single greatest force affecting wildlife and wildlife habitat in the state. To understand the various ethics regarding private property, we must understand the land and its history.

The Landscape

Presettlement Texas can best be described as a huge plain, mixed with open savannahs of scattered mesquite, live oak or post oak, or open forests. Early Spanish explorers entered Texas from the south, through New Spain (present-day Mexico). Francisco de Coronado searched for the fabled Seven Cities of Gold in 1540–42. The expedition crossed the Panhandle and Palo Duro Canyon, describing huge treeless grasslands with large herds of buffalo. The first usable records of vegetative conditions can be gleaned from the diaries of Spanish explorers in the period between 1675 and 1722 as they traveled through South Texas toward San Antonio and east to Nacogdoches in the Piney Woods.

The Spanish explorers and early settlers described the eastern Texas Piney Woods area as an oak-pine forest with an open understory, or a prairie under widely spaced pine trees. Three areas of shortleaf pine–hardwood forest occurred in the northeast, while an oak-hickory forest dominated the redlands in the central part of this area. Amos Parker described in 1834 the longleaf pine barrens in the southeast part of this area, "the trees straight and tall, but standing so far apart, that a carriage might go almost anywhere among them" (Truett and Lay 1984). A strip along the southern edge of the Piney Woods was called the Big Thicket and was a loblolly pine–oak–hickory forest with a thick understory of shade-loving trees. It was unique in that it was unlike the rest of the open forests and savannahs of Texas.

The Post Oak Savannah was predominantly an open tallgrass prairie or oak savannah. In some areas, particularly described by the Spanish explorer Alonzo de León in 1675, the southern portion was plains or open savannahs that ran right up to widely scattered blocks of dense post oak woods, "scrubby woods that were an impediment to travel" (Inglis 1964). Mesquite and live oak occurred as savannahs and mottes but less frequently in this area.

The Spanish characterized the South Texas uplands as plains. Inglis (1964) suggested that nearly ½ of these uplands contained mesquite, though the average density was probably low, ranging from very few shrubs in some areas to scattered mottes or extensive sparse stands. Most drains and small creeks had mesquite, often in dense thickets, while wooded riparian areas were directly adjacent to the rivers and creeks. Lehmann (1984) added that early records indicate the extremely cyclic rainfall patterns and drought conditions inherent in the area.

Live oak was the dominant woody vegetation in the Edwards Plateau of Central Texas, forming scattered low brush or savannahs in the predominantly open grasslands. Juniper and other woody plants were mostly confined to riparian areas and canyons.

The tallgrass prairies of the midcontinent United States ran south into Texas as the Blackland Prairies. This fairly narrow corridor mostly lay just west of the post oak belt, except for a small sliver that cut the post oak on its southeast side.

The coastal plains, or the Gulf Prairies and Marshes parallel to the Gulf of Mexico, were uniformly described as a large expanse of nearly level treeless prairie. The prairie was interspersed with wet or "muddy prairies," with marshes and wetlands near the coast (Inglis 1964; Truett and Lay 1984; Lay and Culbertson 1978). Everything else west of these areas was mostly described as a huge expanse of open grasslands. Post oak was the seldom seen but predominant characteristic woody plant of the Cross Timbers ecological area in North-central Texas on the sandy soils, while sparse live oak dominated limestone soils. Two north-south bands of dense post oak woods cut the prairies, giving rise to the name Cross Timbers. Open midgrass prairies with very little or only widely scattered mesquite were characteristic of the Rolling Plains in North Texas. Both the Cross Timbers and the Rolling Plains had occasional savannahs of live oak, post oak, or mesquite.

The High Plains was an unbroken shortgrass prairie dotted by numerous ephemeral potholes called playas. The Trans-Pecos was a dry, desert grassland with a mix of the Chihuahuan Desert and Rocky Mountains. In these western areas, trees were confined to riparian areas and the infrequent higher elevations of the mountains in the Trans-Pecos region of West Texas.

The wide-open prairies, savannahs, and open understories of the Piney Woods were maintained by frequent periodic fires. Numerous lightning strikes and fires set deliberately by the Indians regularly burned the brush and trees off the prairies.

Settlement

Texas was first settled by Spanish missionaries who attempted to convert the native Indians to Christianity. The padres organized *rancheros* around churches and schools, teaching the Indians about raising livestock and farming crops (Trefethen 1976). These missions were mainly confined to the southern part of Texas but extended into East Texas at

Nacogdoches to provide a Spanish presence on the northeastern frontier to deter the French (Inglis 1964; Truett and Lay 1984). These self-sufficient communities prospered and were more Indian than Spanish. Horses and cattle were driven to these areas, and many escaped along the way to provide the source for the large herds of wild mustangs and longhorn cattle that subsequently developed. The wild, free-roaming herds established migration patterns similar to those of the native bison (Trefethen 1976). Many of these animals were captured from Texas for use by the Plains Indians throughout the country. This was probably as significant a change for the Indian culture as the invention of the automobile was to our present-day society.

Some influential Spaniards were given large blocks of choice grasslands, mostly along the Rio Grande, amassing large herds of longhorn cattle (Trefethen 1976). The ranches of this time adopted an approach very similar to the mission communities, and their headquarters formed the original nucleus for many of the later towns. The Spanish land grants are still the basis for many of the property lines in Texas.

The first major effort to provide a large number of immigrants to colonize the state was made by Stephen F. Austin in the 1820's and 1830's on the fertile coastal prairies. After independence from Mexico in 1836 and through the mid-1800's, settlement was growing in earnest. Farmers moved from the eastern United States, where soils had worn thin from continuous cotton cropping, and cleared forests in the areas of East Texas (Burger 1978). The invention by John Deere of the steel moldboard plow in 1838 permitted settlers to break out the grass-bound sod of the tallgrass prairies; by 1857 John Deere was producing over 10,000 steel plows annually (Westemeier and Edwards 1987). "Wrong side up" was the comment of a Sioux chieftain about the sod busting on the prairies (Cadieux 1987). The eastern ⅓ of the state was occupied by 2 or more people per square mile by 1850 (Trefethen 1976). Europeans landed on the coast and settled in groups, moving inward into Central Texas. The elimination of the huge migratory herds of bison by market shooters and the subsequent control of the Indian threat to settlers by the 1870's to 1880's stimulated an ever-increasing flood of people to Texas. Wildlife, especially game species and predators, were viewed as subsistence food, marketable commodities, and/or competitors. Little thought was given to the declining populations of wildlife or the disappearance of vast natural resources as early Texans struggled to survive in the harsh environment.

The East Texas Forests were treated much like the rest of the southeastern United States with almost all of the highly marketable timber in the virgin forests cut and removed with no thought of the losses or consequences. Almost all the virgin forests were cut by the early 1900's (Truett and Lay 1984). Cotton and grain crops became a dominant feature on the landscape in the entire eastern half of Texas and replaced much of the forest. Many poor sharecroppers and small farmers barely eked out an existence on the poorer, shallow soil sites in this area. They used wildlife as an important source of food.

Expansive farming communities continued to develop on the deep soils of the Panhandle and North Texas, as well as those large early farming areas of East-central and coastal Texas. Many rich natural prairie vegetative communities specific to these rich soils almost completely disappeared under the plow. Many wildlife species specific to these prairies also disappeared, but other animals, such as quail and rabbits, adapted to the broken farm communities and prospered. Matthiessen (1987) noted in the course of this invasion of the New World that "the forests and rivers, plains and prairies suffered changes more drastic than those undergone in all the hundred centuries since the last glacier, and even creatures never preyed upon directly declined rapidly in his wake." Manmade intrusions, drainage, land leveling, filling, and dredging converted valuable wetlands to farmlands (Lay and Culbertson 1978).

In North, Central, West, and South Texas, farming was a risky venture on the shallow soil sites with the constant threat of drought. Only riparian and alluvial areas were consistently productive farm sites. Cattle ranching, however, was a very profitable enterprise in early Texas. Legendary ranches such as the XIT and King Ranch developed around the escaped Spanish longhorns. The industry generated historic cattle drives. Famous routes developed such as the Goodnight Loving Trail from West Texas to Cheyenne and the Chisholm Trail from Central Texas to Abilene, Kansas (Trefethen 1976). The events and western folklore that surrounded the cowboy helped shape the independent philosophy of the cattle ranchers. Drives were common from large ranching communities to early shipping centers and railheads, reaching their peak in the mid-1870's. However, expansion of the rail systems created increased competition from other sections of the country, and Texas's monopoly was short-lived.

The advent of barbed wire in the late 1870's was the catalyst that solidified the private land ethic in the western part of Texas. The saying "Good fences make good neighbors" is considered as true today as it was a hundred years ago. Property lines became as firmly established and as clearly identified as a plowed field. Where disagreements arose over a boundary, feelings could run high, sparking long-running feuds and even deaths. Hollywood legend-making blends with the reality of the bitter disputes that formed part of the philosophy of a fierce privacy ethic in the western half of the state.

Cattle, sheep, and goats, which had once roamed open ranges, were grazed continually behind the fences. Overgrazing the grasslands helped to reduce the hazard of dangerous wildfires. However, range-lands began to change slowly but dramatically under the constant pressure. Overgrazing through the years encouraged extensive brush invasions, reduced the quality and vitality of the grasslands, and caused extensive soil losses in many areas. Again, the wildlife community changed, favoring those species adapted or adjusting to these mostly degraded conditions, while species that could not adapt declined.

Private Lands Conservation

The fledgling conservation movement of the late 1800's and early 1900's had little effect on Texas's private landowners. However, soil and water conservation began in earnest in many farming communities after the Dust Bowl in the 1930's. Hugh Bennett, first chief of the Soil Conservation Service (SCS), urged farmers to change and "help keep the raindrops on the land." The SCS helped develop contour farming, strip cropping, terracing, and permanent cover plantings, as well as farm ponds, shelterbelts, hedgerows, and wildlife plantings (Trefethen 1976). Some Texas farm communities changed radically, helping to hold the soil and moisture on the land. However, this began to change again in the 1960's as expensive equipment, farmlands, and chemicals continued to drive the smaller farmer off the land and into more lucrative job opportunities in urban areas or the oil industry. Larger farms again plowed and planted fencerow to fencerow in monoculture crops to enhance efficiency and profitability. Traditions and/or economics continue to drive decisions by the bulk of Texas farmers, and wildlife and its habitat are a concern only to a small minority.

Detrimental ranching practices begin to receive critical review during the 1930's. Recommended stocking rates for livestock began to be developed that provided for range recovery. However, it was not until the 1950's and 1960's that range-friendly practices were being regularly used by a minority in the ranching industry. This small group of people were generally the wealthier landowners who had large landholdings or bought their ranches with oil money. There was also an educated new generation of ranchers and ranch managers, many of whom returned to the family place. Still, most ranchers continued to run too many cattle, sheep, and goats, and range practices encouraged the clearing of trees and other native vegetation in riparian areas and the planting of nonnative monoculture "tame" or "improved" pastures of bermudagrass, bufflegrass, and other species. Large scale root plowing temporarily removed brush in South Texas, but the brush soon returned more densely than before but with only ½ the diversity.

Hunting demand increased in the growing urban segment, and landowners leased their properties during the relatively brief hunting seasons for a small fee that provided extra income. In South Texas, higher lease fees were generated by the lucrative oil industry. Deer and quail became important commodities. Consequently, interest in white-tailed deer management began to increase, and biologists were writing management plans for ranch managers to improve their deer herds or quail populations. Interest accelerated in other game species, and wildlife management plans were implemented on several large ranches. These plans were aimed at directly addressing the food resources—the habitat—and focused on relieving overgrazing problems. The continued demand for quality hunting areas drove an economic boon for wildlife. A severe decline in livestock and crop prices shook the ranching and farming industries in the late 1970's and early 1980's. Hunting lease revenues provided many landowners with their only positive cash flow in these lean times. Farm and ranch real estate prices were higher for quality wildlife habitats. The nonresident landowner segment increased substantially and began to emerge as a factor on the landscape. These individuals pursued a recreational approach to ranching and wildlife and sought to enhance the aesthetic experience. Attitudes are changing in some areas to incorporate wildlife planning. Still, most ranch land in Texas is committed to livestock, with wildlife and habitat seldom considered in most decision making.

Outlook

A private land stewardship ethic continues to grow in Texas. Landownership patterns will continue to change over the next 25 years, favoring enhancement and restoration of wildlife habitats. The Conservation Resource Program has grown to almost 4 million acres in Texas. Although initially a soils program, using primarily nonnative grass cover, the program has produced wildlife successes. With management, these areas can be greatly enhanced for wildlife. The 1995 Farm Bill promises to provide even greater wildlife benefits.

Less intrusive, less expensive ranch practices, such as short duration/longer rest rotational grazing systems and prescribed burning that simulate functions of the original ecosystems, may ultimately be more profitable as well as aesthetically and environmentally acceptable. Continuing education for farmers, ranchers, and nonresident landowners is critical to ensure landscape improvement and instill a sound land ethic. Groups such as the Texas Wildlife Association, Farm Bureau, and Texas and Southwestern Cattle Raisers Association are becoming actively involved with agencies in wildlife management and education. These groups have incorporated land stewardship recognition programs to further wildlife goals. Natural resource professionals continue to benefit by more extensive multidiscipline training to provide a broader base of expertise to private landowners, while agencies must enhance their commitment to private lands work in a state that is 97% private lands. Farm corporations and agribusiness will continue to come under closer scrutiny and pressure by a broad-based conservation community, not just environmentalists, to develop responsible long-term, nondegrading land management goals that provide reasonable economic returns. These trends have already begun in Texas and appear to be expanding.

Wildlife belongs to the public under common law, but private landowners are the caretakers of 97% of Texas's habitats. Private landowner participation has generated some monumental successes in wildlife recovery and restoration, but neglect, disregard, or self-interest has also created some irrecoverable losses and has pushed some species into severe decline or to the brink of extinction, while some have vanished forever. Public opinion and legislation will likely demand a closer accounting on private lands. It is time for a proactive approach of local community-based action in the rural areas to address wildlife and conservation. A voluntary landscape approach to ecosystem management developed at the local community level will be far preferable to heavy-handed, impractical regulations imposed by the majority of the citizenry of the state who live in cities and have little knowledge but a soft heart for wildlife. This proactive approach to good management must be taken or ensured immediately to protect the existing private land rights and heritage of Texans. Such an approach protects, manages, restores, and connects the pieces to once again produce functioning ecosystems on the landscape (Leopold 1966).

Literature Cited

Burger, G. V. 1978. Agriculture and wildlife. Pp. 89–107 in H. P. Brokaw, ed., Wildlife and America, contributions to an understanding of American wildlife and its conservation. Counc. Environ. Qual. Washington, D.C.: U.S. Govt. Printing Office.

Cadieux, C. L. 1987. Pronghorn antelope: Great Plains rebound. Pp. 133–43 in H. Kallman, C. P. Agee, W. R. Goforth, and J. P. Linduska, eds., Restoring America's wildlife, 1937–1987. U.S. Fish and Wildl. Serv. Washington, D.C.: U.S. Govt. Printing Office.

Gould, F. W. 1975. Texas plants—a checklist and ecological summary. Tex. Agric. Exp. Stn. Misc. Publ. 585 (revised). 121 pp.

Inglis, J. M. 1964. A history of vegetation on the Rio Grande Plain. Bull. No. 45, Tex. Parks and Wildl. Dep., Austin. 122 pp.

Lay, D. W., and K. F. Culbertson. 1978. Wildlife of the Texas coastal zone. Tex. Parks and Wildl. Dep., Austin. 72 pp.

Lehmann, V. W. 1984. Bobwhites in the Rio Grande plain of Texas. College Station: Texas A&M Univ. Press. 371 pp.

Leopold, A. 1966. A Sand County almanac with essays on conservation from Round River. New York: Ballantine Books. 295 pp.

Matthiessen, P. 1987. Wildlife in America. New York: Viking Penguin. 332 pp.

Trefethen, J. B. 1976. The American landscape: 1776–1976, two centuries of change. Wildl. Manage. Inst., Washington, D.C. 91 pp.

Truett, J. C., and D. W. Lay. 1984. Land of bears and honey: A natural history of east Texas. Austin: Univ. Texas Press. 176 pp.

Westemeier, R. L., and W. R. Edwards. 1987. Prairie-chickens: Survival in the Midwest. Pp. 119–31 in H. Kallman, C. P. Agee, W. R. Goforth, and J. P. Linduska, eds., Restoring America's wildlife. 1937–1987. U.S. Fish and Wildl. Serv. Washington, D.C.: U.S. Govt. Printing Office.

Murray T. Walton
Texas Department of Agriculture
Box 12847
Austin, Texas 78711

16. Nuisance Wildlife and Land Use

Abstract: Nuisance wildlife cause millions of dollars worth of damage to crops, livestock, forests, and structures each year. Land use and adjacent habitat contribute to the type of damage and species involved. Only a small number of species is responsible for a majority of the damage. A systems approach should be applied to reduce nuisance situations.

Wildlife can be considered a nuisance whenever it conflicts with the health, welfare, or desires of humans. In the context of this paper, the word "nuisance" is used to cover a wide range of conflicts from simple annoyance to physical harm. Nuisance situations frequently arise from simple competition for food and space, but some of the most serious problems such as disease transmission, automobile collisions, and physical attack (a rarity) are a matter of close association between humans and wildlife regardless of the type of land use. Only a portion of a wildlife population may become a nuisance, and certainly there are differences in opinion as to the severity of such problems, depending on economic and aesthetic perspectives. Indeed, wildlife that may be a nuisance may also be highly valued for other qualities. Furthermore, only a small percentage of the wildlife species in Texas ever constitutes a significant nuisance, with an even smaller number of species responsible for most of the damage.

How land is used or altered contributes to conflicts between humans and wildlife. Food and fiber production from natural habitats bring about competition with indigenous and exotic wildlife for food and

259

shelter. Habitat alteration may give rise to population increases of both native and exotic species of wildlife that are adapted to farming or urban environments. Peripheral habitat may allow for wildlife nuisance situations on adjacent areas. Also, control of one species may give rise to problems from another.

Several large animals that have a high potential for conflict with current land uses have been extirpated in Texas (grizzly bear, gray wolf, red wolf), reduced to remnant populations primarily in remote areas (mountain lion and black bear), or reduced to small numbers kept behind fences as livestock (bison or buffalo). Of these, mountain lions are increasing in Texas, probably due to reduced predator control and changes in land use (Texas Parks and Wildlife Department 1990).

In some ways, we are victims of our own recent successes in wildlife conservation. For instance, the American beaver was nearly extinct due to fur trapping in past years, has been widely restocked, and is now a major nuisance species. Recovery of the American alligator from an endangered species to a frequently unwelcome visitor in towns is also an example. A conservation ethic that has reduced indiscriminate shooting and poisoning of wildlife has allowed many species to increase in numbers. Lands are set aside solely to provide wildlife habitat, and an increase in agricultural efficiency (production per acre) has idled many acres (now in wildlife habitat) while production has increased. Wildlife conservation measures are incorporated in many public works projects.

Wildlife damage costs Texans millions of dollars in property damage and lost income each year. Undoubtedly, the cost would be far greater without extensive control and management measures. The Texas Animal Damage Control Service alone had a budget of $5,553,613 for fiscal year 1989 (U.S. General Accounting Office 1990). Additional funds are spent by other government agencies and private organizations and individuals.

Agricultural Lands

At the Texas Chapter of The Wildlife Society 1982 annual meeting entitled "Texas Wildlife Resources and Land Use," Glen Jones (1982), representing the Texas Farm Bureau, stated: "Most farm problems with wildlife are not with game animals and birds but with pest species— blackbirds and coyotes. Predators and rodents can be very destructive, but the real destruction occurs when government prohibits efficient control methods for these animals." Undoubtedly, the lease-hunting system in Texas, whereby many landowners receive income from game animals, makes their presence more welcome. However, government prohibitions on some control methods, particularly pesticides, still (and will continue to) remain.

Texas is a leading agricultural state with a diverse mix of crops and livestock enterprises made possible by a wide range of climatic, soil, and topographic conditions. Farm numbers peaked at 506,000 farms in 1931 and have steadily declined to 186,000 farms in 1990 (Texas Agricultural Statistics Service n.d.b). Since the Texas Agricultural Statistics Service (n.d.b) began reporting farm acreage figures in 1950, total farm acres peaked at 154 million acres in the mid-1950's and now total approximately 132 million acres. The diversity of Texas agriculture also gives rise to a diversity of nuisance wildlife problems.

Aquaculture

Aquaculture ponds provide a highly attractive food source for a number of fish-eating birds due to the concentration of fish or shellfish. The double-crested cormorant is of most concern at present in regard to total damages to the fish-farming industry. Cormorants breeding in Canada and the Great Lakes region have traditionally wintered along the Gulf of Mexico. Stickley and Andrews (1990) state that fishermen who raided double-crested cormorant colonies and organochlorine pesticides formerly controlled cormorant numbers, but this species has experienced a population growth coincidental to the growth in the 1970's and 1980's of catfish ponds in Mississippi. Cormorants have also adapted use of Texas fish farms and farm ponds managed for sport fishing. Not only do cormorants eat large quantities of fish but they also damage fish with their beaks. Other birds attracted to fish farms include great blue and tricolored herons, gulls, snowy and great egrets, and terns. Also, white-faced and white ibises and night-herons will congregate to feed in crayfish ponds. In addition to birds, raccoons, river otters, western cottonmouths, water snakes, frogs, and turtles are sometimes attracted to feed at aquaculture facilities.

Cropland

In 1989, approximately 23 million acres were in cropland with 6 crops (winter wheat, cotton, hay, sorghum, corn, and oats) accounting for about 21.4 million acres (Texas Agricultural Statistics Service n.d.a). There have been sizable shifts downward in the acreage of most major crops as well as regional shifts in primary growing areas. The movement to dryland and irrigated agriculture on the High Plains and consolidation of production areas has insulated most major crop production from serious damages by nuisance mammals. Small territorial birds with food habits providing a potential for damage do not pose a serious threat to these large blocks of crops. Only flocking migratory birds that occur in large numbers pose a serious threat in most areas. Blackbirds are most frequently involved, but waterfowl will also feed on crops. Snow geese that formerly wintered almost exclusively in coastal marshes began a shift to agricultural plants several decades ago, first in California, then the Midwest, followed by Texas, and most recently, Louisiana (Bellrose 1980). More recently, a diversification trend, particularly into specialty crops grown in small patches by producers randomly distributed throughout the state, complicates vertebrate pest management considerably as it subjects crops to attack from peripheral habitat.

Normal cultivation for row crop production destroys burrows and prevents build-up of field rodents. However, with the increasing popularity of no-tillage farming, more rodent damage problems can be expected. Cropland with peripheral habitat to support rabbits and hares, black-tailed prairie dogs, deer, beavers, feral pigs, or raccoons is frequently subject to severe damage from these species. Irrigated crops in arid areas and small grains and ryegrass that are green in winter are attractive to a number of species. High value crops, particularly orchards, in areas of deer abundance usually have exclusion fencing and avoid losses. Cotton, which has accounted for from 4 to 8 million acres over the last decade, is seldom bothered by vertebrate pests. Some of the most important species in terms of damage to crops as reported to the Texas Animal Damage Control Service in fiscal year 1990 (Hobbs 1990) are listed in Table 16.1. These figures are far from a complete tally of damages but demonstrate a portion of reported losses.

The Rio Grande Valley with its year-round growing season and variety of grain and vegetable crops interspersed in small fields with native brush tracts and urban development provides a unique situation for damage by great-tailed grackles. Grackles use residential areas, chaparral, and citrus groves for nesting, commencing in April and declining in October, with use of feedlots peaking in the intervening months (Rappole et al. 1989). Damages by grackles in 1989 to a wide variety of vegetable, grain, and fruit crops (especially citrus) were esti-

Table 16.1. IMPORTANT CROP-DAMAGING WILDLIFE IN TEXAS, 1990

Crop	Species	Value of loss (in $)
Alfalfa	Pocket gopher	29,746
Cabbage	Blackbirds	517,900
Cabbage	Grackles	497,400
Corn	Deer	300,000
Milo (sorghum)	Blackbirds	450,600
Milo	Grackles	59,575
Pecan trees	Beaver	24,175
Wheat	Geese	22,185
Rice	Blackbirds	61,600

mated to exceed $4 million (Hobbs 1990). Peak grackle use in crops reflects seasonal rhythms of specific fields, with flocks feeding on soil organisms behind machinery working fields, then later on the crops and insects in the fields (Rappole et al. 1989).

The Conservation Reserve Program (CRP), covering about 8 million acres of erodible Texas cropland, has been referred to as the "coyote reserve program" by Rollins (1989). The interspersion of grassland with little disturbance with cropland and pastures does provide habitat for coyotes and other wildlife that may become a nuisance on adjacent lands. Ed Dowty, Texas Department of Agriculture pesticide specialist at Vernon (pers. commun.), reported sighting coyote dens during a flight over CRP lands near farms in the Vernon area that suffered coyote predation on calves.

Feedlots and Farm Storage

Confinement of hogs and poultry under modern production methods greatly reduces predation by avian and large mammalian predators. However, farm structures and areas where livestock and poultry are confined provide ideal feeding areas for the "Old World" commensal rodents (house mouse, Norway rat, roof rat) and birds (house sparrow, feral pigeon or rock dove, European starling) as well as several native species (skunks, raccoons, and opossum). The National Wildlife Damage Association (1989a) reported that roof rats on a single chicken layer operation in Texas caused $176,000 worth of damage to structures and feed, and a nearby hog operation had $38,000 in damages.

Rangelands/Pastures

About half of the state of Texas is rangeland, with approximately 110 million acres being used for livestock production. On January 1, 1990, there were 13.4 million cattle, 2.09 million sheep, and 1.9 million goats in Texas (Texas Agricultural Statistics Service n.d.b). Most sheep, goats, and cattle in Texas are produced under range operations without intensive management. Nuisance wildlife situations affecting the range livestock industry are primarily predation and competition for forage.

The primary sheep- and goat-raising area is the Edwards Plateau and surrounding counties. Rangelands of other areas of Texas are well suited to sheep and/or goat production, but ineffective means of preventing predation forestall large-scale use (Rollins 1990b). In Zapata County (South Texas), Guthery and Beasom (1978) estimated predation loss to be as high as 95% of the Angora kid crop in a pasture without predator control and as high as 59% predation loss even on an area where control measures reduced predator activity by 80%. The Edwards Plateau was virtually coyote free for several decades (Nunley 1985) due to intensive areawide predator control to protect livestock. However, the reduction in sheep and goat producers, a transition to cattle-only operations requiring lower levels of protection, and an increase in acreage for recreational use have contributed to an encroachment of coyotes that began in the 1960's. Sheep and Angora goat predation losses during 1990 totaled 177,000 head valued at $7.5 million, with coyotes accounting for more than half of the damages (Texas Agricultural Statistical Service 1991b). Other important predators on sheep and goats include red fox, gray fox, bobcat, cougar, raccoon, feral pig, and golden eagle.

Clearing of large areas reduces cover desired by bobcats, cougar, raccoon, and gray fox, but coyotes thrive on open prairie habitat. Clearing of forested land for pasture and crops (along with elimination of wolves) has aided in the expansion of the range of this species to the east. Bolen (1975) found a higher incidence of lambs in the diet of golden eagles in areas with a greater amount of brush and speculated that this may be due to increased difficulty in eagles catching hares and rabbits in brushy habitat. Also, excessive clearing of brush removes valuable forage for goats and reduces habitat for valuable wildlife such as white-tailed deer and wild turkey.

Because of their size, cattle are less vulnerable to predation. Cattle losses to predators, primarily coyotes, consists mainly of calves under 400 pounds and cows that are down giving birth. About 1% of the calf crop is lost annually to predators (Stalcup 1988). Ranchers on the eastern half of the Panhandle and adjacent Red River Valley to the east appear to be especially hard hit. Much of this area is in large ranches with few sheep or goats, and the availability of natural prey (especially deer in the more open habitat) may be less than in other areas of the state.

Losses to livestock production due to competition with wildlife for forage are far harder to quantify than predation losses, and in some instances, such as management of white-tailed deer and mule deer for sport hunting, there is a deliberate management decision to allocate forage. Even under excellent range conditions there is competition between white-tailed deer and sheep and goats during the fall and winter for browse and winter and early spring for forbs and any time immature grass is available (Bryant et al. 1979). Predator control may increase productivity of white-tailed deer, and harvest may need to be adjusted to prevent overuse of range forage (Guthery and Beasom 1977).

A number of exotic ungulates including axis deer, fallow deer, sika deer, blackbuck antelope, nilgai antelope, ibex, mouflan sheep, and aoudad sheep can also compete with domestic livestock and native wildlife for forage. Ibex can interbreed with domestic goats, and mouflan can interbreed with domestic sheep. Also, these exotics can carry a number of diseases and parasites.

Foster and Stubbendieck (1980) found that gophers reduced forage production by 18–49% on sandy and silty range sites in western Nebraska. Blacktailed-prairie dogs in shortgrass ecosystems may depress habitat suitability for cattle while enhancing habitat for desert cottontails and prairie rattlesnakes (Hansen and Gold 1977). Aboveground herbage eaten and made unavailable from soil disturbance by prairie dogs and cottontails was estimated by Hansen and Gold (1977) to be about 24% of total potential annual production. Texas rangelands with similar conditions may be expected to be affected likewise. Damage to pastures by prairie dogs reported to the Texas Animal Damage Control Service in 1990 was over $400,000 (Hobbs 1990).

Forest

Effects of wildlife on forests may be highly visible immediately, as in the case of beaver damage from flooding and timber cutting, or may be virtually unnoticed but expressed in long-term changes in stand composition due to browsing by rodents, white-tailed deer, and rabbits. Damage to standing trees reported by Texas Animal Damage Control Service cooperators in fiscal year 1990 attributed nearly $400,000 in losses to beavers (Hobbs 1991), and this probably represents only a fraction of total timber losses. Very little damage by other species was reported.

Jackson (1990) listed 20 species of mammals and birds that can cause economic loss to intensive pine culture in nurseries or seed orchards as follows:

MAMMALS

Voles	Cotton rat
White-footed mice	Pocket gopher
Squirrels	American beaver
Rabbits	Nine-banded armadillo
White-tailed deer	Eastern mole

BIRDS

Evening grosbeak
Red-winged blackbird
Yellow-bellied sapsucker

Damage includes a range of effects, including feeding on leaves, feeding on roots, chewing stems, eating seeds, trampling, and uprooting of seedlings.

Urban/Suburban/Industrial

Highly modified habitats such as cities, industrial plants, suburban housing, electrical and communications systems, and transportation facilities are subject to nuisance wildlife. The Old World commensals are being joined by a small number of native species which are adapting well to human environments—raccoons, opossums, skunks, tree squirrels, house finch, and grackles. Problems from these species include structural damage, consumption and fouling of human and pet food, raiding gardens and orchards, odor, and disease transmission. Older wooden structures, structures with crawl spaces opening to the outside, structures with large ledges, flat roofs, wood or composition shingle roofs, and openings to the attic are more vulnerable to invasion by one or more of these species. Pigeons are usually closely tied to manmade structures and usually roost on building ledges and flat roofs or under bridges. Roosting Brazilian free-tailed bats may also invade buildings and present problems due to droppings and fear of rabies transmission. Poor sanitation, large amounts of shrubbery and/or trees, and location adjacent to parks, green belts, water courses, bird feeders, landfills, etc., may also contribute to the attractiveness of an area to urbanized pest species. Grain elevators, food-processing facilities, food storage warehouses, and port facilities also attract these species due to the large amounts of food available.

Mature trees in urban areas give rise to bird roosts with associated noise and dropping problems. House sparrows, grackles, blackbirds, herons, and cattle egrets are among the common offenders. The cattle egret is a recent arrival to the Americas, and Telfair (1983) discussed various authors' speculations that cattle production allowed the colonization of the Americas by cattle egrets. However, Telfair found no direct relationship between cattle density and cattle egret numbers in Texas.

Beaver damage is becoming common in cities. Beaver will eat a large array of ornamental plants, garden vegetables, and fruit trees found in urban areas. Willging and Sramek (1989) reported that complaints received by the Texas Animal Damage Control Service concerning beaver damage in the Dallas–Fort Worth area increased from 12 in 1984 to 64 in 1988 and attributed part of the problem to the abundance of water resources in the area, including 6 major manmade reservoirs. One beaver was found to be living in a drain pipe and traveling through a storm sewer to feed on neighborhood trees (Willging and Sramek 1989). Also, beaver and nutria burrowing in levees and embankments cause extensive damages.

The boom era of the 1970's and early 1980's gave rise to many housing additions that have failed to be fully developed. Also, many of these developments contain acreage lots. This rapid expansion of urban and suburban areas into the rural community has caused the nuisance wildlife problem to become much more complex (Mapston 1989). More people are coming in contact with wildlife and not always in a welcomed manner—skunks and armadillos root up yards, skunks spray dogs, raccoons and opossums turn over garbage cans and eat pet food off porches, and coyotes eat pets. Snakes (of any type) in the yard or alligators in the swimming pool can also be unsettling.

Auto-wildlife collisions usually relate to adjacent habitat. Runoff from pavement, plantings to control soil erosion during construction (especially winter grasses), and ornamental plantings that produce wildlife food attract wildlife to roadway areas. Due to size and abundance, white-tailed deer is the species of most concern. Rollins (1990a) reported the average repair cost of a deer-auto collision as $1,800. Increasingly, a problem regarding collisions are urban deer herds, especially in the Austin and San Antonio metropolitan areas, where some residents feed and water deer while their neighbors complain about deer eating their shrubbery and flowers. Terrain including steep slopes, gullies, and water courses that prevent dense development are conducive to maintaining escape cover for urban deer.

Airplane-wildlife collisions are of concern due to human safety, equipment damage, and wildlife mortality. Airports with large grassy areas provide ideal soaring and feeding areas for raptors, and runways provide excellent loafing areas for shorebirds. White-tailed deer and coyotes on runways also cause collision hazards on many small community and military airports with basically rural settings. Location of airports near water or wetland areas gives rise to a hazard from (and to) waterfowl. One Texas airfield near a rendering plant has a problem with soaring turkey and black vultures in the flight path.

Rodents will gnaw on buried electrical and communication cables, and shorts of electrical transformers and lines have been attributed to a wide variety of birds, mammals, and snakes. Even purple martins have been implicated. Large numbers of martins roosting on a cable at an aluminum plant (in Texas) caused a short with damages estimated at $500,000 (National Animal Damage Control Association 1989b). Woodpeckers and northern flickers frequently damage transmission poles.

Miscellaneous Lands

Areas set aside for wildlife management areas, parks, green belts, and refuges and "abandoned" lands may also give rise to wildlife damage problems. Including national forests and national grasslands, government-owned parks and preserves totaled about 2.45 million acres in the mid-1980's (Carls 1984), and sizable additions have been made. Also, private organizations own or manage a number of refuges and sanctuaries. The primary purpose of management sometimes gives rise to conflicts. In some instances, one species of native wildlife may damage another native species, such as coyotes preying on nesting birds and eggs on islands along the Gulf Coast managed by the National Audubon Society or grackles eating white-winged dove eggs and young from native brush nesting sanctuaries managed by the Texas Parks and Wildlife Department in the Rio Grande Valley. The brown-headed cowbird is implicated as a major threat to survival of black-capped vireos, a recently listed endangered species, and the Texas Animal Damage Control Service is now trapping cowbirds on vireo nesting areas (Texas Animal Damage Control Service 1991). Cowbirds have undoubtedly benefited from production of small grain, opening of woodlands for cattle production, feedlots, and backyard birdfeeders. The increased management of land for recreational hunting of native and exotic species also brings conflicts with predatory species.

Wildlife from areas where they are protected may cause problems on adjacent lands or produce surplus animals that disperse to cause problems on adjacent lands. Windberg and Knowlton (1988) stated that "the presence of a reservoir of transient animals available to occupy vacant territories emphasizes the logistical problems associated with resolving coyote depredation problems through population reduction, especially on small areas." This is true for other species as well. However, these dispersing animals may be easier to control than established residents. Young coyotes are more likely to be killed by automobiles, and both young and transient coyotes are more vulnerable to trapping than coyotes with established territories (Windberg and Knowlton 1990).

Fur harvest has long been a secondary use of rural lands in Texas. Not only has this produced economic benefits but it has also reduced populations of nuisance animals. The highest harvest in the last two decades, 1,272,462 wild furs in the 1979–80 season, was followed by a downward trend in prices and harvest to a low of 156,682 in 1989–90 (Perkins 1990). From the 1979–80 season to the 1989–90 season, the estimated coyote harvest dropped from 105,797 to 19,975, the raccoon harvest from 465,145 to 69,767, and the opossum harvest from 401,340 to 16,048 (Perkins 1990). In 1989–90, the number of trapper licenses issued by the Texas Parks and Wildlife Department was 57% below the 1979–87 average (Perkins 1990). This reduction in harvest creates a significant potential for increased damages to livestock and crops by furbearers.

Management Considerations

Three things happen every time a wildlife damage problem occurs: (1) a human activity, desire or need is interfered with; (2) the experience fosters an opinion about a wild animal, usually negative; and (3) a decision is made to tolerate the situation or control it (Johnson 1990). Means of control and public acceptance of control are not always easy matters. Wildlife damage is not evenly distributed, causing considerable divergence of opinion on need to control between those who are affected and the unaffected public, and perceptions of wildlife nuisance may differ even among individuals with similar experiences. Also, species of wildlife causing damage may have high economic or ecological values.

Most methods of lethal control are highly controversial, especially using toxicants to kill predators. Arthur et al. (1977) found that 23% of individuals sampled indicated a farmer should not be allowed to kill an animal that killed livestock, but of those who approved of killing such predators, only 43% approved of killing other animals of the same species to prevent further predation. Trapping and slow-acting poisons were judged least humane. Kellert (1979) found that both informed and uninformed members of the general public disapprove of using poison as the cheapest means of coyote control if other species would be killed. In a survey of Dallas–Fort Worth area beaver damage complainants, 25% of respondents were opposed to lethal control, and of these only 50% would permit lethal control as a last resort (Willging and Sramek 1989). The public sentiment is for methods of nonlethal control and targeting only individual offending animals, not populations. However, where legal methods of control are ineffective or unavailable, illegal and unsafe lethal controls are often attempted by the affected public.

Most animal damage control efforts and tools are aimed at one or a few species. Furthermore, there is little planning or coordination for prevention of problems. Vertebrate pest control is mostly reactive after damages have been sustained. A systems approach to vertebrate pest management, including the consideration of all potential problem species in an area or situation and integrating damage prevention and control strategies that minimize damage caused by those species identified as economically or socially detrimental, has been advocated by Hygnstrom (1990). Pest-proof construction, exclusion with fencing, facility location, sanitation, habitat modification, damage-resistant varieties of crops and ornamentals, alteration of planting and harvesting dates, crop rotation and cultural practices, herd management, and livestock-guarding animals are some of the practices to be considered in conjunction with population reduction techniques. Such an approach should be applied in Texas, but success in a systems approach would necessitate greater cooperation between adjoining landowners and some changes in land use. A greater investment in public education, research, and professional management would be required but should be repaid due to reduced damages. Additional advantages of a systems approach should be greater protection for endangered species and broader public acceptance of wildlife and wildlife management.

Literature Cited

Arthur, L. M., R. L. Gum, E. H. Carpenter, and W. W. Shaw. 1977. Predator control: The public viewpoint. Trans. N. Amer. Wildl. and Natural Resources Conf. 42:137–45.

Bellrose, F. C. 1980. Ducks, geese, and swans of North America. 3rd ed. Harrisburg, Pa.: Stackpole Books. 540 pp.

Bryant, F. C., M. M. Kothman, and L. B. Merrill. 1979. Diets of sheep, Angora goats, Spanish goats and white-tailed deer under excellent conditions. J. Range Mgmt. 32(2):412–17.

Bolen, E. G. 1975. Eagles and sheep: A viewpoint. J. Range Mgmt. 28(1):11–21.

Carls, E. G. 1984. Texas natural diversity: The role of park and preserves. Pp. 51–60 in Protection of Texas natural diversity: An introduction for natural resource planners and managers. Tex. Agric. Exp. Stn., College Station. MP-1557.

Foster, M. A., and J. Stubbendieck. 1980. Effects of the plains pocket gopher (*Geomys bursarius*) on rangelands. J. Range Mgmt. 33(1): 74–78.

Guthery, F. S., and S. L. Beasom. 1977. Response of game and nongame wildlife to predator control in south Texas. J. Range Mgmt. 30(6):404–9.

———. 1978. Effects of predator control on Angora goat survival in south Texas. J. Range Mgmt. 31(3):168–73.

Hansen, R. M., and I. K. Gold. 1977. Blacktail prairie dogs, desert cottontails and cattle trophic relations on shortgrass range. J. Range Mgmt. 30(3):210–14.

Hobbs, J. M. 1991. Texas animal damage control program annual report, fiscal year 1990. Texas Animal Damage Control Service. 69 pp.

Hyngstrom, S. E. 1990. The evolution of vertebrate pest management—the species versus the systems approach. Proc. Vertebr. Pest Control Conf. 14:20–24.

Jackson, J. J. 1990. Controlling vertebrate animal damage in southern pines. Proc. Vertebr. Pest Control Conf. 14:199–202.

Johnson, R. J. 1990. The human element in wildlife damage situations. Proc. Vertebr. Pest Control Conf. 14:16–19.

Jones, G. G. 1982. Farmers' view of wildlife and wildlife users. Texas Wildlife Resources and Land Use. Proc. Symp. Texas Chapter of The Wildlife Society, pp. 104–6.

Kellert, S. R. 1979. Public attitudes toward critical wildlife and natural habitat issues. Phase I. USDI Fish and Wildl. Service and School of Forestry and Environmental Studies, Yale Univ., Washington, D.C.: U.S. Govt. Printing Office. 138 pp.

Mapston, M. E. 1989. Urban wildlife damage: A complex problem. Proc. Great Plains Wildl. Damage Control Workshop. 9:70–72.

Nunley, G. 1985. The extirpation and re-establishment of coyotes in the Edwards Plateau of Texas. Proc. Great Plains Wildl. Damage Control Conf. 7:9–27.

Perkins, J. R. 1990. Evaluation of annual fur harvest. Federal Aid Project No. W-125-R-1, Job No. 2. Tex. Parks and Wildl. Dep. 11 pp.

Rappole, J. H., A. H. Kane, R. H. Flores, A. R. Tipton, and N. Koerth. 1989. Seasonal variation in habitat use by great-tailed grackles in the lower Rio Grande Valley. Proc. Great Plains Wildl. Damage Control Workshop 9:138–41.

Rollins, D. 1989. And more on coyotes. On the wild side. Tex. Agric. Ext. Serv. 3(1):n.p.

———. 1990a. Life (and death) in the fast lane. On the wild side. Tex. Agric. Ext. Serv. 4(2):n.p.

———. 1990b. Coping with coyotes. Tex. Agric. Ext. Serv. 12 pp.

Stalcup, L. 1988. Public perception of predator control has direct impact on livestock producers. Cattleman 75(5):148–50, 153, 154, 156, 158.

Stickley, A. R., and K. J. Andrews. 1990. Survey of Mississippi catfish farmers on means, effort, and cost to repel fish-eating birds from ponds. Proc. Eastern Wildl. Damage Control Conf. 4:105–8.

Telfair, R. C., II. 1983. The cattle egret: A Texas focus and world view. Tex. Agric. Exp. Stn. 144 pp.

Texas Agricultural Statistics Service. 1991. Predator losses totaled $7.5 million to Texas farmers and ranchers. Tex. Agric. Stat. Serv., Austin. SM-10-91:3.

———. n.d.a. 1867–1989 Texas historical crops statistics. Texas Dep. Agric. & U.S. Dep. Agric. Austin. 108 pp.

————. n.d.b. 1867–1990 Texas historic livestock statistics. Texas Dep. Agric. & U.S. Dep. Agric. Austin. 92 pp.

Texas Animal Damage Control Service. 1991. ADC around Texas. Trapline March/April: 1–4.

Texas Parks and Wildlife Department. 1990. Mountain lion numbers may be on the increase. Talkin Texan. Tex. Parks and Wildl. Dep. July 6, 1990: 1.

National Animal Damage Control Association. 1989a. Roof rat. Probe (93): 2.

————. 1989b. Purple martins. Probe (95): 9.

U.S. General Accounting Office. 1990. Effects of animal control program on predators. GAO/RCED-90-149. 31 pp.

Willging, B., and R. Sramek. 1989. Urban beaver damage and control in Dallas–Fort Worth, Texas. Proc. Great Plains Wildl. Damage Control Workshop 9: 77–80.

Windberg, L. A., and F. F. Knowlton. 1988. Management implications of coyote spacing patterns in southern Texas. J. Wildl. Manage. 52(4): 632–40.

————. 1990. Relative vulnerability of coyotes to some capture procedures. Wildl. Soc. Bull. 18(3): 282–90.

Fred S. Guthery
Caesar Kleberg Wildlife
Research Institute
Texas A & M University-Kingsville
Kingsville, TX 78363

Nova J. Silvy
Department of Wildlife
and Fisheries Sciences
Texas A & M University
College Station, TX 77843

17. Wildlife Research in Texas, 1981–1990

Abstract: We examine the status of wildlife research in Texas and compare research needs identified in 1980 with research activity during 1981–90. Wildlife research is essential because it moves wildlife management from the realm of art to that of science. During the past decade, the number of wildlife research organizations in Texas remained constant at 15, but funding levels for research appeared to have decreased. Texas authors published 129 papers in the *Journal of Wildlife Management* and the *Wildlife Society Bulletin* during 1981–90. Of these, 2.3% were multidisciplinary and 96.1% were descriptive (lacked hypothesis). Thus, identified needs for multidisciplinary efforts and research on process and cause and effect were not met. All levels of the wildlife management profession need greater training in mathematics, statistics, and the philosophy of science if research and management are to become more effective.

Aldo Leopold (1933:3) defined game management as the "art of making land produce sustained annual crops of wild game for recreational use." *Webster's New World Dictionary* defines art, in the sense Leopold probably intended, as "any craft, trade, etc., or its principles: as, the cobbler's art." The dictionary defines science as "systematized knowledge derived from observation, study, and experimentation carried on in order to determine the nature or principles of what is being studied." Obviously, research is essential to the orderly accumulation of systematized knowledge. The raison d'être for research is to move wildlife management away from art and toward science. Therefore, this discussion of the status of wildlife research in Texas is relevant to natural resource issues in the state.

Herein, we recapitulate selected information on wildlife research provided by Guthery et al. (1982) in the Texas Chapter's first symposium. We analyze research in Texas during 1981–90 relative to needs identified by Guthery et al. (1982). Lastly, we speculate on future needs concerning the nature and direction of wildlife research in Texas.

Research Programs, Goals, and Issues

Fiscal Considerations

In 1981, 15 research groups (6 federal, 7 state, 2 private) were actively involved in wildlife research (Guthery et al. 1982). Total statewide expenditures on wildlife research were about $5.6 million in fiscal year 1981. Federal, private, and state agencies contributed 44.8, 35.9, and 19.3% of these funds, respectively.

All research groups except one remain active as of this writing. The Great Plains Wildlife Research Laboratory, U.S. Forest Service, headquartered at Texas Tech University, Lubbock, was closed because of budget restrictions during the Carter administration. However, Texas Tech has obtained a Cooperative Wildlife and Fisheries Research Unit, so there has been no net loss in the state's research unit base.

We did not obtain a recent estimate of total statewide expenditures on research. However, because of state budget cuts during the mid-1980's, efforts to trim the federal budget deficits during the late 1980's, and elimination of Caesar Kleberg Foundation monies to Texas A & M University and Texas Tech University and reduced support for Texas A & M University-Kingsville, research budgets were probably less during this decade than the previous decade.

Conduct of Research

Guthery et al. (1982:149) wrote, "The current economic, social, and political indicators point out dramatically that decreasing public revenues will be available for future wildlife research. At the same time, the need for the results of research has never been greater, because more pressure is being applied to the land for commodity and noncommodity products."

Guthery et al. (1982) felt that, because financial support for wildlife research was declining and the need for research information was expanding, research would have to become more efficient. To improve efficiency, they advocated multidisciplinary efforts and collaboration and coordination across agencies (the latter to reduce redundant efforts). Neither of these circumstances has occurred in the past decade. No group has taken the lead in planning and collaboration. Of 129 Texas-based articles (Table 17.1) published in the *Journal of Wildlife Management* (JWM) and the *Wildlife Society Bulletin* (WSB) during 1981–90, only 3 were clearly multidisciplinary (wildlife biologists collaborated with chemists in 2 papers and a geologist in the other).

Relative to the conduct of research, Guthery et al. (1982) felt more effort should be devoted to understanding relationships and processes and that in accord with this need, basic as opposed to applied research should be given more emphasis. Recognition of the process-relationship need by Texas researchers was not apparent based on JWM and WSB articles in the last decade. Only 5 of 129 studies had clearly defined, a priori hypotheses, and the remainder were descriptive

Table 17.1. AFFILIATION OF SENIOR AUTHORS (%) ON TEXAS-BASED[a] STUDIES PUBLISHED IN THE *Wildlife Society Bulletin* (N = 59) AND THE *Journal of Wildlife Management* (N = 70) DURING 1981–90

Affiliation	Wildl. Soc. Bull.	J. Wildl. Manage.	Total
University			
Texas A & M	27.1	30.0	28.7
Texas A & I	35.6	22.9	28.7
Texas Tech	18.6	34.3	27.1
Other	3.4	1.4	2.3
Federal agency	10.2	11.4	10.8
State agency	5.1	0.0	2.3

[a] Senior author was a Texas resident during the study, and the research was conducted in Texas.

A. Journal of Wildlife Management

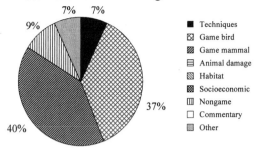

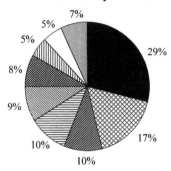

B. Wildlife Society Bulletin

Fig. 17.1. *Subject matter of Texas-based articles in (A)* The Journal of Wildlife Management *(N = 70) and (B)* Wildlife Society Bulletin *(N = 59) during 1981–1990 (senior authors were residents of Texas and the research was conducted in Texas).*

studies or commentaries. Eighty-seven percent of articles in WSB were applied in nature, compared to 16% in JWM. These differences reflect subject matter content of the journals. That 84% of JWM articles was basic in nature indicates wildlife researchers in Texas undertook a major effort in this line of study.

Content of Research

Guthery et al.'s (1982) analysis indicated that about 51% of the fiscal year 1981 research budget was expended on game animals, 27% on environmental and ecological topics, 19% on nongame, and 3% on other items. These percentages did not hold during the decade 1981–90 based on Texas-based studies in JWM and WSB (Fig. 17.1). Because most of the techniques papers dealt with game animals, about 85% of the articles in JWM and 55% of those in WSB were on game animals. However, our survey did not include major journals such as *Auk, Wilson Bulletin, Condor, Journal of Mammalogy, Southwestern Naturalist,* and others which publish information on nongame animals.

Discussion

The opinions advanced by Guthery et al. (1982) were merely that—opinions. Those authors did not necessarily identify salient shortcomings of the research effort at that time or crucial research needs. However, their work served as a benchmark against which to compare research activities in the past decade. Insofar as their observations and recommendations were consistent with the protocols and traditions of science, the observations were timeless and appropriate.

Collaboration and Cooperation

The need for multidisciplinary and collaborative efforts seems as intense today as a decade ago, and the failure of Texas wildlife researchers to recognize and respond to this need is distressing. In virtually any discipline, the knowledge base is too great for a scientist from outside the discipline to be fully functional in the different subject matter. A seemingly simple study, like validation of an auditory index of abundance, deals with the physics of sound and statistical matters that are, necessarily and appropriately, beyond the expertise of a wildlife researcher. An auditory index study of enduring value would meld the expertise of the physicist, the statistician, and the biologist. Numerous, if not most, wildlife studies have a need for multidisciplinary input. Lacking input from specialists outside the field, results of these studies may be superficial if not spurious. Probably the most important reason that multidisciplinary wildlife research is not done is the insufficient monetary support for such studies. Only when granting agencies and/or administrators provide the incentives for such research will multidisciplinary wildlife research be accomplished. Granting agencies must encourage multidisciplinary research through their grant programs. The partitioning of monies by research administrators to individual scientists so each will have research monies also has discouraged multidisciplinary research.

Lack of collaboration among research groups is not so distressing from the standpoint of redundant efforts as from the standpoint of contributions to knowledge. Geographic and ecological differences within the state indirectly reduce redundancies of effort. Collaboration among researchers from different geographic and ecological regions could well result in greater insight into nature's processes and wildlife responses to those processes.

Causes and False Causes

Perhaps the greatest failure of the Texas wildlife research establishment in the past decade has been its negligence in addressing causes and effects, processes, and relationships. This is a common problem in wildlife research (Romesburg 1981; Gavin 1989). Recall that 96.1% of Texas-based articles published in The Wildlife Society's periodicals were descriptive studies or commentaries. As a result, wildlife management operates—without a doubt—on some false premises.

As a profession, we have been too ready to accept and apply speculation or descriptive findings as principle. We did not know that our research arm should have been building models or developing hypotheses and then vigorously trying to destroy them.

Processes

Understanding processes and relationships is intimidating to the wildlife researcher, because nature is extremely complex. The number of potentially relevant variables may be too great to measure. Even if all relevant variables could be measured with high accuracy and precision, the human mind is too limited to process the information. The situation seems hopeless, but it is not.

In the face of complexity, the proper scientific approach is to create a simple model or hypothesis based on a few arbitrary elements; the model or hypothesis should make definite predictions about the future (Hawking 1988:9). If the predictions hold, the model or hypothesis is accepted but indefinitely regarded as tentative (all knowledge is tentative) (Bronowski 1973:353). Even the theorems of calculus, which have proven acceptable for 400–600 years, are still called *theorems* because of the chance of exceptions.

Remedies

All sciences have descriptive beginnings, and descriptive natural history was a necessary precursor of wildlife science. After the descriptive phase, researchers should begin searching for patterns in the descriptive knowledge base, searching for order in apparent chaos, rendering complexity simple with arbitrariness, and finding faults with cherished "truths."

We believe the failure of the Texas wildlife research establishment (this is not limited to Texas) to conduct studies with more scientific elegance and greater enduring value, i.e., to address process and cause and effect and to attack what is held to be true, stems from inadequate training in mathematics, statistics, and the philosophy of science.

Four events must occur for research on (and management of) Texas wildlife to become more effective.

1. All levels of the wildlife profession must become more comfortable with mathematics—a language of science. Undergraduate students should take more math, statistics, and biometrics. Graduate students should receive training in advanced statistics, sampling techniques and research design, and probability theory.

   Mathematics training will confer important skills on the wildlife biologist. He or she will be able to think in new patterns and gain experience in the mental process. This training will allow better communication with statisticians who may not understand the biological limits of the data.

2. All levels of the wildlife profession should be exposed to philosophy of science issues. Graduate students should receive intense training in these issues, e.g., an in-depth seminar. This will promote skepticism about our knowledge base, and it will help shift research away from descriptive studies toward hypothetico-deductive studies (Romesburg 1981).

3. All levels of the wildlife profession must become more skeptical of what passes for fact or knowledge. Many papers in the wildlife literature arrive at questionable or false conclusions. The best protection from spurious literature is strong skepticism. With a suspicious outlook, research and management biologists alike will be better able to identify and correct false information. Researchers, in particular, should operate under the assumption that knowledge is suspect.

4. Above all, wildlife researchers must maintain their objectivity. Scientists must not set out to "prove" a hypothesis. Philosophically, nothing can ever be proved correct, but something can be proved wrong. Research should involve a frontal assault on hypotheses and theories. Sound knowledge grows as defective knowledge is identified and discarded and better theories are developed.

Literature Cited

Bronowski, J. 1973. The ascent of man. Boston, Mass.: Little, Brown and Co. 448 pp.

Gavin, T. A. 1989. What's wrong with the questions we ask in wildlife research? Wildl. Soc. Bull. 17:345–50.

Guthery, F. S., E. G. Bolen, and F. A. Stormer. 1982. Wildlife research programs, goals and issues. Pp. 142–56 in J. I. Baccus, ed., Texas wildlife resources and land use. Texas chapter, Wildlife Society, Austin.

Hawking, S. W. 1988. A brief history of time. New York: Bantam Books. 198 pp.

Leopold, A. 1933. Game management. New York: Charles Scribner's Sons. 481 pp.

Romesburg, H. C. 1981. Wildlife science: Gaining reliable knowledge. J. Wildl. Manage. 45:293–313.

V. WILDLIFE MANAGEMENT ON PUBLIC LANDS

Spencer L. Reid
Deputy Commissioner
for Asset Management
Texas General Land Office
1700 N. Congress
Austin, Texas 78701

18. Texas General Land Office

Abstract: Wildlife programs on upland properties managed by the General Land Office (GLO) are implemented through leases to private parties. Leases require management plans prepared in consultation with the U.S. Soil Conservation Service. Wildlife management in coastal areas occurs primarily through leases to private organizations for management of estuarine preserves and through the Texas Coastal Preserve Program operated in conjunction with the Texas Parks and Wildlife Department.

Wildlife Programs

GLO's wildlife programs are tailored to 2 different types of public lands: uplands and submerged lands. The public lands to which I refer are lands dedicated to the Permanent School Fund (PSF). The PSF upland surface estate consists of over 809,938 acres of land, of which approximately 79% (640,000 acres) is under lease to other entities. There are another 5 million acres of submerged lands, of which approximately 1 million acres are in the state's bays and estuaries. Wildlife management options on the upland fee PSF lands are determined by the constitutional and statutory responsibilities under which we operate. The PSF is a trust fund for the public education system, and we serve as trustees for the purpose. As trustees, we have 2 distinct but related responsibilities. We must generate income to the trust as well as preserve, protect, and enhance the land asset that is the portion of the corpus of that trust under our jurisdiction.

Upland Management

During the Clinton administration, we have attempted to accomplish the following goal regarding state uplands under GLO's jurisdiction: to manage state uplands for optimum, sustained yields of livestock and wildlife while upgrading and improving the range resource. Management of all PSF uplands occurs through the vehicle of a lease to a private individual or other public agency. PSF lands are generally not public in the sense of public accessibility, although a significant portion of tracts have been opened under the Public Hunting Program by lease to the Texas Parks and Wildlife Department (TPWD).

Management of the PSF uplands is complicated by the fact that the properties are scattered throughout the state, frequently in small, noncontiguous parcels. The vast majority of this land lies in the Trans-Pecos region of West Texas. It often lacks legal and, in some cases, practical access. PSF lands were intended to be sold, but for decades these lands were leased merely as a warehouse maneuver between sales. Early in this century, oil and gas became the primary income producer, resulting in a cessation of land sales around 1952. By that time, the original allotment of 42 million acres dedicated to the PSF had dwindled to approximately 800,000 acres of the poorest land in the state. Passage of the first trade statute in 1971 acknowledged that the surface estate of PSF land had value as a manageable resource. This statute allowed the block-up of noncontiguous parcels into manageable units. Efforts in resource management have steadily increased since the first trade.

In terms of wildlife management, a key assumption in our program is that quality, quantity, and diversity of wildlife will improve coincidentally with active management of range resources for other purposes. Generally, a mixture of both livestock and wildlife objectives are included in a lease. In some instances, range conditions for wildlife are improved as a consequence of management directed primarily at livestock, but there are some cases where efforts are aimed directly at the wildlife resource.

Since 1983, several tangible steps have been taken to improve the overall management of state land resources.

1. In 1985, GLO secured legislation that requires a Soil Conservation Service (SCS) plan for every surface lease. The plan can be developed by either the SCS or GLO staff. SCS management is required

on the larger tracts and includes complete floral and faunal inventories. Wildlife resource harvests are based on densities, ratios, and increment rates. Our lessees are encouraged to consult regularly with GLO or SCS staff. GLO staff assistance is made available to private landowners to assist in multiple-use plans.

2. Also in 1985, the legislature appropriated to GLO the income that can be collected from surface impacts of mineral development to be allocated to state lessees to construct improvements such as game fencing and to develop water sources for range management. Another mechanism used to construct improvements on PSF lands is encouraging lessees to construct improvements on property financed by offsetting rental fees due the state.

3. GLO has entered into a formal memorandum of understanding with the SCS whereby each agency formally agrees to work together to enhance and improve state lands administered by GLO.

Wildlife management is an integral part of GLO's overall scheme of multiple-use management, which we feel derives maximum benefit from our land resources. When terrain requires that wildlife resources receive the major thrust of management, then livestock management becomes secondary. Staff members initiate the process of preparing a management and development plan after an inventory of the range is completed. This management and development plan generally becomes part of the lease. Lease terms also provide compliance with game survey findings through limits on hunting, thus ensuring that our wildlife resource is not degraded. All phases of the lease are monitored by GLO field staff.

GLO now has 13 units of PSF land comprising 125,111 acres under active range management with specific-interest wildlife plans. Nearly all of these tracts have been blocked up or acquired since 1973 through our trade programs (Table 18.1). We conduct an annual population census and provide big game quotas on 243,397 acres that include most of these units and other leases (Table 18.2). We are especially pleased that several of our lessees have received awards from their local soil and water conservation districts for their work in improving range resources. In all of our management efforts, we never sacrifice the wildlife resource to increase income production from other sources.

In addition to the programs we have implemented on existing tracts in the inventory, we are also making efforts to upgrade the inventory to

Table 18.1. STATE LEASES WITH MANAGEMENT PLANS SPECIFICALLY FOR WILDLIFE

Unit lessee	Acreage	County
Hackberry Creek Ranch	9,540.00	Briscoe
Ernest Angelo, Sr.	1,705.11	Pecos
Indian Cliffs Ranch	18,978.78	El Paso
Martin Lettunich	10,420.20	El Paso
Quail Unlimited	640.00	El Paso
Paul Lettunich	5,760.00	El Paso
Indian Hot Springs	2,566.00	Hudspeth
Pennzoil Sulphur Co.	2,095.56	Culberson
Ronald Herrmann	14,560.00	Brewster
Reagan Canyon Ranch	16,677.68	Brewster
Terlingua Ranch, Inc.	4,660.00	Brewster
Texas Parks and Wildlife Department	22,400.26	Brewster
Sanderson/Mund	9,508.08	Presidio
Yerro Ranch	5,600.00	Duval
Total: 14 units	125,111.67 acres	8 counties

create other opportunities for management. Of considerable importance in this regard is the blocking of state fee lands into manageable tracts. Where possible, all scattered and/or unproductive tracts in our inventory are disposed of, and the money obtained is used to purchase more manageable properties. When leased, these properties provide a greater return to the PSF. Additionally, comprehensive, multiple-use management criteria are developed and implemented to ensure that all ranges are improved to reach and maintain their potential.

GLO has taken the first steps in an extensive program to upgrade range resources of our surface estate. It is our intention that those management programs which have been implemented to date and those to be initiated will become so firmly entrenched that they will never be eliminated. Wildlife management and range resource programs must be institutionalized to protect our natural resources for generations to come.

Table 18.2. LEASES ON WHICH BIG GAME HARVEST QUOTAS ARE SET ANNUALLY

Unit lessee	Acreage	County
Ronald Herrmann	12,000.20	Brewster
Texas Parks and Wildlife Department	22,400.26	Brewster
Texas Parks and Wildlife Department	80,975.92	Hudspeth
Hackberry Creek Ranch	9,540.00	Briscoe
Martin Lettunich	10,420.20	El Paso
Paul Lettunich	5,760.00	El Paso
Reagan Canyon Ranch	16,677.68	Brewster
Double L Cattle Co.	10,115.50	Hudspeth
Wylie McMillan	3,680.00	Hudspeth
L. R. Talley, Jr.	18,956.90	Hudspeth
L. R. and K. W. Talley	15,849.00	Hudspeth
Richard Weinberg	12,154.21	Hudspeth
Russell Wilbanks	9,760.00	Hudspeth
Sanderson/Mund	9,508.08	Presidio
Yerro Ranch	5,600.00	Duval
Total: 15 units	243,397.95 acres	6 counties

Coastal Management

Coastal wildlife management is manifest in the active preservation and protection of our coastal wetlands and estuarine areas. Generally, GLO issues permits for numerous marinas, pipelines, channels, and other coastal structures. Environmental assessments are conducted by GLO staff on all permits, and mitigation is required when an activity results in habitat loss.

In 1941, the legislature placed all state-owned, submerged tidelands in the PSF. Many laws have been enacted since then that affect tidelands management. Most significantly, the Coastal Public Lands Act of 1973 established a comprehensive authority for permitting activities on school lands. One activity authorized by the act is the lease of submerged land to TPWD for management of wildlife refuges. The law also allows the lease of coastal public lands to private organizations for the creation and management of sanctuaries and estuarine preserves. The 2 most significant efforts resulting from the Coastal Public Lands Act are the Coastal Preserve Program and the National Audubon Society sanctuaries.

TEXAS COASTAL PRESERVE PROGRAM

The Texas Coastal Preserve Program was founded in 1987 by the GLO and TPWD to protect unique and fragile natural areas on coastal public lands. Under a cooperative agreement, GLO leases designated preserves to TPWD to manage. Coordinators from each agency evaluate proposed sites, present candidate sites to the Texas Parks and Wildlife Commission and Texas School Land Board for approval, and determine management goals and permissible activities for approved sites.

The first 2 coastal preserves, established in 1988, were South Bay in Cameron County and Welder Flats in Calhoun County. South Bay is a 3,420-acre estuarine area bordering the U.S. Fish and Wildlife Service's Loma Ecological Preserve at the southernmost extreme of Laguna Madre. The bay contains seagrasses, algal flats, mangroves, and oyster reefs. A unique feature of the preserve is an oyster population adapted to the bay's unusually high salinity, which approaches that of seawater.

Welder Flats comprises 1,480 acres of submerged land in San Antonio Bay adjacent to the Welder Ranch. The preserve lies across the bay from the Aransas National Wildlife Refuge and is an important wintering habitat for the endangered whooping crane. In 1991, Armand Bayou in Harris County and Christmas Bay in Brazoria County were added to the program. Designation of these preserves was supported by the Galveston Bay National Estuary Program. Both preserves are within the Galveston Bay system, one of the nation's most heavily used and biologically productive estuarine areas. Intensive urban and industrial growth in the region makes the protection of Armand Bayou and Christmas Bay especially timely.

THE NATIONAL AUDUBON SOCIETY SANCTUARIES

The Audubon Society, either directly or through its local chapters, manages 30 sanctuaries along the Texas Coast comprising over 15,000 acres. They are listed in Table 18.3.

The future of wildlife management on the Texas Coast has been brightened significantly by the passage of SB 1053 by the 72nd Legislature in 1991. SB 1053 establishes a framework for the preparation of

Table 18.3 AUDUBON SANCTUARIES ALONG THE TEXAS COAST

Name	Acreage	County
Sydney Island	126.49	Orange
Deadman's Island	87.00	Aransas
Sundown Island	45.00	Matagorda
Rattlesnake Island Ayres Island Roddy Island	668.00	Aransas
Matagorda Island	3,638.00	Aransas
Bludworth Island Spoil Area	262.00	Aransas
Green Island Spoil Area	1,090.00	Cameron/Willacy
Rollover Pass	136.59	Galveston
Big Bayou Spoil #1	543.61	Nueces
Big Bayou Spoil #2	71.98	Nueces/Aransas
East Shore Spoil	334.49	Nueces
West Nueces Bay Spoil #1	235.70	Nueces
West Nueces Bay Spoil #2	493.57	Nueces
West Nueces Bay Spoil #3	285.24	Nueces
East Nueces Bay Spoil #1	182.83	Nueces
East Nueces Bay Spoil #2	61.66	Nueces
Pita Island Spoil	567.59	Nueces
Rabbit Island	146.50	Kenedy
Southland Cut	572.66	Kenedy
Arroyo Colorado Spoil	228.31	Cameron
Three Island Spoil	275.23	Cameron
Laguna Vista Spoil	560.40	Cameron
Port Isabel Spoil	233.66	Cameron
Lydia Ann Island	156.00	Aransas
Vingt-et-un Islands	61.00	Chambers
Second Chain of Islands	241.00	Aransas
West Bay Bird Island	120.00	Brazoria
Green Island	1,584.00	Cameron
Three Islands	2,287.00	Cameron
Bolivar Flats (Houston chapter)	555.00	Galveston
Total: 30 sanctuaries	15,850.51 acres	11 counties

a comprehensive coastal management plan and establishes the Coastal Coordinating Council with representation by all major state agencies with environmental responsibilities. The General Land Office is the lead agency for this effort. The primary goal of the Coastal Coordinating Council is to establish a coastal plan that will comply with the requirement of the federal Coastal Zone Management Program. Acceptance in the program should result in a significant infusion of federal funds to enhance our abilities to manage wildlife on coastal-area public lands.

Acknowledgments

Portions of this paper were reproduced from several internal memorandums and brochures published by the General Land Office.

I especially thank Bob Blumberg, Paul Loeffler, Christine Ritter and all GLO Coastal staff for their generous assistance in the writing of this document.

Andrew Sansom
Executive Director
Texas Parks and Wildlife Department
4200 Smith School Road
Austin, Texas 78744

19. Texas Parks and Wildlife Department

Abstract: Texas offers many opportunities for people to enjoy numerous activities that involve our diverse fish and wildlife resources. However, there are many challenging problems ahead. These problems include accelerating landscape alterations and fragmentation; increasing human population, especially in urban areas; less accessibility of public access to outdoor opportunities; and declining budgets. Some possible solutions to these problems involve incentives for private landowners to manage and conserve their natural resources, expanded opportunities for public access to resource-oriented outdoor recreation, incentives to promote land acquisition, establishment of endowments, and reduction of governmental red tape.

In the days of naturalist Aldo Leopold and the formation of state game and fish agencies across the nation, things were relatively simple. Management concerns during the first half of this century centered primarily on a limited number of game species, and the primary tools were law enforcement and restocking of depleted populations.

To a great extent, it worked. We have been very successful. In Texas, we now have the largest population of white-tailed deer in existence, including plentiful numbers in locations where the species had been totally exterminated. We have stocked over a billion fish in the public waters of Texas since the formation of Texas Parks and Wildlife, and, each year now, as a direct result of management, we harvest more wild turkey than existed in our state prior to World War II.

Today, Texas ranks first among the states in hunting opportunities and second in fishing. It is the number 1 destination in the world for birdwatchers. The impact of these activities on the economy of the state is substantial: in 1993 alone, visitors to Texas state parks spent nearly $200 million, while hunters, anglers, and other wildlife enthusiasts spent almost $4 billion. Texas's natural advantages form the resource base for a 20-billion-dollar tourism and outdoor recreation industry that is now the third-largest industry in the state and a cornerstone of the new economy. And yet, as rich and varied and wonderful as Texas is, seemingly inexorable changes are threatening our natural treasure even as the demands to use and enjoy it proliferate and climb ever higher.

The landscape of Texas itself has changed. Very little is pristine now. At one time, it was mostly grassland, the southern reaches of the Great Plains, but through the past 2 centuries or so it has almost all been altered in some way. Thanks to generally enlightened management for the past couple of generations, Texans enjoy an unparalleled variety of outdoor uses and a level of access to them that is equally unexcelled.

Besides its diversity, the most significant characteristic of the land in Texas is that it is privately owned. Unlike other states, Texas entered the Union as an independent nation and thus was in a position to negotiate the retention of its public lands. The early leaders of our state did so, then promptly sold those lands off to retire indebtedness, to finance the fledgling government, to build the capitol, and to endow the public schools. As a result, some 97% of the land area of Texas today is in private ownership, and this fact, more than anything else, accounts for its healthy condition.

On the other hand, in times past, the outdoors was more accessible to us because we lived there. Before World War II, 80% of all Texans lived on farms and ranches or in rural communities; today, 80% of us live in cities. Thus, even though good stewardship by private owners has left a legacy of natural wealth, that treasure is less accessible to the majority of Texans than ever before.

The fastest growing segments of our population in Texas are African American and Hispanic, and yet less than 3% of them have ever hunted or fished. Women make up the majority of our population, and yet they are woefully underrepresented in the outdoors, particularly among hunters. At the same time, dogged economic forces threaten stewards of both public and private lands in their efforts to protect the legacy for future generations of Texans and to meet the demands of the present one.

The single most destructive force in the biological environment of Texas today is the continued breakup of family lands brought about by changing economies, inheritance taxes, and a state financial structure that is extremely dependent on property taxes. Throughout much of Central Texas, where only tiny remnants of the native landscape survive today, the average tract size has dropped in this generation alone from thousands of acres to fewer than 100 in many counties. These areas, which once provided large blocks of land for habitat and outdoor recreation, now consist of tiny plots of introduced vegetation that cannot sustain the native wildlife. Meanwhile, the fear of litigation and regulation has closed off lands whose owners once welcomed outdoor enthusiasts.

At the same time, the 3% of Texas that is set aside for the public is also under stress. Declining budgets have reduced the ability of public outdoor recreation agencies at the local, state, and federal levels to operate conservation lands efficiently or even to maintain the vital infrastructure necessary for public use. Because of the reduced opportunity imposed by the sheer paucity of public land in Texas, what we have is taking a beating even as a new generation of city dwellers, increasingly desperate to enjoy the outdoors, places more and more demands on it, and in spite of what, at first glance, may seem to be signals to the contrary today. Texans support conservation of natural resources as never before, and all measures of public opinion in recent years are consistent in this finding. It is reflected in the fact that our understanding and acceptance of responsibility for the land are producing results, as private landowners, nonprofit organizations, and public agencies each develop increased capacity and, more important, strengthened commitment to stewardship. Nonetheless, much more must be done.

In Texas, no foreseeable event or circumstance will ever change the fundamental reality that the vast majority of our natural heritage will always be in private hands. Therefore, we must reinforce the ability of private landowners to protect the resources in their care. One priority should be the establishment of federal inheritance tax relief in exchange for public conservation benefits; thereby, the breakup of family lands, which is the result more often than not of forced sales conducted to meet tax obligations, could be restrained.

We must enhance public access to the outdoors, not just to meet the burgeoning demand but also to encourage access without regard to color, gender, or socioeconomic status and to continue building a constituency for conservation among a population increasingly cut off from exposure to its natural heritage. This is particularly true of children. No amount of effort to introduce children to the joys of resource-oriented outdoor recreation is too much. Whether it be hunting, fishing, camping, hiking, wildlife viewing, canoeing, or rock climbing, the efforts of professional wildlife managers to introduce young people to the joys of exposure to the natural world can never be enough.

Thoughtful and well-constructed incentives can motivate private owners to open their lands to greater outdoor recreational use. And we must make the use of our public lands more efficient both by investing in additional infrastructure and by emphasizing, wherever possible, multiple outdoor recreational use. This emphasis is manifest in efforts to provide expanded opportunity for hunters on state park lands and for enhanced wildlife viewing and other forms of resource-oriented recreation on wildlife management areas (Fig. 19.1).

We must continue to build our preservation inventory by taking advantage of critical acquisition opportunities whenever they arise and by employing nontraditional techniques, such as conservation easements that guarantee permanent protection for the landscape while perpetuating private ownership. Even if we cannot gain immediate use from such procurement, we must never lose sight of our obligation to those who will succeed us. Issues of local property taxes and operational expenses must be high on our list as we consider additional lands in our management inventory, be they wildlife management areas, natural areas, or parks. One tool which can be used to ameliorate these concerns is the establishment of endowments dedicated to these purposes at the time of acquisition. Policymakers must support responsible means of securing the necessary funds for this purpose, because the maintenance of our natural heritage and diversity requires it.

The ability of both public and private land stewards to manage biological resources should be augmented through creation of incentives and reduction in red tape. Finally, we must acknowledge that everyone has a way to contribute and a role to play. Neither public nor private entities have a premium on responsibility. There is too much to be done, and the potential of each should be expanded.

Without exposure to wild places, urban Texans may not gain an appreciation for them. Without an appreciation for the outdoors, conserving and managing biological resources is not a priority. The irony is that temporary interludes of escape to the wild through hunting, wildlife viewing, or just nature contemplation may represent a key to maintaining sanity in the increasing urban condition of our state.

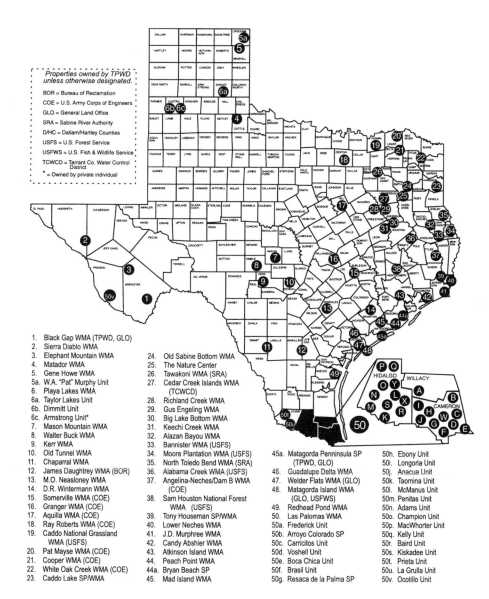

Properties owned by TPWD unless otherwise designated.

BOR = Bureau of Reclamation
COE = U.S. Army Corps of Engineers
GLO = General Land Office
SRA = Sabine River Authority
D/HC = Dallam/Hartley Counties
USFS = U.S. Forest Service
USFWS = U.S. Fish & Wildlife Service
TCWCD = Tarrant Co. Water Control District
* = Owned by private individual

1. Black Gap WMA (TPWD, GLO)
2. Sierra Diablo WMA
3. Elephant Mountain WMA
4. Matador WMA
5. Gene Howe WMA
5a. W.A. "Pat" Murphy Unit
6. Playa Lakes WMA
6a. Taylor Lakes Unit
6b. Dimmitt Unit
6c. Armstrong Unit*
7. Mason Mountain WMA
8. Walter Buck WMA
9. Kerr WMA
10. Old Tunnel WMA
11. Chaparral WMA
12. James Daughtrey WMA (BOR)
13. M.O. Neasloney WMA
14. D.R. Wintermann WMA
15. Somerville WMA (COE)
16. Granger WMA (COE)
17. Aquilla WMA (COE)
18. Ray Roberts WMA (COE)
19. Caddo National Grassland WMA (USFS)
20. Pat Mayse WMA (COE)
21. Cooper WMA (COE)
22. White Oak Creek WMA (COE)
23. Caddo Lake SP/WMA

24. Old Sabine Bottom WMA
25. The Nature Center
26. Tawakoni WMA (SRA)
27. Cedar Creek Islands WMA (TCWCD)
28. Richland Creek WMA
29. Gus Engeling WMA
30. Big Lake Bottom WMA
31. Keechi Creek WMA
32. Alazan Bayou WMA
33. Bannister WMA (USFS)
34. Moore Plantation WMA (USFS)
35. North Toledo Bend WMA (SRA)
36. Alabama Creek WMA (USFS)
37. Angelina-Neches/Dam B WMA (COE)
38. Sam Houston National Forest WMA (USFS)
39. Tony Houseman SP/WMA
40. Lower Neches WMA
41. J.D. Murphree WMA
42. Candy Abshier WMA
43. Atkinson Island WMA
44. Peach Point WMA
44a. Bryan Beach SP
45. Mad Island WMA

45a. Matagorda Penninsula SP (TPWD, GLO)
46. Guadalupe Delta WMA
47. Welder Flats WMA (GLO)
48. Matagorda Island WMA (GLO, USFWS)
49. Redhead Pond WMA
50. Las Palomas WMA
50a. Frederick Unit
50b. Arroyo Colorado SP
50c. Carricitos Unit
50d. Voshell Unit
50e. Boca Chica Unit
50f. Brasil Unit
50g. Resaca de la Palma SP

50h. Ebony Unit
50i. Longoria Unit
50j. Anacua Unit
50k. Taomina Unit
50l. McManus Unit
50m. Penitas Unit
50n. Adams Unit
50o. Champion Unit
50p. MacWhorter Unit
50q. Kelly Unit
50r. Baird Unit
50s. Kiskadee Unit
50t. Prieta Unit
50u. La Grulla Unit
50v. Ocotillo Unit

Fig. 19.1. *Wildlife management areas (WMA), wildlife research and demonstration areas (WRDA), and state parks (SP) managed by the Texas Parks and Wildlife Department Wildlife Division, September 1997).*

More than anything else, we must always remember that the primary beneficiaries of our work are not born yet, and we should be willing to make sacrifices on their behalf. That is the greatest privilege we have, and therein lies the opportunity to extend our abiding love of Texas beyond our own lifetimes and into the future.

F. Stephen Hartmann
Director, West Texas Operations
University Lands—Surface Interests
The University of Texas System
P.O. Box 553
Midland, Texas 79702

20. University Lands

Abstract: The University of Texas System (University Lands—Surface Interests) manages over 2.1 million acres of land located in 19 counties in West Texas. Management of wildlife resources has intensified since the mid-1970's. Under current leasing policies, all lessees are required to "develop and carry out a sound conservation, range, and wildlife improvement program." Aerial surveys of the wildlife resources were initiated in 1979 and have continued on a yearly basis. The information from these surveys is the basis for which many of the management decisions are made. An average of 600,000 acres of white-tailed and mule deer range are surveyed each year using a helicopter. An airplane is used to survey another 500,000 acres of pronghorn habitat. Animal densities, buck-to-doe ratios, fawn-to-doe ratios, estimates of animal quality, and overall range conditions are determined. Wildlife research and habitat improvement projects on University Lands are numerous. Recently, pronghorn research has been conducted in Hudspeth County, predator/prey research involving coyotes has been done in Andrews County, and Ward County has been the site of scaled quail research. Wildlife "guzzlers" are being installed in arid areas where water availability is a limiting factor for desert mule deer and pronghorn. Many brush control, reclamation, and desirable plant establishment projects are also improving conditions for wildlife on University Lands.

The University of Texas System owns and manages over 2.1 million acres of land in West Texas. One million acres of these University Lands were set aside by the Texas Legislature in 1876. The 1876 constitution also established the Permanent University Fund to receive all proceeds from the sale of land, all grants, donations, and appropriations. Another 1 million acres of land were appropriated by the 1883 Legislature, and this legislature removed the lands from sale and authorized the leasing of the land. Today, the University Lands—Surface Interests Office has the responsibility of supervising all activities on the surface of these lands. Its stated mission is "to maximize the revenue from University Lands while applying intensive management and conservation programs to improve the sustained productivity of the land."

Currently, there are 123 combination grazing/hunting/recreation leases on these University Lands. Our current leasing system is known as the "flexible grazing lease," where a lease holder pays rent based on the actual amount, kind, and market value of the livestock that is grazed on the lease. The holder also pays a per-acre hunting and recreation lease charge. Under this leasing system, all lessees are required to "develop and carry out a sound conservation, range, and wildlife improvement program."

A "conservation plan" is required for each grazing lease and is developed jointly by the grazing lessee, a University Lands representative, and the U.S. Soil Conservation Service. The plan includes land treatments such as proper grazing use, deferred grazing, and brush control, all of which directly impact wildlife resources and habitat. This plan provides for perpetuation of range and wildlife resources through management practices.

Realizing that the management practice of brush control can be critical for wildlife, we require our lessees to contact us before any major brush work is started. The area is then inspected, and decisions are made based on the actual need for brush control, the presence or absence of endangered species or suitable habitat, and the amount of work to be done. If brush control is determined to be needed, then generally the lessee is required to pattern the brush work and leave key habitat areas.

We are fortunate to have one or more species of native game animals occurring on almost all areas of University Lands. These include white-tailed deer, mule deer, pronghorn, collared peccary, wild turkey, scaled quail, northern bobwhite, and mourning dove. Many of our management practices and decisions revolve around these animals. However, nongame and endangered species receive appropriate consideration and influence the decision-making process. The importance of managing for these species continues to grow.

The mid- to late 1970's were the formative years of the University Lands wildlife management program(s). It was during this time that the expertise of the Texas Parks and Wildlife Department, the Texas A & M Extension Service, the U.S. Soil Conservation Service, and several private management consultants were put to use. We were fortunate in that we had a wealth of agency expertise from which to obtain assistance to develop a plan and set goals for a management program. With their help, we began doing our own aerial survey work to determine where and how many native big game species live on University Lands.

These surveys serve a 2-fold purpose. First, they provide the means to determine the number and kinds of animals on the leases, which, in turn, allows us to make sound harvest recommendations. Valuable information such as buck-to-doe ratios, doe-to-fawn ratios, deer densities, and a general estimate of the number of other wildlife on a lease is also obtained. Second, they give us a unique opportunity to observe the leases and note the overall condition of the fences, waterings, pens, and other physical improvements as well as the general condition of the land resource.

An average of 600,000 acres of white-tailed deer and mule deer range is surveyed each year using a helicopter. With knowledge gained from these surveys, we are better able to properly manage the deer herds and assist lessees in setting up good deer management programs.

An additional 500,000 acres of pronghorn habitat is surveyed each year using an airplane. Most of this acreage is located in Hudspeth County, but small herds are also found in Crockett, Reagan, and Culberson Counties. From the survey data, the number of animals to be harvested is determined, and the appropriate number of permits are issued to each lessee. This enables us to control the harvest, a key element of our pronghorn management program.

Range and wildlife personnel work with oilfield and research personnel to reclaim rangeland previously disturbed by oilfield activity or other surface disturbance activities. Revegetation studies of the Texas Agricultural Experiment Station have been used to develop reclamation techniques for salt-affected areas on University Lands. Reserve pits, created during the drilling process, are being revegetated successfully using fourwing saltbush, an indigenous, salt-tolerant plant species. This plant is high in crude protein content and is a desirable browse species for both deer and livestock. Caliche pit reclamation and revegetation projects also provide wildlife habitat. Abandoned pits are shaped using heavy machinery and seeded to native grasses and shrubs. Using these techniques allows us to create wildlife habitat on previously unproductive sites.

Other wildlife research and habitat improvement projects on University Lands are numerous. Desirable plant establishment projects in Crockett, Reagan and Ward Counties are being conducted by Texas A & M University. Again, native plants including grasses, forbs, and shrubs are being planted in areas to diversify the plant community and enhance wildlife habitat. Texas Tech University in conjunction with the Welder Wildlife Foundation has conducted pronghorn research in Hudspeth County as well as predator/prey research involving coyotes in Andrews County. Scaled quail research in Ward County has also taken place. With the aid of SCS personnel, wildlife "guzzlers" are being installed in arid areas where water availability is a limiting factor for desert mule deer.

University Lands range and wildlife personnel are members of The Wildlife Society, the Society for Range Management, and the Texas Wildlife Association. Much importance is placed on attendance at annual meetings, symposia, round table meetings, and training sessions. Thus, as resource managers we are better able to stay informed on range and wildlife management practices, research, and environmental and legal issues and make the right decisions for University Lands.

Craig A. Steffens
Texas Department of Transportation
DeWitt C. Greer State Highway
Building
Austin, TX 78701

21. Texas Department of Transportation

Abstract: A memorandum of understanding (MOU) has been negotiated between the Texas Department of Transportation (TxDOT) and the Texas Parks and Wildlife Department (TPWD) in part to create and preserve wildlife habitat on the roadsides under the jurisdiction of TxDOT. A proposal was requested by TxDOT from TPWD for a Roadsides for Texas Wildlife Program. The following is the subject proposal written by Gene T. Miller and James D. Ray, wildlife biologists of TPWD, and is hereby submitted by Craig A. Steffens, chief landscape architect for TxDOT. This proposal is currently under review for adoption and incorporation into the integrated Vegetation Management Standards for roadsides by TxDOT.

Wildlife biologists in Texas and throughout the nation recognize that roadsides are an important wildlife habitat, especially in high agricultural use areas. Intensive cultivation has reduced the amount and quality of nesting cover available to ground-nesting birds and mammals (i.e., pheasants, ducks, rabbits, and songbirds, in many areas in the High Plains), causing road rights-of-way to become of even greater value to wildlife production. Although these ribbons of green comprise only a small fraction of our land area, researchers have found them to be highly productive nesting sites for more than 40 species of birds and small mammals that nest on the ground or in low vegetation. Roadsides can receive almost continuous nesting use from March through August. Disturbance of roadside cover by early mowing, farm tillage, haying, or vehicle and tractor encroachment during the peak nesting months (April, May, June, July, variable within the state) significantly lowers production for roadside nesting species. However, roadsides with natural vegetative cover (grasses, wildflowers, and legumes) not only provide valuable wildlife habitat but also serve to enhance aesthetic beauty, retard "noxious" weed growth, improve water quality, reduce erosion, and provide proper drainage. This increases the life of roads and reduces maintenance costs.

With the exception of the wildflower program, roadside management in Texas has historically favored the clean, "manicured" look. However, due to current financial constraints, roadside managers in the Texas Department of Transportation (TxDOT) are now faced with a dilemma; budgets are not likely to increase, fuel and contract mowing costs continue to rise, and environmental and health concerns are causing reevaluation of herbicide use. In Texas, mowing costs on 750,000 acres of rights-of-way have increased from $10 million in 1969 to $35 million in 1988. Mowing costs were reduced by millions of dollars in 1984 and 1985, when the TxDOT's Vegetation Management System (VMS), which calls for a greatly reduced mowing scenario, was fully implemented. However, with a relaxation of VMS policy (i.e., greatly increased mowing activity), costs again escalated from $21 million in 1984 and 1985 to an all-time high of $35 million in 1988. Since then, spending on mowing has decreased to $27 million in 1989 and 1990 due to a budgetary ceiling.

Opportunity for Action

In view of these facts, especially with rising concern over state government expenditures, a great opportunity exists for TPWD to form a partnership with TxDOT to develop a Roadsides for Texas Wildlife initiative, incorporating specific wildlife concerns/recommendations and principles of integrated roadside management into the VMS.

Goal

The goal of a Roadsides for Texas Program is to maintain and improve wildlife values on Texas's rights-of-way consistent with safe travel by the public. Suggested program objectives are

1. to provide information to the public and roadway authorities (state and county levels) to build an awareness of the importance of roadsides as wildlife habitat, as well as the other environmental and economic benefits of integrated roadside management;
2. to reduce disturbance and destruction of roadside wildlife habitat, especially during the spring and summer nesting season; and

3. to improve the quality of roadside habitat for the benefit of wildlife and people.

Strategy

A memorandum of understanding (MOU) involving roadside vegetation management has been signed by both TxDOT and TPWD commissions. This will help to insure perpetual implementation of key points of the Roadsides for Texas Wildlife concept. Also, the stage is set for work with county roadway departments and noxious weed control districts in areas where some of the greatest benefits to ground-dwelling wildlife can be achieved.

Justification

Some important benefits from a Roadsides for Texas Wildlife initiative to all citizens are

1. millions of taxpayers' dollars saved annually;
2. improvement of aesthetics (i.e., wildflower program in place over parts of the state);
3. increased wildlife production for viewing and hunting; and
4. an increased awareness, especially on the part of children, of our natural heritage and wildlife values that are so important to our quality of life.

Within the High and Rolling Plains, there exists considerable opportunity for increased pheasant/duck production with the implementation of such a program which could connote millions of dollars pumped into local economies in a region where hunting-related income is becoming increasingly more important to landowners and local communities.

Key Wildlife Considerations and Recommendations

Key recommendations for incorporation into the revision of TxDOT "Standards of Vegetation Management" (the manual for VMS) include the following.

- Delay roadside mowing of the ditch bottom and backslope until after August 1. Where possible, leave roadsides undisturbed year around. Reason: by August 1, most species can nest successfully.
- Use rotational mowing for brush control. Reason: mowing only once every third year, with the exception of extremely high rainfall

areas, will normally retard brushy growth while reducing roadside habitat disturbance.

- Use spot treatment (spraying) to manage sites for noxious weed control, safety, and snow drifting. Reason: spot spraying leaves cover intact, is less costly, and decreases the chance of causing nest destruction or abandonment.
- Roadsides mowed after September 1 should be clipped "high." Reason: a minimum of 12 inches of erect, residual cover is necessary for the following year's early nesters. Establish "no-mow" areas where possible.
- Avoid indiscriminate roadside burning. Reason: under prescribed conditions, burning can be an effective management tool for enhancement of native vegetation in these areas. However, widespread and indiscriminate burning may remove essential cover.
- Jointly develop appropriate "site-specific" grass/legume/wildflower seeding mixtures for different ecological regions of the state. Reason: rights-of-way requiring seeding should be planted to locally adapted mixtures best suited for wildlife, low maintenance, and aesthetic beauty and could serve as demonstration plots.

These key points can be easily incorporated into the revision of VMS's Level #3, Moderate Maintenance Areas, and Level #4, Low Maintenance Areas, which comprise most of the state's rural road system.

Potential Conflicts

Several real or perceived problems must be addressed. Weeds require spot control; snow drift problems can be considered on east-west roads in the Panhandle; and wildlife/vehicle interaction will be a safety concern. (Research in several states has found this to be no more of a problem on mowed than unmowed roadsides.) The greatest resistance to elements of this initiative will come from row-crop farmers in the intensively cultivated areas of the state because of the weed issue. What they must acknowledge is that their continual disturbance of roadsides perpetuates the problem. They may contact legislators, Agricultural Stabilization and Conservation Service (ASCS) officials, highway commissioners, and their local noxious weed control district, if one exists, to combat our efforts. However, we must gain their support if we are to achieve our goal and objectives in these localities. Our overall expectation of results in this initiative is to gain key concessions for wildlife and reach compromise on other points.

James E. Walters
Chief, Branch of Resource Operations
Division of Ranger Activities
Southwest Region
National Park Service
P.O. Box 728
Santa Fe, New Mexico 87504-0728

22. National Park Service

Abstract: Six of 13 National Park Service units in Texas have significant wildlife management programs. Four units allow hunting and fishing activities. There are policies to perpetuate native plant and animal diversity, to rely on natural processes to control their populations, to control problem animals, to restore or reintroduce native species, and to eliminate exotic species. Some management policies are controversial and are not easy to implement, especially issues that involve emotional public relations. Examples of these policies are discussed in the context of the documents upon which they are based.

Of the 13 units administered by the National Park Service (NPS) in Texas (Fig. 22.1), 6 areas have identified significant wildlife management programs in their resource planning documents. Four of the Texas units permit the taking of certain fish and wildlife following the Texas Parks and Wildlife Department's season and bag limits.

It is true that most people in the United States are surprised to learn that people can actually enter some NPS lands with guns and fishing gear and legally kill wildlife. These activities do appear to fly in the face of the 1916 National Park Service Organic Act, which chartered the agency to "conserve the scenery and the natural and historic objects and the wildlife therein and to provide for the enjoyment of the same in such manner and by such means as will leave them unimpaired for the enjoyment of future generations."

National Park System Areas

NHP	National Historical Park
NHS	National Historic Site
NM	National Monument
N MEM	National Memorial
NP	National Park
N PRES	National Preserve
NRA	National Recreation Area
NS	National Seashore
WSR	Wild and Scenic River

  * = parks with significant wildlife management issues.
** = nps areas which permit the taking of certain wildlife.

Fig. 22.1. *National Park Service units in Texas.*

Hunting and Fishing Authorization

The fact that hunting and fishing are permitted in some areas of the National Park System, not just in Texas but throughout the United States, is usually a reflection of the specific wording in the unit's congressional enabling legislation. Thus, hunting is permitted at Big

Thicket National Preserve, Lake Meredith National Recreation Area, and Amistad National Recreation Area, and hunting and fishing are major recreational activities at Padre Island National Seashore.

However, these hunting and fishing activities are taking place in national "recreation areas," "preserves," and "seashores" rather than in national parks and national monuments. These special designations were, in fact, created to accommodate the fact that, whereas the Congress desired establishment of the unit as part of the National Park System, it also recognized that authorization of consumption activities such as hunting and fishing would not be in keeping with the traditional mission of the National Park Service as prescribed in the Organic Act of 1916.

Accordingly, most national parks and monuments prohibit hunting and fishing. We have to emphasize the word "most" because fishing is a permitted, although controversial, activity in some national parks. You may be familiar with the growing controversy over fishing within Yellowstone National Park, and you may also be aware of the incredible trout fishery in the Colorado River within Grand Canyon National Park. There is no specific authorization for fishing in these units. Fishing was simply a traditional use in the parks which somehow became "grandfathered" into the day-to-day business of these areas. There is a strong feeling among many park service traditionalists that this consumptive use is wrong.

On the other hand, the Alaska National Interest Lands Conservation Act (ANILCA) of 1980 specifically identified subsistence hunting and fishing as being permitted in most of the newly established Alaskan parks. But because the Alaskan parks are unusual in many ways compared with the rest of the National Park Service (use of aircraft, active mining operations, etc.), my comments will be based upon wildlife management policies pertinent to the "lower" 49 states and, specifically, to Texas.

Most National Park Service employees find it very difficult to explain to a visitor who has just been handed a ticket for picking a flower or for walking off a trail and, therefore, "impacting" (trampling) vegetation about the fragility of a park's ecology when the same park unit may allow hunters and fishermen to periodically enter the area to remove major vertebrate species from that same ecosystem. This is especially true when one realizes that most of the game populations in the parks is being harvested with only a rudimentary understanding of the population dynamics of the game animal and an even shallower understanding of the impacts of removing this component of the ecosystem. Still, most National Park Service employees do what the Congress directs and are well aware of the pressures which dictate how some park units are to be operated.

Wildlife Management Policies

The service attempts to administer wildlife within Texas parks in the same manner the rest of the parks are administered. Wildlife management policies are basically refined from the mission statement contained in the 1916 Organic Act (mentioned above) to more specific policy statements identified in the 1988 *Management Policies* handbook. The wildlife management statements identified in the policies handbook itself evolved from a brief but important document commissioned by Interior Secretary Stuart Udall in 1962.

The Leopold Report

In response to the extremely controversial practice of park rangers shooting hundreds of elk within Yellowstone National Park as a population control measure, Secretary Udall asked a group of 5 eminent biologists, chaired by A. Starker Leopold, to form a board whose charter was to provide guidance and direction concerning wildlife management in the National Park System. Their findings, generally referred to as *The Leopold Committee Report* (1963) or more simply as the *Leopold Report,* has subsequently served as the foundation upon which all NPS wildlife management practices are based. It is this report which established the objective of managing national parks "and the wild life therein" as a "vignette of primitive America." This meant that the NPS should use the time prior to European settlement of the continent as a standard by which to gauge the natural processes which constantly modify the biological scene within the parks. It was not, as some people interpret, a mandate to return park biosystems to this period.

The *Leopold Report* also established the extremely important premise that wildlife present on the continent before the coming of Europeans would be considered as natural, or native, and those animals introduced by Europeans would be classified as exotic. Exotic species are subsequently considered as fundamentally undesirable within all national park areas and have been the source of massive expenditures of labor and dollars in attempts to eradicate them.

National Park Service Guidelines

The National Park Service attempted to further refine the directives of both the *Leopold Report* and its own *Management Policies* handbook (USDI 1988) for park managers in a recent additional planning document entitled *NPS-77 Natural Resource Management Guideline* (USDI 1991). Thus, through a tiering process, a park manager dealing with wildlife is provided a set of directives which distills the "preserve and protect" mandate of the Organic Act into policy statements such as the following:

> The National Park Service will seek to perpetuate the native animal life as part of the natural ecosystem of parks. (Chap. 2:5)

> Natural processes will be relied on to control populations of native species to the greatest extent possible. Unnatural concentrations of native species caused by human activities may be controlled if the activities causing the concentration cannot be controlled. (Chap. 4:6)

> Animal populations or individuals will be controlled in natural, cultural, and development zones when they present a direct threat to visitor safety and health, and in cultural and development zones when necessary to protect property or landscaped areas. (Chap. 4:6)

Wildlife policy statements are further refined in the *Natural Resource Management Guideline* and provide the park manager steps needed to develop a program to maintain biological and genetic diversity; procedures recommended to consider the restoration of native species; steps necessary for augmentation of diminished populations, for predator management, and for immobilization and restraint procedures; and methods used for surveying and estimating populations, for disease control, for scientific collecting, for management of endangered and threatened species, etc.

Obviously, there is no manual which can provide answers to even the simplest ecological questions confronting wildlife managers. The purpose of the NPS wildlife planning documents is intended to ensure, as much as possible, that national park units are managing wildlife by following a standardized set of academically recognized procedures so that wildlife issues throughout the system are managed in essentially the same manner. Individual problems will vary, but procedures to resolve these problems are standard. The goal of this program is to encourage the park manager to take full advantage of available information in scientific literature to ensure that wildlife management techniques prescribed by the scientific and professional communities are used in developing management decisions. The planning documents also attempt to ensure that pertinent laws are followed in development and implementation of management decisions. Accordingly, park personnel experiencing bear problems are aware of a range of acceptable management alternatives; the procedures which must be followed to develop a management program, including public involvement; and the realization that they will be expected to use the best available science in their decisions. They are also made aware that, all too often, wildlife management is not a simple matter of science and that they are dealing with extremely emotional public relations issues.

These management alternatives often include the controversial decision of needing to destroy certain problem animals and the equally controversial decision regarding reintroduction of native species into park ecosystems. The above policy documents and directives mandate that the park superintendent be aware of his or her responsibility to inventory his or her wildlife resources and, when it is "reasonable and practical" to do so, reintroduce those native wildlife species which were extirpated during historic periods and to remove those which are considered exotic.

These policy mandates drive the current controversy concerning reintroduction of the Mexican gray wolf to Big Bend National Park, the gray wolf to Yellowstone National Park, the desert bighorn sheep to Guadalupe Mountains National Park and Big Bend, and the black bear and wild turkey to Big Thicket National Preserve. To the National Park Service, the issue is not whether we should or should not consider these reintroductions; rather, our own policies and our understanding that these animals represent important missing components of the native ecosystems require that we must. The real questions which drive most wildlife management issues are those of regional and national politics and the feasibility that such reintroductions can be accomplished successfully. Politics as a major influence of NPS wildlife management programs is illustrated by headlines that appeared on 7–15 January 1992, in Washington, Wyoming, and Montana newspapers addressing attempts by the park service to remove the mountain goat from Olympic National Park and the destruction of bison, suspected of carrying the brucellosis virus, immediately outside the boundary of Yellowstone National Park. Closer to home, we are attempting to learn more about the local population of mountain lions and understand what prompted these animals to attack park visitors in Big Bend National Park. This study does not set well with some people who view the solution as simply to kill all the lions in the park. We are also attempting to control the feral pigs in Big Thicket National Preserve. Politics has led to the present ironic situation wherein park rangers are attempting to totally eliminate these animals from Big Thicket by encouraging hunters to shoot all the pigs they see during the hunting season but must ticket someone caught shooting them any other time.

All of these issues offer testimony to National Park Service managers that wildlife management problems are never easy and require the integration of professional information and skill in the business of people management if they are to be successfully resolved.

Literature Cited

Leopold, A. S., S. A. Cain, C. M. Cottam, I. N. Gabrielson, and T. L. Kimball. 1963. Wildlife management in the national parks. Trans. N. Amer. Wildl. and Nat. Resour. Conf. 28:29–42.

USDI. 1988. Management policies. Natl. Park Serv. 77 pp.

———. 1991. NPS-77 natural resources management guideline. Natl. Park Serv. 381 pp.

Joseph P. Mazzoni
Assistant Regional Director, Refuges
and Wildlife
U.S. Fish and Wildlife Service
Room 3018
500 Gold Avenue, SW
Albuquerque, New Mexico 87103

23. National Wildlife Refuges

Abstract: National wildlife refuges play an increasingly important role in the protection and management of wildlife habitats of national significance throughout the country. The National Wildlife Refuge System embraces over 92 million acres within 510 individual units located in all 50 states. Refuges have contributed to conservation of Texas's vast natural resources for over 50 years. Nineteen areas totaling over 480,000 acres are now located in the state. Management of Texas's refuges involves management of wildlife populations, habitat, public use, economic use, and technical assistance. The purposes and management of each refuge are described. The importance of effective partnerships between public and private interests to the success of refuge programs and the preservation of Texas's wildlife resources generally are stressed.

National wildlife refuges play an increasingly important role in the protection and management of wildlife habitats of national significance throughout the country. Beginning with establishment of the first refuge in 1903, the 3-acre Pelican Island National Wildlife Refuge in Florida, the National Wildlife Refuge System (Refuge System) has grown to the point where it now embraces over 92 million acres, with 80 million of them located in Alaska. As the only national system of lands specifically dedicated to the needs of wildlife, the Refuge System consists of over 510 individual units, with at least 1 located in each of our 50 states. The special mission of the Refuge System is to "provide, preserve, restore, and manage a national network of lands and waters sufficient in size, diversity, and location to meet society's need for areas where the widest possible spectrum of benefits associated with wildlife and wildlands is enhanced and made available."

Individual refuges and refuge purposes are as varied as the wildlife they seek to protect and support. They range from island habitats in Hawaii to the prairie potholes of the Midwest, from the Alaskan tundra to the coastal marshes of Texas, and from the Sonoran Desert of Arizona to the suburbs of some of our largest cities.

Management of this great national system of wildlife habitats is dedicated primarily to maintenance of natural flora and fauna and their associated habitats. However, service policy permits the full range of wildlife and wildlife habitat management activities and strategies, depending upon what is most appropriate for each refuge and what is required to meet individual refuge objectives. On colonial bird-nesting islands along the Pacific Coast, our management is geared toward simply protecting the birds and their habitat from human development and disturbances. On other areas, particularly in the lower 48, prescribed fire, livestock grazing, mowing, intensive farming, native plant restoration, and other techniques are used to enhance nesting and migration habitat and supplement natural food supplies.

Within the Refuge System, there are 75 areas totaling 20.6 million acres that have been designated by Congress as wilderness. On these areas, our management is designed to maintain natural ecological systems, with management guided by the "minimum tool" concept. That is, we use whatever technique we feel is minimally necessary to fulfill the wildlife management purposes of the refuge. On many of our Alaskan refuge wilderness areas, for example, prescribed fire along with natural fire is used extensively to manage habitat for moose. On desert wilderness in the Kofa and Cabeza Prieta National Wildlife Refuges in Arizona, natural water seeps are enhanced and artificial water facilities developed to help meet desert bighorn sheep population objectives. While we have no designated wilderness in Texas, in this region we are involved with wilderness management in Oklahoma, New Mexico, and Arizona.

The National Wildlife Refuges of Texas

National wildlife refuges have played a role in the conservation of Texas's vast natural resources for over 50 years. The first refuge in Texas was established in 1935 with acquisition of the 5,800-acre Muleshoe National Wildlife Refuge. Since that time, 19 refuges have been established totaling over 480,000 acres (Fig. 23.1). The diversity of

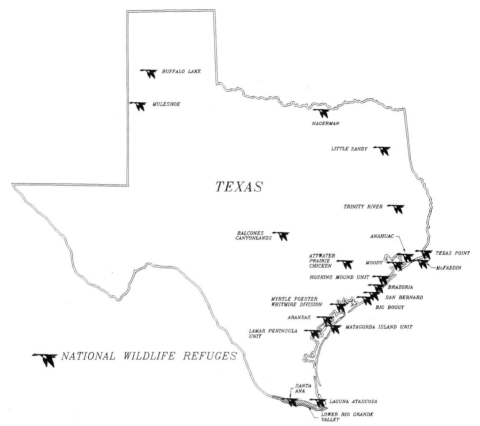

Fig. 23.1. *National Wildlife Refuges in Texas.*

Texas's refuges and their associated wildlife mirrors the diversity of the
Refuge System itself. While most have been created for the protection
and management of coastal marsh waterfowl wintering habitat, others
have been established for such varied species as the Attwater's greater
prairie-chicken and neotropical migrants such as the black-capped
vireo and golden-cheeked warbler. Management of Texas's refuges can
be divided into 5 basic categories: wildlife population management,
habitat management, public use management, economic use management, and technical assistance.

The Anahuac Refuge Complex consists of Anahuac, Texas Point,
and McFaddin Refuges, comprising 96,000 acres. These refuges were
established primarily to provide habitat for wintering waterfowl and

other waterbirds. Wildlife management involves a combination of water management (in this case, to regulate water levels and salinity), livestock grazing, and prescribed burning to provide favorable feeding and loafing conditions. Grazing use is monitored. We have also been involved with the Texas Parks and Wildlife Department in a cooperative effort to restore and enhance the Salt Bayou drainage. This work is designed to restore much of these upper coastal marshes to their historical complex of fresh, brackish, and saline conditions.

Perhaps the single most important resource problem we face in this area, as with 7 of our 11 refuges located on the Texas coast, is the shoreline erosion and saltwater intrusion caused by the Gulf Intracoastal Waterway. Solutions to this problem are costly, and our progress to date has been very limited. Only through large infusions of funds and the assistance of the Corps of Engineers will we even begin to address the magnitude of this problem.

These refuges have an annual, regulated harvest of American alligators as a means of maintaining desired population levels. A limited amount of rice farming is also practiced to provide supplemental food for geese and ducks.

The Brazoria Refuge Complex consists of Brazoria, San Bernard, and Big Boggy Refuges and the recently acquired Hoskins Mound unit, comprising a total of 75,000 acres. These refuges were also established primarily to provide wintering habitat for waterfowl and other waterbirds. In addition to deep marsh management, Brazoria Refuge also manages several moist soil units, which require a more intensive level of water manipulation. These areas are especially attractive to wintering ducks. Prescribed burning and livestock grazing are also used to enhance browse conditions for geese and field-feeding ducks.

With the recent addition of the 28,000-acre Hoskins Mount unit to this refuge complex, a comprehensive management planning process has been initiated that will outline long-term goals, objectives, and management strategies for habitat, wildlife, and public use. A draft plan will soon be available for public review and comment. Management of the refuge's 28-acre rookery island in east Matagorda Bay is designed to provide protection to the various nesting species from human disturbances and predation during the nesting season. We are also working to stabilize island shoreline erosion.

The Aransas Refuge and nearby Matagorda Island unit of Aransas Refuge are the winter home for the Woods Buffalo/Aransas flock of some 157 whooping cranes. While these areas were established for waterfowl and all other migratory birds, management emphasis has been on providing a secure wintering area for the whooper.

Prescribed fire is the primary habitat management tool on Aransas Refuge where it is used to control woody vegetation encroachment and maintain a healthy grassland community. Burned areas also provide very attractive feeding areas for whoopers. Efforts are also under way to restore the historic Attwater's greater prairie-chicken habitat in the Tatton unit of the refuge through a combination of prescribed burning and controlled grazing. A 2-year study of the impacts of bay commercial and recreational activities on whooping cranes and other water birds was recently completed. With completion of the study report, we are hopeful that this study will provide insight into the effects of these activities and, where they may be harmful, suggestions as to how we might minimize adverse impacts.

With elimination of grazing from Matagorda Island, prescribed fire has become our primary habitat management tool. A long-term, comprehensive study of fire effects on both plants and animals is being completed on the island through Texas Tech University and the Texas Cooperative Research Unit for the purpose of developing information on how this management technique can best be applied to meet refuge objectives. Given the purposes of refuge lands on Matagorda Island, our management emphasis will be on endangered species such as the whooping crane and piping plover and on migratory birds, including neotropical migrants, wading birds, and shorebirds, and on maintaining the natural ecological components of a coastal barrier island. With the recent adoption of a comprehensive island management plan, we have embarked on a unique cooperative relationship with the Texas Parks and Wildlife Department, the Texas General Land Office, and the Texas Nature Conservancy for management of the island's ecological, educational, and recreational resources.

Management of the Laguna Atascosa Refuge has historically been focused on providing freshwater marsh habitat for redhead ducks using the Lower Laguna Madre and supplemental food for wintering geese. Providing wintering habitat through marsh management for migrating and wintering shorebirds has also been an important part of the program. A major problem at Laguna Atascosa Refuge is the lack of adequate water rights to provide consistent freshwater inflow needed for proper management of the resacas and marsh units. We are currently pursuing alternative ways of acquiring needed high quality fresh water.

The Laguna Atascosa Refuge now has the lead in the recovery of the endangered ocelot. As a result, ocelot research and the restoration and management of native brush habitat have become an important part of the program. The refuge now handles the entire farming program to free up former share-cropped fields for reestablishment of native brush. It is also working to establish native brush corridor linkages with ocelot habitat to the north of the refuge and south to the Rio Grande and Mexico. Restoration of native brush will also enhance migration habitats of neotropical migratory birds.

Reduced freshwater inflow and open bay disposal of dredge material are also a concern at Laguna Atascosa Refuge, because of the threats to refuge and state-owned wetlands, sea grass beds, and the overall quality and productivity of the Lower Laguna Madre. Our refuge staff is working with the affected state agencies and other interests in cooperative efforts to address these concerns.

The Lower Rio Grande Valley Refuge Complex comprises an ongoing land acquisition project designed to restore and preserve a corridor of habitat for the wide diversity of wildlife that inhabits the Lower Rio Grande Valley from Falcon Dam downstream nearly 200 miles to the Lower Laguna Madre. This complex currently contains over 60,000 acres of acquired land and will ultimately embrace over 100,000 acres.

Management is designed to protect remaining native habitat and restore areas altered by farming and other developments. Restoration of former farm fields to native vegetation is a major part of the program. The refuge is also working with ways to simulate the historic flood regime that played such an important role in maintaining the wildlife habitat values of this riverine habitat.

An extremely important part of the programs at both the Lower Rio Grande Valley and Laguna Atascosa Refuges is the staffs' efforts to develop cooperative habitat management partnerships with adjacent private landowners. The Otha Holland Wildlife Corridor is an outstanding example. As a result of a cooperative agreement between the Lower Rio Grande Valley Refuge and the Delta Lake Irrigation District, a 25-mile continuous stretch of district canal system is being managed to provide a 1,200-acre corridor of improved wildlife habitat. The district has agreed to limit its canal bank maintenance to create habitat linkages that will benefit wildlife from throughout the valley.

The Attwater Prairie Chicken Refuge was established for the restoration of its endangered namesake. The refuge was envisioned as serving as a "core" area where habitat management practices could be developed that ideally would serve as a demonstration of what needs to be done to recover a population of birds that is clearly on the brink of extinction. The refuge has developed a very intensive management program that includes prescribed burning and livestock grazing to produce favorable habitat conditions, predator control during the critical nesting season, research, and an education and outreach effort involving private landowners.

Texas Tech University and the Texas Cooperative Wildlife Research Unit are assisting with evaluations of prescribed burning techniques. Grazing is intensively managed to achieve desired vegetative conditions. Grazing use is very carefully monitored, and the grazing prescription is designed with the flexibility to react quickly to changing habitat conditions.

Recognizing that public land management alone cannot prevent the loss of this subspecies, cooperation of private ranchers in the management of native prairie habitat is critical to population recovery. The refuge staff is working with the Texas Parks and Wildlife Department in efforts to develop cooperative programs with private landowners. Such partnerships are essential if we are to succeed with our cooperative efforts to save this unique member of Texas's bird life.

The 7,600-acre Buffalo Lake Refuge Complex in the Panhandle includes the Muleshoe and Grulla Refuges (with the latter located almost entirely across the state line in New Mexico) for a total of 16,700 acres in the 3 areas. All are managed for migratory birds, with an emphasis on waterfowl and sandhill cranes. Farming and livestock grazing are the principal management practices.

The 11,300-acre Hagerman Refuge is an overlay on the Corps of Engineers' Lake Texoma. It is managed for feeding and nesting waterfowl as mitigation for the impacts of dam construction. Included are marsh management, farming, and livestock grazing.

The Little Sandy Refuge involves a nondevelopment easement on the 3,800-acre privately owned Little Sandy Hunting and Fishing Club. The easement was negotiated to help preserve the area's outstanding hardwood bottomland habitat and associated wildlife.

The 14,000-acre Balcones Canyonland Refuge, located on the outskirts of Austin, is projected to be 46,000 acres in size upon completion of acquisition. It is designed to serve as the core of an effort to preserve habitat for the endangered golden-cheeked warbler and black-capped vireo. Management efforts will focus on maintaining and restoring the natural diversity of wildlife and plant communities found in this unique ecosystem. It is our hope that habitat management practices developed on the refuge will serve as models that can be applied on privately owned lands where these species occur. Again, cooperative relationships with private landowners will be key to the ultimate success of this effort.

The last refuge to be added to our system of wildlife preserves in Texas is the projected 12,000-acre Trinity River Refuge, located on the Trinity River in the southeastern part of the state. With 4,400 acres currently included in this area, management objectives are to maintain and restore, in some cases, the bottomland hardwoods habitat associated with this unique riverine system.

Oil and gas exploration and development rights were reserved on the majority of our refuges in Texas. Obviously, such activities have potential for adversely affecting wildlife and its habitat. Fostering cooperation with oil and gas operators has been important to our success in minimizing the harmful effects of these activities.

Public use is also an important part of our management program, not only from the standpoint of providing educational and recreational opportunities and benefits but also to ensure that such use occurs in a manner that is compatible with wildlife management objectives. Given that over 600,000 people annually use refuge lands in Texas, the potential for such impacts is substantial.

Conclusion

As we look to the future of wildlife in Texas, I believe existing and future national wildlife refuges will play an increasingly important role in protection of habitat critical to preservation of the rich biological diversity of this state. However, ours is only one of many efforts that will be necessary if Texas's great legacy of wildlife is to be preserved. Success will lie in the effectiveness of partnerships forged between all of us, especially private landowners, with a stake in protection of the state's fish and wildlife resources. Private lands will continue to support the vast majority of the state's wildlife resources. The success of our program and the success of the wildlife profession in helping to preserve these resources will generally depend on effective partnerships between public and private lands.

John L. Steele, Jr.
U.S. Army Corps of Engineers (Retired)
Fort Worth District
Operations Divison

24. U.S. Army Corps of Engineers

Abstract: The U. S. Army Corps of Engineers (Corps) administers 25 flood control projects in North-central Texas. Costs of operation and other expenses are shared with local sponsors. In the public interest, Corps policy requires project management, protection, and enhancement of the natural, cultural, and developed resources in order to provide opportunities for safe and healthful recreation. Stewardship oversight of outgrants, licenses, etc., provided conservation land use benefiting resident wildlife from 1950 to 1986. Prior to 1986, the Corps granted four licenses to the Texas Parks and Wildlife Department (TPWD) for wildlife management and hunting on 72,000 acres. Passage of the 1986 and 1990 Water Resources Development Acts (WRDA) authorized the Corps to mitigate for losses of wildlife habitat. The Corps purchased 25,500 acres in the White Oak Creek area and leased it to TPWD with 10,000 acres of land at Cooper Lake. The Corps constructed wetland structures for watering the prime waterfowl management areas. An additional 150 acres at Ray Roberts Lake and 200 acres at Lake O' the Pines are managed for wintering waterfowl and wood duck nesting habitat. Restoration of 28,000 acres of prime waterfowl habitat at Wright Patman Lake was highly recommended by TPWD and federal wildlife personnel. The project was dropped by the Corps for lack of a cost-share partner and agreement.

This chapter is an account of the multiple uses that have been carried out on U.S. Army Corps of Engineers water projects. The primary purpose of Corps projects is flood control. The Corps is not a land management agency. All use of project lands is subordinate to its primary purpose and must be managed with that understanding. Corps projects are authorized by Congress and are limited in exercising any use that cannot coexist with floodwater impoundments. Early projects were for multiple uses such as water supplies, power generation, and navigation. At a later date, recreation was authorized and developed as a special use.

Corps projects were developed to achieve perceived needs sought by communities with help from the U.S. Congress. The nongovernment sponsor may be a river authority, water district, or entity that is able to cost-share with the federal government to buy the land, construct the project, and operate it. The Corps locates a dam site, designs the dam, and determines the amount of land necessary to impound a flood that may occur once in a 50-year period. Contractors build the dam, access roads, parks, and recreational facilities (U.S. Army Corps of Engineers 1996a, 1996b).

The Corps and its cost-sharing partners operate and maintain 25 flood control projects in the Fort Worth District. Four projects are in the East Texas Pine/Hardwood Timberlands, 2 in the West Texas Rangelands, 15 in the Blackland Prairies and Cross Timbers and Prairies, and 4 in the Texas Hill Country. Water covers over 397,000 acres at the normal pool elevations. The area of land above the operating pool (normal conservation pool) is about 389,000 acres. Project operations and park areas utilize 116,000 acres (29.82%) of land, leaving 273,000 acres available for wildlife use (70.18%).

Project Environment

Project lands provide a limited area suited to year-long wildlife use. Most of the projects have narrow upland borders above the lakes and a larger area of land within the upper part of the flood zone. Species with small home ranges such as cottontails and both gray and fox squirrels can establish territories on project lands. White-tailed deer, wild turkey, furbearers, and bobwhites use project lands for part of their habitat needs or make seasonal use of the areas. Annual floods for 3 years after 1988 temporarily evicted nearly all resident species of wildlife from 15 of the 25 projects.

Developments on adjoining lands are impacting wildlife and recreational use on project lands. Housing developments have cut off travel lanes that wildlife need to reach project lands. Residents in housing developments are seeking ways to stop hunting on project areas that have long been available and free for that recreational use. In addition to those developments, project lands are intensively used by public utilities, city water and sanitation departments, state and county highway departments, oil and gas production and distribution companies, and state and city park departments, as well as being used for hay production and grazing or agricultural crops on an interim basis.

The Corps Management Policy

The policy 327.1(a) is stated in title 36, chapter 3, part 327—rules and regulations government public use of water resources development projects administered by the chief of engineers. Paraphrased, it is to manage natural resources of each project in the public interest while providing safe and healthful recreational opportunities to the public and protecting and enhancing these resources (Code of Federal Regulations 1985).

The Corps Stewardship Program

The Corps built and operated its Fort Worth District project lakes in Texas from the early 1950's until 1972 with only 1 operations biologist on the district staff. After Congress passed the National Environmental Policy Act (NEPA) on December 31, 1969, the Corps hired a staff of natural resource–trained specialists to evaluate lake project operations for adverse impacts (Public Law PL 91-190 1970). Since then, the Natural Resources Management Section in Operations has served to analyze all proposed uses of project lands and to recommend construction or management activities that can minimize adverse impacts to the resources.

The natural resource staff recommends a course of management for all land-use proposals. Staff members follow the project master plan and operational management plans in making a decision for internal programs and for private proposals to use project lands or waters. Engineer Regulation (ER) 1130-2-540 provides for the application of approved management techniques to improve vegetative conditions for wildlife, recreation, scenic value, timber, cultural resources, and other project uses (U.S. Army Corps of Engineers 1996a). The regulation also provides for watershed protection, pest control, and prevention of wildfires.

The Corps's recognition of natural resources values is demonstrated in the construction of new reservoirs. Bottomland timber is left in most of the impoundment zone for fish and waterfowl habitat. Old fields or overgrazed pastures are revegetated to protect the soil and thus keep it from washing into the reservoir, where it would displace space designed for storing water. The projects constructed after 1970 have all been fenced to prevent damage to the soil and vegetation by trespass livestock and off-road vehicles.

The history of natural resource management on Corps projects has evolved from nearly total private use to controlled public uses. Lands on projects constructed and operated between 1950 and 1970 were leased to former landowners for grazing because there were no fences separating federal from private lands. The grazing leases were let with a conservation requirement that the vegetative resource would be protected from overuse and further provided for payment of rental by planting approved grasses. Most of the grass was planted as agreed. The conservative grazing requirement was generally ignored during year-long use and a series of droughts.

Following passage of NEPA in 1969, grazing leases were allowed to expire, and the pastures were rested between 1972 and 1976. Eventually, grazing leases were advertised for controlled numbers of livestock for up to 8 months of the year or for rotational grazing. Lease rental was paid in labor to accomplish fencing, firebreaks, mowing undesirable vegetation, mesquite control, planting grass, and planting green cover to protect bare-earth firebreaks. Hay production tracts were limed as needed and fertilized according to soil tests. Grazing lessees are required to practice soil conservation and conservative use as recommended by the U.S. Soil Conservation Service (SCS).

Some project programs are conducted on a large scale. The outgrant program for rights-of-way covers use of project lands for electric lines, water lines, oil and gas collection and distribution, and sewer lines. Oil and gas production sites are covered under separate easements than those for their line rights-of-way. Most of these easements are analyzed by project personnel for potential impacts and damages. They then submit proposals to the district office for the uses listed above, along with their survey reports. Easement requests may be refused if the requester does not agree to fulfill specific conditions the Corps requires for site protection and restoration. Where possible, corridor widths and routes are reduced to avoid use of important wildlife habitat, e.g., mature shrub/tree stands, wetlands, and drainage areas. Replacement vegetation is selected for site conditions and wildlife food and cover value. The lessee may be required to restore the site to the original contour and plant a protective cover on it. Some rights-of-way require fencing to protect new tree and cover plantings.

Some easement requests are a challenge to the stewardship concept.

They may require special mitigation efforts and cooperation between the Corps and lessee to make the result valuable to wildlife.

Public Access

The federal lands at 23 Corps projects are open to the public for free hunting, fishing, and other recreational uses. Some projects limit the number of hunters by requiring possession of a Corps permit and proof of taking a hunter safety course. Projects at Canyon Lake and Joe Pool Lake are in densely developed areas and are closed to hunting. The projects at Town Bluff Dam and B. A. Steinhagen Lake and Somerville, Granger, and Ray Roberts Lakes are licensed in part to TPWD for wildlife management and hunting. The Cooper Lake and White Oak Creek mitigation lands were closed to hunting until the TPWD leased them in 1992 and initiated operations under a Corps outgrant.

Wildlife Management

The Corps land available for wildlife use is about 273,000 acres, including some water, but the land suited to wildlife management and hunting is limited to 186,000 acres. Project management for wildlife is very limited and is not performed by all field projects. Individual projects have at some time applied all of the common habitat management techniques, including food and cover plantings, vegetative manipulations with plows, mowers, saws, and fire, and nest boxes for wood ducks, but most of the management is on a small scale. Project areas have been protected from damage by trespass livestock and wildfire, but protection is not enough to produce the wildlife needed to meet the increasing demands for recreational hunting.

Some recent and significant cooperative events have involved Corps projects with individuals and conservation groups (Shoreline Releaf 1991). Examples include tree salvage and planting projects, which save thousands of dollars and provide scenic restoration and wildlife habitat. Some Texas projects have won national awards in Corps management competitions.

The Corps is a party to a cooperative management agreement for the protection, preservation, and perpetuation of prairie sites and vegetation. The cooperative management agreement was signed by TPWD, the State Soil and Water Conservation Association (SSWCA), and the Corps to accomplish common goals. The Native Prairie Association was invited to join the cooperative group because it needs prairie research areas and sites for conducting educational tours. The TPWD and SSWCA have the lead in establishing and maintaining prairie sites at Granger Lake and the Culp Branch Prairie at Ray Roberts Lake. Surveys for other potential prairie restoration sites are continuing programs.

Operations Division conducted an emergency timber salvage effort at the Sam Rayburn and Wright Patman projects during 3 years of near record flood impoundment. Large numbers of pines and hardwoods were subjected to flood water beginning in 1989. Salvage cuts were organized, and pines were sold at a damage discounted rate for timber and pulpwood. The total salvage effort earned approximately $2 million. Salvaged areas at the Sam Rayburn and Wright Patman Projects are each being replanted with 80,000 water-tolerant oaks and bald cypress per year; replanting began in 1993 and will end by 1998.

Major Outgrants

This category excluded individual grazing leases and easements for roads, utilities, etc. Our most unusual lease is for the Experiment Station and Research Center at the O. C. Fisher Lake project north of San Angelo, Texas (U.S. Army Corps of Engineers 1972; Vincent 1974). The station includes 4,645 acres typical of West Texas rangeland topography and vegetation and conducts research to improve range conditions and to discover ranch management techniques that permit joint use and production of wildlife, sheep, and cattle (Menzies 1974).

The Texas Parks and Wildlife Department (TPWD) has parts of 4 Corps projects under license, including Town Bluff Dam and B. A. Steinhagen Lake (Dam B) and Granger, Somerville, and Ray Roberts Lakes.

Dam B

Dam B is in the East Texas Pine/Hardwood Timberlands where the Neches and Angelina Rivers come together. The upper end of the lake is much like the setting and vegetation typical of the Big Thicket National Preserve farther west. Pines and hardwoods on low upland sites and water-tolerant trees and shrubs form a hardwood bottomland forest interlaced with sloughs and swampy grounds.

TPWD manages 16,000 plus acres in the Angelina/Neches Dam B Wildlife Management Area (WMA) for public hunting. Hunters are not limited and are free to hunt after they register at one of several entry stations. The major game species are gray squirrel, white-tailed deer, and waterfowl. Local people have hunted at Dam B for several generations and claim that privilege as a traditional right. They overhunted it for years using hounds and boats to take deer until dogs were outlawed in the 1970's. Wood ducks were consistently hunted after shooting hours; the area is difficult to police and easy to hide in. Active wildlife management has been restricted to a release of eastern wild turkeys and installation of nest boxes for wood ducks.

An active management plan for the WMA was developed by Dan Lay, a premier forester and wildlife manager, now retired from TPWD (Lay 1973). He regarded the WMA as the last remnant of a prime river bottom hardwood forest. There are pure stands of pine and hardwoods and some mixed stands. Dan Lay's recommendations for managing the WMA are valid and should be applied when TPWD is able to do so.

Granger Lake

The Corps licensed Granger Lake to TPWD for wildlife management and hunting on January 1, 1977. The management area covers over 11,300 acres of former cropland in eastern Williamson County. Prior to granting the license, the Corps fenced the project boundary and contracted for planting 4,000 acres of grass, 400 acres of sweet clover and millet, and 8,000 trees (Brazos Valley Nursery, Inc. 1980). Prior to government purchase, the prairie soils produced good crops of cotton and sorghums, but when farming ceased, Johnsongrass soon dominated the land. Woody cover is limited and generally restricted to narrow borders of 2 major creeks and the San Gabriel River. An open stand of pecan and cottonwood south of the dam site is similar to other sites that turkeys choose for roosting.

The TPWD wildlife managers have applied a classic management plan at Granger Lake for mourning doves, bobwhite quail, ring-necked pheasant, Rio Grande turkey, ducks, and geese. Fire and fallow disking produced forb foods for upland game birds but failed to control dense stands of Johnsongrass. Renewing farm operations with 20 share-crop lessees opened strips that were dispersed throughout the area and planted to corn, sorghum, or wheat. Strips of green wheat close to the lakeshore provided geese with popular feeding areas. Clearing a stand of black willow on the shoreline provided a safe loafing area heavily used by geese (Boyd 1984; Welch 1989, 1990a).

Large-scale share-crop farming was reduced with the expiration of lease agreements in 1992. Johnsongrass was such a mangement problem that TPWD decided to utilize it in a grazing program. Some of the share-crop fields were fenced so that strip farming could be conducted inside the overall 5,100-acre grazing area. Work payments were substituted for cash rent as part of the management program.

A cooperative effort by TPWD and the Wetland Habitat Alliance of Texas (WHAT) enhanced the lakeshore by installing nest boxes for wood ducks. General management for water fowl and upland wildlife was enhanced by the Koch Oil Pipeline Company when it agreed to build 3 ponds on sites selected by the TPWD manager. Koch built the ponds in trade for the right to construct a pipeline through the Willis Creek area.

The Panhandle is generally considered to be the only suitable range for ring-necked pheasants in Texas, but TPWD decided Granger Lake might change that. It decided to make a trial release of 49 wild pheasants from the Panhandle with several thousand pen-reared birds. The pheasants increased enough to TPWD to open a special season in 1986. Hunters were selected in a special drawing, and 4,244 applicants were authorized to make 4 trips with a rest period between each trip. Hunting was permitted for 2 consecutive days on each trip. A total bag of 323 pheasants, including 183 cocks and 140 hens, was reported. The special season was not extended after 1986, but hunts may be resumed in the future if TPWD can find a source of birds (Wallace 1987).

The TPWD has established a successful state wild turkey program by releasing the Rio Grande species in many ranges west of East Texas. Fifty-four of the Rio Grande species were released in a potential roost area south of the dam site along the San Gabriel River (Welch 1990). By itself, the Granger Lake Wildlife Management Area (WMA) is too small to meet the year-round needs of these big birds. By combining the acreage of adjoining private lands with the WMA, TPWD established an area large enough for a year-round turkey range.

The wildlife management area at Granger Lake has one of the most diversified and active programs developed by TPWD. The brief account given above does not address the full range of the management activities.

Somerville Lake

Somerville Lake began operations in 1966 as a closed hunting and trapping area (Texas Parks and Wildlife Commission 1966). Deer multiplied during the following 15 years, and the habitat began to show signs of overuse. In 1981, the TPWD opened wildlife management areas to hunting at Nail's Creek (1,500 acres) and Yegua Creek

(2,000 acres) and the state park units at Birch Creek and Nail's Creek. Hunters took 1,000 deer from the overall 8,700-acre area before TPWD closed the 2 park units to further hunting. Deer hunting is still permitted by special permits, selected in a computer drawing, for the 2 WMAs. The number of regular season permits issued is based on data developed from transect counts and an estimate of the number required to return a hunter success rate of 12–15%. Hunting permission is not limited for small game or waterfowl (Lehmann 1992).

Management for deer has been simplified from use of food plots and burning to burning only up to 200 acres a year in August. These fires result in a growth of fall forbs and woody browse that the deer rely on in their daily diet (Rideout 1990).

A research study has been under way since the 1,000 deer were removed from the WMAs and state park lands. After that hunt, reproduction of the remaining herd was suppressed for reasons that were not readily apparent. Technicians collected muscle and liver tissues, blood samples, and doe reproductive organs for studies of genetics, nutrition levels, diseases, conception dates, and reproductive rates. The deer used to stock the WMAs had been captured in areas of Texas with different rutting seasons, and that may be related to why so few does were pregnant after what is considered to be the local rutting season (Lehmann 1992).

Waterfowl are the other species of major management interest at Somerville Lake. The creek bottoms and ponds are natural fall and wintering areas for ducks. Some ducks stop over on their spring migrations and eat a high protein diet of crayfish. Several ponds and wetlands have been developed on the WMAs to mitigate the use of the land for oil-drilling sites. The ponds have been designed for experimental study and easy drainage, but most of them depend on runoff or floodwater from the creeks to fill them in the fall and winter when ducks use them. Sedges, smartweeds, and oak mast are available in the different pond areas.

Wood duck nest boxes have long been considered a productive method for attracting this species to suitable brood-rearing habitat. At Somerville, the TPWD and Corps have tried in vain to get wood ducks to use nest boxes; they conducted the program for 5 years without any success (Gustafson 1991).

The Corps lands are closed to hunting outside of the state licensed area, except for a special 1- to 2-day deer hunt organized by volunteers for handicapped hunters in wheelchairs. This annual handicapped deer hunt is popular with the hunters and strongly supported by the local community of Brenham, Texas (Houston 1991).

The Corps also permits waterfowl hunting from 50 blinds located in areas picked by Corps project employees. Hunters draw for permits, and winners must deposit $50 for a lakeshore permit prior to constructing their blinds. Forty dollars will be refunded if the blind is removed by the owner within 30 days after the hunting season. Otherwise, the $40 fee is forfeited; the other $10 is kept for a handling fee.

Ray Roberts Lake

Ray Roberts Lake is licensed to TPWD for a WMA and hunting. The WMA includes 41,600 acres of the 43,000 acres in the project. TPWD has access to most of the project other than parks, the dam embankment, the spillway, and outlet facilities.

The wildlife management program uses an active farming operation with small grains, corn, and wheat. Over 200 acres of corn, milo, and wheat are planted in plots and strips. Forb foods are produced by fallow disking and prescribed burns; the latter also create a supply of green forage (Dillard 1990).

The Ray Roberts WMA has been very attractive to ducks and some geese. The corn and small grain plots also attract many ducks. Harvest data show a steady increase in the number of ducks taken at the WMA since it opened. In 1987, Ray Roberts WMA had 51% of all waterfowl killed on all lakes in the same TPWD program; percentages for 1988–90 were 60, 73, and 71, respectively. Hunting for all species was expected to attract up to 20,000 hunters over a 5-year period (Dillard 1990). The acreage of quail habitat diminished as the lake filled and probably will be limited to 9,286 acres above the 632.5-foot lake elevation. In the future, doves and waterfowl are expected to attract most hunters. The only mitigation authorized for habitat lost in constructing Ray Roberts was to develop wetlands for waterfowl (U.S. Army Corps of Engineers 1983).

Surveys by the TPWD at Ray Roberts Lake WMA indicated a potential for management of ring-necked pheasant and Rio Grande wild turkey. The management plan included a release of wild, trapped pheasants when a source of birds is available. Rio Grande turkeys have been released on the uplands of the Wolf Creek and Indian Creek drainages (Dillard 1990–1991). A nest box program for wood ducks and eastern bluebirds has been under way for several years. Den boxes for raccoon have been installed and are being evaluated as a management technique.

The Ray Roberts Lake WMA is a high quality feeding and wintering area for migratory waterfowl. The Corps constructed a 150-acre wetland on Range Creek as partial mitigaton for loss of wildlife habitats due to water storage. Water level controls include low levees to confine water and a weir in an outlet structure to discharge surplus runoff from the watershed. Ongoing studies of the project and basic structure are being evaluated for design improvements. Research studies employing college graduates are documenting changes in water quality, sedimentation rates, the success of planted aquatic vegetation, and the densities and success of volunteer native species. Waterfowl use is also documented for comparison with other natural areas at RRWMA that attract waterfowl.

Mitigation Projects

Cooper Lake

Cooper Lake was the center of a court battle that delayed its construction until 25,500 acres of land were purchased to mitigate its taking of wildlife lands. The court ruled that the acreage was justified and was necessary to compensate for the wildlife productivity lost by impounding water in a hardwood bottomland habitat. The Corps purchased 25,500 acres of similar habitat on the White Oak Creek area 60 miles below Cooper Dam. Another 10,000 acres of land at Cooper Lake were also designated for management as partial mitigation for taking the bottomland habitat from wildlife production (U.S. Corps of Engineers 1990).

Cooper Lake is located in the central part of Delta and Hopkins Counties on the South Sulphur River. The topography is best described as rolling hills. The major vegetation includes pine woods, post oak savannahs, and species typical of the Blackland Prairies. The wildlife spectrum includes white-tailed deer, both gray and fox squirrels, mourning dove, bobwhite quail, cottontail, and swamp rabbit. Furbearers such as beaver, river otter, mink, muskrat, raccoon, nutria, and opossum provide an insight into the area's habitat diversity.

Prior to impoundment, the bed of Cooper Lake was partially cleared. Standing timber within a mile of the dam was removed and used to construct 22 large fish shelters close to the shoreline. Timber in the upper ½ of the lake and in coves was left for prime fish and waterfowl habitat.

Habitat developments at Cooper Lake include nearly 1,200 acres of former croplands and pastures that are scheduled for extensive management. Routine management will involve vegetation manipulation, planting plots of trees and small grains, and thinning and clearing trees to favor trees producing mast and fruit. Installation of some of the above wildlife management measures have been completed by TPWD (U.S. Army Corps of Engineers 1987).

A special management development for waterfowl habitat utilizes moist soil compartments and a wood duck nest box program. The dikes are separated by two side-by-side compartments with surface areas of 74 and 144 acres, respectively. Water from the South Sulphur River can be diverted into a 220-acre reservoir and released as needed to fill the compartments to a depth of 1–4 feet. In addition to existing aquatic vegetation, wetland species have been planted in the compartments and wood duck nest boxes erected over the deeper water (U.S. Army Corps of Engineers 1987).

White Oak Creek

The Water Resources Development Act of 1986 (PL99-662) authorized the purchase and development of the mitigation area at White Oak Creek (WOCMA). The WOCMA is a 25,500-acre bottomland formerly part of the flowage easement utilized by Wright Patman Lake. It is in the Sulphur River drainage of Bowie, Cass, Morris, and Titus Counties. Most of it is timbered and subject to frequent flooding. The area includes 17 miles of the Sulphur River and 26 miles of White Oak Creek. There are over 16,000 acres of bottomland hardwoods and 2,800 acres of mixed pine-hardwoods in the mitigation area. The small, widely dispersed wetlands generally dry up during late summer, but permanent water is well distributed and available in creeks, oxbow sloughs, beaver ponds, stock ponds, and the river (U.S. Fish and Wildlife Service 1985). WOCMA is part of the nation's most important waterfowl wintering grounds and a top production area for wood ducks. It is also part of the area that provides wintering habitat for 30% of the nation's mallards (U.S. Fish and Wildlife Service 1984). The hardwood bottomland habitat of East Texas is of international importance to waterfowl. According to information included in the North American Waterfowl Management Program (NAWMP), the East Texas area is one of the major waterfowl habitats in North America and ranks with the Gulf Coast in importance for wintering and migrating waterfowl (U.S. Department of the Interior, Fish and Wildlife Service and Environment Canada, Canadian Wildlife Service 1986).

The White Oak Creek mitigation plans also involve construction of facilities that will permit sophisticated water and moist soil management. A 224-acre supply reservoir fed by Caney Creek can deliver water to 3 contiguous compartments via a controlled outlet and diversion channel. Each compartment has an inlet facility with controls that can be set to deliver specific volumes of water for management needs. The 3 compartments are separated by earthen dikes. The perimeter dikes were designed for vehicle use and planted with flood-tolerant forbs and grasses. The dikes were designed to withstand frequent inundation in the event that Wright Patman Lake goes into flood stage. The compartments have individual surface areas of 205, 147, and 198 acres, respectively.

The dikes were built with soil excavated from inside the compartments. A number of 1- to 2-acre pits of similar depth were excavated within each moist soil management compartment to hold water when most of the area dries out. Nest boxes for wood ducks have been installed on posts over the pits at a rate of 3 boxes per acre and set about 5 feet above the mean spring and summer water level (U.S. Army Corps of Engineers 1990).

The Water Resource Development Acts (WRDA) of 1986 and 1990

These acts authorized the secretary of the army to review the operation of water resources projects constructed by the secretary before the date of enactment of WRDA 1986, section 1135. Reviews were to determine the need for modifications in the structures and operation of such projects to improve the environmental quality in the public interest. Section 304 of WRDA 1990 deletes a 2-year time limit that section 1135 had assigned to modifying the projects and provides a continuing authority for project reviews. WRDA projects require the Corps to have a cost-sharing partner to pay for construction and agree to fund 100% of the operation and maintenance after construction (Public Law PL 99-662, 100 Stat. 4082, Water Resources Development Act of 1986; Public Law PL 101-640, Water Resources Development Act of 1990, Section 307a).

Lake O' the Pines

The first application of WRDA 1986 Section 1135, as amended by WRDA 1990 Section 304, was a feasibility study to restore wetland habitat for waterfowl at the Lake O' the Pines. An area known as the Cypress Creek Wildlife Management Area (CCWMA) was surveyed by representatives of TPWD, the Corps, the U.S. Fish and Wildlife Service (USFWS), and the North American Waterfowl Management Program. They identified 3,900 acres of hardwood bottomland and lacustrine wetlands and 1,100 acres of shallow water habitat. They also recommended enhancing the areas with wood duck nest boxes and establishment of waterfowl feeding areas (U.S. Army Corps of Engineers 1991b).

Reconnaissance indicated that the site has high potential for wetland and waterfowl management. The area is upstream of Highway 155 in Camp, Morris, Marion, and Upshur Counties. It is located on the upper end of Lake O' the Pines where Cypress Creek discharges into the lake. The project is situated in the Piney Woods of the East Texas forest region on gently rolling to hilly terrain drained by numerous streams. Intermittent swamps, cropland, and pastures lie close to the drainages. Wide river bottoms and bayous add to the wealth of waterfowl habitat in the CCWMA.

The wet soils of the alluvial floodplain and terrace flats are covered with bottomland hardwoods. Trees in the wetland have a moderately open canopy and are associated with water-tolerant shrubs, sedges, and grasses that make it a high quality area for rearing broods of wood ducks (U.S. Army Corps of Engineers 1991). A management plan for the area was activated when the Corps thinned 200 acres of bottomland oaks to increase mast production and installed wood duck nest boxes (Wiese 1997). TPWD and U.S. Fish and Wildlife Service officials estimated that management in the area could produce up to 750 new adult birds per year within 3–5 years of initiation (U.S. Army Corps of Engineers 1991).

Wright Patman Lake

The lake is a natural attraction for nesting wood ducks and wintering waterfowl. The U.S. Fish and Wildlife Service and TPWD surveyed 28,000 acres of water-tolerant bottomland hardwoods and wetlands on the upper end of the lake and recommended enhancing it for waterfowl. Their planners estimated that management could increase wood duck populations by 5,000 new adult birds per year, as well as benefit white-tailed deer, squirrels, and other birds and mammals, including bald eagles (U.S. Army Corps of Engineers 1991c).

The Corps cannot unilaterally manage the area as proposed above. The 1986 and 1990 Water Resources Development Acts cover improving natural habitats in the public interest, but they will not authorize development and management by the Corps without a cost-share partner. An operational waterfowl project of this scope at Wright Patman Lake would add a significant area to the North American Waterfowl Management Program (Sansom 1991).

Literature Cited

Boyd, C. E. 1984. Performance report, Federal Aid Project W-27-D-38 Granger Lake Wildlife Unit, Williamson County, Texas. Tex. Parks and Wildl. Dep., Austin.

Brazos Valley Nursery, Inc. 1980. Letter to Corps of Engineers for special provisions article 13(e) (1). Contract No. DACW63-79-C-0122 for Wildlife Area improvement, Granger Dam and Lake; total funding available for contract through 30 September 1980. U.S. Army Corps of Eng.

Code of Federal Regulations (CFR) 36. 1985. Chapter III, part 327. Rules and regulations governing public use of water resource development projects administered by the chief of engineers. Sept. 3.

Dillard, J. E. 1990. Strategic plan for Ray Roberts Lake Wildlife Management Area 1990–1994. Tex. Parks and Wildl. Dep. and Corps of Eng. Coop., Tex. Parks and Wildl. Dep., Wildl. Div., Austin.

———. 1991. Summary of activities, Ray Roberts Lake Wildlife Management Area, September 1, 1990 to August 31, 1991. Tex. Parks and Wildl. Dep., Austin.

Gustafson, M. H. 1991. Wood duck/whistling duck project letter report to director, Tex. Parks and Wildl. Dep., Austin. U.S. Army Corps of Eng., Somerville Lake Reservoir Manager.

Hathorn, P. M. 1991. Research proposals for the artificial wetlands being created at Ray Roberts Lake. Letter to George Litton, Reg. Wildl. Dir., Tex. Parks and Wildl. Dep., Waco. Planning Div., Fort Worth Dist., U. S. Army Corps of Eng.

Houston, C. F. 1991. Fourth annual Somerville Lake handicap deer hunt. Memorandum to Operations Div., Fort Worth Dist., U.S. Army Corps of Eng.

Lay, D. W. 1973. Annual management plan. September 1, 1973, to August 31, 1974. Town Bluff Dam (B. A. Steinhagen Lake), unnumbered license (amendment number 3). Tex. Parks and Wildl. Dep.

Lehmann, R. 1992. Telephone conversation concerning deer populations, waterfowl and ponds on TPWD licensed land at Somerville Lake Wildlife Management Area with John Steele, Oper. Div., Fort Worth Dist., U.S. Army Corps of Eng.

Menzies, C. 1974. Management plans for the Texas Agricultural Experiment Station and Research Station Area subleased from Angelo State University on the O. C. Fisher Dam and Lake, a Corps of Eng. Proj., San Angelo, Texas. Letter to Dr. Lloyd D. Vincent, president, Angelo State Univ.

Public Law PL 91-190. 1970. National Environmental Policy Act of 1969 (42 USC 4321 et seq.), 1 Jan.

Public Law PL 99-662. 1986. 100 Stat. 4082, Water Resources Development Act.

Public Law PL 101-640. 1990. Water Resources Development Act, Section 307 (a).

Rideout, D. W. 1990. Management plan for deer on Somerville Lake project land in Burleson, Washington, and Lee Counties. Tex. Parks and Wildl. Dep., Tyler.

Sansom, A. 1991. Texas Parks and Wildlife interest in development and management of wetlands at Lake O' the Pines and Wright Patman Lake, U.S. Army Corps of Eng. Proj., Fort Worth Dist. Letter to Colonel William D. Brown, Dist. Eng., U.S. Army Corps of Eng.

Shoreline Releaf. 1991. Metroplex lakes tree planting project. Multiple memorandum, Oper. Div., Fort Worth Dist., U.S. Army Corps of Eng.

Texas Parks and Wildlife Commission. 1966. The Trinity-Brazos hunting, fishing and trapping proclamation No. H-14, Somerville Lake Proj., Austin, Tex.

U.S. Army Corps of Engineers. 1972. Department of Army Lease No. DACW63-1-72-0333 for management, research, and instruction purposes related to animals, plants, wildlife, conservation, restricted agriculture, grazing, and recreation at O. C. Fisher Lake, Texas. Fort Worth Dist., U.S. Army Corps of Eng.

———. 1983. Ray Roberts Lake, Elm Fork, Trinity River, Texas, design memorandum no. 8, master plan. Planning Branch of the Eng. and Planning Div., Fort Worth Dist., U.S. Army Corps of Eng.

———. 1987. Cooper Lake, Sulphur River, Texas, master plan design memorandum no. 60. Plan. Div., Fort Worth Dist., U.S. Army Corps of Eng.

———. 1990. Cooper Lake Sulphur River, Texas. Supplement no. 1 to master plan design memorandum no. 10, White Oak Creek Mitigation Area. Plan. Div., Fort Worth Dist., U.S. Army Corps of Eng.

———. 1991a. Solicitation No. DACW63-91-B-0098, April 1991. Ray Roberts Lake Elm Fork Trinity River Plans and Specifications for Developed Wetlands. Construct. Div., Fort Worth Dist., U.S. Army Corps of Eng.

———. 1991b. Section 1135 project modifications report for Lake O' the Pines waterfowl habitat restoration, Texas. U.S. Army Corps of Eng. in cooperation with Tex. Parks and Wildl. Dep., Plan. Div., Fort Worth Dist.

———. 1991c. Section 1135 project proposal fact sheet for Wright Patman Lake waterfowl habitat restoration, Bowie and Cass Counties, Texas. Plan. Div., Fort Worth Dist., U.S. Army Corps of Eng.

———. 1996a. Engineer regulation ER 1130-2-540 establishes guidance for management of environmental stewardship-related operations and maintenance activities at USACE civil works water resource projects. Nov. 15.

———. 1996b. Engineer regulation ER 1130-2-550 recreation operations and maintenance policies. Nov. 15.

U.S. Fish and Wildlife Service. 1984. Report of the waterfowl habitat strategy team. Washington, D.C.

———. 1985. Texas bottomland hardwood preservation program—final concept plan. U.S. Fish and Wildl. Serv., Albuquerque, N.M.

U.S. Department of the Interior, Fish and Wildlife Service and Environment Canada, Canadian Wildlife Service. 1986. North American waterfowl management plan: A strategy for cooperation.

Vincent, L. D. 1974. Range management program letter to Real Estate Div., Fort Worth Dist., U.S. Army Corps of Eng.

Wallace, J. D. 1987. Performance report, Fed. Aid Proj. W-27-D-41. Granger Lake Wildlife Management Area, Williamson County, Texas. Tex. Parks and Wildl. Dep., Austin.

Welch, R. D. 1989. Annual wildlife management plan, Granger Lake Wildlife Management Area, Williamson County, Texas 1989–1990. Tex. Parks and Wildl. Dep., Austin.

———. 1990a. Annual report, Granger Wildlife Management Area maintenance and operations, September 1, 1989–August 31, 1990. Tex. Parks and Wildl. Dep., Austin.

———. 1990b. Memorandum, mitigation plan for Koch Oil Pipeline, Granger Lake Wildlife Management Area. Tex. Parks and Wildl. Dep., Austin.

Larry H. Bonner
Resources Team Leader
U.S. Forest Service
701 North First Street
Lufkin, Texas 75901

25. National Forests and Grasslands

Abstract: Forests and wildlife biologists have long accepted as a truism the statement that "forest management is wildlife management." Any management activity that alters the structure and composition of forest vegetation vitally alters wildlife habitats and associated wildlife communities and populations. Whether these habitat alterations result in good or bad wildlife management depends on the forest manager's foresight and ability to consider and plan for wildlife requirements when scheduling habitat manipulations. In the not too distant past, wildlife management was synonymous with game management, and the forest manager's job was relatively simple. Scheduling forest management treatments required consideration of the needs of only a handful of game birds and mammals. However, legislative action over the past decade has significantly increased the public forest manager's responsibilities toward all wildlife, especially on federal lands (USDA Forest Service 1982).

Background

Management of wildlife on public lands and, in particular, the U.S. Forest Service (USFS) has been directed to consider all species of wildlife. This includes game and nongame, as well as vertebrate and invertebrate species (USDA Reg. 9500-4). Planning any management program for the number of species this concept entails has fueled much debate. Further guidance has been directed through U.S. code of federal regulation (36CFR 219) of the National Forest System Land and

Resource Management Planning regulations. Comprehensive wildlife planning got a boost from the Sikes Act (PL 93-452, Title II, October 1974), which specifies cooperative planning between the state wildlife resource agencies and the USFS.

Early managers of federal lands recognized that management of all native animals on every acre is not possible. Therefore, the Featured Species System was adopted and implemented by the USFS in February 1971. This concept is detailed in a management handbook which has been regularly updated and expanded (FSH 2609.23R, chap. 20). The Featured Species System was developed for use with an even-aged system of silviculture. Even-aged timber management with well-distributed regeneration and intermediate cuts insures an age-class distribution of stands and productive understory habitat conditions. Even-aged management, when combined with growing forest types that are suitable to the site and meet the planned objectives for land and resource management, sustains diversity of both plants and animals (FSH 2609.23R, chap. 10).

As stated in the 1976 Final Environmental Impact Statement (FEIS) and Unit Plan for the Sam Houston National Forest (Fig. 25.1), management of the wildlife resource on national forests was performed both by the USFS and the Texas Parks and Wildlife Department. The USFS was responsible for habitat management, while the state was responsible for setting seasons, harvest regulations, and game law enforcement. This clear division of responsibility for management of animal and habitat vanished with the signing of the memorandum of understanding between the two agencies in May 1981. The USFS entered this agreement to end years of independent management. Since the termination of the first agreement in 1973, current coordination looks promising. FSM 12/81 R-8 Supp 40 states: "it is the mutual desire of the U.S. Forest Service and the Texas Parks and Wildlife Department to work in harmony for the common purpose of developing, maintaining and managing all of the wildlife resources on the National Forests and National Grasslands for the best interest of the people of Texas and the United States." This agreement applies only to 5 wildlife management areas (WMAs) comprising the Alabama Creek WMA, Bannister WMA, Moore Plantation WMA, Caddo WMA, and Sam Houston WMA totaling 247,074 acres.

According to a recent Wildlife Management Institute (WMI 1990) report submitted to the USFS recommendation item #16: "The USFS should work with other landowners (State, private, etc.), where neces-

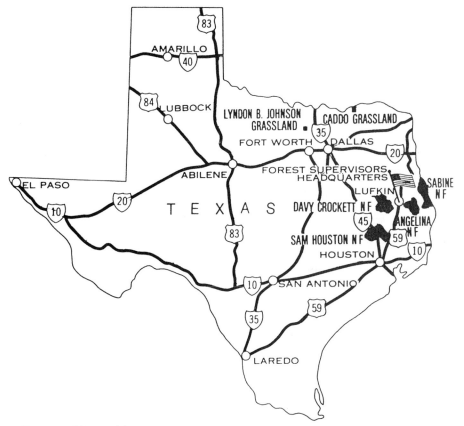

Fig. 25.1. *National forests and grasslands in Texas.*

sary to improve wildlife and fish habitats on lands near National Forests." This concept is further clarified according to the USFS Action
Plan in response to WMI Report 1989 Recommendations.

A national forest or grassland can have over 300 different species of
vertebrates occupying dozens to hundreds of different kinds of habitats.
There may be thousands of invertebrate species. The Committee of
Scientists, therefore, recommended the use of Management Indicator
Species to reduce the complexity (FSH 2609.13, Section 214, draft
4/12/85). Management Indicator Species are plants or animals whose
"population changes are believed to indicate the effects of management
activities" (36 CFR 219). The set of Management Indicator Species
should represent the major goals and concerns for wildlife and fish di-

versity and production at that level. There are many terms used for species that are selected for planning or management attention: featured species, game species, emphasis species, special interest species, ecological indicator species, etc. These terms clarify the purpose or primary use of Management Indicator Species.

The Forest Plan utilized the Featured Species as found in the regional wildlife handbook as well as other ecological indicators in an effort to provide maintenance and enhancement of a diversity of habitats to support the species indigenous to the forest. A full range of habitats, including early and late successional stages, old growth, and special features such as snags and den trees, was proposed. This is implemented along with direct habitat improvements to provide essential elements such as water supplies and permanent food plots, which help enhance habitat, disperse populations, and promote better habitat utilization. The overall objective is to maintain viable populations of all native species.

Within the Featured Species framework, the forest emphasizes management of demand species, including white-tailed deer, eastern gray squirrel and eastern fox squirrel, northern bobwhite, and warm water game fish. Native wild turkey populations are low to nonexistent, but population improvements through restocking efforts and protection are emphasized. The pileated woodpecker and the endangered red-cockaded woodpecker are selected as Management Indicator Species to represent the requirements of other species. It is the philosophy in the Forest Plan that the habitat managed to support these demand species will provide for the diversity of species native to the NFGT.

Current Situation

Since the approval of the Forest Plan, the NFGT has been in an accelerated Threatened and Endangered Species Program. Budgets received are augmented with the reprogramming of funds from other National Forest Wide Funds (NFWF) and from timber dollars in order to meet the recovery effort for the red-cockaded woodpecker (RCW). This emphasis to manage for the RCW is a combination of the forests' initiative and the court order issued by Judge Parker in 1988. Table 25.1 represents the budget summary since development of the Land Management Plan, 1987.

Since 1987, the NFGT has entered into Challenge Cost Share projects to enhance the wildlife program (Table 25.2). These programs enhance the habitat and other wildlife management opportunities without additional budgetary outlays. The NFGT entered into agreements with state, private, and other federal agencies on a dollar-for-dollar ratio, with challenger contributions often exceeding that of the forests.

Nonstructural wildlife improvements consist of habitat improvements that benefit wildlife measured in acres. For the NFGT, this work is primarily prescribed burning, which creates earlier plant successional stages. Other nonstructural habitat work includes seeding and plantings, thinnings, and releases which improve or encourage existing food or cover plants (1986–90 Management Information Handbook, FSH 1309.11a).

Nonstructural fish improvements measured in acres consist of habitat fertilization treatments to change the water chemical composition to increase biological productivity for fish production, treatment to control aquatic plants, and fish population controls mainly in the form of stocking. Structural improvements include all structural habitat improvements which directly benefit specified wildlife, fish, or threatened and endangered animal and plant species. This activity is measured in structures and includes water developments (ponds), nest structures, den development, and greentree reservoir construction, etc.

Staffing

The professional biologist staff of the national forests and grasslands in Texas has increased substantially since 1970. Table 25.3 reflects the changes in the past 25 years. Many of the staffing changes have been the result of requirements to protect, manage, and enhance habitat for the RCW. Many other benefits to a variety of wildlife species have resulted from this increase in wildlife staffing.

Habitat and Species Management

In the development of NFGT compartment prescriptions, a wide range of wildlife management activities may be proposed. These projects range from habitat management for timber or rangeland, to inventory and assessment, to development of ponds for fisheries enhancement. Texas Parks and Wildlife Department, by agreement, participates in these prescription reviews and provides direct exchange of information to ensure the agencies coordinate to the fullest extent possible. During fiscal year 1990, Texas Parks and Wildlife Department partici-

Table 25.1. WILDLIFE BUDGET ALLOCATION FOR THE

Activity codes	Land mgmt. plan	Year		
		1987	1988	1989
FISHERIES				
Nonstructural	*	—	5	2
Structural	*	—	4	1
Fish operations	*	—	20	37
THREATENED & ENDANGERED				
Operations	*	—	30	171
Structural	*	—		
Nonstructural	*	—	455	350
Habitat maintenance	*	—		
WILDLIFE HABITAT IMPROVEMENT				
Operations	*	—	89	37
Structural	*	—	99	95
Nonstructural	*	— *	287	255
FY total	738*	874	989	949

*Plan total is all operations/habitat improvement combined.

pated in 13 prescription reviews (Kruger 1990). In addition, 58 project plans or decision notices were reviewed that related to specific actions within the RCW 1200m zones. This cooperative effort has benefitted both agencies and will continue in the future.

Since the Forest Plan was approved, a number of activities have been promoted that were not described in that document. One management action that has been somewhat controversial is the closing of certain roads in response to hunting management and the turkey restoration program. One of the considerations in site selection for turkey reintroductions involves public access and control. Closure of some roads to restrict traffic and disturbance is one requirement that has to be made

NATIONAL FORESTS AND GRASSLANDS IN TEXAS USING 1989 BASELINE DOLLARS (thousands).

1990	1991	1992	1993	1994	1995
25	30	(20)	15	21	36
1	12	(20)	11	5	31
12	10	(26)	43	78	99
200	270	(136)	247	311	290
25	6	(38)	92	137	80
595	669	(728)	393	454	622
4	21				
12	68	(109)	46	80	44
75	74	(41)	106	127	127
285	235	(83)	377	471	388
1,234	1,395	(1,201)	1,330	1,684	1,717

before turkeys can be restocked on NFGT lands. Road closures have other benefits such as reduced dumping and vandalism.

Many other habitat management activities are considered and utilized on the NFGT. Most of these activities are in conjunction with other multiple-use objectives. Timber management and range improvement are generalized practices that supply most of the habitat activities. Other management practices, such as that directed by the court order for RCW, have direct and positive influences on a variety of other wildlife species. These habitat management activities also consider the adjacent non-USFS lands. Continued monitoring and consideration for these concerns are included during the revision process.

Table 25.2. WILDLIFE ACCOMPLISHMENTS* FOR

Land activity	Mgt. plan	Year		
		1987	1988	1989
Wildlife habitat	6.4	31.1	29.6	22.6
Fisheries habitat	1.4	0.1	1.2	0.03
Threatened/endangered species habitat	0.8	0.4	2.4	6.5
Wildlife structures (all)	3–15	42	60	80

*From monitoring and evaluation reports since 1987.

Areas Where Change May Be Needed

1. Change: consider closer coordination for wildlife and habitat management betwen the Texas Parks and Wildlife Department and the USFS. Coordination should be addressed through the Forest Plan by linking goals and objectives in 5-year operating plans between TPWD and NFGT. Reason: the requirement to meet the Sikes Act is through the forest-planning process. Coordinate management and improvement of wildlife, fish, and endangered and threatened species habitat through implementation of Forest Plans. New guidance was recently identified in the FSM 2600 revision specifically related to habitat planning and evaluation and integration of Sikes Act planning and forest-planning actions. Implement Sikes Act schedules as 5-year operating plans for accomplishing wildlife and fisheries goals identified in Forest Plans. Link these operating plans with the program planning and budgeting process. Ensure Sikes Act agreements are consistent with Forest Plans (FSM 2624, Sikes Act Planning, July 19, 1991). Specific objectives are to
   A. integrate habitat planning into land management and project plans to meet national, regional, and local objectives for wildlife and fish, including threatened, endangered, and sensitive animal and plant species and their habitats,
   B. provide a sound base of information to support management decision making affecting wildlife and fish, including endan-

ENHANCING HABITAT ON NATIONAL FOREST GRASSLANDS IN TEXAS

1990	1991	1992	1993	1994	1995	1996
11.9	20.0	13.3	16.0	34.0	22.0	4.7
0.2	1.3	24.6	4.0	0.25	0.3	0.2
5.7	7.9	0.14	14.2	14.3	10.7	3.6
242	333	920	401	1,726	1,464	454

gered, threatened, and sensitive animal and plant species and their habitats,

C. identify opportunities and management strategies to maintain and improve habitats throughout the National Forest System, and

D. coordinate forest planning for wildlife and fish with state comprehensive planning conducted pursuant to the Fish and Wildlife Conservation Act, as amended by the Sikes Act (FSM 2601, item 6). Include in Forest Plans and projects objectives required by the act.

2. Change: achieve USFS-wide consistency in how habitats of wildlife, fish, sensitive, threatened, and endangered species are evaluated and considered in land and resource management planning. Reason: many National Forest Plans have initiated or are in the process of initiating amendments or revisions. Many of the forests must deal with the same or similar wildlife needs according to guidance directed by NMFA. Consistency between these developing plans would benefit the quality and reliability of these plans in the future.

3. Change: consistency of wildlife programs in national forests should be maintained through professionals that are familiar with that area's needs. This consistency should be considered through administrative and personnel decisions at the forest level. Reason: a recent study completed by the Wildlife Management Institute identified several points that would improve the capability of the

Table 25.3. WILDLIFE STAFFING ON TEXAS NATIONAL FORESTS AND GRASSLANDS, 1970–95

Position	Year				
	1971	1981	1988	1990	1995
Supervisor's office biologist	2	2	1	2	3
District biologist	0	1	3	7	6
Trainee biologist	0	1	3	1	1
Biological technician	0	0	1	1	1
Fisheries biologist*	0	0	.50	.50	.75
Trainee-botanist/ecologist	0	0	0	1	1
Botanist/ecologist	0	4	0	1	1
Total	2	8	8.5	13.5	13.75

USFS to manage wildlife. These recommendations include the following:

A. The USFS should employ sufficient biologists and technicians to meet wildlife and fish management needs. These personnel should have equivalent status with other resource professionals.

B. Wildlife and fish biologists and other resource specialists should be allowed to receive grade promotions in place on ranger districts, on national forests, and in regional and the Washington offices.

C. The USFS should provide Series 482 and 486 biologists greater opportunity to move into line officer and staff officer positions throughout all levels.

4. Change: consider a revision of the existing cooperative agreement/MOU with Texas Parks and Wildlife Department. Reason: there is a need to enter into a management agreement with the Texas Parks and Wildlife Department to expand management to cover the entire national forests and grasslands in Texas. Success in the mutual management of the 5 wildlife management areas is the foundation for this need for change. The Angelina National Forest and the LBJ Grasslands should be priority targets for this type of cooperative management if complete commitment of the forest is not possible. In addition to the changes considered for wildlife management

areas, more direct dialogue and cooperation may be needed to address the FSM 2624 changes as they relate to consistent USFS and state agency comprehensive planning.

5. Change: consider full evaluation and amendments as needed to ensure the wildlife habitat management direction and philosophy is consistent between the featured species concept, biodiversity, and guidance for endangered or threatened species. Reason: featured species concept could possibly conflict with the direction to maintain viable populations of existing native and desired nonnative fish, wildlife (36, CFR219.19), and plant species generally well distributed throughout their current range (FSH 2622; FSH 2602; 1987 LMP, IV7). New information indicated that management should be directed or in consideration of groups, communities, guilds, etc., instead of individual species (see chap. 2). Habitat fragmentation will need to be addressed in the revision of the plan. This subject matter is often addressed when discusssing neotropical birds and, in particular, when addressing the problems associated with the recovery of the RCW. As this subject is discussed in the plan, it must be emphasized that the landownership pattern in itself has created a fragmented forest. Forest Plan guidance pertaining to wildlife management should consider these ownership patterns and fragmentation of habitat in the evaluation process for both programmatic as well as site-specific impacts.

6. Change: consider more detailed descriptions of wildlife-related monitoring and evaluation needs in the revision process. Reason: monitoring and evaluation is an area where improvement is vital. The public wants to be more informed on how wildlife is being affected by implementation of the plan. Reporting accomplishments via local media contact and annual reports to the region is imperative. Those items of most interest to the public need to be developed. Some of these areas are neotropical birds, nongame species management, diversity, hardwood development, and work associated with the strategies for declining species such as wood ducks and mallards. With the reduction of clearcutting and site preparation techniques, i.e., rake and windrow, there will be a need to look for alternative techniques to provide habitats for species such as the American woodcock. Monitoring and evaluation of these impacts due to changes in regeneration practices should be included due to the perceived effect on certain special interest species.

Literature Cited

Krueger, M. 1990. Wildlife resource planning. Fed. Aid Proj. Rpt. No. W-107-R-16. Job No. 9. Tex. Parks and Wildl. Dep., Austin. 5pp.

USDA Forest Service. 1982. General technical report. SE For. Exper. St. No. Se-22.

Wildlife Management Institute. 1990. Recommendations to improve wildlife and fish programs of the USDA Forest Service. Misc. Publ. 98pp.

Dennis M. Herbert
Chief, Natural Resources Branch
Directorate Public Works
Department of Army
Fort Hood, Texas 76544-5707

26. U.S. Department of Defense

Abstract: Public lands held by the U.S. Department of Defense (DoD),
including army, navy, air force, marines, and reserve components, play
an increasingly important role in the protection and management of
wildlife habitats throughout the country. The DoD has a huge responsibility for the management of some of our nation's finest natural trea-
sures among its almost 25 million acres. These lands not only provide
the training and testing grounds for those who must defend our way of
life, but they include some of our nation's finest wildlife habitats and
provide excellent outdoor recreation. DoD lands have contributed to
conservation of Texas's vast natural resources for over half a century.
The major DoD land steward in Texas, in terms of acres, is the army,
with holdings totaling over 1.4 million acres. The navy follows with
over 16,000 acres. Management of DoD installations in Texas involves
management of wildlife populations, habitat, public use, antiquities,
economic use, research, and defense preparedness. The purposes and
management of each of the service holdings are described. DoD's natural resource management is characterized as stewardship. In general,
important, effective land management practices support the training
mission and preservation of Texas's wildlife resources.

Public lands held by the U.S. Department of Defense (DoD) play an
increasingly important role in the protection and management of wildlife habitats in Texas and throughout the country. In general, the primary mission of military installations located throughout Texas is

training, housing, and support for the active duty units that provide for our nation's defense. Installations also provide support for other assigned and tenant organizations, the reserve, National Guard, and Reserve Officer Training Corps. The military mission also provides community facilities and services to the large number of military retirees living in the communities surrounding an installation. When speaking of the military mission, one must also speak of collective natural resource management programs, which support all other missions. DoD is steward for 25 million acres of federal land. DoD lands represent all of our country's major land types and contain sensitive ecosystems and endangered species, irreplaceable historic and archaeological sites, and many other important natural cultural resources. Defense faces the challenging task of protecting these resources while supporting the primary military mission. DoD recognizes that protection of these resources and compliance with environmental laws ensure the continued availability of lands and waters to support training critical to mission performance and readiness. As part of this conservation strategy, DoD is committed to

1. comply with all applicable laws and standards for natural resources;
2. identify all significant and sensitive natural resources;
3. promote ecosystem-based management on all military lands;
4. provide training, education, and staffing to build a strong conservation ethic;
5. enhance coordination and consultation with federal and state agencies, the public, and other stakeholders; and
6. provide for public access to our conservation programs whenever possible.

For more than 30 years, the Sikes Act has proven instrumental in helping the department manage its unique natural resources. The approximately 250 cooperative fish and wildlife management plans military installations have developed under the Sikes Act in coordination with the U.S. Fish and Wildlife Service and state fish and game agencies have been the cornerstone for many of the natural resources management initiatives in DoD. The Sikes Act also provides authorization to charge users for access to utilize natural resources on military installations. There is a wide disparity between installations in terms of the fees each charges for similar activities, such as hunting and fishing. Fees run the gamut from no charge to more than $100 for 1 person for 1 season.

User fees, although very important on some installations, are a small part of the overall budget to support natural resource programs. Historically, other funding sources included base operational and maintenance funds, agriculture outlease accounts, and forestry accounts. The last 10 years have seen access to or advent of other funding such as A-106, Legacy, and Land Rehabilitation and Maintenance. Each of these programs was originally designed to fill a particular need in maintaining the natural environment while directly or indirectly supporting the training mission. In the early years, all of these funding programs may not have been coordinated into an integrated effort, but they each in their own way supported the natural environment as well as the overall mission.

Today, ecosystem management represents a new chapter in our understanding of the interrelationships between land and species. The goal of ecosystem management is to restore and maintain the health, sustainability, and biological diversity of ecosystems while supporting sustainable economies and communities. Under the Fiscal Year 1996–2001 Defense Planning Guidance, Military Departments are required to develop an Environmental Security Strategic Plan for conservation that will serve as the basis for programming and budgeting. This plan requires, at a minimum that by FY 1996, components will ensure that at least 60% of all Integrated Natural Resource Management Plans for installations determined by the component to have sufficient natural resources to require a management plan are prepared and implemented to provide for the effective management of natural resources and for the protection of threatened and endangered species, wetlands, and biodiversity. Components will complete inventories of natural and cultural resources entrusted to DoD on a timeline consistent with the National Biological Survey.

The army's Integrated Training Area Management (ITAM) program is an excellent example of an initiative to integrate training needs with land conditions and capabilities to reduce impacts. ITAM is used to establish base-line data, inventory land condition and capabilities, match mission use with land capabilities, program land restoration and rehabilitation, and provide environmental education training to land users. Another integrated initiative is the establishment of procedures with the National Biological Survey (NBS) to conduct biological inventories on DoD lands. The department is committed to working with the NBS to inventory and monitor the nation's biological resources. Through these efforts, we will evaluate the status and trends of biological resources on DoD lands and identify how these resources can best be used to meet our environmental, economic, and social needs.

Within the context of training individuals and units to provide for this country's national defense, integrated management of the natural environment is dedicated primarily to maintenance of natural flora and fauna and their associated habitats. However, department regulation permits the full range of wildlife and wildlife habitat management activities and strategies, depending upon what is most appropriate for each installation and what is required to meet individual installation objectives. Multipurpose use of our lands requires multipurpose management of these lands, such as prescribed burning, timber harvests, native plant restoration, livestock grazing, mowing, farming, brush management (cutting, dozing, chaining, burning), and other techniques used to maintain training areas, enhance habitats, and supplement natural food supplies.

DoD Installations of Texas

DoD installations have played an important role in the conservation of Texas's vast natural resources for over 50 years even though military installations have been a part of Texas history since before Texas was a state. Nine major installations and a number of minor landholdings make up a total of over 1.4 million acres in the state of Texas (Fig. 26.1).

Fort Hood

Fort Hood (FH) covers 339 square miles in Central Texas just west of Killeen, midway between Waco and Austin. Named for Confederate general John Bell Hood, the Great Place, as the post is now known throughout the United States Army, is the largest armored installation in the free world.

Fort Hood is located at the southernmost extension of the Cross Timbers and Prairies vegetational area. Area ecology is influenced by this and two other nearby vegetational areas. The Blackland Prairie vegetational area is adjacent to and east of Fort Hood, and the Edwards Plateau vegetational area is just to the southwest. Woodlands of Fort Hood are most closely representative of Edwards Plateau associations, and the grasslands are representative of both the tall-grass associations of the Blackland Prairies and the mid- and short-grass associations of the Cross Timbers and Prairies areas.

Fig. 26.1 *United States Department of Defense installations in Texas.*

The character of the vegetation at Fort Hood reflects such human disturbances as accidental fire, military training operations, and cattle grazing. However, areas in the northeastern portion of the post have not been routinely subjected to these events and are therefore relatively undisturbed. Areas in the adjacent Live Fire Area (LFA) are subject to accidental fires started as a result of training operations. These fires clear much of the existing vegetation, effectively initiating a new successional sequence at the burned site. Training operations, especially involving tracked vehicles, cause direct destruction of ground vegetation, especially along established roads.

The various habitat types in the Fort Hood area provide for wildlife communities characteristic of the Edwards Plateau and the other vegetational areas on which Fort Hood borders. Terrestrial wildlife habitats follow closely the vegetation communities described but also follow clines from upland down to riparian habitats. Wetland habitat is limited on the installation, but where it does occur, aquatic wildlife is typical of the particular habitat.

In 1988, the DoD entered into a memorandum of agreement (MOA) with the Nature Conservancy. The purpose of this agreement is to protect endangered species and to promote natural diversity nationwide. The agreement encourages the use of geographic information systems (GISs) and allows for DoD funding to accomplish the agreement's goals on DoD lands.

In August 1991, a supplemental MOA was drafted between the Texas Nature Conservancy, the Texas Parks and Wildlife Department Biological Conservation Data System, the Fort Worth District of the U.S. Army Corp of Engineers, Fort Sam Houston, and Fort Hood. The supplemental MOA was signed in May 1992. Under the supplemental MOA, participants create GIS map layers for vegetative cover types, soils topography, roads, institutional boundaries, and other spatial variables. The GIS is linked to the Biological Conservation Data System's natural resource database. This database contains information from field surveys of threatened and endangered species and rare or unique habitats. Data are maintained by the Texas Parks and Wildlife Department for the Texas Nature Conservancy and include spatial referencing. Fort Hood's environmental staff, along with U.S. Fish and Wildlife Service (USFWS) and other participants in the supplemental MOA, will confirm the GIS map layers, including vegetative mapping of endangered species habitats. The shared GIS database allows a unified assessment of known and potential endangered species habitat on Fort Hood. This should reduce future agency conflicts as well as facilitate agency cooperation on issues potentially affecting all species.

High tech is not the only form management takes on Fort Hood. FH follows an integrated natural resource management plan (INRMP), which covers a 5-year period, and cooperative agreements developed with the state and the USFWS. Wildlife management involves a combination of aquatic management, livestock grazing, prescribed burning, brush management, trapping and translocating, erosion management, farming, annual surveys, endangered species protection, public hunting, and natural resource law enforcement.

Aquatic Management. FH has 247 water impoundments varying in size from 0.5 acre to 30 acres. Most provide wildlife/livestock water, slow storm water run-off and trap silt, or are storage for fire-fighting capabilities; only about 10% are intensely managed annually. Annual projects include electro-fishing surveys, aquatic herbicide application, placement of underwater fish structures, construction and repair of fencing enclosures around dams, fertilizing, and fish stocking. Ponds fill with silt over time, so at least 1 per year is renovated, and at least 1 new impoundment is built each year.

Livestock Grazing. The present grazing lease is managed under a program of controlled grazing that is executed in coordination with the Central Texas Cattlemen's Association and the USDA Natural Resource Conservation Service (NRCS). Yearly grazing limits (stocking rates) are based on annual range condition surveys and recommendations of range specialists from the NRCS. Under the terms of the present lease, the stocking rate shall not exceed 1 animal unit per 45.7 acres of land included in the lease area.

Prescribed Burning. Burning is one of the least expensive and most often employed management tools to renovate grasslands; control regrowth of Ashe juniper, also known as cedar; protect endangered species habitat; and provide favorable feeding and loafing areas.

Brush Management. Even though thousands of acres of juniper are protected for the preservation of the golden-cheeked warbler, approximately 6,000 acres annually are removed by mechanical means (chaining, dozing, shredding) to provide better forage, conserve water, and open training areas.

Trapping and Translocating. Game animal populations expand and exceed the carrying capacity of the land in areas that can't be hunted and sensitive and off-limits areas. Annually, deer or turkeys are moved from a nonuse area of the installation to a high use area.

Erosion Management. Concentrated vehicular traffic during training maneuvers denudes soils of vegetative cover. Repeated traffic on some training areas has almost eradicated the native plant community. This traffic has mechanically altered physical characteristics of training area soils. Ultimately, affected soils are subjected to excessive erosion, downstream sedimentation is significantly increased, and the training area's usefulness for achieving the army's mission is compromised. A memorandum of understanding was executed and dated April 16, 1992, identifying the U.S. Department of Army and the U.S. Department of Agriculture, Natural Resource Conservation Service as cooperating agencies to formulate and accomplish the objective of the Fort Hood Erosion and Sedimentation Reduction Project. The objectives are to maintain training areas for the army's training mission; establish, sustain, or improve vegetation; protect soil resources; enhance water quality; and prolong useful storage capacity of water reservoirs. The project's vegetative and structural components are to establish 4,930 acres of herbaceous vegetation; manage 18,300 acres of juniper; construct 38 debris basin-grade stabilization structures; and upgrade 62.8 miles of tank roads with 37 hard stream crossings and 11 hillside access points. These accomplishments were realized in the years 1993–98 with NRCS technical assistance and private contracts.

Farming. Wildlife feeding areas (food plots) have been farmed annually since the early 1960's. Annuals (small grains) and perennials (fruit and seed-producing shrubs/trees) are planted, fertilized, and maintained on approximately 50 sites across the reservation each year.

Annual Surveys. Surveys are used to monitor numerous wildlife populations such as deer census or game bird counts. Some are extensive and mandated by law (e.g., endangered species such as the black-capped vireo), and some are minor and requested by the National Biological Service, such as Monitoring Avian Productivity and Survival stations.

Endangered Species Protection. Significant numbers of 2 listed neotropical migrants, the black-capped vireo and the golden-cheeked warbler, nest on FH. The bald eagle winters on FH from November through April each year. One category I plant, Texabama croton, occurs in limited densities in the northeast section of the reservation. Extensive research has been under way on these and other sensitive species since 1987. In September 1993, FH and the USFWS signed an agreement, the biological opinion, that spells out specific protection and research that FH will carry out. The caretaker status of the army at FH has been beneficial to these species.

Public Use. One of the oldest wildlife management tools to manipulate wildlife numbers is hunting. Hunting has been allowed at FH since the late 1940's. The first deer hunt occurred in 1957; Rio Grande turkey were first hunted in 1962. Early wildlife management was provided directly as a result of the army or by volunteers. Between 1947 and 1952, the army moved white-tailed deer from Camp Bullis, Texas, and Fort Sill, Oklahoma, to stock FH, which had no deer. Today, over 5,000 people hunt and fish on FH annually.

Law Enforcement. Any number of laws, regulations, and programs can be developed for the benefit of wildlife, but they are only as good as the natural resource law enforcement program that supports them. FH has a combination of full-time, civilian, DoD police (game wardens), and temporary, rotational, and military police that provide law enforcement.

Other DoD installations in Texas manage extensive landholdings, and from close working relations with some of these managers it is known that they engage in the same types of wildlife management programs. Wildlife habitats and species vary widely across this great state, but managers use many of the same management techniques and certainly follow the same laws and regulations promulgated by DoD for the preservation of our wildlife heritage.

Other DoD Installations in Texas

Wildlife management plans are being implemented for several DoD installations in Texas.

Fort Sam Houston. This facility is the hub of support to many commands and tenant activities on the post, including a school that trains thousands of medical personnel for army and other military services. As part of its support, the command manages Camp Bullis, a 27,880-acre area. Besides the continuous training at the camp, 20,400 acres are under agricultural grazing leases, and approximately 6,000 acres are home to the endangered golden-cheeked warbler. The entire area is managed for both game and nongame wildlife.

Army Depots. Corpus Christi Army Depot covers 180 acres and is located on the Corpus Christi Naval Air Station. It is the army's only complete overhaul and repair facility for helicopters. Red River Army Depot at Texarkana occupies 50 square miles and receives, stores, reconditions, and issues all types of army ordnance, general supplies, and ammunition.

Fort Bliss. Located at El Paso in the vast expanse of West Texas and New Mexico, Fort Bliss is the home of the U.S. Army Air Defense Artillery Center, largest air defense center in the free world (1,125,000 acres). It provides the key training, development, and support activities for the army's vital guided missile and air defense artillery programs.

Longhorn Army Ammunition Plant. The Department of the Army has approved funding for a project on the 8,500-acre Longhorn Army Ammunition Plant (LHAAP) under the DoD Legacy Program. Applications for additional Legacy Programs are pending with DoD. LHAAP has a number of significant environmental areas on their property, and implementing the Legacy Program will contribute to conserving those resources.

The approved project will fund a survey of breeding birds at LHAAP. The objective of this study is to determine the presence and distribution of breeding birds at LHAAP. The Breeding Bird Survey will be conducted in coordination with Louisiana State University at Shreveport.

Additional projects for which funds have been applied for include a bluebird nature trail and a waterfowl habitat enhancement study.

Eastern bluebirds are cavity-nesting birds that are displaced by aggressive nonnative starlings. Nest box programs for bluebirds have been very successful at reestablishing the species. The LHAAP bluebird project would establish nest boxes along the roadways at LHAAP to increase the number of bluebirds locally.

The waterfowl study will consist of placing wood duck prothonotary warbler boxes designed to accommodate both species simultaneously. When properly placed and maintained, these nest boxes have been successful at increasing local populations of these birds. The prothonotary warbler, a cavity-nesting neotropical migrant which shares habitat with the wood duck, faces habitat losses due to clearing of bottomland forest. These boxes would be placed in the Harrison Bayou area at LHAAP and be evaluated for nesting success of each species.

Implementing conservation programs on the LHAAP lands will complement the research efforts on adjoining state and private lands around Caddo Lake and contribute to an ecosystem approach to managing the watershed.

U.S. Navy and Naval Reserve. There are 7,222 active-duty military and 2,213 civilian employees stationed throughout the state, but they are concentrated in 4 principal locations: Corpus Christi, Kingsville, Beeville, and Dallas. Tom Burst of the Naval Facilities Engineering Command in Charleston, North Carolina, offered the following limited information about naval facilities in Texas that provide various forms of wildlife management on their holdings. A total of 11 sites in and around the 4 principal locations comprise a total of 16,798 acres controlled by the navy. Integrated natural resource management plans, fish and wildlife management plans, or land management plans are in place on 9 of the 11 sites. Endangered species surveys and environmental impact statements are in progress or are complete for 9 of the 11 sites. For security reasons, public access is allowed on only 1 of the sites, the Escondita Ranch near Kingsville. A limited amount of deer hunting is allowed on the Escondita.

U.S. Air Force. Air force bases in Texas as of July 1, 1994, include Brooks near San Antonio, Carswell in Fort Worth, Dyess in Abilene, Goodfellow at San Angelo, Kelly near San Antonio, Lackland near San Antonio, Laughlin near Del Rio, Randolph at San Antonio, Reese at Lubbock, and Sheppard at Wichita Falls.

Conclusion

Many military training operations, by their nature, can be very destructive in terms of vegetation loss, increased erosion, and habitat alteration. When speaking of the military mission one must also speak of collective natural resource management programs, which support these missions. Defense faces the challenging task of protecting these resources while supporting the primary military mission. DoD recognizes that protection of these resources ensures the continued availability of lands and waters to support training critical to mission performance and readiness as well as providing the nation's sportsmen with quality outdoor experiences and protection of the varied natural resources.

Joe C. Truett
P.O. Box 211
Glenwood, NM 88039

Daniel W. Lay
P.O. Box 4608
SFA Station
Nacogdoches, TX 75951

Prognosis

Abstract: Degradation of wildlife habitat and loss of wildlife on Texas lands continue with little abatement. The underlying causes are the growth of human populations and consumer expectations, which lead to greater and greater demands for food, raw materials, and energy. As these demands escalate, landowners intensify production of beef, trees, and other commodities, and wildlife declines in abundance and diversity. Even most landowners who lease land for hunting or viewing wild animals exert little effort to manage their lands for wildlife. In the coming decades, as trespass restrictions tighten and more and more people lose access to wildlife, public motivation to preserve wildlife will undoubtedly decline. Wildlife agencies can best counteract such apathy by increasing the acreage of land purchased or leased specifically for wildlife, thereby reversing the decline in public access. In the long term, constraints on both human reproductive and consumptive behavior, coupled with maintenance of a wildlife tradition in young people, will be required to halt wildlife decline on Texas lands. These adjustments come only with major changes in societal values, changes set in motion by new directions in the education and orientation of youth.

As the third millennium approaches, many who value wildlife in Texas fear for the future. The timber men continue the felling of hardwoods and the planting of pines. Cattle and pasturelands push back the wildlands with increasing speed. Dams have already flooded or dried out the best of the bottomlands. Town folks build houses where Grandpa hunted deer. Coal fields, oil wells, power plants, and transmission corridors pock-mark the hinterlands so cities can shine like comets on the way toward darkness.

One of us has worked with Texas wildlife since armadillos constituted table fare in the 1930's. One has lived in recent years in other
places but grew up on Texas land. This one remembers:

> When I was twelve and my brother was eleven, my father and grandfather
> put their heads together and decided to have the hardwood hammock
> cleared on our 50 acres in Jasper County. The bulldozer came in, and that
> afternoon when we got off the school bus we could hear the trees cracking
> and groaning. For several days afterward we watched the D-7 cat fight the
> tangled woods. Near the end the tractor stalled at a big beech, 4 feet
> through at shoulder height and one of the few trees ever to frustrate our
> efforts to climb it. The caterpillar blade ripped the roots on every side, then
> lifted high to push and push and finally bring it down. At dusk we climbed
> among its fallen branches, running ironwood switches into hollows where
> the gray squirrels used to get away. Nothing came out of the holes, and,
> leaning in to listen, my brother said he heard nothing, but I thought I heard
> waves beating on a distant shore.
>
> Years passed, and other woodlots fell. Neighbors strived to be the first
> to clear their land, buy a tractor and a bush-hog, and bring in Brahma cows.
> One morning my grandfather was mowing the cleared land with his John
> Deere tractor when the machine hit a hidden stump, flipped, and fell on
> him. Later in the day my father smelled the smoke from the grass fire that
> started, saw the rear wheel of the tractor thrust into the air, and ran down
> to see. To attend the funeral I came home from college, where they were
> teaching us about hardwood trees and squirrels and the nature of habitat.
>
> In the early 1990's, 30 years after Granddaddy died, I drove around the
> Southeast Texas countryside, and it looked like sacrificial ground. The land
> I'd known in childhood had been mostly stripped to grow pines and beef.
> Along the highways and back roads, mile after mile, I saw a 50-inch-rainfall
> farm, patchwork and ragged to be sure, but busily and purposefully grow-
> ing food and fiber for human use.

Census records show our population's persistent growth. Television
ads identify us as voracious consumers. These facts disclose the basic
problem: a growing population of humans, each with growing expectations to consume material goods and energy, leads inexorably to a
farmed and mined landscape that yields only cardboard, coal, and calo-
ries. We will be thwarted in our attempts to conserve wildlife habitat
over the long term as long as these uses of the land take precedence over
its use by wildlife.

Resource decisions that influence wildlife in Texas echo an economic philosophy that promotes the continuous growth of human population and enterprises. Worship of growth plays no geographic favorites—every community, large and small, answers to its siren call, and growth continues. The 1980 population of Texas totalled 14.2 million, the 1990 population 16.9 million, a 19.4% increase that challenges the growth rates of Third World nations.

State agencies with influence on wildlife respond to the wishes of elected officials and their appointees. These appointees invariably promote growth, and most contribute generously to politicians before receiving an appointment—seed money spent in hopes of gaining more money. This is not new and is unlikely to change.

With few exceptions, wildlife has become a by-product of, or fugitive from, economic enterprise. Most wildlife planners seek compromise year after year with the army of developers that wants to dig channels, create reservoirs, convert complex ecosystems to monocultures, drain wetlands, and build new smelters, chemical plants, and houses. Wildlife and its habitats diminish.

A more insidious problem threatens to escalate this trend: most of us in America seem to be entering an era of declining personal affluence. The resources that support our material well-being have been high-graded, and high-graded again, and each succeeding generation pays more in real dollars to buy them. Warren Johnson (1978), chairman of the Geography Department at San Diego State University, summed it up well: "to maintain the heavy flow of raw materials now being cranked through our economy will become an increasingly laborious and ultimately desperate task."

The resulting decline in the average standard of living could have been predicted on ecological grounds. It is the result of more and more people feeding on a diminishing supply of life-sustaining resources such as oil, coal, fertile soils, fresh water, timber, and, ultimately, food. As resource scarcities widen the gap between what we want and what we get of these resources, we up the ante for landowners to convert land to food and fiber production. Significantly, extractive pursuits constitute almost all the phenomena leading to wildlife habitat degradation in Texas (Table P.1). Although a few kinds of wildlife may prosper as farms, pastures, and cities push aside wildlands, the majority suffer.

People show little sign that their affection for wild animals is likely to reverse this conversion of land to commodity production. Increasingly fewer Texans even think about wildlife conservation because more of them than previously live in cities long vacated by species com-

Table P.1. MAJOR CAUSES OF WILDLIFE HABITAT LOSS BY VEGETATIVE REGION IN TEXAS

Causes of wildlife habitat loss[a]	Vegetative region (see frontispiece)								
	1	2	3	4	5/6	7/8	9	10	11
Intensive farming/monocultures[b]	X	X	X	X	X		X	X	X
Short-rotation timber monocultures	X								
Intensive pasture development[b]	X	X	X						
Overgrazing	X	X	X	X	X	X	X	X	X
Mining (coal, oil, stone, minerals)	X	X	X	X	X	X	X	X	X
Urban/industrial expansion/transportation	X	X	X	X	X	X			
Reservoir construction/aquifer use	X	X	X	X	X	X	X	X	X
Fragmentation by patchwork ownership	X	X	X	X		X			
Toxic chemical use/disposal (agriculture, industry)	X	X	X	X	X			X	X
Drainage/dredging/channelization[c]		X	X	X					
Recreation/tourism development (localized)	X	X	X	X	X	X			X

1 = East Texas Pine and Hardwood Forests	5/6 = South Texas Brushlands/ Coastal Sand Plains
2 = Post Oak Savannah and Cross Timbers and Prairies	7/8 = Edwards Plateau–Llano Uplift
3 = Blackland Prairies	9 = Rolling Plains
4 = Gulf Coast Prairies and Marshes	10 = High Plains
	11 = Trans-Pecos

Adapted and updated from Frentress 1985.

[a] The changes shown do not cause habitat loss for all species; almost invariably, a few species benefit.

[b] Involves intensive clearing of native vegetation.

[c] Also involves major metropolitan areas and associated streams.

mon on Grandfather's farm. Even those who continue to mingle with wild animals almost invariably opt for more dollars over more deer (Clark 1982; Teer 1982).

We view this trend with apprehension. Even though a present owner may not value squirrels or ducks, his progeny or the next owner might. This dilemma—created when people seeking short-term gain curtail options for the long term—has recurred again and again among people who share resources. Garret Hardin (1868) dubbed it the "tragedy of the commons."

This trend probably will worsen as the average Texan loses affluence in the years ahead. Many examples worldwide demonstrate the incompatibility between hungry people and abundant wildlife. The larger wild animals often are overhunted even when habitats remain intact; we know this from local situations in Africa (Eltringham 1990) and other places where people suffer desperate hunger. Older biologists may remember the wildlife scarcity in Texas during our own Great Depression in the 1930's.

Many of us today like to believe that landowner enlightenment about wildlife values will guarantee a future for diverse and abundant wildlife worldwide. There is little indication that this holds true even in our own well-fed society.

Given the strong personal drive for economic gain, what are the best political strategies for preserving wildlife populations and values in Texas landscapes? Authoritarian protection by a centralized government finds little support in Texas, where 98% of the land is privately owned, and powerful ownership rights are legally mandated and culturally pervasive. Landowner consensus for land-use regulations that benefit wildlife—a form of Garret Hardin's proposed "mutual coercion mutually agreed upon"—is certainly possible, but truly effective agreements seem unlikely. We agree with DeYoung and Kaplan (1988), who saw that neither authoritarianism nor conventional democratic consensus will be very effective solutions.

Three options seem feasible, and all have already worked to some extent. The best long-term option seems to be fee acquisition by government agencies or private groups of lands earmarked for wildlife management or protection. Leasing of lands, as the Audubon Society has done (Ahrns 1982), or obtaining conservation easements, as done by the U.S. Fish and Wildlife Service, is a second option for obtaining control, though it seems less dependable in the long term than outright purchase of land. The third is capitalizing on the market value of wildlife per se.

Most people concerned about wildlife applaud the acquisition or leasing of Texas lands for wildlife preservation, conservation, or research. State and federal ownership of wildlife management areas and parks resolves to a great extent the problem of wildlife habitat losses in those areas. Clark (1982) lists habitat preservation and acquisition about halfway down a prioritized list of 13 goals of the Texas Parks and Wildlife Department; we believe it deserves a much higher rank, particularly in high rainfall areas of the state where intensive food and fiber production are competing options and in other regions where the presence of surface water or other special features elevates habitat values.

Legal control by conservation interests is the only method guaranteeing that wildlife habitat will be preserved on private lands in most of the eastern third of the state. Places in East Texas owned for many years by the state, such as the Engeling and Murphy Wildlife Management Areas, are rapidly becoming natural gems in a farmed landscape. The recent purchase of the Blount Farm, a bottomland hardwood tract in Nacogdoches County, lends encouragement that such acquisitions can continue. Private gifts of land have not been encouraged but should be.

Long-term leases to protect wildlife habitat may be less dependable from the wildlife standpoint but politically more expedient than land purchase. The North Toledo Waterfowl Project operates on lands leased from the Sabine River Authority, and the Dam B Wildlife Management Area is managed under a long-term lease from the U.S. Army Corps of Engineers.

Finding some way to improve wildlife habitat on the remaining vast acreages has geographic potential far greater than purchasing or leasing small acreages. It may work best for low rainfall regions where intensive farming cannot venture. Already, many such landholdings support hunting leases, and some of the landowners (though not many) improve wildlife habitat to enhance the value of their leases (Teer 1982).

Clearly, if human populations continue to grow and living standards to decline, as appears almost inevitable, most people will be strongly motivated to use land ever more intensively for economic gain. But it is difficult for us to believe that everyone will operate strictly from economic motivations. Many Texans have grandmothers and grandfathers who lived daily in the open and talked before winter fires of deer and birds and mysterious long-tailed cats slinking down creek bottoms. These interests may appear dead in the grandsons and granddaughters, but surely they languish just below the surface, waiting to be awakened by a cardinal feeding young or a coyote howling near a weekend campsite. The task of wildlife conservation is to stir these latent responses.

People fall into 1 of 2 groups in terms of what practical steps can be taken to motivate them to conserve wildlife. The most populous group comprises the landless, those who have vocal and voting power but no access to private land with wildlife. The second group contains the owners and lessees of private lands.

Let's look at the first group, the landless public. In a democratic society, considerable power to manage private lands can be exerted by them. If they can be motivated toward land management for wildlife, various legal restrictions or incentives to favor wildlife on private lands could result.

We believe that such motivation has lagged in recent years because these people no longer own the wildlife on private lands, and they know it. If this is true, how did it happen? How can its effects be reversed? It is instructive to review the history that eroded the public's ownership of wildlife.

Texans and other Americans traditionally have regarded wildlife as a resource to be shared by all the people, a common property that all may use. This view probably developed as a rejection of the European feudal system of land tenure, in which a privileged few owned the game. Early European migrants to America, being mostly from common stock, did not want such a situation to arise in their new home with its newfound freedoms. Thus, the tradition of a wildlife "commons" took root in America.

These early immigrants, mostly peasant stock, came also with a great land hunger, conceived in the same feudal system where they had labored as peasants on the lands of lords. Thus, private ownership of land developed its own tradition of America, side by side with public ownership of the wildlife.

These 2 traditions operated well together as long as the landowner allowed free trespass by others upon his land. But as human populations grew and landholdings per capita shrank, landowners became more possessive of the land's economic potential. They used their right of ownership to prevent trespass.

One version of Genesis maintains that the sons of Adam inherited an equal division of the world: Cain the ownership of all the land, Abel of all animals. Cain, the farmer, eventually slew Abel, the manager of beasts, for trespassing.

In any case, we have inherited a predicament. Though the landless have a legal right to harvest or view the wildlife on private lands, they cannot legally reach it if a landowner desires to post his or her land. Because the tradition of hunting, fishing, and looking for wildlife has kept its hold, a fee system has arisen whereby the new landless class can buy access to the wildlife.

Many of those in the wildlife profession, among others, have resented this "privatization" of wildlife. It has seemed somehow unethical for landowners to benefit financially from a public resource. Some believe we are headed back to the system our ancestors migrated overseas to escape (Geist 1988).

The problem worsens as escalating trespass fees prohibit more and more people from buying access (Clark 1982; Teer 1982). This trend probably will continue if, as many predict, our society loses most of its middle economic class to a poorer class and only a small wealthy class retains the ability to buy access. Those with no access to wildlife lose interest in its preservation.

This collision of social values is only one of the many that have arisen as our legal system and our traditions, developed largely when populations were sparse and resources were plentiful, face a crowded world. It is time we moved beyond convention in our efforts to deal with the contradictions that have emerged. It is time we realize that, unless Texas laws and traditions of landownership change, most of the wildlife really does not and will not belong to the public and thus will have little support from the public. Strategies to return a measure of wildlife ownership to the landless are imperative if wildlife conservation is to gain their support.

Now let's look at those people who own land. What can motivate them to manage it for wildlife? Economic returns from hunting leases may currently provide the greatest incentive to landowners, but even where the connection between wildlife and income is clear, most landowners practice little or no habitat management (Teer 1982). However, it is our observation that some landowners go to considerable effort and expense to maintain wildlife on their property when they clearly see wildlife respond to their efforts. Often the efforts serve a nourishing function—feeding birds or deer, or building bird nest boxes—and often are motivated by women. Frequently, these efforts are extended with little thought of monetary gain.

Why then do the same landowners cut the hardwoods on the back 40 acres when they need cash? Why do lessors not institute brush management for deer? This is indeed an enigma and may relate to the landowners' poor understanding of how wildlife interacts with habitat. Perhaps the average landowner cannot be expected to delve into the intricacies of ecology any more than the average voter shows interest in political issues more complicated than slogans.

The hesitancy by nonecologists to hear and act upon complex habitat management strategies for conserving wildlife seems pervasive in our society. For many years we ecologists have touted the benefits of fire, but untrained fans of wildlife remain horrified by the Yellowstone Inferno of 1989. Bulldozers on the landscape represent devastation to many self-made conservationists, whether the objective is to build cities or to thin brush for wildlife.

Perhaps one reason this problem exists is that people often hear contradictory messages about the benefits brought about by habitat change. Paper companies and the Texas Parks and Wildlife Department often disagree publicly about the wildlife benefits of pine plantations. The ranching industry and wildlife biologists sometimes send different messages about cattle grazing. Nongame biologists and deer biologists may advertise opposing views about cutting trees.

How can we simplify and agree upon ecological messages to motivate both the landless and the landed toward sound management for wildlife? Is it even possible, given the complexity of land-animal relations and the tendency for those with interests in the land's use to contradict each other? Our view is that it may be difficult, but it is necessary. The best progress may come from biologists who work daily with the public.

For example, it may be possible to send simple and palatable messages about maintaining habitat diversity. Explaining that wildlife needs variety in food sources and cover types seems relatively straightforward: the corollary is that activities that reduce these kinds of diversity are bad. Specific features of diversity can be illustrated as needed by species of particular interest, e.g., suitable nest holes for red-cockaded woodpeckers.

Attitudes develop young. Preschool and grade-school children often display more receptiveness to the importance of wild animals than do older age groups culturally attuned to milking the land's economic potential. Further, the complexity of ideas youngsters can understand about their world often exeeds that of the pap fed to their parents by politicians. Can currently unpopular ideas such as human population control and economic frugality be introduced in the public schools? Or by example at home?

Only by better educating children can we help change the cultural values that are the key to saving tomorrow's wildlife. It will be a Herculean task, for the very classroom youngsters need is the land from which most of them have been excluded. Raised apart from landscapes with snakes, frogs, raccoons, quail, and deer, they inevitably receive their images of a "proper" world from city streets and television screens.

Having summed up some of the major trends in wildlife on Texas lands and touched some of the problems that hinder its conservation, we could easily be depressed. We are most uneasy with the seemingly inexorable growth of human populations and human appetites for commodities.

But positive signs continue to surface. More lands than before are being bought or leased by public agencies or conservation groups, so that the wildlife on them really can belong to the public. Management agencies recognize the importance of educating Texans about how to retain wildlife on the land and now promote lobbying for legislation that puts legal constraints on habitat loss (e.g., Clark 1982, first 5 of 13 priorities). Ecological succession is our relentless ally, particularly in the very places watered well enough to encourage intensive farming of the land, and wildlife habitat and many species of wildlife quickly move in again once the farmer's ardor becomes cooled or his or her operation bankrupted. Some industries responsible for habitat destruction now work diligently not only to restore the land but to educate landowners about the values of wildlife (e.g., White 1977). Much of Texas is too arid to attract most kinds of extensive landscape alteration in any case and by default always will have some wildlife habitat and wildlife. Most important, calls for limiting human populations and economic growth are gaining greater respectability and more media coverage.

Today in Jasper County, hardwoods reach modest heights in neglected patches on the 50-acre home place bulldozers cleared for pasture 40 years ago. Squirrels have found the trees; oaks that sprouted since the land was cleared bear acorns. Bush-hog and tractor keep the trees at bay on fewer and fewer acres each year. Cattle haven't grazed it now for more than a decade.

The old magnolia saved from the bulldozer hasn't grown, it seems, but maybe that's because even middle-sized trees looked big to very young eyes. It holds its waxen blossoms high and guards the jonquils by the driveway leading to the weathered house.

Each spring a garden grows still, though no one lives here now. Somehow it seems worth the commute from 15 miles away where the owners live beside the lake. The raccoons and the proliferating herd of deer help eat the peas and squash, meantime waiting for the pears to ripen. The woodland isn't back to where it used to be, but it seems to know its way. Only

*time and the wants of people later on will tell which direction it will go
from here.*

Literature Cited

Ahrns, J. 1982. Nonconsumptive wildlife uses. Pp. 83–92 in J. T.
Baccus, ed., Proc. symposium on Texas wildlife resources and land
use, 14–16 April, Austin.

Clark, T. L. 1982. Wildlife management programs, goals, and issues—
the state perspective. Pp. 116–31 in J. T. Baccus, ed., Proc. symposium on Texas wildlife resources and land use, 14–16 April, Austin.

DeYoung, R., and S. Kaplan. 1988. On averting the tragedy of the commons. Environ. Manage. 12:273–83.

Eltringham, S. K. 1990. Wildlife carrying capacities in relation to human settlement. Koedoe 33(2):87–97.

Frentress, C. D. 1985. Letter from the Resolution Committee of the
Texas chapter of the Wildlife Society to Fred Bryant, president. Cop-
ies to contributing committee members Dan W. Lay, William J. Sheffield, and Ray C. Telfair II.

Geist, V. 1988. How markets in wildlife meat and parts, and the sale of
hunting privileges, jeopardize wildlife conservation. Conserv. Biol.
2(1):15–26.

Hardin, G. J. 1968. The tragedy of the commons. Science 162:
1243–48.

Johnson, W. 1978. Muddling toward frugality. San Francisco: Sierra
Club Books. 252 pp.

Teer, J. G. 1982. Texas Wildlife: Now and for the future. Pp. 9–20 in
J. T. Baccus, ed., Proc. symposium on Texas wildlife resources and
land use, 14–16 April, Austin.

White, R. L. 1977. Land reclamation in Texas: An opportunity. Pp.
199–208 in W. R. Kaiser, ed., Proc. Gulf Coast lignite conference:
Geology, utilization, and environmental aspects. Univ. Texas Bur.
Econ. Geol. Rep. Invest. No. 90.

Lee Ann Johnson Linam
Texas Parks and Wildlife Department
Endangered Resources Branch
4200 Smith School Road
Austin, Texas 78744

Appendix A. Conservation Organizations in Texas

Texans interested in wildlife have access to a wide variety of organizations addressing wildlife and conservation issues. Many Texans support wildlife conservation through membership in such organizations. A recent report found that at a national level, membership in environmental organizations in the 1990's was at an all-time high, with the 44 largest organizations totaling over 15 million (Hendee and Pitstick 1992). In 1989, over 5,800 environmental organizations were reported in the United States (National Center for Charitable Statistics 1990). Clearinghouses for information on environmental organizations in Texas report that over 200 state and local organizations are also active within the state (Texas Environmental Center 1991; pers. commun., Alan Allen, Sportsman Conservationists of Texas; NWF 1994).

There are several types of wildlife organizations in Texas. A survey of Texas state and local organizations conducted in 1992 revealed some common characteristics, as well as differences, between these groups. Some examples of the different types of wildlife organizations are presented below. Most Texas organizations came into existence after 1960; however, a few groups, especially local sportsmen clubs, were formed much earlier (the earliest reported group was formed in 1936). Membership costs vary, but the overwhelming majority of annual fees are $25 or less. Number of members varies greatly—a number of clubs have over 500 members, but many groups also have less than 200 members. Reported club activities include regular meetings, field trips, fund raising, research projects, socials, education activities, review and comment on environmental issues, land management, and publications.

General Interest Conservation Groups

Many of these organizations are familiar to Texans. Although these groups address a variety of conservation issues, many of them originated as efforts to conserve wildlife species, such as the National Audubon Society's early efforts on behalf of waterbirds. Often these organizations, such as the National Audubon Society, National Wildlife Federation, Sierra Club, and Izaak Walton League of America, have a large network of state and local organizations which enable much grassroots involvement. Others, such as the Nature Conservancy, are organized primarily through state offices. Others, though familiar to many people, operate primarily at a national level. Some familiar groups in this category include World Wildlife Fund, Wilderness Society, Natural Resources Defense Council, Environmental Defense Fund, and Defenders of Wildlife. Some organizations serve as an umbrella organization for other clubs. Sportsmen's Conservationists of Texas (SCOT), a Texas affiliate of the National Wildlife Federation, serves this role in Texas.

Texas also has some unique conservation organizations without national origins. Texas Wildlife Association membership is composed primarily of landowners and wildlife managers in the state, sponsors a variety of activities, and provides input regarding wildlife policy. Texas Committee on Natural Resources sponsors a large annual meeting, along with numerous volunteer task forces, and is extensively involved in reviewing and commenting on natural resources issues. The Texas Organization for Endangered Species is a statewide organization with both professional and lay membership dedicated to conservation and awareness activities on behalf of rare species and natural communities in the state. The Native Plant Society of Texas is dedicated to the conservation, preservation, and utilization of the native plants and plant habitats of Texas. In addition, there are a handful of local or regional independent wildlife conservation and outdoor clubs. The Big Bend Natural History Association is one example.

Professional Natural Resource Groups

The largest organization of professional wildlife biologists in the state is the Texas Chapter of The Wildlife Society. This organization conducts annual meetings, recognizes outstanding professional achievement, reviews and comments on current wildlife issues, offers scholarships, and conducts educational activities for professionals, landowners, students, and the general public. The Society of American Foresters and Society for Range Management also have state chapters with similar activities in Texas, and the Tejas Chapter of the Society for Conservation Biology was recently formed in the Austin area. Finally, the Texas Forestry Association is an example of several agriculture-related organizations that promote conservation and use of natural resources.

Species-Oriented Groups

Several of these groups are among the earliest and most effective wildlife conservation efforts, both at a grass-roots level through local affiliates and at statewide and national levels. Some examples of national organizations with active chapters in Texas include Ducks Unlimited, National Wild Turkey Federation, Quail Unlimited, and Trout Unlimited. Chapters of these groups are often active in fund raising, member socials, and funding scholarships and habitat improvement projects. A similar Texas-based organization is Wetland Habitat Alliance of Texas (WHAT), although WHAT promotes wetland conservation for a variety of species. A few specialized organizations dedicated to nongame species also exist. One example is HEART (Help Endangered Ridley Turtles), based in the Galveston area. In addition, the Texas Ornithological Society, Texas Herpetological Society, and Texas Society of Mammalogists are all groups oriented toward specific groups of species and are composed of both professional biologists and lay members.

Hunting-Oriented Groups

As noted above, local hunting sports organizations were some of the earliest conservation groups formed in Texas. Many of these organizations continue to be active in their local area. Several larger organizations focused on hunting, such as chapters of Safari Club International in Houston and Dallas, are also actively involved in supporting wildlife conservation in the state.

For More Information

In addition to the examples listed above, there are many more organizations dedicated to wildlife conservation in Texas. Similarly, many additional organizations are dedicated to related issues such as pollution control, fisheries, and outdoor recreation. Larger cities, such as

Austin and Houston, have organizations that serve as clearinghouses for information on local conservation groups, or individuals interested in becoming involved in wildlife conservation may want to contact sportsmen or outdoor enthusiasts in the local community. A more complete list of environmental organization in the state, along with addresses for groups mentioned above, are available from the following sources:

Sportsmen's Conservationists of Texas (SCOT)
311 Vaughn Building
805 Brazos St.
Austin, Texas 78701

National Wildlife Federation
1996 Conservation Directory
1400 Sixteenth Street, N.W.
Washington, D.C. 20036-2266

Literature Cited

Hendee, J. C., and R. C. Pitstick. 1992. The growth of environmental and conservation-related organization: 1980–91. Renewable Res. J. 10:6–19.

National Center for Charitable Statistics. 1990. Special analysis: National survey on giving and volunteering in the United States. In a profile of giving and volunteering to environmental causes and a national profile of environmental organizations. National Center for Charitable Statistics at INDEPENDENT SECTOR, Washington, D.C.

National Wildlife Federation. 1994. Conservation directory. Washington, D.C. 477 pp.

Appendix B
Plants Cited in the Text

Common name	Scientific name
FORBES	
* Alfalfa	*Medicago sativa*
* Alligator-weed	*Alternanthera philoxeroides*
Arrowhead	*Sagittaria* spp.
Balsamscale, Pan American	*Elyonurus tripsacoides*
Bladderpod, White	*Lesquerella pallida*
Broomweed	*Amphiachyris* and *Gutierrezia* spp.
Bundleflower	*Desmanthus* spp.
Bur-Reed	*Sparganium* spp.
Cattail	*Tyha* spp.
Celery, Wild	*Vallisneria americana*
* Clover	*Trifolium* spp.
* Cowpea	*Vigna unguiculata*
Croton	*Croton* spp.
Croton, Grassland	*Croton dioicus*
Croton, Texabama	*Croton alabamensis texana*
Daisy, Englemann	*Engelmannia pinnatifida*
* Elodea	*Egeria densa* (=*Elodea densa*)
Featherfoil, American	*Hottonia inflata*

Common name	Scientific name
Frogbit, Common	*Limnobium spongia*
* Hyacinth, Water	*Eichornia crassipes*
Sunflower	*Helianthus* spp.
* Sweetclover	*Melilotus* spp.
* Vetch	*Vicia* spp.
Waterlettuce	*Pistia stratiotes*
Waterlily	*Nymphaea* spp.
Water-primrose	*Ludwigia* spp.
* Winterpea	*Pisum* spp.
* Winterpea, Austrian	*Pisum sativum*
Wolfberry	*Lycium* spp.

GRASSES, RUSHES, AND SEDGES

* Bahiagrass	*Paspalum notatum*
* Bermudagrass	*Cynodon dactylon*
* Bermudagrass, Coastal	*Cynodon dactylon* (cultivar)
Bluestem, Big	*Andropogon gerardii*
Bluestem, Little	*Schizachyrium ischium*
Bluestem, Seacoast	*Schizachyrium scoparium* var. *littorale*
Bluestem, Silver	*Bothriochloa laguroides*
Bristlegrass, Plains	*Setaria macrostachya*
* Brome	*Bromus* spp.
Buffalograss	*Buchloe dactyloides*
* Bufflegrass	*Cenchrus ciliaris*
Bulrush	*Scirpus* spp.
Burrograss	*Scleropogon brevifolius*
* Canarygrass, Reed	*Phalaris arundinacea*
Carpetgrass	*Axonopus* spp.
* Chufa	*Cyperus esculentus*
Cordgrass, Gulf	*Spartina spartinae*
Cordgrass, Smooth	*Spartina alterniflora* var. *glabra*
Crinkleawn	*Trachypogon secundus*

Common name	Scientific name
* Dallisgrass	*Paspalum dilatatum*
Deertongue (see Rosettegrass)	
Dropseed	*Sporobolus* spp.
Dropseed, Sand	*Sporobolus cryptandrus*
Dropseed, Silveanus	*Sporobolus silveanus*
* Fescue	*Festuca* spp.
Fluffgrass	*Dasyochloa pulchella*
Gamagrass, Eastern	*Tripsacum didactyus*
Grama	*Grama* spp.
Grama, Sideoats	*Bouteloa curtipendula*
Indiangrass	*Sorghastrum* spp.
Indiangrass, Yellow	*Sorghastrum nutans*
* Johnsongrass	*Sorghum halepense*
* Kleingrass	*Panicum coloratum*
* Lovegrass (nonnative)	*Eragrostis* spp.
Marshmillet	*Zizaniopsis miliacea*
* Millet, Broomcorn	*Panicum miliaceum*
* Millet, Foxtail	*Setaria italica*
* Millet, Japanese	*Echinochloa crusgalli* var. *frumentacea*
* Millet, Pearl	*Perrisetum typhoideum*
Muhly, Ear	*Muhlenbergia arenacea*
Muhly, Sand	*Muhlenbergia arenicola*
Needlegrass	*Stipa* spp.
Panicum	*Panicum* spp.
Pappusgrass	*Pappophorum* spp.
Paspalum	*Paspalum* spp.
Reed, Common	*Phragmites communalis*
* Rice, Wild	*Zizania aquatica*
Rosettegrass, Deertongue	*Dichanthelium clandestinum*
Rush	*Juncus* spp.
* Ryegrass	*Lolium* spp.
Saltgrass, Coastal	*Distichalis spicata* var. *spicata*

Common name	Scientific name
Sandbur	*Cenchrus* spp.
Sawgrass, Jamaica	*Cladium jamaicense*
Sea-oats	*Uniola paniculata*
Indigo, Western	*Indigofera miniata* var. *leptosepala*
Ladies'-Tresses, Navasota	*Spiranthes parksii*
* Lespedeza	*Lespedeza* spp.
Lotus, American	*Nelumbo lutea*
Morningglory	*Ipomia* spp.
Pea, Partridge	*Chamaecrista fasciculata*
* Pea, Singletary	*Lathyrus hirsutus*
Phlox, Texas Trailing	*Phlox nivalis texensis*
Pickerelweed	*Pontederia cordata*
Pondweed	*Potamogeton* spp.
Poppymallow, Texas	*Callirhoe scabriuscula*
Potato, Duck	*Sagittaria latifolia*
Prairie Clover, Comanche Peak	*Dalea reverchonii*
Purslane, Sea	*Sesuvium* spp.
Sagebrush	*Artemisia* spp.
Sagewort (see Sagebrush)	
Saltwort, Dwarf	*Salicornia virginica*
Sand Verbena, Large-fruited	*Abronia macrocarpa*
Smartweed	*Polygonum* spp.
Snakeweed	*Gutierrezia* spp.
Sphagnum	*Sphagnum* spp.
Sedge	*Carex* spp.
Signalgrass	*Brachiaria arizonica*
Sprangletop, Green	*Leptochloa dubia*
Switchgrass	*Panicum virgatum*
Threeawn	*Aristida* spp.
Tobosa	*Hilaria mutica*
Wheatgrass	*Elytrigia* spp.
Wheatgrass, Western	*Elytrigia smithii*

Common name	Scientific name
Windmillgrass	*Chloris* spp.
Wintergrass, Texas	*Stipa leucotricha*

VINES

Creeper, Virginia	*Parthenocissus quinquefolia*
Dewberry/Blackberry	*Rubus* spp.
Grape	*Vitis* spp.
* Honeysuckle	*Lonicera* sp.
Peppervine	*Ampelopsis* spp.
Trumpet-Creeper	*Campsis radicans*

SHRUBS

Acacia	*Acacia* spp.
Acacia, Blackbrush	*Acacia rigidula*
* Arborvitae	*Thuja* spp.
Beautyberry	*Callicarpa* sp.
Buttonbush	*Cephalanthus* sp.
Cactus, Tobush Fishhook	*Echinocactus tobuschii*
Ceniza	*Leucophyllum* spp.
Coralberry	*Symphoricarpos orbiculatus*
Creosotebush	*Larrea tridentata*
Elderberry	*Sambucus* sp.
* Eleagnus	*Eleagnus* spp.
Farkleberry	*Vaccinium arboretum*
Greasebush	*Glossopetalon* spp.
Guajillo	*Acacia berlandieri*
Huisache	*Acacia smallii*
* Indigo	*Indiogofera* sp.
Lotebush	Zizyphus obtusifolia
Palmetto, Texas	*Sabal mexicana*
Pricklyash	*Zanthoxylum* spp.
Pricklypear	*Opuntia* spp.
* Pyracantha	*Pyracantha* sp.

Common name	Scientific name
Rattlebush	*Sesbania* spp.
* Rose, Macartney	*Rosa bracteata*
Sagebush, Sand	*Artemisia filifolia*
Saltbush, Fourwing	*Atriplex canescens*
Sesbania (see Rattlebush)	
Snake-eyes	*Phaulothamnus spinescens*
Sumac	*Rhus* spp.
Tarbush	*Flourensia cernua*
Viburnum	*Viburnum* spp.
Wax-myrtle	*Myrica* sp.
Yaupon	*Ilex vomitoria*
Yucca	*Yucca* spp.

TREES

Anacua	*Ehretia anacua*
Ash	*Fraxinus* spp.
Baldcypress	*Taxodium distichum*
Beech, American	*Fagus grandifolia*
Birch, River	*Betula nigra*
Blackgum	*Nyssa sylvatica*
Bluewood	*Condalia hookeri*
Bumelia	*Bumelia* spp.
* Catalpa	*Catalpa* spp.
* Coffee Tree, Kentucky	*Gymnocladus dioica*
Cottonwood	*Populus* spp.
Cottonwood, Eastern	*Populus deltoides*
Dogwood	*Cornus* spp.
Ebony, Texas	*Pithecellobium flexicaule*
Elm	*Ulmus* spp.
Hackberry	*Celtis* spp.
Hackberry, Sugar	*Celtis laevigata*
Hawthorn	*Crataegus* spp.
Hickory	*Carya* spp.

Common name	Scientific name
Holly	*Ilex* spp.
Juniper	*Juniperus* spp.
Juniper, Ashe	*Juniperus ashei*
* Locust, Black	*Robinia pseudo-acacia*
Magnolia, Southern	*Magnolia grandiflora*
Maple	*Acer* spp.
Mesquite	*Prosopis* spp.
Mesquite, Honey	*Prosopis glandulosa*
Mulberry, Red	*Morus rubra*
Oak	*Quercus* spp.
Oak, Blackjack	*Quercus marylandica*
Oak, Escarpment Live	*Quercus fusiformis*
Oak, Havard	*Quercus havardii*
Oak, Live	*Quercus virginiana*
Oak, Mohr (Shinnery)	*Quercus mohriana*
Oak, Post	*Quercus stellata*
Oak, Sand Live	*Quercus oleoides* x *Q. fusiformis*
Oak, Southern Red	*Quercus falcata*
Oak, Water	*Quercus nigra*
* Olive, Russian	*Elaeagnus angustifolia*
Osage Orange	*Maclura pomifera*
Pecan	*Carya illinoensis*
Persimmon	*Diospyros* spp.
Pine	*Pinus* spp.
Pine, Pinyon	*Pinus edulis*
Pine, Ponderosa	*Pinus ponderosa*
Pine, Loblolly	*Pinus taeda*
Pine, Longleaf	*Pinus palustris*
Pine, Shortleaf	*Pinus echinata*
* Pine, Slash	*Pinus elliotii*
Plum	*Prunus* spp.
Redbud	*Cercis canadensis*

Common name	Scientific name
Red Cedar, Eastern	*Juniperus virginianus*
* Saltcedar, French	*Tamarix gallica*
Soapberry, Western	*Sapindus saponaria*
Sweetgum	*Liquidambar styraciflua*
Sycamore, American	*Plantanus americanus*
* Tallow Tree, Chinese	*Sapium sebiferum*
Tupelo, Water	*Nyssa aquatica*
Willow	*Salix* spp.
Willow, Black	*Salix nigra*

* Introduced species in Texas (nonnative, i.e., exotic).

Appendix C

Animals Cited in the Text

Common name	Scientific name
INVERTEBRATES	
* Ant, Red Imported Fire	*Solenopsis invicta*
Fly, Screwworm	*Cochliomyia hominivorax*
FISHES	
Bass, Guadalupe	*Micropterus treculi*
Bass, Largemouth	*Micropterus salmoides*
Blindcat	*Satan* and *Trogloglanis* spp.
* Carp, Common	*Cyprinus carpio*
Catfish, Channel	*Ictalurus punctatus*
Darter, Fountain	*Etheostoma fonticola*
Gambusia, Amistad	*Gambusia amistadensis*
Gambusia, Big Bend	*Gambusia gaigei*
Gambusia, Clear Creek	*Gambusia heterochir*
Gambusia, San Marcos	*Gambusia georgei*
Pupfish, Comanche Springs	*Cyprinodon elegans*
Pupfish, Leon Springs	*Cyprinodon bovinus*
Shiner, Bluntnose	*Notropis simus*
Sunfish	*Lepomis* spp.
* Trout, Rainbow	*Oncorhynchus mykiss*

Common name	Scientific name
AMPHIBIANS	
Bullfrog	*Rana catesbiena*
Frog	*Rana* spp.
Frog, Cliff Chirping	*Syrrhophus marnocki*
Salamander, Cave	*Eurycea* and *Typhlomolge* spp.
Toad, Houston	*Bufo houstonensis*
REPTILES	
Alligator, American	*Alligator mississippiensis*
Cooter	*Pseudemys* spp.
Cottonmouth, Western	*Agkistrodon piscivorus*
Lizard, Dunes Sagebrush	*Sceloporus arenicolus*
Lizard, Gray-checkered Whiptail	*Cnemidophorus dixoni*
Lizard, Texas Horned	*Phrynosoma cornutum*
Rattlesnake	*Crotalus* spp.
Rattlesnake, Prairie	*Crotalus viridis viridis*
Rattlesnake, Western Diamondback	*Crotalus atrox*
Sea Turtle, Atlantic Ridley	*Lepidochelys kempii*
Sea Turtle, Green	*Chelonia mydas*
Sea Turtle, Hawksbill	*Eretmochelys imbricata*
Sea Turtle, Leatherback	*Dermochelys coriacea*
Sea Turtle, Loggerhead	*Caretta caretta*
Slider	*Trachemys* spp.
Slider, Red-eared	*Trachemys scripta elegans*
Snake, Brazos Water	*Nerodia harteri*
Snake, Concho Water	*Nerodia paucimaculata*
Snake, Milk	*Lampropeltis triangulum*
Snake, Water	*Nerodia* spp.
Terrapin, Texas Diamondback	*Malaclemys terrapin littoralis*
Turtle, Cagle's Map	*Graptemys caglei*
Turtle, Common Snapping	*Chelydra serpentina*
Turtle, Painted	*Chrysemys* spp.

Common name	Scientific name
BIRDS	
Blackbird, Brewer's	*Euphagus cyanocephalus*
Blackbird, Red-winged	*Agelaius phoeniceus*
Blackbird, Rusty	*Euphagus carolinus*
Bluebird, Eastern	*Sialis sialis*
Bobwhite, Northern	*Colinus virginianus*
Chachalaca, Plain	*Ortalis vetula*
Coot, American	*Fulica americana*
Cormorant	*Phalacrocorax* spp.
Cormorant, Double-crested	*Phalacrocorax auritus*
Cowbird, Brown-headed	*Molothrus ater*
Crane	*Grus* spp.
Crane, Canadian Sandhill	*Grus canadensis rowani*
Crane, Greater Sandhill	*Grus canadensis tabida*
Crane, Lesser Sandhill	*Grus canadensis canadensis*
Crane, Sandhill	*Grus canadensis*
Crane, Whooping	*Grus americana*
Curlew, Eskimo	*Numenius borealis*
Dove, Mourning	*Zenaida macroura*
* Dove, Rock (Feral Pigeon)	*Columba livia*
Dove, White-tipped	*Leptotila verreauxi*
Dove, White-winged	*Zenaida asiatica*
Duck, Redhead	*Aythya americana*
Duck, Wood	*Aix sponsa*
Eagle, Bald	*Haliaeetus leucocephalus*
Eagle, Golden	*Aquila chrysaetos*
* Egret, Cattle	*Bubulcus ibis*
Egret, Great	*Ardea alba*
Egret, Reddish	*Egretta rufescens*
Egret, Snowy	*Egretta thula*
Falcon, Aplomado	*Falco femoralis*
Falcon, Arctic Peregrine	*Falco peregrinus tundrius*

Common name	Scientific name
Falcon, Peregrine	*Falco peregrinus*
Finch, House	*Carpodacus mexicanus*
Flicker, Northern	*Colaptes auratus*
Flycatcher, Scissor-tailed	*Tyranus forficatus*
Gallinule	*Gallinula* and *Porphyrula* spp.
Goose, Snow	*Chen caerulescens*
Grackle, Great-tailed	*Quiscalus mexicanus*
Grosbeak, Evening	*Coccothraustes vespertinus*
Grouse, Sharp-tailed	*Pedioecetes phasianellus*
Gulls	*Larus* spp.
Hawk, White-tailed	*Buteo albicaudatus*
Heron, Great Blue	*Ardea herodias*
Heron, Tricolored	*Egretta tricolor*
Ibis, White	*Eudocimus albus*
Ibis, White-faced	*Plegadis chihi*
Kite, Swallow-tailed	*Elanoides forficatus*
Mallard	*Anas platyrhynchos*
Martin, Purple	*Progne subis*
Night-Heron	*Nycticorax* spp.
Owl, Northern Spotted	*Strix occidentalis caurina*
Parakeet, Carolina	*Conuropsis carolinensis*
Pelican, Brown	*Pelecanus occidentalis*
* Pheasant, Ring-necked	*Phasianus colchicus*
Pigeon, Band-tailed	*Columba fasciata*
Pigeon, Feral (See Dove, Rock)	
Pigeon, Passenger	*Ectopistes migratorius*
Pigeon, Red-billed	*Columba flavirostris*
Plover, Piping	*Charadrius melodus*
Prairie-Chicken, Attwater's Greater	*Tympanuchus cupido attwateri*
Prairie-Chicken, Greater	*Tympanuchus cupido*
Prairie-Chicken, Lesser	*Tympanuchus pallidicinctus*
Quail, Gambel's	*Colinus gambelii*

Common name	Scientific name
Quail, Montezuma	*Cyrtonyx montezumae*
Quail, Scaled	*Callipepla squamata*
Rail	*Porzana* and *Rallus* spp.
Robin, American	*Turdus migratorius*
Sapsucker, Yellow-bellied	*Sphrapicus varius*
Snipe, Common	*Capella gallinago*
* Sparrow, House	*Passer domesticus*
* Starling, European	*Sturnus vulgaris*
Tern	*Sterna* spp.
Tern, Interior Least	*Sterna antillarum athalassos*
Turkey, Wild	*Meleagris gallopavo*
Turkey, Eastern Wild	*Meleagris gallopavo silvestris*
Turkey, Merriam's Wild	*Meleagris gallapavo merriami*
Turkey, Rio Grande Wild	*Meleagris gallopavo intermedia*
Vireo, Black-capped	*Vireo atricapillus*
Vulture, Black	*Coragyps atratus*
Vulture, Turkey	*Cathartes aura*
Warbler, Golden-cheeked	*Dendroica chrysoparia*
Warbler, Prothonotary	*Protonotaria citrea*
Woodcock, American	*Scolopax minor*
Woodpecker	*Dryocopus, Melanerpes,* and *Picoides* spp.
Woodpecker, Ivory-billed	*Campephilus principalis*
Woodpecker, Pileated	*Dryocopus pileatus*
Woodpecker, Red-cockaded	*Picoides borealis*

MAMMALS

* Antelope, Blackbuck	*Antilope cervicapra*
* Antelope, Nilgai	*Boselaphus tragocamelus*
Armadillo, Nine-banded	*Dasypus novemcinctus*
Badger, American	*Taxidea taxus*
* Barasingha	*Cervis duvanceli*
Bat, Brazilian Free-tailed	*Tadarida brasiliensis*

Common name	Scientific name
Bear, Black	*Ursus americanus*
Bear, Grizzly	*Ursus arctos*
Beaver, American	*Castor canadensis*
Bison, American	*Bos bison*
* Boar, European Wild	*Sus scrofa*
Bobcat	*Lynx rufus*
Cottontail, Desert	*Sylvilagus auduboni*
Cottontail, Eastern	*Sylvilagus floridanus*
Cougar (see Lion, Moutain)	
Coyote	*Canis latrans*
* Deer, Axis	*Cervus axis*
Deer, Carmen Mountains White-tailed	*Odocoileus virginianus carminis*
Deer, Desert Mule	*Odocoileus hemionus crooki*
* Deer, Eurasian Red	*Cervus elephus* spp.
* Deer, Fallow	*Cervus dama*
Deer, Mule	*Odocoileus hemionus*
* Deer, Rocky Mountain Mule	*Odocoileus hemionus hemionus*
*Deer, Sika	*Cervus nippon*
Deer, White-tailed	*Odocoileus virginianus*
Elk	*Cervus elaphus*
Elk, Manitoba	*Cervus elaephus manitobensis*
Elk, Merriam	*Cervus elaphus merriami*
* Elk, Rocky Mountain	*Cervus elaphus nelsoni*
Ferret, Black-footed	*Mustela nigripes*
Fox, Common Gray	*Urocyon cinereoargenteus*
Fox, Kit	*Vulpes velox*
* Fox, Red	*Vulpes vulpes*
* Goat, Mountain	*Oreamnos americanus*
Gopher, Pocket	*Geomys* spp.
Hare	*Lepus* spp.
* Ibex	*Capra ibex*
Jackrabbit, Black-tailed	*Lepus californicus*

Common name	Scientific name
Jaguar	*Panthera onca*
Jaguarundi	*Felis yagoauroundi*
Javelina (see Peccary)	
Lion, Mountain (Cougar)	*Felis concolor*
Manatee, West Indian	*Trichechus manatus*
Margay	*Felis wiedii*
Mink	*Mustela vison*
Mole, Eastern	*Scalopus aquaticus*
* Moose	*Alces alces*
* Mouse, House	*Mus musculus*
Mouse, Palo Duro	*Peromyscus truei comanche*
Mouse, Pinõn	*Peromyscus truei*
Mouse, White-footed	*Peromysus leucopus*
Muskrat	*Ondatra zibethicus*
* Nutria	*Myocastor coypus*
Ocelot	*Felis pardalis*
Opossum, Virginia	*Didelphis virginiana*
Otter, Northern River	*Lutra canadensis*
Peccary, Collared (Javelina)	*Tayassu tajacu*
* Pig, Feral	*Sus scrofa*
Prairie Dog, Black-tailed	*Cynomys ludovicianus*
Pronghorn	*Antilocapra americana americana* *Antilocapra americana mexicana*
Rabbit	*Sylvilagus* spp.
Rabbit, Swamp	*Sylvilagus aquaticus*
Racoon, Common	*Procyon lotor*
Rat, Cotton	*Sigmodon hispidus*
* Rat, Norway	*Rattus norvegicus*
* Rat, Roof	*Rattus rattus*
Rat, Texas Kangaroo	*Dipodomys elator*
Ringtail	*Basariscus astutus*
* Sheep, Aoudad (Barbary)	*Ammotragus lervia*
* Sheep, Barbary (Aoudad)	*Ammotragus lervia*

Common name	Scientific name
Sheep, Bighorn	*Ovis canadensis*
Sheep, Desert Bighorn	*Ovis canadensis mexicana*
	Ovis canadensis nelsoni
* Sheep, Mouflon (Barbados)	*Ovis musimon*
Squirrel	*Sciurus* spp.
Squirrel, Eastern Fox	*Sciurus niger*
Squirrel, Eastern Gray	*Sciurus carolinensis*
Skunk, Eastern Spotted	*Spilogale putorius*
Skunk, Striped	*Mephitis mephitis*
Vole	*Microtus* spp.
Wolf, Gray	*Canis lupus*
Wolf, Mexican Gray	*Canis lupus baileyi*
Wolf, Plains Gray	*Canis lupus monstrabilis*
Wolf, Red	*Canis rufus*

* Introduced species and subspecies in Texas (nonnative, i.e., exotic).

Appendix D. Texas Threatened and Endangered Species, November 1997

Animals

In 1973 the Texas legislature authorized the Texas Parks and Wildlife Department to establish a list of endangered animals in the state. Endangered species are those species which the executive director of the Texas Parks and Wildlife Department has named as being "threatened with statewide extinction." Threatened species are those which the TPW Commission has determined are likely to become endangered in the future. Laws and regulations pertaining to endangered or threatened animal species are contained in chapters 67 and 68 of the Texas Parks and Wildlife (TPW) Code and Sections 65.171–65.184 of the Title 31 of the Texas Administrative Code (TAC).

Plants

In 1988 the Texas Legislature authorized the Department to establish a list of threatened and endangered plant species for the state. An endangered plant is one that is "in danger of extinction throughout all or a significant portion of its range." A threatened plant is one which is likely to become endangered within the foreseeable future. Laws and regulations pertaining to endangered or threatened plant species are contained in chapter 88 of the TPW Code and Sections 69.01–69.14 of the TAC.

Regulations

TPWD regulations prohibit the taking, possession, transportation, or sale of any of the animal species designated by state law as endangered or threatened without the issuance of a permit. State laws and regulations prohibit commerce in threatened and endangered plants and the collection of listed plant species from public land without a permit issued by TPWD. In addition, some species listed as threatened or endangered under state law are also listed under federal regulations. These animals are provided additional protection by the U.S. Fish and Wildlife Service.

Listing and Recovery

Listing and recovery of endangered species in Texas is coordinated by the Endangered Resources Branch. The department's Permitting Section is responsible for the issuance of permits for the handling of listed species. The following pages list those species which have been designated as threatened or endangered in Texas. The range of the species within the state can be referenced by the map of Texas ecological regions below.

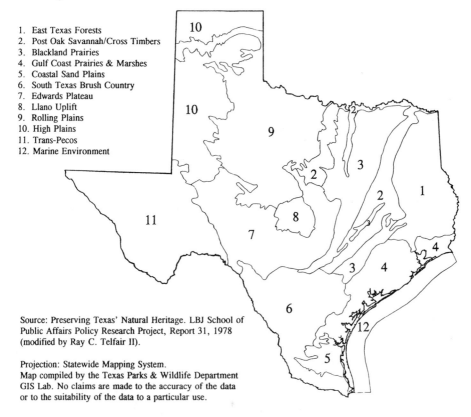

1. East Texas Forests
2. Post Oak Savannah/Cross Timbers
3. Blackland Prairies
4. Gulf Coast Prairies & Marshes
5. Coastal Sand Plains
6. South Texas Brush Country
7. Edwards Plateau
8. Llano Uplift
9. Rolling Plains
10. High Plains
11. Trans-Pecos
12. Marine Environment

Source: Preserving Texas' Natural Heritage. LBJ School of Public Affairs Policy Research Project, Report 31, 1978 (modified by Ray C. Telfair II).

Projection: Statewide Mapping System.
Map compiled by the Texas Parks & Wildlife Department GIS Lab. No claims are made to the accuracy of the data or to the suitability of the data to a particular use.

Fig. A.1. *Ecological regions of Texas.*

Common name	Scientific name	State Status	Federal Status	Ecoregions of Occurrence
***MAMMALS				
BATS				
Greater Long-nosed Bat	Leptonycteris nivalis	E	LE	11
Southern Yellow Bat	Lasiurus ega	T		6
Spotted Bat	Euderma maculatum	T		11
Rafinesque's Big-eared Bat	Corynorhinus rafinesquii	T		1
RODENTS				
Texas Kangaroo Rat	Dipodomys elator	T		9
Coues' Rice Rat	Oryzomys couesi	T		6
Palo Duro Mouse	Peromyscus truei comanche	T		10
MARINE MAMMALS				
Gervais' Beaked Whale	Mesoplodon europaeus	T		12
Goose-beaked Whale	Ziphius cavirostris	T		12
Pygmy Sperm Whale	Kogia breviceps	T		12
Dwarf Sperm Whale	Kogia simus	T		12
Sperm Whale	Physeter macrocephalus	E	LE	12
Atlantic Spotted Dolphin	Stenella frontalis	T		12
Rough-toothed Dolphin	Steno bredanensis	T		12
Killer Whale	Orcinus orca	T		12
False Killer Whale	Pseudorca crassidens	T		12
Short-finned Pilot Whale	Globicephala macrorhynchus	T		12
Pygmy Killer Whale	Feresa attenuata	T		12
Finback Whale	Balaenoptera physalus	E	LE	12
Blue Whale	Balaenoptera musculus	E	LE	12
Black Right Whale	Eubalaena glacialis	E	LE	12

Common name	Scientific name	State Status	Federal Status	Ecoregions of Occurrence
West Indian Manatee	Trichechus Manatus	E	LE	(4,12)
CARNIVORES				
Red Wolf	Canis rufus	E	LE	(1–4,7)**
Gray Wolf	Canis lupus	E	LE	(6–11)
Black Bear	Ursus americanus	T	T/SA	(1,2,4,6–8),11
Louisiana Black Bear	Ursus americanus luteolus	T	LT	(1)
Grizzly Bear	Ursus arctos		LT	(10,11)
White-nosed Coati	Nasua narica	T		4,6,7,11
Black-footed Ferret	Mustela nigripes	E	LE	(9–11)**
Ocelot	Felis pardalis	E	LE	(4),6
Margay	Felis wiedii	T		(6)
Jaguarundi	Felis yaguarondi	E	LE	(4),6
Jaguar	Panthera onca	T	LE	(6,11)
***BIRDS				
WATERBIRDS				
Brown Pelican	Pelecanus occidentalis	E	LE	4
Reddish Egret	Egretta rufescens	T		4
White-faced Ibis	Plegadis chihi	T		2–11
Wood Stork	Mycteria americana	T		1,2,4,6
Whooping Crane	Grus americana	E	LE	4
RAPTORS				
Swallow-tailed Kite	Elanoides forficatus	T		1,4
Bald Eagle	Haliaeetus leucocephalus	T	LT	1–4,7–11
Common Black-Hawk	Buteogallus anthracinus	T		6,11
Gray Hawk	Buteo nitidus	T		6
White-tailed Hawk	Buteo albicaudatus	T		4–6
Zone-tailed Hawk	Buteo albonotatus	T		6,7

Common name	Scientific name	State Status	Federal Status	Ecoregions of Occurrence
Northern Aplomado Falcon	Falco femoralis septentrionalis	E	LE	6
Peregrine Falcon	Falco peregrinus	E,T	E/SA	4,7–11
American Peregrine Falcon	Falco peregrinus anatum	E	LE	7–11
Arctic Peregrine Falcon	Falco peregrinus tundrius	T	E/SA	4
Cactus Ferruginous Pygmy-Owl	Glaucidium brasilianum cactorum	T		5,6
Mexican Spotted Owl	Strix occidentalis lucida	T	LT	11
UPLAND BIRDS				
Attwater's Greater Prairie-Chicken	Tympanuchus cupido attwateri	E	LE	4
SHOREBIRDS				
Piping Plover	Charadrius melodus	T	LT	4
Eskimo Curlew	Numenius borealis	E	LE	4
Interior Least Tern	Sterna antillarum athalassos	E	LE	6,9
Sooty Tern	Sterna fuscata	T		4
WOODPECKERS				
Red-cockaded Woodpecker	Picoides borealis	E	LE	1
Ivory-billed Woodpecker	Campephilus principalis	E	LE	(1)
SONGBIRDS				
Northern Beardless-Tyrannulet	Camptostoma imberbe	T		6
Southwestern Willow Flycatcher	Empidonax traillii extimus	E	LE	11
Rose-throated Becard	Pachyramphus aglaiae	T		6
Black-capped Vireo	Vireo atricapillus	E	LE	7,11
Bachman's Warbler	Vermivora bachmanii	E	LE	(1)

Common name	Scientific name	State Status	Federal Status	Ecoregions of Occurrence
Tropical Parula	Parula pitiayumi	T		6
Golden-Cheeked Warbler	Dendroica chrysoparia	E	LE	7
Bachman's Sparrow	Aimophila aestivalis	T		1
Botteri's Sparrow	Aimophila botterii	T		4
***REPTILES				
TURTLES				
Loggerhead Sea Turtle	Caretta caretta	T	LT	12
Green Sea Turtle	Chelonia mydas	T	LT	12
Atlantic Hawksbill Sea Turtle	Eretmochelys imbricata	E	LE	12
Kemp's Ridley Sea Turtle	Lepidochelys kempii	E	LE	12
Alligator Snapping Turtle	Macroclemys temminckii	T		1–4
Leatherback Sea Turtle	Dermochelys coriacea	E	LE	12
Chihuahuan Mud Turtle	Kinosternon hirtipes	T		11
Texas Tortoise	Gopherus berlandieri	T		4–6
LIZARDS				
Reticulated Gecko	Coleonyx reticulatus	T		11
Reticulate Collared Lizard	Crotaphytus reticulatus	T		6
Texas Horned Lizard	Phrynosoma cornutum	T		2–11
Mountain Short-horned Lizard	Phrynosoma hernandesi	T		11
SNAKES				
Scarlet snake	Cemophora coccinea	T		1,4–6
Black-striped Snake	Coniophanes imperialis	T		6
Indigo Snake	Drymarchon corais	T		4–7

Common name	Scientific name	State Status	Federal Status	Ecoregions of Occurrence
Speckled Racer	Drymobius margaritiferus	T		6
Northern Cat-eyed Snake	Leptodeira septentrionalis	T		4
Brazos Water Snake	Nerodia harteri	T		2,9
Concho Water Snake	Nerodia paucimaculata	T	LT	8,9
Smooth Green Snake	Liochlorophis vernalis	T		4
Louisiana Pine Snake	Pituophis melanoleucus ruthveni	T		1
Big Bend Blackhead Snake	Tantilla rubra	T		7,11
Texas Lyre Snake	Trimorphodon biscutatus	T		11
Timber (Canebrake) Rattlesnake	Crotalus horridus	T		1–4

***AMPHIBIANS

SALAMANDERS

Cascade Caverns Salamander	Eurycea latitans	T		7
San Marcos Salamander	Eurycea nana	T	LT	7
Comal Blind Salamander	Eurycea tridenifera	T		7
Barton Springs Salamander	Eurycea sosorum		LE	7
Texas Blind Salamander	Eurycea rathbuni	E	LE	7
Blanco Blind Salamander	Eurycea robusta	T		7
Black-Spotted Newt	Notophthalmus meridionalis	T		4–6
South Texas Siren (Large Form)	Siren sp 1	T		4–6

Common name	Scientific name	State Status	Federal Status	Ecoregions of Occurrence
FROGS AND TOADS				
Houston Toad	Bufo houstonensis	E	LE	2,4
Mexican Treefrog	Smilisca baudinii	T		6
White-lipped Frog	Leptodactylus labialis	T		6
Sheep Frog	Hypopachus variolosus	T		5,6
Mexican Burrowing Toad	Rhinophrynus dorsalis	T		6
***FISHES**				
LARGE RIVER FISH				
Shovelnose Sturgeon	Scaphirhynchus platorynchus	T		1
Paddlefish	Polyodon spathula	T		1
MINNOWS				
Mexican Stoneroller	Campostoma ornatum	T		11
Devils River Minnow	Dionda diaboli	T	C1	7
Rio Grande Chub	Gila pandora	T		11
Rio Grande Silvery Minnow	Hybognathus amarus	E	LE	(11)
Chihuahua Shiner	Notropis chihuahua	T		11
Arkansas River Shiner	Notropis girardi		PE	9
Bluehead Shiner	Notropis hubbsi	T		1
Bluntnose Shiner	Notropis simus	T		(11)*
Proserpine Shiner	Cyprinella proserpina	T		7,11
SUCKERS				
Blue Sucker	Cycleptus elongatus	T		1–4,6,7
Creek Chubsucker	Erimyzon oblongus	T		1
CATFISH				
Widemouth Blindcat	Satan eurystomus	T		7
Toothless Blindcat	Trogloglanis pattersoni	T		7

Common name	Scientific name	State Status	Federal Status	Ecoregions of Occurrence
KILLIFISHES				
Leon Springs Pupfish	Cyprinodon bovinus	E	LE	11
Comanche Springs Pupfish	Cyprinodon elegans	E	LE	11
Conchos Pupfish	Cyprinodon eximius	T		11
Pecos Pupfish	Cyprinodon pecosensis	T	C1	11
LIVEBEARERS				
Big Bend Gambusia	Gambusia gaigei	E	LE	11
San Marcos Gambusia	Gambusia georgei	E	LE	(7)*
Clear Creek Gambusia	Gambusia heterochir	E	LE	8
Pecos Gambusia	Gambusia nobilis	E	LE	11
Blotched Gambusia	Gambusia senilis	T		(7,11)**
PERCHES				
Fountain Darter	Etheostoma fonticola	E	LE	7
Rio Grande Darter	Etheostoma grahami	T		7,11
Blackside Darter	Percina maculata	T		1
COASTAL FISHES				
Opossum Pipefish	Microphis brachyurus	T		12
River Goby	Awaous tajasica	T		4,6,12
Blackfin Goby	Gobionellus atripinnis	T		6,12
***INVERTEBRATES**				
CRUSTACEANS				
Peck's Cave Amphipod	Stygobromus pecki		PE	7
INSECTS				
American Burying Beetle	Nicrophorus americanus		LE	1
Comal Springs Riffle Beetle	Heterelmis comalensis		PE	7
Tooth Cave Ground Beetle	Rhadine persephone		LE	7

Common name	Scientific name	State Status	Federal Status	Ecoregions of Occurrence
Kretschmarr Cave Mold Beetle	Texamaurops reddelli		LE	7
Coffin Cave Mold Beetle	Batrisodes texanus		LE	7
Comal Springs Dryopid Beetle	Stygoparnus comalensis		PE	7
SPIDERS				
Tooth Cave Spider	Neoleptoneta myopica		LE	7
Bee Creek Cave Harvestman	Texella reddelli		LE	7
Bone Cave Harvestman	Texella reyesi		LE	7
Tooth Cave Pseudoscorpion	Tartarocreagris texana		LE	7
MOLLUSKS				
Ouachita Rock-Pocketbook Mussel	Arkansia wheeleri	E	LE	2
***PLANTS				
CACTI				
Tobusch Fishhook Cactus	Ancistrocactus tobuschii	E	LE	7
Bunched Cory Cactus	Coryphantha ramillosa	T	LT	11
Lloyd's Hedgehog Cactus	Echinocereus lloydii	E	PDL	11
Black Lace Cactus	Echinocereus reichenbachii var albertii	E	LE	4,6
Davis' Green Pitaya	Echinocereus viridiflorus var davisii	E	LE	11
Chisos Mountains Hedgehog Cactus	Echinocereus chisoensis var chisoensis	T	LT	11
Lloyd's Mariposa Cactus	Neolloydia mariposensis	T	LT	11
Nellie Cory Cactus	Coryphantha minima	E	LE	11

Common name	Scientific name	State Status	Federal Status	Ecoregions of Occurrence
Sneed Pincushion Cactus	Coryphantha sneedii var sneedii	E	LE	11
Star Cactus	Astrophytum asterias	E	LE	6
TREES, SHRUBS, AND SUBSHRUBS				
Walker's Manioc	Manihot walkerae	E	LE	6
Hinckley's Oak	Quercus hinckleyi	T	LT	11
Johnston's Frankenia	Frankenia johnstonii	E	LE	6
Texas Ayenia	Ayenia limitaris	E	LE	6
Texas Snowbells	Styrax texanus	E	LE	7
WILDFLOWERS				
South Texas Ambrosia	Ambrosia cheiranthifolia	E	LE	4,6
Texas Prairie Dawn	Hymenoxys texana	E	LE	4
Ashy Dogweed	Thymophylla tephroleuca	E	LE	6
Terlingua Creek Cat's-Eye	Cryptantha crassipes	E	LE	11
White Bladderpod	Lesquerella pallida	E	LE	1
Slender Rush-Pea	Hoffmannseggia Tenella	E	LE	4,6
McKittrick Pennyroyal	Hedeoma apiculatum	T	DL	11
Texas Poppy-Mallow	Callirhoe scabriuscula	E	LE	9
Large-Fruited Sand-Verbena	Abronia macrocarpa	E	LE	2
Texas Trailing Phlox	Phlox nivalis ssp texensis	E	LE	1
Chaffseed	Schwalbea americana		LE	?
ORCHIDS				
Navasota Ladies'-Tresses	Spiranthes parksii	E	LE	1,2

Common name	Scientific name	State Status	Federal Status	Ecoregions of Occurrence
GRASSES AND GRASSLIKE PLANTS				
Texas Wild-Rice	Zizania texana	E	LE	7
Little Aguja Pondweed	Potamogeton clystocarpus	E	LE	11

KEY

State Status
E=Endangered
T=Threatened

Federal Status
LE=Listed Endangered
LT=Listed Threatened
PE=Proposed Endangered
PT=Proposed Threatened
DL=Delisted
PDL=Proposed Delisted

E/SA, T/SA=Endangered/Threatened by Similarity of Appearance
C1=Candidate Species (category 1—awaiting listing)
Ecoregion—( )=Species extirpated from ecoregion within Texas
*=Species extinct
**=Species extinct in the wild (except some experimental populations)

If a species is listed, all its subspecies have same listing status, by default

In 1983, the Texas Legislature created the Special Nongame and Endangered Species Conservation Fund. This fund may be used for nongame wildlife and endangered species research and conservation, habitat acquisition and development, and dissemination of information pertaining to these species. Money for the fund is obtained through private donations and sale of nongame wildlife art prints, decals and stamps. For more information on the fund or endangered species, call 1-800-792-1112 or 512-912-7011.

PWD-LF-W3000-017 (11/97)